Authors, Consultants, Partners

[Authors]

James West Davidson
Dr. James Davidson is coauthor of *After the Fact: The Art of Historical Detection* and *Nation of Nations: A Narrative History of the American Republic.* Dr. Davidson has taught at both the college and high school levels. He has also consulted on curriculum design for American history courses. Dr. Davidson is an avid canoeist and hiker. His published works on these subjects include *Great Heart,* the true story of a 1903 canoe trip in the Canadian wilderness.

Michael B. Stoff
Dr. Michael Stoff received his Ph.D. from Yale University and teaches history at the University of Texas at Austin. He is the author of *Oil, War, and American Security: The Search for a National Policy on Foreign Oil, 1941–1947,* coauthor of *Nation of Nations: A Narrative History of the American Republic,* and coeditor of *The Manhattan Project: A Documentary Introduction to the Atomic Age.* Dr. Stoff has won numerous grants, fellowships, and teaching awards.

[Contributing Author]

Jennifer L. Bertolet
Jennifer L. Bertolet is a Professorial Lecturer at George Washington University, where she teaches American history courses, among them Introduction to American History. She received her Ph.D. from George Washington University. In addition to teaching, she has served as an education consultant, a subject matter expert for online teaching and learning, and as an historian and policy consultant specializing in Indian policy and environmental issues.

[Program Consultant]

Dr. Kathy Swan is an Associate Professor of Curriculum and Instruction at the University of Kentucky. Her research focuses on standards-based technology integration, authentic intellectual work, and documentary-making in the social studies classroom. Swan has been a four-time recipient of the National Technology Leadership Award in Social Studies Education. She is also the advisor for the Social Studies Assessment, Curriculum, and Instruction Collaborative (SSACI) at CCSSO.

[Program Partners]

NBC Learn, the educational arm of NBC News, develops original stories for use in the classroom and makes archival NBC News stories, images, and primary source documents available on demand to teachers, students, and parents. NBC Learn partnered with Pearson to produce the myStory videos that support this program.

Constitutional Rights Foundation
Educate. Participate.

Constitutional Rights Foundation is a nonprofit, nonpartisan organization focused on educating students about the importance of civic participation in a democratic society. Constitutional Rights Foundation is the lead contributor to the development of the Civic Discussion Topic Inquiries for this program. Constitutional Rights Foundation is also the provider of the Civic Action Project (CAP) for the *Economics* and *Magruder's American Government* programs. CAP is a project-based learning model for civics, government, and economics courses.

Reviewers & Academic Consultants

Pearson American History Beginnings Through Reconstruction was developed especially for you and your students. The story of its creation began with a three-day Innovation Lab in which teachers, historians, students, and authors came together to imagine our ideal Social Studies teaching and learning experiences. We refined the plan with a series of teacher roundtables that shaped this new approach to ensure your students' mastery of content and skills. A dedicated team, made up of Pearson authors, content experts, and social studies teachers, worked to bring our collective vision into reality. Kathy Swan, Professor of Education and architect of the new College, Career, and Civic Life (C3) Framework, served as our expert advisor on curriculum and instruction.

Pearson would like to extend a special thank you to all of the teachers who helped guide the development of this program. We gratefully acknowledge your efforts to realize Next Generation Social Studies teaching and learning that will prepare American students for college, careers, and active citizenship.

[Program Advisors]

Campaign for the Civic Mission of Schools is a coalition of over 70 national civic learning, education, civic engagement, and business groups committed to improving the quality and quantity of civic learning in American schools. The Campaign served as an advisor on this program.

Buck Institute for Education is a nonprofit organization dedicated to helping teachers implement the effective use of Project-Based Learning in their classrooms. Buck Institute staff consulted on the Project-Based Learning Topic Inquiries for this program.

[Program Academic Consultants]

Barbara Brown
Director of Outreach
College of Arts and Sciences
African Studies Center
Boston University
Boston, Massachusetts

William Childs
Professor of History Emeritus
The Ohio State University
Columbus, Ohio

Jennifer Giglielmo
Associate Professor of History
Smith College
Northhampton, Massachusetts

Joanne Connor Green
Professor, Department Chair
Political Science
Texas Christian University
Fort Worth, Texas

Ramdas Lamb, Ph.D.
Associate Professor of Religion
University of Hawaii at Manoa
Honolulu, Hawaii

Huping Ling
Changjiang Scholar Chair Professor
Professor of History
Truman State University
Kirksville, Missouri

Jeffery Long, Ph.D.
Professor of Religion and Asian Studies
Elizabethtown College
Elizabethtown, Pennsylvania

Gordon Newby
Professor of Islamic, Jewish and
    Comparative Studies
Department of Middle Eastern and South
    Asian Studies
Emory University
Atlanta, Georgia

Mark Peterson
Associate Professor
Department of Asian and Near Eastern
    Languages
Brigham Young University
Provo, Utah

William Pitts
Professor, Department of Religion
Baylor University
Waco, Texas

Benjamin Ravid
Professor Emeritus of Jewish History
Department of Near Eastern and Judaic
    Studies
Brandeis University
Waltham, Massachusetts

Harpreet Singh
College Fellow
Department of South Asian Studies
Harvard University
Cambridge, Massachusetts

Christopher E. Smith, J.D., Ph.D.
Professor
Michigan State University
MSU School of Criminal Justice
East Lansing, Michigan

John Voll
Professor of Islamic History
Georgetown University
Washington, D.C.

Michael R. Wolf
Associate Professor
Department of Political Science
Indiana University-Purdue University Fort
    Wayne
Fort Wayne, Indiana

Realize Results. Social studies is more than dots on a map or dates on a timeline. It's where we've been and where we're going. It's stories from the past and our stories today. And in today's fast-paced, interconnected world, it's essential.

Instruction Your Way!

Comprehensive teaching support is available in two different formats:

- **Teacher's Edition:** Designed like a "T.V. Guide," teaching suggestions are paired with preview images of digital resources.

- **Teaching Support Online:** Teaching suggestions, answer keys, blackline masters, and other resources are provided at point-of-use online in Realize.

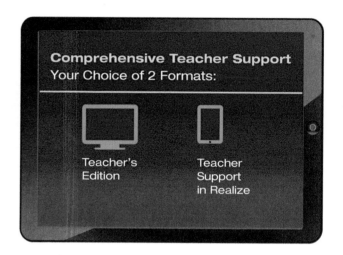

Comprehensive Teacher Support
Your Choice of 2 Formats:

Teacher's Edition

Teacher Support in Realize

Pearson Mastery System

This complete system for teaching and learning uses best practices, technology, and a four-part framework—Connect, Investigate, Synthesize, and Demonstrate—to prepare students to be college-and-career ready.

- Higher-level content that gives students support to access complex text, acquire skills and tackle rigorous questions.

- Inquiry-focused Projects, Civic Discussions, and Document-Based Questions that prepare students for real-world challenges;

- Digital content on Pearson Realize that is dynamic, flexible, and uses the power of technology to bring social studies to life.

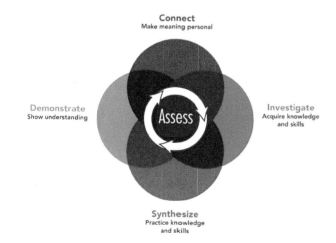

Connect
Make meaning personal

Assess

Demonstrate
Show understanding

Investigate
Acquire knowledge and skills

Synthesize
Practice knowledge and skills

Table of Contents for Today's Learners

Today's learners research new information by using a search engine and browsing by topic. Breaking out of a book metaphor of "chapters," this table of contents is organized by:

- **Topic:** As you decide what you want to teach, you search first for the topic.

- **Lesson:** Within each topic are several lessons where you will find a variety of diverse resources to support teaching and learning.

- **Text:** Each lesson contains chunked information called Texts. This is the same informational text that appears in the print Student Edition.

This organization saves time, improves pacing, and makes it easy to rearrange content.

» Go online to learn more and see the program overview video.

PEARSON • • •
realize™

CONNECT! Begin the Pearson Mastery System by engaging in the topic story and connecting it to your own lives.

Preview—Each Topic opens with the Enduring Understandings section, allowing you to preview expected learning outcomes.

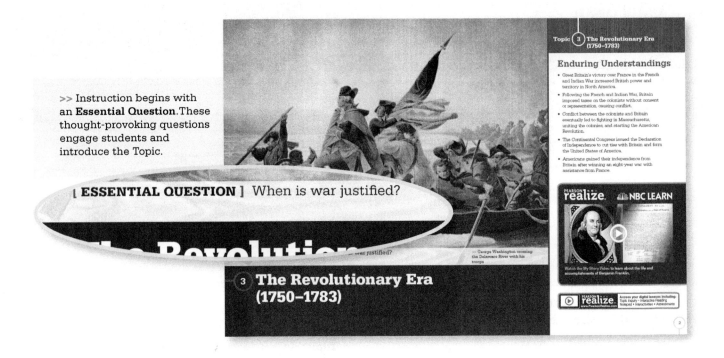

>> Instruction begins with an **Essential Question**. These thought-provoking questions engage students and introduce the Topic.

[**ESSENTIAL QUESTION**] When is war justified?

Developed in partnership with NBCLearn, the **My Story** videos help students connect to the Topic content by hearing the personal story of an individual whose life is related to the content students are about to learn.

INVESTIGATE! Step two of the Mastery System allows you to investigate the topic story through a number of engaging features as you learn the content.

>> **Active Classroom Strategies** integrated in the daily lesson plans help to increase in-class participation, raise energy levels and attentiveness, all while engaging in the story. These 5-15 minute activities have you use what you have learned to draw, write, speak, and decide.

>> **Interactive Primary Source Galleries:** Use primary source image galleries throughout the lesson to see, analyze, and interact with images that tie to the topic story content.

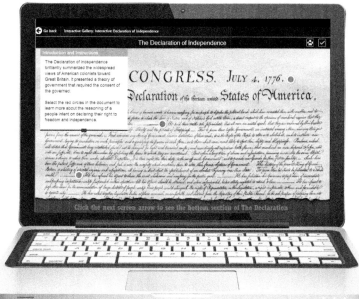

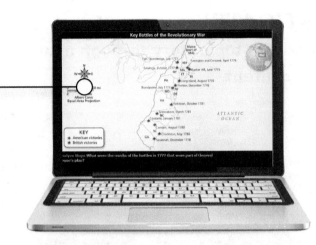

>> Feel like you are a part of the story with **interactive 3-D models**.

>> Continue to investigate the topic story through **dynamic interactive maps**. Build map skills while covering the essential standards.

>> Learn content by reading narrative text online or in a printed Student Edition.

Synthesize: Practice Knowledge and Skills

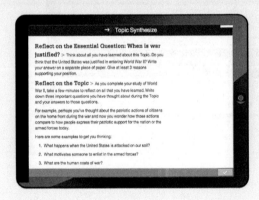

SYNTHESIZE!

In step three of the Mastery System, pause to reflect on what you learn and revisit an essential question.

DEMONSTRATE! The final step of the Mastery System is to demonstrate understanding of the text.

PEARSON **realize**™

>> **The digital course on Realize!** The program's digital course on Realize puts engaging content, embedded assessments, instant data, and flexible tools at your fingertips.

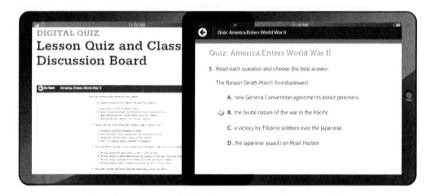

>> **Assessment**. At the end of each lesson and topic, demonstrate understanding through Lesson Quizzes, Topic Tests, and Topic Inquiry performance assessments. The System provides remediation and enrichment recommendations based on your individual performance towards mastery.

>> **Class and Data** features on Realize make it easy to see your mastery data.

Digital Course Content

Topic 3   The Revolutionary Era (1750–1783)   **76**

Topic 4   A Constitution for the United States (1776–Present)   **114**

Digital Course Content

Digital Course Content

Topic 8 Sectionalism and Civil War (1820–1865) 291

Many types of digital resources help you investigate the topics in this course. You'll find biographies, primary sources, maps, and more. These resources will help bring the topics to life.

Core Concepts

Culture

- What Is Culture?
- Families and Societies
- Language
- Religion
- The Arts
- Cultural Diffusion and Change
- Science and Technology

Economics

- Economics Basics
- Economic Process
- Economic Systems
- Economic Development
- Trade
- Money Management

Geography

- The Study of Earth
- Geography's Five Themes
- Ways to Show Earth's Surface
- Understanding Maps

- Earth in Space
- Time and Earth's Rotation
- Forces on Earth's Surface
- Forces Inside Earth
- Climate and Weather
- Temperature
- Water and Climate
- Air Circulation and Precipitation
- Types of Climate
- Ecosystems
- Environment and Resources
- Land Use
- People's Impact on the Environment
- Population
- Migration
- Urbanization

Government and Civics

- Foundations of Government
- Political Systems
- Political Structures
- Conflict and Cooperation
- Citizenship

History

- How Do Historians Study History?
- Measuring Time
- Historical Sources
- Archaeology and Other Sources
- Historical Maps

Personal Finance

- Your Fiscal Fitness: An Introduction
- Budgeting
- Checking
- Investments
- Savings and Retirement
- Credit and Debt
- Risk Management
- Consumer Smarts
- After High School
- Taxes and Income

Landmark Supreme Court Cases

- *Korematsu* v. *United States*
- *Marbury* v. *Madison*
- *McCulloch* v. *Maryland*
- *Gibbons* v. *Ogden*
- *Worcester* v. *Georgia*
- *Dred Scott* v. *Sandford*
- *Plessy* v. *Ferguson*
- *Schenck* v. *United States*
- *Brown* v. *Board of Education*
- *Engel* v. *Vitale*

- *Sweatt* v. *Painter*
- *Mapp* v. *Ohio*
- *Hernandez* v. *Texas*
- *Gideon* v. *Wainwright*
- *Wisconsin* v. *Yoder*
- *Miranda* v. *Arizona*
- *White* v. *Regester*
- *Tinker* v. *Des Moines School District*
- *Roe* v. *Wade*

- *Baker* v. *Carr*
- *Grutter* v. *Bollinger*
- *Edgewood* v. *Kirby*
- *Texas* v. *Johnson*
- *National Federation of Independent Businesses et al.* v. *Sebelius et al.*
- *Mendez* v. *Westminster* and *Delgado* v. *Bastrop*

Interactive Primary Sources

Biographies

- Abigail Adams
- John Adams
- John Quincy Adams
- Samuel Adams
- James Armistead
- Crispus Attucks
- Moses Austin
- Stephen F. Austin
- James A. Baker III
- William Blackstone
- Simón Bolívar
- Napoleon Bonaparte
- Chief Bowles
- Omar Bradley
- John C. Calhoun
- César Chávez
- Wentworth Cheswell
- George Childress
- Winston Churchill
- Henry Clay
- Bill Clinton
- Jefferson Davis
- Martin De León
- Green DeWitt
- Dwight Eisenhower
- James Fannin
- James L. Farmer, Jr.
- Benjamin Franklin
- Milton Friedman
- Betty Friedan
- Bernardo de Gálvez
- Hector P. Garcia
- John Nance Garner
- King George III
- Henry B. González
- Raul A. Gonzalez, Jr.
- Mikhail Gorbachev
- William Goyens

- Ulysses S. Grant
- José Gutiérrez de Lara
- Alexander Hamilton
- Hammurabi
- Warren Harding
- Friedrich Hayek
- Jack Coffee Hays
- Patrick Henry
- Adolf Hitler
- Oveta Culp Hobby
- James Hogg
- Sam Houston
- Kay Bailey Hutchison
- Andrew Jackson
- John Jay
- Thomas Jefferson
- Lyndon B. Johnson
- Anson Jones
- Barbara Jordan
- Justinian
- John F. Kennedy
- John Maynard Keynes
- Martin Luther King, Jr.
- Marquis de Lafayette
- Mirabeau B. Lamar
- Robert E. Lee
- Abraham Lincoln
- John Locke
- James Madison
- John Marshall
- George Marshall
- Karl Marx
- George Mason
- Mary Maverick
- Jane McCallum
- Joseph McCarthy
- James Monroe
- Charles de Montesquieu

- Edwin W. Moore
- Moses
- Benito Mussolini
- José Antonio Navarro
- Chester A. Nimitz
- Richard M. Nixon
- Barack Obama
- Sandra Day O'Connor
- Thomas Paine
- Quanah Parker
- Rosa Parks
- George Patton
- John J. Pershing
- John Paul II
- Sam Rayburn
- Ronald Reagan
- Hiram Rhodes Revels
- Franklin D. Roosevelt
- Theodore Roosevelt
- Lawrence Sullivan Ross
- Haym Soloman
- Antonio Lopez de Santa Anna
- Phyllis Schlafly
- Erasmo Seguín
- Juan N. Seguín
- Roger Sherman
- Adam Smith
- Joseph Stalin
- Raymond L. Telles
- Alexis de Tocqueville
- Hideki Tojo
- William B. Travis
- Harry Truman
- Lech Walesa
- Mercy Otis Warren
- George Washington
- Daniel Webster

- Lulu Belle Madison White
- William Wilberforce
- James Wilson
- Woodrow Wilson
- Lorenzo de Zavala
- Mao Zedong

21st Century Skills

- Identify Main Ideas and Details
- Set a Purpose for Reading
- Use Context Clues
- Analyze Cause and Effect
- Categorize
- Compare and Contrast
- Draw Conclusions
- Draw Inferences
- Generalize
- Make Decisions
- Make Predictions
- Sequence
- Solve Problems
- Summarize
- Analyze Media Content
- Analyze Primary and Secondary Sources
- Compare Viewpoints
- Distinguish Between Fact and Opinion
- Identify Bias
- Analyze Data and Models

- Analyze Images
- Analyze Political Cartoons
- Create Charts and Maps
- Create Databases
- Read Charts, Graphs, and Tables
- Read Physical Maps
- Read Political Maps
- Read Special-Purpose Maps
- Use Parts of a Map
- Ask Questions
- Avoid Plagiarism
- Create a Research Hypothesis
- Evaluate Web Sites
- Identify Evidence
- Identify Trends
- Interpret Sources
- Search for Information on the Internet
- Synthesize
- Take Effective Notes
- Develop a Clear Thesis
- Organize Your Ideas

- Support Ideas With Evidence
- Evaluate Existing Arguments
- Consider & Counter Opposing Arguments
- Give an Effective Presentation
- Participate in a Discussion or Debate
- Publish Your Work
- Write a Journal Entry
- Write an Essay
- Share Responsibility
- Compromise
- Develop Cultural Awareness
- Generate New Ideas
- Innovate
- Make a Difference
- Work in Teams
- Being an Informed Citizen
- Paying Taxes
- Political Participation
- Serving on a Jury
- Voting

Atlas

- United States: Political
- United States: Physical
- World Political
- World Physical
- World Climate
- World Ecosystems
- World Population Density
- World Land Use
- North Africa and Southwest Asia: Political
- North Africa and Southwest Asia: Physical
- Sub-Saharan Africa: Political
- Sub-Saharan Africa: Physical
- South Asia: Political
- South Asia: Physical
- East Asia: Political

- East Asia: Physical
- Southeast Asia: Political
- Southeast Asia: Physical
- Europe: Political
- Europe: Physical
- Russia, Central Asia, and the Caucasus: Political
- Russia, Central Asia, and the Caucasus: Physical
- North America: Political
- North America: Physical
- Central America and the Caribbean: Political
- Central America and the Caribbean: Physical
- South America: Political
- South America: Physical
- Australia and the Pacific: Political
- Australia and the Pacific: Physical

Creating an Active Classroom

This Social Studies program places a strong emphasis on

Inquiry in the form of

- Document-Based Questions
- Project-Based Learning
- Civic Discussions

Each inquiry strand requires students to formulate their own arguments based on evidence. To support this learning approach, the program integrates **Active Classroom strategies** throughout each lesson. These strategies encourage students to begin building their own arguments and collecting evidence about the past and present at even the earliest stages of a lesson.

You can use these strategies to help students participate in their own learning as you call upon them to

- draw
- write
- speak
- decide

You'll find a rich variety of these strategy suggestions throughout both the Teacher's Edition and online **Teacher Support** for each lesson.

ACTIVE CLASSROOM STRATEGIES

ACTIVITY NAME	HOW TO ACTIVATE
Quickdraw	· Pair students and give them 30 seconds to share what they know about a concept or Key Term by creating a symbol or drawing.
Graffiti Concepts	· Ask students to reflect on the meaning of a concept or idea and create a visual image and/or written phrase that represents that concept. Allow approximately 3–5 minutes. · Next ask students to post their "graffiti" on the board or on chart paper and ask students to look at all the various responses. · Next discuss similarities and differences in the responses as a group.
Word Wall	· Ask students to chose one of the Key Terms for the lesson and create a visual image with a text definition. Allow approximately 3–5 minutes. · Ask students to post their words on the board or on chart paper and ask students to look at all the various responses. · Discuss similarities and differences in the responses as a group. · Pick a few favorites and post them on the class "Word Wall" for the year.
Cartoon It	· Ask students to make a quick drawing of one compelling image from this lesson on a piece of paper. · Next ask students to turn their drawing into a political cartoon that illustrates a key concept or main idea from the lesson by adding a text caption or text "bubbles." · Ask students to share their cartoons with a partner or within small groups.
Wallpaper	· Ask students to review information they have learned in a topic and design a piece of "wallpaper" that encapsulates key learnings. · Then have students post their wallpaper and take a "gallery" walk noting what others have written and illustrated in their samples.
Quick Write	· Ask students to write what they know about a key idea or term in 30 seconds.
Make Headlines	· Have students write a headline that captures the key idea in a map, photo, timeline, or reading. · Ask students to share their headline with a partner.
Circle Write	· Break into groups and provide a writing prompt or key question. · Have students write as much as they can in response to the question or prompt for 1 minute. · Next have students give their response to the person on their right. That person should improve or elaborate on the response where the other person left off. · Continue to pass each response to the right until the original response comes back to the first person. · Each group then reviews all the responses and decides which is the best composition and shares that with the larger group.

Creating an Active Classroom

ACTIVE CLASSROOM STRATEGIES

ACTIVITY NAME	HOW TO ACTIVATE
Write 1-Get 3 (or Write 5-Get 4)	· Ask a question with multiple answers, such as: What are 4 key characteristics of _____ (a dictator)? What are the 5 key causes of _____? · Have students write down 1 response and then go around the room asking for 3 other responses. If they think a response is correct, ask them to write it down. · Have students keep asking and writing until they have 3 more responses on their page. · Have students share and discuss responses with the class.
Sticky Notes	· Ask students to spend three minutes jotting down their response to a critical thinking question on a sticky note. · Ask students to work in pairs and share their responses. · Next ssk students to post their sticky notes on the board or on chart paper and read all the notes. · Discuss similarities and differences in the responses as a group.
Connect Two	· Select 10 to 12 words or phrases you think are important for students to know prior to reading a selection. · List the words on the board. · Ask students to "Connect Two" or choose two words they think might belong together, and state the reason. "I would connect _____ and _____ because _____." Consider posting their Connect Two statements on the board. · As students read the text they should look for evidence to support or refute their Connect Two statements.
Conversation With History	· Ask students to choose one of the people mentioned or pictured in the text and write down a question they would like to ask that person if they could. · Next ask students to write what they think that person would say in response and then what they would say in response to that.
Walking Tour	· Post passages from a reading around the room. · Ask small groups to tour the room and discuss each passage. · Summarize each passage as a class. · Alternatively, assign each small group to a passage and have them summarize that passage for the rest of the class.
Audio Tour	· Ask students to work in pairs. Have the first student give the second a verbal "tour" of a map or graph or infographic. · Have the second student give the first an explanation of what the graphic shows.

ACTIVITY NAME	HOW TO ACTIVATE
My Metaphor	· Post the following metaphor on the board: This (map, timeline, image, primary source) shows that _____ is like _____ because _____. · Ask students to fill in the metaphor prompt based on their understanding of the source.
Act It Out	· Choose an image in the lesson and ask students to think about one of the following questions as appropriate to the image: · What may have happened next in this image? · What may have happened just before this image? · What do you think the people in this image are thinking? · What do you think the people in this image are saying to each other?
If Photos/Images/Art Could Talk	· Ask the following questions about an image in the course: What do you think the person in this photo would say if they could talk? What's your evidence?
See-Think-Wonder	· Ask students to work in pairs. · Ask them to look at an image, map, or graph and answer these questions: · What do you see? · What does that make you think? · What are you wondering about now that you've seen this? · Have students share their answers with the class.
A Closer Look	· Project a map or image on the board and divide it into four numbered quadrants. · Have students count off from 1 to 4 into four small groups. Have each group look closely at the part of the image in their quadrant. · Have each small group report on what they observed and learned as a result of their focus on this part of the image.
Take a Stand	· Ask students to take a stand on a yes-or-no or agree/disagree critical thinking question. · Ask students to divide into two groups based on their answer and move to separate areas of the classroom. · Ask students to talk with each other to compare their reasons for answering yes or no. · Ask a representative from each side to present and defend the group's point of view. · Note: you can adapt this activity to have students take their place on a continuum line from 1 to 10 depending on how strongly they agree or disagree.

Creating an Active Classroom

ACTIVE CLASSROOM STRATEGIES

ACTIVITY NAME	HOW TO ACTIVATE
Rank It	· List a group of items/concepts/steps/causes/events on the board. · Ask students to rank the items/steps . . . according to X criteria (which is most important, which had the greatest impact . . . most influential, essential, changed, affected). · Ask students to provide a justification for the ranking decisions they made. · Then ask students to work in pairs to share their rankings and justifications. · Poll the class to see if there is agreement on the ranking. OR · Place stickies on the board with key events from the lesson or topic. · Break students into small groups and ask each group to go up and choose the sticky with what they think is the most significant event. · Ask the group to discuss among themselves why they think it is most significant. · Ask one person from each group to explain why the group chose that event.
Sequence It	· Place key events from a lesson or topic on sticky notes on the board. · Ask students to place the events in chronological order. · You could do this activity with multiple groups in different parts of the classroom.
PMI Plus/Minus/Interesting	· Place students in groups and give each group a 3-column organizer with headings Plus/Minus/Interesting for recording responses. · Ask students to analyze a text or examine an issue and then answer these three questions in their organizer: 1. What was positive about this text/issue? 2. What was negative about this text/issue? 3. What was interesting about this text/issue?

Celebrate Freedom

Objective 1: Understand the intent, meaning, and importance of the Declaration of Independence; 2: Recite the opening text from the Declaration of Independence.

Quick Instruction

Using these materials, students can prepare for Celebrate Freedom Week, by thinking about the importance of the Declaration of Independence and the Bill of Rights. The materials will help you make links between the Declaration and your course of study.

Aa Vocabulary Development: Before students recite the words from the Declaration, review key terms the key terms "self-evident," "endowed," "unalienable," "deriving," and "consent." Ask students to compose a sentence using each word. Then have students paraphrase the excerpt from the Declaration, putting the ideas into their own words.

Further Instruction

Have students recite the key section from the Declaration of Independence, "We hold these truths…" to each other or as a whole class.

Summarize *all men have rights; no one can take them away, because they are unalienable.*

Paraphrase *Sample: Governments are set up in order to protect people's rights.*

Analyze *Sample: They recite the words to remember that our country started because of a beliefs in our rights and we still believe that people have rights today.*

Bill of Rights Teach

Plan Help student review the Bill of Rights found in the U.S. Constitution in the Reference Center or in the back of their books. They might be particularly interested in the First (freedom of religion, speech, press, assembly, and petition), Second (bearing arms), Fourth (searches and seizures). Fifth (criminal proceedings; due process; eminent domain), Sixth (criminal proceedings), and Eighth (punishment for crimes). You might suggest students work in pairs as they consider the provisions of the amendments. This closer study will help each student choose the Amendment on which they want to focus their research.

Explore Students might begin their research with the local newspaper, or they could conduct an online search using key words related to the Amendment they have chosen. As they do their research, remind students to use several sources and to be sure the sources are reliable. Remind them to keep track of information about their sources, such as source name, date, location, and so on.

Communicate Remind students of the basics of a good essay. Have them sketch a rough outline. The thesis statement should directly respond to the assignment. Tell students to start their essay with a clear statement of the thesis, to use specific examples and details to support it, and to finish with a strong conclusion.

■ ADDITIONAL LESSON RESOURCES

- Print student text
- Declaration of Independence
- United States Constitution
- Pledge of Allegiance to the U.S. Flag
- Celebrate Freedom Resources

Topic 1

The Early Americas and European Exploration (Prehistory–1550)

TOPIC 1 ORGANIZER	PACING: APPROX. 1 PERIOD, .5 BLOCKS
	PACING
Connect	1 period
MY STORY VIDEO — Austin Celebrates His Heritage	10 min.
DIGITAL ESSENTIAL QUESTION ACTIVITY — How Much Does Geography Affect People's Lives?	10 min.
DIGITAL MAP ACTIVITY — Physical Features of the United States	10 min.
TOPIC INQUIRY: DOCUMENT-BASED QUESTION — How Reliable is This Account of the Easter Mutiny?	20 min.
Investigate	1–3 periods
TOPIC INQUIRY: DOCUMENT-BASED QUESTION — How Reliable is This Account of the Easter Mutiny?	Ongoing
LESSON 1 — The Early Americas	30–40 min.
LESSON 2 — Early Europe, Africa, and Asia	30–40 min.
LESSON 3 — European Exploration in the Americas	30–40 min.
Synthesize	1 period
DIGITAL ACTIVITY — Reflect on the Essential Question and Topic	10 min.
TOPIC INQUIRY: DOCUMENT-BASED QUESTION — How Reliable is This Account of the Easter Mutiny?	20 min.
Demonstrate	1–2 periods
DIGITAL TOPIC TEST — The Early Americas and European Exploration	10 min.
TOPIC INQUIRY: DOCUMENT-BASED QUESTION — How Reliable is This Account of the Easter Mutiny?	20 min.

NOTES

Topic

How Reliable is This Account of the Easter Mutiny?

While Ferdinand Magellan led the first successful expedition to circumnavigate the world, it was not without significant difficulty and sacrifice on the part of his crew. Magellan had difficulty maintaining his leadership, and a mutiny broke out in 1520. Written accounts of the mutiny exist, but in this Inquiry, students will examine the account of the voyage's record keeper, Antonio Pigafetta, to evaluate its veracity.

STEP 1: CONNECT
Develop Questions and Plan the Investigation

Watch the Entry Event and Discuss
Explain to students that they will evaluate the validity of a primary source about the mutiny that took place during Ferdinand Magellan's voyage in 1520 based on language, corroboration with other sources, and information about the author. They will decide whether or not this account of the mutiny is a reliable description of what took place. Review the primary source, including the language it uses, and the corroborating sources on Magellan's expedition. Then have students view the information about the author.

Suggestion: You can have students watch the biography together in class, or assign them to view it on their own.

Discuss: Have students discuss the video as a class or in small groups. Ask students to explain the reasons for Magellan's expedition and why his route matters today. Students should also imagine what challenges the expedition held for Magellan and his crew. Remind students to use examples from the biography in their discussion.

Suggestion: If you'd prefer students to work outside of class time, you can assign them to write down their thoughts or share them on a class blog or discussion board.

STEP 2: INVESTIGATE
Apply Disciplinary Concepts and Tools

Analyze the Documents
Students will work independently to analyze six sources relating to the expedition. Guide students to write down key facts and observations about each source.

Suggestion: Tell students to make a separate list of notes for each source to help them organize their thinking.

Check Your Understanding
Students will answer the multiple choice and short answer questions attached to each document. Students can discuss the answers in pairs or as a class to ensure understanding.

Suggestion: To save time, students can complete the questions on their own and then check their answers in class.

⏻ PROFESSIONAL DEVELOPMENT

Document-Based Question
Be sure to view the Document-Based Question Professional Development resources in the online course.

STEP 3: SYNTHESIZE
Evaluate Sources
and Use Evidence to Formulate Conclusions

Write Your Essay

Have students prepare the first draft of their essay. Tell students to gather the relevant information from each source and review the notes they took as they examined the documents. Remind students to include evidence from at least one document with information about the author of the primary source and at least two documents that corroborate or conflict with the primary source.

STEP 4: DEMONSTRATE
Communicate Conclusions
and Take Informed Action

Complete Your Essay

Have students revise and submit their essays. Remind students to read over their essays for any errors before turning it in.

Suggestion: When students finish drafting their essays, have them exchange essays with a partner to review. Students should look for topic sentences, organization, evidence, facts, and integration of opposing arguments, as well as correct spelling, grammar, and punctuation.

Suggestion: Have students share with the class whether or not they think Pigafetta's account of the mutiny is valid, or reliable, giving evidence from their essays to support their argument.

INTRODUCTION

The Early Americas and European Exploration (Prehistory–1550)

The United States is a vast country encompassing different geographic regions, from icy mountains to some of the driest, hottest deserts on Earth. The first people to settle in the Americas had their way of life shaped by the environment and resources where they lived. The arrival of the first Europeans brought many changes, with both positive and negative results.

■ CONNECT

MY STORY VIDEO
Austin Celebrates His Heritage

Watch a video about a brother and sister as they learn more about their ancestry.

Check Understanding What musical instrument is essential to Native American culture? *(Drum)*

Determine Point of View What words best describe Austin's perspective about his heritage? *(pride, eagerness to find out more, desire to set a good example)*

DIGITAL ESSENTIAL QUESTION ACTIVITY
How Much Does Geography Affect People's Lives?

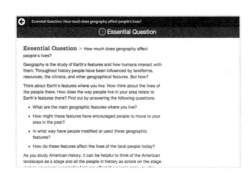

Ask students to think about the Essential Question for this Topic: How much does geography affect people's lives? Geography is the study of Earth's features and how humans interact with them. What role does it play in shaping societies?

If students have not already done so, ask them to think about the questions in the activity. Then go over the answers as a class.

Compare and Contrast Ask students to pick two areas in the United States with dissimilar geographies and explain how life would differ in each area as a result. *(Midwestern plains and northeastern woodlands; in the Midwest the flat land makes farming easier.)*

Support Ideas with Examples Do you think the amount that geography affects people's lives has changed over time? Why or why not? Provide examples to support your view. *(Geography may affect people's lives less now than in the past. For example, heating and air conditioning mean people can live more comfortably year-round in hot and cold climates)*

DIGITAL MAP ACTIVITY
Physical Features of the United States

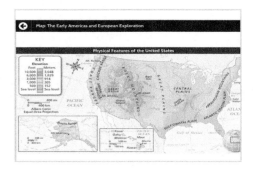

Display the map showing the physical features of the United States. During this Topic students will learn about the early peoples of North America. This map will help them understand the regions in which Native Americans lived.

Analyze Information What region of the United States has the highest elevation? What does this tell you about that area? *(The west; this area is mountainous)*

Analyze Maps Describe three things you notice about the physical features of the United States, based on this map. *(Elevation changes; extensive plains; several large rivers)*

Topic Inquiry
Launch the Topic Inquiry DBQ with students after introducing the topic.

The Early Americas

Supporting English Language Learners

Use with Digital Text 6, **Early North American Societies.**

Learning, Speaking

Ask one or more volunteers to read aloud the first paragraph of the reading. Then point out certain key words in the text, and invite students to share how prior knowledge helps them to understand the meanings of these words. Ask students to use vocabulary from the reading to ask for more information about the reading content. Prompt students to use a range of vocabulary, from key words and expressions needed for basic communication to more abstract, content-based vocabulary during speaking assignments.

Beginning Identify basic words in the text, such as "complex," "culture," and "migrating." Ask students to work in pairs, using those words in questions and responding to them using prior knowledge related to the content.

Intermediate Have students focus on the second sentence in the reading. Ask students to work in pairs, asking what the words in the sentence mean, and responding with examples from previous lessons of each of the items mentioned in the sentence.

Advanced Have students work in pairs and take turns speaking for a couple of minutes each. Have them use vocabulary to state questions they had about the reading and to explain how prior knowledge, from previous lessons or outside the course, enriches their understanding of the content.

Advanced High Invite students to give extended spoken presentations to one another or to the class. Have them share their questions about the content that use abstract, content-based vocabulary, and have them respond to those questions drawing on prior knowledge in ways that enrich students' understanding of the content.

Use with Digital Text 7, **Culture and the Physical Characteristics of North America.**

Writing

Read aloud the section *Cultures of the Northwest Coastal Region*, or invite volunteers to do so. Prompt students to write explanations with increasing specificity and detail to fulfill content area writing needs.

Beginning Have students reread the first paragraph of this reading aloud. Invite students to ask questions about parts of the paragraph that they do not understand. Then have students explain briefly in writing why people in the Northwest stayed in permanent villages.

Intermediate Ask students to write a brief paragraph explaining how the physical environment affected the ways of life of people in the Northwest.

Advanced Have students write a paragraph explain in detail how the environment of the Northwest was related to the customs of its people.

Advanced High Invite to write an essay explaining in detail how the physical environment of the Northwest was connect to the people's culture, including the custom of potlatches.

▣ Differentiate Instruction

Use the Differentiated Instruction notes throughout the lesson plan to support the varied skill sets, levels of readiness, and interests in the mixed-ability classroom.

Challenge These notes include suggestions for expanding the activity for advanced students.

On-Level These notes include suggestions for modifying the activity to address different interests or learning styles.

Extra Support These notes include ideas for providing more scaffolding or reading spuport.

Special Needs These notes provide ideas for adapting instruction to support the needs of various special needs students.

■ NOTES

Topic ① Lesson 1

The Early Americas

Objectives

Objective 1: Explain how people first reached the Americas.

Objective 2: Describe early civilizations and cultures of the Americas.

Objective 3: Identify the human and physical characteristics of regions.

Objective 4: Analyze how physical characteristics influenced population distribution and settlement patterns.

LESSON 1 ORGANIZER		PACING: APPROX. 1 PERIOD, .5 BLOCKS			
				RESOURCES	
		OBJECTIVES	**PACING**	**Online**	**Print**
Connect					
DIGITAL START UP ACTIVITY **Physical Geography Affects Ways of Life**			5 min.	●	
Investigate					
DIGITAL TEXT 1 **The First Americans**		Objective 1	10 min.	●	●
DIGITAL TEXT 2; DIGITAL TEXT 3 **Olmecs Develop a Civilization; Mayan Civilization**		Objective 2	20 min.	●	●
DIGITAL TEXT 4; DIGITAL TEXT 5 **Aztec Civilization; Incan Civilization**		Objective 2	20 min.	●	●
DIGITAL TEXT 6; DIGITAL TEXT 7 **Early North American Societies; Culture and the Physical Characteristics of North America**		Objective 3	20 min.	●	●
INTERACTIVE MAP **Native American Culture Regions of North America**			10 min.	●	
DIGITAL TEXT 8; DIGITAL TEXT 9 **Religion; The Iroquois League**		Objective 4	20 min.	●	●
INTERACTIVE GALLERY **Housing Adaptations Based on Environment**			10 min.	●	
Synthesize					
DIGITAL ACTIVITY **Adapting to the Environment**			5 min.	●	
Demonstrate					
DIGITAL QUIZ **Lesson Quiz and Class Discussion Board**			10 min.	●	

CONNECT

DIGITAL START UP ACTIVITY
Physical Geography Affects Ways of Life

Project the Start Up Activity Ask students to look at the map as they enter and get settled. Then have them discuss their answers with another student, either in class or through a chat or blog space.

Discuss What would people do if they lived somewhere very cold? What about somewhere very hot? *(Use furs for warm clothing; build settlements in shade)* How might people find food if they lived near water? What about in the hills? *(Fishing, hunting, trapping game, gathering plants)*

Tell students that in this lesson they will be learning about how the physical characteristics of the environment shaped where Native Americans settled and how they lived.

Aa **Vocabulary Development:** Use the Interactive Reading Notepad to preview the Key Terms and Academic Vocabulary in the lesson with students.

↑↓ FLIP IT!
Assign the Flipped Video for this lesson.

STUDENT EDITION PRINT PAGES: 4–20

INVESTIGATE

DIGITAL TEXT 1
The First Americans

Objective 1: Explain how people first reached the Americas.

Quick Instruction
Project the image on the whiteboard. Explain to students that the physical characteristics of the environment influenced population distribution and early settlements in North America.

Categorize Ask students to describe the physical characteristics of different environments in the United States, such as deserts, mountains, and forests.

D **Differentiate: Challenge** Ask students to describe the physical characteristics of their environment and explain how these characteristics influence their community.

Further Instruction
Go through the Interactive Reading Notepad questions and discuss the answers with the class. To extend the lesson, have students go through the additional resource Geography: People and Their Environments.

Sequence Events Have students explain the process by which Native Americans spread across and came to settle in North America. *(They arrived on foot over land exposed by lower sea levels, or by sea, and spread across the continent in search of food, eventually building settlements around farming.)*

Make Predictions Ask students to predict how the different geographical regions of North America will impact Native American groups. *(Native Americans will adapt differently to their regions, developing different settlements and ways of life.)*

DIGITAL TEXT 2
Olmecs Develop a Civilization

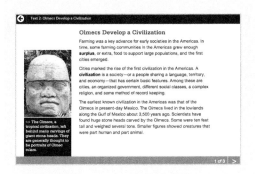

Objective 2: Describe early civilizations and cultures of the Americas.

Quick Instruction
Project the image on the whiteboard. Explain that the Olmecs and the Mayas were two different tropical civilizations that were shaped by the physical characteristics of their environment in Central America. In both civilizations, farmers supported nearby cities and leaders built temples of stone. The Olmecs also built giant stone heads.

Compare and Contrast How might the Olmec and Maya civilizations differ from a civilization built in a colder region? Why? *(There would be more opportunities for farming. The clothing, food, and houses would differ.)*

Further Instruction
Go through the Interactive Reading Notepad questions for *Olmec Civilization and Maya Civilization* with the class, including the graphic organizer asking students to describe the features of the Olmec civilization. Review the features of the civilization on the whiteboard as you go.

Be sure that students understand that the physical characteristics of the environment in Central America influenced features of Olmec civilization. Discuss how both Olmec and Maya settlements were shaped by the geographic region in which the civilizations lived.

The Early Americas

DIGITAL TEXT 3

Mayan Civilization

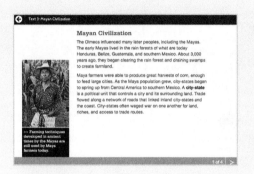

Mayan Civilization

The Olmecs influenced many later peoples, including the Mayas. The early Mayas lived in the rain forests of what are today Honduras, Belize, Guatemala, and southern Mexico. About 3,000 years ago, they began clearing the rain forest and draining swamps to create farmland.

Maya farmers were able to produce great harvests of corn, enough to feed large cities. As the Maya population grew, city-states began to spring up from Central America to southern Mexico. A **city-state** is a political unit that controls a city and its surrounding land. Trade flowed along a network of roads that linked inland city-states and the coast. City-states often waged war on one another for land, riches, and access to trade routes.

>> Farming techniques developed in ancient times by the Mayas are still used by Maya farmers today.

1 of 4 >

DIGITAL TEXT 4

Aztec Civilization

Aztec Civilization

Long after the Maya cities were abandoned, a new civilization arose to the northwest. Its builders were the Aztecs. The early Aztecs were nomads, people who moved from place to place in search of food. In the 1300s, the Aztecs settled around Lake Texcoco (tays koh) in central Mexico. From there, they built a powerful empire.

Tenochtitlán On an island in the middle of the lake, the Aztecs built their capital, Tenochtitlán (tay nawch tee TLAHN). They constructed a system of **causeways**, or raised roads made of packed earth. The causeways linked the capital to the mainland.

The Aztecs learned to farm the shallow swamps of Lake Texcoco. In some places, they dug canals, using the mud they removed to fill in parts of the lake. In other places, they attached floating reed mats to the lake bottom with long stakes. Then, they piled mud onto the mats to create farmland. Aztec farmers harvested several crops a year on these chinampas, or floating gardens.

>> Aztecs adapted to life on an island in the middle of a lake with limited land area by using chinampas for agriculture, even planting trees to better anchor them to the lake bed.

1 of 4 >

DIGITAL TEXT 5

Incan Civilization

Inca Civilization

Far to the south of the Aztecs, the Incas built one of the largest empires in the Americas. By 1550, their empire stretched for almost 2,500 miles along the west coast of South America.

An Impressive Capital The center of the Inca empire was the magnificent capital at Cuzco (KOOS koh), located high in the Andes in present-day Peru. Cuzco was a holy city to the Incas. All nobles in the empire tried to visit it at least once in their lifetimes. The city had massive palaces and temples made of stone and decorated with gold ornaments. At the center was the palace of the emperor, who was known as the Sapa Inca. The emperor was regarded as a god who was descended from the sun god.

>> This ancient Inca stone wall remains standing today.

1 of 4 >

Identify Cause and Effect How did farming cause Olmec cities to grow? *(Farming allowed people to build permanent settlements. Having sufficient food enabled larger populations to grow.)*

Generate Explanations Have students explain why the Mayas' successful farming enabled the civilization to make developments in mathematics and astronomy. *(Successful harvests meant not everyone had to farm. Priests therefore had the time to study.)*

Objective 2: **Describe early civilizations and cultures of the Americas.**

Quick Instruction

Project the image of Machu Picchu. Explain that the Aztecs were a civilization in present-day Mexico, while further south, the Incas built a civilization along the west coast of South America. The Aztecs settled near shallow swamps, and the Incas in the mountains. Both civilizations altered the land in order to farm.

Analyze Information Ask students to examine the image of Machu Picchu and describe the physical environment where the Incas lived. Then ask how and why the Incas modified their physical environment. *(The terrain was mountainous and rugged. The Incas cut flat areas into the mountains where they could build houses and farms.)*

Further Instruction

Go through the Interactive Reading Notepad questions for *Aztec Civilization and Inca Civilization* with the class.

Be sure that students understand how the physical characteristics of the environment influenced both the Aztecs and the Incas. Discuss the different environments where the two groups lived and the ways these differences were reflected in the civilizations.

Compare and Contrast where the Incas and the Aztecs lived and how they utilized their environments. *(The Aztecs settled around a lake. They built causeways, canals, and chinampas to farm and get around. The Incas built terraces with stone walls to farm in the mountains. They also built bridges and roads to travel through different regions.)*

Determine Relevance Why is it relevant to know about the physical characteristics of the region in which a civilization lived? *(The characteristics can explain what resources people had, how they used these resources, and how the resources shaped their way of life.)*

DIGITAL TEXT 6

Early North American Societies

DIGITAL TEXT 7

Culture and the Physical Characteristics of North America

INTERACTIVE MAP

Native American Culture Regions of North America

Objective 3: **Identify the human and physical characteristics of regions.**

Quick Instruction

Interactive Map: Native American Culture Regions of North America Project the map and click through the hotspots. Introduce the map activity by telling students that early North American societies were divided into different culture regions. The physical characteristics of these environments influenced the cultures that called each region home. Prompt students to compare these regions in terms of human characteristics.

☷ ACTIVE CLASSROOM

Ask students to use the *Write 1-Get 3* strategy to describe four ways culture regions shaped early North American societies. *(Culture regions determined food, clothing, shelter, settlement patterns, artwork, and religious ceremonies.)*

Analyze Maps What physical characteristics of the environment led North America to be divided into different culture regions? *(Temperature; rainfall; geography; available natural resources)*

ELL Use the ELL activity described in the ELL chart.

Further Instruction

Go through the Interactive Reading Notepad questions for *Early North American Societies and Culture* and *Physical Characteristics of North America* with the class, including the graphic organizer asking students to explain how each Native American culture adapted to the climate and resources in the area.

Identify Central Issues How did the physical environment determine which Native American groups were nomadic and which groups lived in permanent or semi-permanent settlements? *(Native Americans built more permanent settlements in areas with sufficient food and natural resources throughout the year. When there were not enough resources to survive in one place, groups had to move.)*

Support Ideas with Evidence The Hohokams built irrigation ditches, while the Mount Builders did not use irrigation at all. How does this evidence show that the groups lived in different culture regions? *(The Mound Builders lived in a wetter climate than the Hohokams, evidenced by the fact that they did not need to irrigate their crops.)*

The Early Americas

DIGITAL TEXT 8
Religion

DIGITAL TEXT 9
The Iroquois League

INTERACTIVE GALLERY
Housing Adaptations Based on Environment

Objective 4: Analyze how physical characteristics influenced population distribution and settlement patterns.

Quick Instruction
Remind students that the physical characteristics of regions shaped where people lived and what their lives were like. This includes people's religious practices and housing. It also includes their social and political structures, as with the Iroquois in present-day New York.

Interactive Gallery: Housing Adaptations Based on Environment Project the images. Look at each image individually and then the collection as a whole. Remind students that the human characteristics of each region were different. Native American groups lived in different types of dwellings depending on where they lived.

📷 ACTIVE CLASSROOM
Create a quick copy of one compelling image from the Native American housing adaptations interactive gallery. Label the different features of the dwelling and explain how these features suited the environment in which the dwelling was used.

Analyze Images Ask students to describe the materials used to make the houses in the image gallery. Why was there such wide variety in materials used? *(Houses were made out of snow, clay, trees, and skins. They varied depending on what material were available, whether they needed to be portable, and whether they kept people warm or cool.)*

Further Instruction
Go through the Interactive Reading Notepad questions for *Religion* and *The Iroquios Confederacy* with the class. To extend the lesson, have students go through the additional resource Geography: Population and Settlements.

Remind students that Native American cultures, beliefs, and social structures were shaped by the environments in which people lived.

Draw Conclusions What conclusions about the human characteristics of Iroquois culture and society can you draw based on the fact that they lived in long houses? *(Long houses were built of trees, meaning Iroquois lived in wooded areas. Long houses are sturdy, meaning the Iroquois were not nomadic.)*

Identify Cause and Effect How did the physical environment affect Native American religious practices? *(Native Americans relied on the environment to survive. Ceremonies honored aspects of nature needed for survival, such as rain, fish, and corn.)*

■ SYNTHESIZE

DIGITAL ACTIVITY
Adapting to the Environment

Have students use the Think-Pair-Share strategy to answer the questions in the Adapting to the Environment activity. Poll the class on which culture region that would most want to live in and then discuss why.

Have partners think about the following question. How do people adapt to the physical environments in which they live? Ask students to come up with examples from the lesson, and from their own lives.

■ DEMONSTRATE

DIGITAL QUIZ
Lesson Quiz and Class Discussion Board

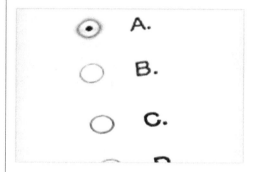

Assign the online Lesson Quiz for this lesson if you haven't already done so. Students will be offered automatic remediation or enrichment based on their score.

Pose these questions to the class on the Discussion Board:

In *The Early Americas*, you read about the first civilizations and cultures of the Americas and how these populations were influenced by the physical characteristics of different regions.

Hypothesize Following the arrival of Europeans to North America, Native American groups were steadily pushed off their land. How do you think relocating to new culture regions impacted Native American traditions? *(Native Americans were forced to adapt their traditions to new physical environments.)*

Pose and Answer Questions What is an additional question that you have about the physical and human characteristics of the early Americas? Write down your question and a possible response.

Topic Inquiry
Have students continue their investigations for the Topic Inquiry.

Early Europe, Africa, and Asia

Supporting English Language Learners

Use with Digital Text 3, **African Cultures and Technologies.**

Speaking
Have students read the section *Ways of Life in Africa*. Encourage students to draw on their own prior experiences to understand the meanings of sentences in the reading.

Beginning Have students, in class or working in pairs, identify words in the subsection that name family members (e.g., *grandparent*). Ask students to draw on their own experience and share the names of their relatives that correspond to these categories.

Intermediate Select one or more key words from the text, such as *extended, loyalty,* or *cooperation*. Provide students with an example from your life that illustrates one of these words. Then ask students, in class or working in pairs, to explain the meanings of other words with examples from their lives.

Advanced In class or working in pairs, have students draw on their own experience of family relationships to make sense of African family structures. Have them compare their own families with African families.

Advanced High Invite students to think about their experiences of family or religion. Invite them to share with the class, or with each other in pairs, how their prior experiences compare and contrast with the information in the reading.

Use with Digital Text 5, **Europe's Renaissance.**

Speaking
Have students read the sections *Portuguese Voyages* and *Further Exploration*, working in pairs. Have students share information from the reading with each other using a range of vocabulary from key words and expressions needed for basic communication to more abstract and content-based vocabulary.

Beginning Display a list of several key vocabulary words that are found in the text. Ask students to choose from these words in order to give information to one another about the text's content.

Intermediate Taking turns, have students say the name of a key figure in Portugal's exploration (e.g., Henry the Navigator). Challenge students to state opinions and give factual information about the person using complete sentences using key words and content-based vocabulary.

Advanced Have students identify three key events during the 1400s that relate to Portugal's exploration. Have students to use transitional words and phrases as they give information about these events in chronological order in extended spoken responses

Advanced High Ask students to infer key themes and concepts from the text. Have each student use abstract and content-based vocabulary to present information about these themes and concepts.

▣ Differentiate Instruction

Use the Differentiated Instruction notes throughout the lesson plan to support the varied skill sets, levels of readiness, and interests in the mixed-ability classroom.

Challenge These notes include suggestions for expanding the activity for advanced students.

On-Level These notes include suggestions for modifying the activity to address different interests or learning styles.

Extra Support These notes include ideas for providing more scaffolding or reading spuport.

Special Needs These notes provide ideas for adapting instruction to support the needs of various special needs students.

■ NOTES

PEARSON
realize™
www.PearsonRealize.com

Go online to access additional resources including:
Primary Sources • Biographies • Supreme Court cases •
21st Century Skill Tutorials • Maps • Graphic Organizers.

Objectives

Objective 1: Describe how Europe changed in the Middle Ages, including through technological innovations.

Objective 2: Describe patterns of trade and technological innovations in the Muslim world, Africa, and East Asia.

Objective 3: Identify the impact of technological innovations on Renaissance Europe.

LESSON 2 ORGANIZER		PACING: APPROX. 1 PERIOD, .5 BLOCKS			
				RESOURCES	
		OBJECTIVES	**PACING**	**Online**	**Print**
Connect					
DIGITAL START UP ACTIVITY **The World is a Smaller Place**			5 min.	●	
Investigate					
DIGITAL TEXT 1 **Europe in the Middle Ages**		Objective 1	10 min.	●	●
DIGITAL TEXT 2 **The Middle East**			10 min.	●	●
DIGITAL TEXT 3 **African Cultures and Technologies**		Objective 2	10 min.	●	●
INTERACTIVE ILLUSTRATION **How an Astrolabe Works**			10 min.	●	
DIGITAL TEXT 4 **Chinese Trade and Technology**		Objective 2	10 min.	●	●
DIGITAL TEXT 5 **Europe's Renaissance**		Objective 3	10 min.	●	●
3-D MODEL **Seafaring Technologies**			10 min.	●	
Synthesize					
DIGITAL ACTIVITY **Technology and Exploration**			5 min.	●	
Demonstrate					
DIGITAL QUIZ **Lesson Quiz and Class Discussion Board**			10 min.	●	

Early Europe, Africa, and Asia

▌CONNECT

DIGITAL START UP ACTIVITY
The World is a Smaller Place

Project the Start Up Activity As students settle in and get ready, ask them to pick an object in the classroom and write a few sentences answering the questions. Then have them discuss their answers with another student, either in class or through a chat or blog space.

Discuss Was your object made in the United States or in a different country? What materials and methods had to be invented to create your object? Has this object improved your life, and if so, how? *(Answers will vary but should mention that many everyday products travel long distances, as innovations continue to make the world smaller and easier.)*

Aa Vocabulary Development: Use the Interactive Reading Notepad to preview the Key Terms and Academic Vocabulary in this lesson with students.

⚑ FLIP IT!
Assign the Flipped Video for this lesson.

▌STUDENT EDITION PRINT PAGES: 21–32

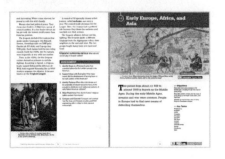

▌INVESTIGATE

DIGITAL TEXT 1
Europe in the Middle Ages

Objective 1: Describe how Europe changed in the Middle Ages, including through technological innovations.

Quick Instruction
Project the image of the mariner's magnetic compass on the whiteboard. Explain that the needle of a magnetic compass points north. Tell students that technological innovations,especially in sailing and navigation, led to changes in Europe and around the world.

D Differentiate: Extra Support Have students draw the four cardinal directions. Explain that before the magnetic compass, people found north by looking at the sun or stars. Ask students why someone navigating a ship would want to locate north.

Draw Conclusions Ask students why they think the development of the magnetic compass was a significant innovation. *(It improved navigation, letting ships travel greater distances. It helped ships determine their direction more accurately.)*

Further Instruction
Go through the Interactive Reading Notepad questions and discuss the answers with the class.

Identify Central Issues Ask students to name three examples of technological innovations that took place in the Middle Ages and explain how they impacted the daily lives of Europeans. *(New methods enabled farmers to produce more food. New sailing*

skills developed. The magnetic compass and the astrolabe helped sailors travel farther from land.)

Identify Cause and Effect What factors caused Europeans to travel greater distances outside Europe? *(Demand for trade; the Crusades; technological innovations)*

Make Predictions Make a prediction about how growing trade in the Middle East will impact life in Europe. *(Demand for Middle Eastern goods will continue to grow, prompting more travel and exploration.)*

DIGITAL TEXT 2
The Middle East

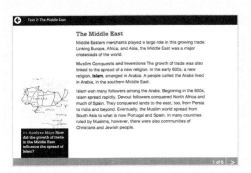

DIGITAL TEXT 3
African Cultures and Technologies

INTERACTIVE ILLUSTRATION
How an Astrolabe Works

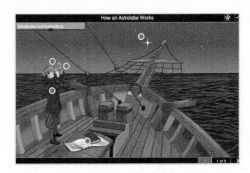

Objective 2: Describe patterns of trade and technological innovations in the Muslim world, Africa, and East Asia.

Quick Instruction
Project the image of the astrolabe on the whiteboard. Explain that technological innovations in sailing and navigation allowed Europeans to travel to the Middle East, Africa, and China. Many technologies we use today were developed in these regions. These innovations spread around the world by merchants, traders, sailors, and other travelers.

Interactive Illustration: How an Astrolabe Works Project the interactive activity on the whiteboard and click through the hotspots. Look at each image individually to make sure students understand the components of the astrolabe.

Summarize Have students explain in their own words how an astrolabe works. *(It measures a ship's location in relation to the sun, moon, planets, or stars. The angle between the horizon and the object in the sky corresponds to the ship's latitude.)*

Draw Conclusions How did the astrolabe enable explorers to find new trade routes? *(It let ships travel further from land without getting lost.)*

📷 ACTIVE CLASSROOM

Pair students and have them use the Audio Tour strategy to go through the activity. Have the first student describe each part of the illustration and the second student explain its significance. *(The alidade aligns with a distant object to measure the angle between the object in the sky and the horizon; the mater and rete also measure this angle; a latitude table gives the latitude based on this angle and the date.)*

ELL Use the ELL activity described in the ELL chart.

Further Instruction
Go through the Interactive Reading Notepad questions for *The Middle East, and African Cultures and Technology*, including the graphic organizer summarizing how Muslim groups created an exchange of cultures between the Middle East, Europe, and Asia. To extend the lesson, have students go through the primary source "Travels," by Ibn Battuta.

Be sure that students understand the patterns of trade and technological innovations that impacted the Middle East, Africa, and China. Discuss the technologies that emerged out of each region and how they impacted life around the world.

Early Europe, Africa, and Asia

DIGITAL TEXT 4	DIGITAL TEXT 5	3-D MODEL

Chinese Trade and Technology

Europe's Renaissance

Seafaring Technologies

Objective 2: Describe patterns of trade and technological innovations in the Muslim world, Africa, and East Asia.

Quick Instruction
Project the image of the Chinese cargo ship on the whiteboard. Explain that technological innovations in sailing and navigation allowed Europeans to travel to China.

Identify Central Issues How did technological innovations give rise to new trade routes? *(Technological innovations enabled explorers to travel greater distances, opening up new trade routes connecting Asia, Africa, Europe, and the Middle East.)*

Further Instruction
Go through the Interactive Notepad questions for *Chinese Trade and Technology*.

Discuss Prompt students to discuss any parallels they see between concurrent technological innovations in China and other regions of the world.

Objective 3: Identify the impact of technological innovations on the Renaissance.

Quick Instruction
Remind students that technological innovations changed European society and increased the contact Europeans had with other cultures. The Renaissance was a burst of learning and technological innovation in Europe that led to greater exploration and trade.

3-D Model: Seafaring Technologies Project the interactivity on the whiteboard and scroll to animate the image for the students. Click to the second screen to reveal the hotspots. Look at each image individually to make sure students understand the different aspects of navigation technology on the ship.

👥 ACTIVE CLASSROOM

Pair students together. Have the first student describe each part of the 3-D Model and the second explain its significance.

ELL Use the ELL activity described in the ELL chart.

Further Instruction
Go through the Interactive Reading Notepad questions for *Europe's Renaissance* with the class. Have students complete the additional resource Elements of Culture.

Support Ideas with Examples What improvements in sailing occurred during the Renaissance, and how did these innovations impact Europe? *(The development of the caravel, in addition to previous inventions like the astrolabe and magnetic compass, enabled Europeans to travel farther and more accurately. Instruction in navigation and shipbuilding also allowed sailors to travel greater distances, opening up new routes for trade.)*

Infer Ask students why they think the Renaissance led to the first European voyages to the Americas. *(Increased interest in exploration and in finding new trade routes led Europeans to cross the Atlantic in search of a new route to Asia.)*

■ SYNTHESIZE

DIGITAL ACTIVITY
Technology and Exploration

Have students select an innovation discussed in the lesson and answer the questions in the Technology and Exploration Activity. Have students share their findings with the class, ensuring a variety of innovations are covered.

At the beginning of this lesson, students considered how the world became a smaller place. Ask students how the technological innovations they learned about in this lesson made the world smaller. Have students share their answers with the class.

■ DEMONSTRATE

DIGITAL QUIZ
Lesson Quiz and Class Discussion Board

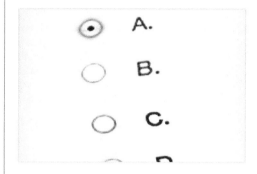

Assign the online Lesson Quiz for this lesson if you haven't already done so. Students will be offered automatic remediation or enrichment based on their score.

Pose these questions to the class on the Discussion Board:

In *Early Europe, Africa, and Asia*, you read about culture and society in early Europe, the Middle East, Africa, and China, and considered technological innovations that changed life around the globe.

Draw Conclusions How did technological innovations lead to greater contact among people in early Europe, Africa, and Asia? *(Improvements in navigation led to voyages of exploration and trade that increased contact among people from different continents.)*

Compare How were the effects of technological innovations in Europe, Asia, Africa, and the Middle East different from the innovations of Native American peoples that you read about in the previous lesson? *(The effects of technological innovations in Europe, Asia, and Africa, unlike those in the Americas, included improvements in navigation. Partly as a result, they spread much more widely among different cultures than innovations in the Americas did.)*

Topic Inquiry
Have students continue their investigations for the Topic Inquiry.

European Exploration in the Americas

Supporting English Language Learners

Use with Digital Text 2, **The Voyages of Columbus.**

Speaking
Review the definition of an opinion. Then have students read the section titled *The Impact of Columbus's Voyages*. Prompt students, in class or working in pairs, to express opinions ranging from communicating single words and short phrases to participating in extended discussions on a variety of social and grade-appropriate academic topics.

Beginning Ask students to state an opinion on whether they think the impact of Columbus's voyages was positive or negative, using single words or short phrases.

Intermediate Invite students to share aloud their opinion about the impact of Columbus's voyages. Provide them with a sentence frame such as: I think that Columbus's voyages _____ because _____.

Advanced Ask students: In your opinion, did the positive impact of Columbus's voyages on Native Americans outweigh their negative impact, or was the opposite true? Have students give reasons for their responses.

Advanced High Pair students that have differing opinions about the impact of Columbus's voyages. Give them time to have an extended discussion of their viewpoints using factual details and persuasive language.

Use with Digital Text 4, **The Columbian Exchange.**

Learning
Have students read the first paragraph in the section *Modifying Environments*. Working in small groups or pairs, have student explain what they have learned. Have students monitor and correct their own speech as needed. Model self-corrective techniques for students by making a statement using incorrect grammar, and poor word choices, then correct yourself. For example, you might say, "Europeans brought animals. The place wasn't never the same after that." Point out the grammar error in the second sentence. Ask students to rephrase your statement using accurate and correct language.

Beginning Pair students. Have each student state one thing that they learned from this reading. Ask students to take turns thinking about what they have said and correcting any mistakes.

Intermediate Ask partners to take turns making statements about the reading. Ask students to identify ways that they could improve their statements, then ask them to rephrase their statement with those improvements.

Advanced In pairs, ask students to take turns making a statement about the reading. Ask students to reflect on what they've said and to rephrase their statement using more academic language and sentences with more than one clause.

Advanced High Invite students, individually or in small groups, to make a statement about the reading using everyday language. Then have students identify ways that academic language differs from everyday language and apply those differences to their statement, rephrasing it using academic language.

▣ Differentiate Instruction

Use the Differentiated Instruction notes throughout the lesson plan to support the varied skill sets, levels of readiness, and interests in the mixed-ability classroom.

Challenge These notes include suggestions for expanding the activity for advanced students.

On-Level These notes include suggestions for modifying the activity to address different interests or learning styles.

Extra Support These notes include ideas for providing more scaffolding or reading spuport.

Special Needs These notes provide ideas for adapting instruction to support the needs of various special needs students.

■ NOTES

PEARSON
realize™
www.PearsonRealize.com

Go online to access additional resources including:
Primary Sources • Biographies • Supreme Court cases •
21st Century Skill Tutorials • Maps • Graphic Organizers.

Objectives

Objective 1: Identify reasons for European exploration of the Americas.

Objective 2: Describe the results of European exploration in the Americas.

Objective 3: Evaluate how exchanges between Europeans and Native Americans modified the physical environment.

LESSON 3 ORGANIZER		PACING: APPROX. 1 PERIOD, .5 BLOCKS			
				RESOURCES	
		OBJECTIVES	PACING	Online	Print
Connect					
DIGITAL START UP ACTIVITY **The Desire to See New Places**			5 min.	●	
Investigate					
DIGITAL TEXT 1 **Early Contact with the Americas**			10 min.	●	●
DIGITAL TEXT 2 **The Voyages of Columbus**		Objective 1	10 min.	●	●
INTERACTIVE CHART **Reasons to Explore**			10 min.	●	
DIGITAL TEXT 3 **Other Spanish Exploration**		Objective 2	10 min.	●	●
DIGITAL TEXT 4 **The Columbian Exchange**		Objective 3	10 min.	●	●
INTERACTIVE MAP **The Columbian Exchange**			10 min.	●	
Synthesize					
DIGITAL ACTIVITY **Exploring the New World**			5 min.	●	
Demonstrate					
DIGITAL QUIZ **Lesson Quiz and Class Discussion Board**			10 min.	●	

European Exploration in the Americas

■ CONNECT

DIGITAL START UP ACTIVITY
The Desire to See New Places

Project the Start Up Activity Ask students to generate their lists as they enter and get settled. Then have them answer the questions alone or in pairs, in class or through a chat or blog space.

Discuss Why did kings and queens want to pay for expensive voyages across the seas? What did they hope to gain? (*Land, wealth, power, knowledge*) Travel in those days was long and filled with dangers. What would make people want to take such risks? (*Curiosity, excitement, desire for wealth or prestige*) What benefits did Europeans expect to gain by traveling? What do you think they found? (*New trade routes; unfamiliar land*)

Aa Vocabulary Development: Use the Interactive Reading Notepad to preview the Key Terms and Academic Vocabulary in this lesson with students.

⇅ FLIP IT!

Assign the Flipped Video for this lesson.

■ STUDENT EDITION PRINT PAGES: 33–40

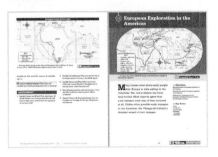

■ INVESTIGATE

DIGITAL TEXT 1
Early Contact with the Americas

Objective 1: Identify reasons for European exploration of the Americas.

Quick Instruction
Interactive Chart: Reasons to Explore Project the image of the interactive chart on the whiteboard and discuss the reasons for European exploration with students. Explain that Europeans did not know America existed until Columbus traveled west searching for a new trade route to Asia.

📖 ACTIVE CLASSROOM

List the following reasons on the board: land, colonies, riches, religion, personal glory, empire. Have students use the Rank It strategy to rank the reasons for European exploration from strongest to weakest. Ask students to justify their ranking decision and then share their rankings and justifications with a partner. Poll the class to see if there is agreement on the ranking.

DIGITAL TEXT 2
The Voyages of Columbus

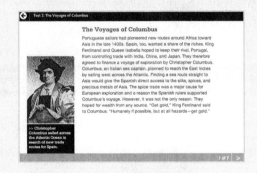

Summarize Have students explain in their own words why they think Europeans traveled to North America and continued exploring the continent once they arrived. (*Europeans were looking for land, wealth, and new trade opportunities. They wanted to convert Native Americans to Christianity and spread European empires.*)

ELL Use the ELL activity described in the ELL chart.

Further Instruction
Go through the Interactive Reading Notepad questions for *Early Contact with the Americas* and *The Voyages of Columbus* and discuss the answers with the class. Make sure students understand why Europeans began exploring the Americas and why Columbus's voyage marked a decisive change in history.

INTERACTIVE CHART

Reasons to Explore

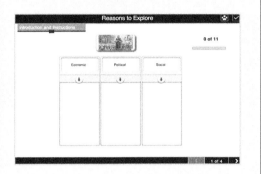

DIGITAL TEXT 3

Other Spanish Exploration

Cite Evidence What evidence does the text give to explain why Ferdinand and Isabella supported Columbus's voyage? *(Spain wanted a share of the riches in Africa and Asia. Ferdinand and Isabella wanted Columbus to increase Spain's access to the spice trade. They also wanted Columbus to get gold.)*

Evaluate Arguments Columbus is often described as "discovering" America. Why is this statement inaccurate? *(People were already living in the Americas when Columbus arrived. Other travelers from Europe and Asia had also set foot in North America before him.)*

Objective 2: Describe the results of European exploration in the Americas.

Quick Instruction

Project the image of Vasco Núñez de Balboa on the whiteboard. Explain that following Columbus, the Spanish exploration moved into North America. Meanwhile, Ferdinand Magellan, Balboa, and others explored the Caribbean and the Pacific.

Infer Why do you think explorers began to explore North America? *(To claim land for Spain; to find new trade routes; because they were curious about the land and people; because they hoped for wealth and fame)*

Hypothesize What difficulties do you think these explorers faced? *(Bad weather and storms; lack of food and water; conflict with Native Americans; disease; getting lost)*

D **Differentiate: Extra Support** Have students locate the following places on a map or globe: Spain, the Atlantic Ocean, the Caribbean, Panama, North America, the Pacific Ocean, Asia. Have students use the map to trace the voyages of European explorers as they read.

Further Instruction

Go through the Interactive Reading Notepad questions and discuss the answers with the class. As students review the voyages discussed in the lesson, be sure they also consider the impact of these voyages in both Europe and the Americas. To extend the lesson, have students go through the additional resource What is Human Geography: Geography.

Infer What does Magellan's death in a battle with local people of the Philippine islands suggest was one result of European exploration? *(Hostile contact with people who lived in the areas that Europeans were exploring)*

Identify Cause and Effect How did European discoveries in the Americas affect the Spanish empire? *(These discoveries expanded the Spanish to include new territory, opened up new trade routes to Asia, and brought riches to Spain.)*

European Exploration in the Americas

DIGITAL TEXT 4
The Columbian Exchange

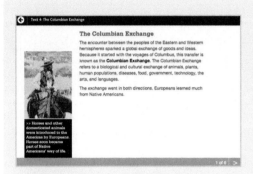

INTERACTIVE MAP
The Columbian Exchange

Objective 3: **Evaluate the consequences of human modification of the physical environment that resulted from exchange between Europeans and Native Americans.**

Quick Instruction

European exploration brought Europeans and Native Americans in contact with one another. This led to a global exchange of goods and ideas that modified cultures on both sides of the Atlantic. It also modified the physical environment of the Americas, with both positive and negative results.

Interactive Map: The Columbian Exchange
Project the Interactive Activity on the whiteboard. Use the slider to show the movement of goods from west to east. Point out that this exchange brought new goods from Europe, Africa, and Asia to the Americas, and spread goods from the Americas in turn. Add that it also spread language, skills, ideas, and even disease.

Use Context Clues Have students define what they think a "global exchange" means. *(The swap of goods and ideas back and forth from different places around the globe)*

Identify Central Issues Have students explain why the Columbian Exchange had both positive and negative consequences. *(Some of the new goods, skills, and ideas that were spread made life better for people. The introduction of new species and new ways of modifying the environment was not always as beneficial. The spread of diseases killed millions.)*

ELL Use the ELL activity described in the ELL chart.

ACTIVE CLASSROOM

Have students use the Wallpaper strategy to draw a key piece of information about the Columbian Exchange. Have students post their drawings and look at what others have created, jotting down ideas as they occur.

Further Instruction

Go through the Interactive Reading Notepad questions and use the graphic organizer to list positive and negative consequences of the Columbian Exchange for Native Americans and for Europeans.

Support Ideas with Examples Give an example of how the Columbian Exchange modified the physical environment of the Americas. *(Farming; mining; the introduction of new crops and animals)*

SYNTHESIZE

DIGITAL ACTIVITY
Exploring the New World

Ask students to recall the list they made in the Digital Start Up Activity considering reasons Europeans wanted to explore. Have them address the consequences of these reasons as they answer the questions in the Exploring the New World activity. Ask students to write down their answers, and then share their findings with a partner.

Have partners think about the final question. Were the overall consequences of European exploration in the Americas positive or negative? Have partners share their answers with the class, explaining their reasoning.

DEMONSTRATE

DIGITAL QUIZ
Lesson Quiz and Class Discussion Board

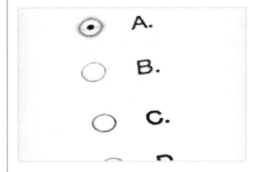

Assign the online Lesson Quiz for this lesson if you haven't already done so. Students will be offered automatic remediation or enrichment based on their score.

Pose these questions to the class on the Discussion Board:

In *European Exploration of the Americas*, you read about the reasons Europeans explored the Americas and the consequences of that exploration.

Support a Point of View with Evidence
Why is Columbus's voyage to the Americas considered a "turning point" in world history? *(His voyage led to sustained contact among peoples of all continents in the world for the first time, to the Columbian Exchange, and to the European colonization of the Americas.)*

Make Predictions How would European exploration continue to affect Native Americans and the physical environment of the New World after the period discussed in this lesson? *(European diseases would kill many Native Americans, and European colonization would displace them from their homelands. The physical environment would be affected by European colonization, agricultural practices, and the Columbian Exchange.)*

Topic Inquiry
Have students continue their investigations for the Topic Inquiry.

The Early Americas and European Exploration (Prehistory–1550)

■ SYNTHESIZE

DIGITAL ACTIVITY
Reflect on the Essential Question and Topic

First, ask students to reconsider the Essential Question for the Topic: How much does geography affect people's lives? Remind students that geography includes the land, climate, environment, resources, and other features of a region.

Have students pick two of the individuals listed in the activity. Ask, "How do you think geography influenced their lives?" Ask them to give at least three examples supporting their position. Discuss their answers as a class or ask students to post their answers on the Class Discussion board.

Next ask students to reflect on the Topic as a whole and jot down one to three questions they've thought about during the Topic. Share these examples if they need help getting started:

- How are people affected by the geography of where they live?
- What motivates someone to move to a faraway place?
- How do people impact the physical environment in which they live, positively and negatively?

■ DEMONSTRATE

DIGITAL TOPIC REVIEW AND ASSESSMENT
The Early Americas and European Exploration (Prehistory–1550)

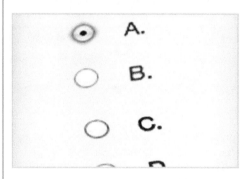

Students can prepare for the Topic Test by answering the questions in the Topic Review and Assessment online or the Assessment questions in the Print Student text. They can also prepare by reviewing their answers to the Interactive Reading Notepad questions or reviewing their notes in the Reading and Notetaking Study Guide.

DIGITAL TOPIC TEST
The Early Americas and European Exploration (Prehistory–1550)

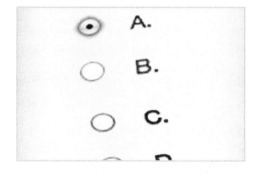

TOPIC TEST
Assign the Topic Test to assess students' understanding of topic content.

BENCHMARK TESTS
Assign these benchmark tests as you complete the relevant topics to monitor student progress toward mastering the course content and as preparation for the End-of-Course Test.

Benchmark Test 1: Topics 1–2

Benchmark Test 2: Topics 3–4

Benchmark Test 3: Topics 5–6

Benchmark Test 4: Topics 7–9

Benchmark Test 5: Topics 10–12

Benchmark Test 6: Topics 13–14

Benchmark Test 7: Topics 15–17

Topic ②

PEARSON **realize**™ ···· www.PearsonRealize.com Access your Digital Lesson

European Colonization of North America (1500–1750)

TOPIC 2 ORGANIZER	PACING: APPROX. 1 PERIOD, .5 BLOCKS
	PACING
Connect	1 period
MY STORY VIDEO **John Smith, Jamestown, and the Roots of America**	10 min.
DIGITAL ESSENTIAL QUESTION ACTIVITY **Why Do People Move?**	10 min.
DIGITAL OVERVIEW ACTIVITY **European Colonization of North America**	10 min.
TOPIC INQUIRY: PROJECT-BASED LEARNING **Publish an ePortfolio of Colonial Data**	20 min.
Investigate	3–7 periods
TOPIC INQUIRY: PROJECT-BASED LEARNING **Publish an ePortfolio of Colonial Data**	Ongoing
LESSON 1 Spanish Colonization and New Spain	30–40 min.
LESSON 2 The First French, Dutch, and English Colonies	30–40 min.
LESSON 3 The New England Colonies	30–40 min.
LESSON 4 The Middle Colonies	30–40 min.
LESSON 5 The Southern Colonies	30–40 min.
LESSON 6 Colonial Society	30–40 min.
LESSON 7 Colonial Trade and Government	30–40 min.
Synthesize	1 period
DIGITAL ACTIVITY **Reflect on the Essential Question and Topic**	10 min.
TOPIC INQUIRY: PROJECT-BASED LEARNING **Publish an ePortfolio of Colonial Data**	20 min.
Demonstrate	1–2 periods
DIGITAL TOPIC REVIEW AND ASSESSMENT **European Colonization of North America**	10 min.
TOPIC INQUIRY: PROJECT-BASED LEARNING **Publish an ePortfolio of Colonial Data**	20 min.

Topic ②

 TOPIC INQUIRY: PROJECT-BASED LEARNING

Publish an ePortfolio of Colonial Data

In this Topic Inquiry, students create and publish an e-Portfolio with data on the geography and economy of the 13 English colonies in North America. They will use the data they collect to create visual representations of social studies information, including thematic maps, graphs, charts, models, and databases to go in their portfolios. Learning about the geography, economy, and population of the colonies will contribute to students' understanding of the Topic Essential Question: Why do people move?

STEP 1: CONNECT
Develop Questions and Plan the Investigation

Read the Project Launch
Explain to students that in this project, they will be collecting data about the English colonies in North America and publishing that data in an e-Portfolio. Have students read the Project Launch and review the fictional proclamation issued by King George II.

Suggestion: To provide extra support, have students restate the proclamation in their own words. Make sure they understand that they are being asked to investigate and organize facts about the colonies.

Discuss
Have students discuss the proclamation as a class or in small groups. Ask students what facts about the colonies might be relevant to this investigation, such as geography, climate, physical features, natural resources, and economic activities.

Suggestion: Students can work together in pairs or small groups to brainstorm what areas their investigation should cover.

Resources
- Project Launch
- Rubric for an e-Portfolio
- Need-to-Know Questions
- Project Contract
- Student Instructions

STEP 2: INVESTIGATE
Apply Disciplinary Concepts and Tools

Identify Needed Information and Conduct Research
Teams will identify information they need to investigate, and research the physical characteristics of the environment in the three colonial regions and how they influenced population distribution and economic activities.

Create a Team Database and Compile Information
Teams will create a database to store their research that is well organized, easy to use, and include sections for all the information gathered.

Suggestion: The database may be electronic or hard copy. Regardless of format, students should develop an organizational system using folders, files, notes, and other methods to keep track of information.

Create Visual Representations of Data (Thematic Maps, Graphs, Charts, and Models)
Teams will create visual representations of their data to present information about the physical features, resources, economies, population, and settlement patterns of the colonies.

Write and Edit Introduction, Captions, and Explanatory Materials
Teams will write and edit material to accompany their visuals. They should have an introduction to their portfolio and provide captions to all images. Students may also wish to include additional explanatory comments to accompany their visual representations.

Resources
- Need-to-Know Questions
- Project Tracker
- Information Organizer

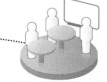

STEP 3: SYNTHESIZE
Evaluate Sources and Use
Evidence to Formulate Conclusions

Build Your e-Portfolio or Book
Have students work as a team to put together their e-Portfolio. Portfolios should include visual information, explanatory materials, and any other relevant visual, audio, or written materials gathered during research.

Suggestion: If your class has limited access to the Internet, you could supply materials for students to make a physical binder or book to present their visuals and accompanying materials.

Write Your Conclusions
Have teams write a conclusion section for their portfolios in which they summarize the reasons for the differences among the colonies. Students should consider the physical environment, population distribution, settlement patterns, and economic activities of each region.

Suggestion: Have teams include at least one conclusion and one additional question that they have.

Resources
• Plan Your Book

STEP 4: DEMONSTRATE
Communicate Conclusions
and Take Informed Action

Present Your e-Portfolio
Have students present their e-Portfolios to the class or an invited audience. To help students structure their presentations, give them a time limit and have them use a clock to monitor their delivery.

Suggestion: As an extension, have students use the data they collected about the environment, population, and economy of the colonies to draw conclusions about why immigrants moved to each region.

Resources
• Give an Effective Presentation   • Self Assessment

INTRODUCTION

European Colonization of North America (1500–1750)

Following Columbus's first voyages, European empires began exploring the Americas. Spain, France, the Netherlands, France, and England wanted to expand their empires, find faster trade routes to Asia, and generate wealth. They established colonies where they could farm, trade, and exploit the region's many natural resources. Over time, England founded 13 colonies, divided into three regions: New England, the Middle Colonies, and the Southern Colonies. As the colonies grew, they developed their own unique cultures, political structures, and ways of life.

■ CONNECT

MY STORY VIDEO	DIGITAL ESSENTIAL QUESTION ACTIVITY	DIGITAL OVERVIEW ACTIVITY
John Smith, Jamestown, and the Roots of America	**Why Do People Move?**	**European Colonization of North America**

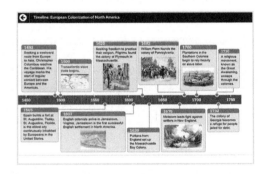

Watch a video about the exploits of John Smith in North America.

Check Understanding What was John Smith's goal in Virginia? *(settling a colony and making money for the Virginia Company)*

Assess Credibility What about John Smith's story of being rescued from his Native American captors would have made it less questionable? *(The story of his rescue is not based on reliable evidence. Historians debate whether it even happened or, if it did, the reason for his rescue.)*

Ask students to think about the Topic Essential Question: Why do people move? People move because they are drawn to certain places (pull factors), and because they want to leave other places behind (push factors). What factors lead people to establish a new home?

If students have not already done so, ask them to think about the questions in the activity. Then go over the answers as a class.

Support a Point of View with Evidence What push or pull factors do you think have the strongest influence on whether people move? Explain your reasoning. *(People move because of economic push factors such as poverty and economic pull factors such as the search for better job opportunities. People also need to be able to meet their basic needs.)*

Identify Central Issues What pull factors do you think drew early settlers to the colonies? *(Land, opportunities to generate wealth, religious freedom, freedom from oppression, and a chance for adventure)*

Display the timeline showing key events in the history of European colonization of North America. This timeline will help provide a framework in which students can place the events they learn about while working on this topic.

Analyze Information Based on the timeline, what reasons led European settlers to move to the Americas? *(Religious freedom, economic gain, seeking refuge, and an interest in exploration)*

Draw Conclusions What conclusion can you draw from the knowledge that Metacom led a fight against New England settlers? *(European colonization led to conflicts between Europeans and Native Americans.)*

Topic Inquiry
Launch the Topic Inquiry with students after introducing the topic.

Spanish Colonization and New Spain

Supporting English Language Learners

Use with Digital Text 4, **The Social Order in New Spain.**

Learning
Read the section titled *Different Social Classes*, or invite volunteers to do so. Tell students that they will be writing about what they've learning and checking their writing to improve it. Tell them that they will need to write complete sentences or paragraphs. Write the following words on the board: "Four social classes in Spanish colony." Ask students what is wrong with this statement. *(It is not a sentence because it lacks a verb, and* colony *should be plural.)* Explain to students that they will be monitoring and correcting their own writing, with your help.

Beginning Have students write a single sentence describing something that they learned from the reading. Ask them to look closely at their sentence and find ways to improve it. Invite them to ask for help as needed.

Intermediate Ask students to write a few sentences describing the creoles. Then ask them to revise their sentences to improve their grammar and to incorporate academic language.

Advanced Have students write a full paragraph about the Spanish colonial social structure. Ask them to check their paragraphs to make sure that they include a clear topic statement and supporting details and to correct any style or grammar errors. Then ask them to revise their paragraphs.

Advanced High Ask students to write a paragraph that compares and contrasts the Creoles and the Mestizos. Have them share their writing with a partner, offer and receive feedback, and revise their paragraph accordingly.

Use with Digital Text 5, **The Transatlantic Slave Trade.**

Speaking
Have students read the text under this heading, including the subheadings. Give students time to gather their thoughts about the transatlantic slave trade, then have them form small groups or pairs. Tell students that they will be expressing ideas by speaking about what they have read. Students should express ideas ranging from communicating single words and short phrases to participating in extended discussions.

Beginning Display a word web with *Bartolomé de Las Casas* written in the center. Ask students to say words and phrases that describe Las Casas and his impact on slave trade in the Americas. Add their responses to the word web.

Intermediate Ask students to express an idea about Bartolomé de Las Casas and his contribution to slave trade in the Americas. Have students' partners ask each of them a follow up question about their ideas, and have students respond orally.

Advanced In pairs or in small groups, have students give a short expressing their ideas about the Atlantic slave trade.. Have students' partners ask each of them a follow up question about their ideas, and have students respond orally.

Advanced High Ask pairs of students to have extended discussions of their ideas about the emergence of the transatlantic slave trade (e.g., what might have happened if Las Casas had not made his suggestion). If appropriate, have them conduct their discussion for the class.

▣ Differentiate Instruction

Use the Differentiated Instruction notes throughout the lesson plan to support the varied skill sets, levels of readiness, and interests in the mixed-ability classroom.

Challenge These notes include suggestions for expanding the activity for advanced students.

On-Level These notes include suggestions for modifying the activity to address different interests or learning styles.

Extra Support These notes include ideas for providing more scaffolding or reading spuport.

Special Needs These notes provide ideas for adapting instruction to support the needs of various special needs students.

■ NOTES

Spanish Colonization and New Spain

Objectives

Objective 1: Describe how conquistadors defeated two Native American empires.

Objective 2: Explain why Spain settled its colonies.

Objective 3: Explain the causes and effects of the transatlantic slave trade.

LESSON 1 ORGANIZER	PACING: APPROX. 1 PERIOD, .5 BLOCKS				
				RESOURCES	
		OBJECTIVES	**PACING**	**Online**	**Print**
Connect					
DIGITAL START UP ACTIVITY **Álvar Núñez Cabeza de Vaca**			5 min.	●	
Investigate					
DIGITAL TEXT 1 **Conquistadors Arrive in the Americas**		Objective 1	10 min.	●	●
DIGITAL TEXT 2 **Exploring Lands to the North**			10 min.	●	●
DIGITAL TEXT 3 **The Colonization of New Spain**			10 min.	●	●
DIGITAL TEXT 4 **Social Order in New Spain**		Objective 2	10 min.	●	●
INTERACTIVE MAP **Spanish Explorers and Settlements**			10 min.	●	
INTERACTIVE CHART **Social Classes in New Spain**			10 min.	●	
DIGITAL TEXT 5 **Transatlantic Slave Trade**		Objective 3	10 min.	●	●
Synthesize					
DIGITAL ACTIVITY **Interaction in the Americas**			5 min.	●	
Demonstrate					
DIGITAL QUIZ **Lesson Quiz and Class Discussion Board**			10 min.	●	

PEARSON realize™
www.PearsonRealize.com

Go online to access additional resources including:
Primary Sources • Biographies • Supreme Court cases •
21st Century Skill Tutorials • Maps • Graphic Organizers.

CONNECT

DIGITAL START UP ACTIVITY

Álvar Núñez Cabeza de Vaca

Project the Start Up Activity Ask students to read the quote as they enter and get settled. Have them discuss the quote with another student and then write a few sentences explaining their opinion.

Discuss Based on what he wrote, what opinion do you think Cabeza de Vaca had of the Indians he met? *(He admired their skills; he thought they were very different; he thought they were resourceful but also led simple lives.)*

Tell students that in this lesson they will be learning about the reasons the Spanish settled in North America, the causes and effects of colonization, and the development of the transatlantic slave trade.

Aa **Vocabulary Development:** Use the Interactive Reading Notepad to preview the Key Terms and Academic Vocabulary in this lesson with students.

⇅ FLIP IT!

Assign the Flipped Video for this lesson.

STUDENT EDITION PRINT PAGES: 46–55

INVESTIGATE

DIGITAL TEXT 1

Conquistadors Arrive in the Americas

Objective 1: Describe how conquistadors defeated two Native American empires.

Quick Instruction

Project the image of the Francisco Pizarro on the whiteboard. Explain that the conquistadors were conquerors who established the first Spanish settlements in the Americas. Identify reasons for colonization of North America such as their quest to find gold and spread the Spanish empire. Point out that had defeated two Native American empires: the Aztecs and the Incas.

Draw Conclusions Ask students why they think the conquistadors were able to defeat two major empires, citing examples from the image to support their views. *(They had substantial resources including swords, horses, and armor and were well trained in fighting.)*

D **Differentiate: Extra Support** Tell students that *conquistador* is the Spanish word for conqueror. A conqueror is someone who conquers, or takes control of, a place and its people. Have students draw on these definitions to explain what they think happened when the conquistadors encountered Native American empires.

Further Instruction

Go through the Interactive Reading Notepad questions and discuss the answers with the class, including the graphic organizer on the factors that influenced Spanish military success over the Aztecs and Incas.

Compare Points of View How did Spain view the defeat of the Aztecs and the Incas? How did the Aztecs and Incas view the same events? *(The Spanish viewed the defeat of the empires as a victory. The Native Americans viewed it as a tragedy.)*

Identify Cause and Effect How did the Spanish defeat of Native American empires lead to the development of Spanish colonies? *(Spain was able to take over Native American lands and create new settlements under Spanish rule, which led to colonies.)*

Draw Conclusions What were the reasons the conquistadors came to the Americas? *(They hoped for gold and glory for Spain and wanted to serve the king.)*

Spanish Colonization and New Spain

DIGITAL TEXT 2

Exploring Lands to the North

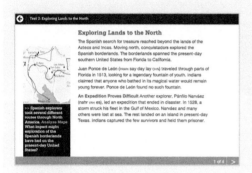

DIGITAL TEXT 3

The Colonization of New Spain

DIGITAL TEXT 4

Social Order in New Spain

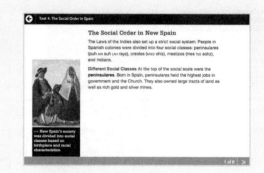

Objective 2: Explain why Spain settled its colonies.

Quick Instruction

Interactive Map: Spanish Explorers and Settlements Project the map on the whiteboard. Explain that Spanish explorers traveled throughout the southeastern and southwestern United States, establishing settlements. Tell students that in this lesson, they will learn about the reasons for Spanish colonization of North America.

Interactive Chart: Social Classes in New Spain Project the Interactive Chart on the whiteboard. Explain that Spanish colonies were settlements that included different racial and ethnic groups. Identify ethnic groups that settled in the colonies and explain their reasons for immigration. These colonies developed their own social systems and methods of organization.

Generate Explanations Point out that the text identifies the founding of St. Augustine in Florida as the beginning of the era of colonization in the present-day United States, which ended when the United States declared independence in 1776. Ask students to explain why historians refer to this period as the era of colonization. *(During this period, the United States did not yet exist as a nation, but was instead part of colonies belonging to European nations.)*

Identify Cause and Effect As students read Texts 2 through 4, ask them to identify both the causes and the effects of colonization by the Spanish. *(Causes: desire for adventure; desire for more land; interest in searching for riches. Effects: Spanish settlement in the Americas, the spread of Spanish customs and ways of making a living, the spread of Christianity, loss of land and culture for Indians, development of a social system based on people's backgrounds.)*

🖳 ACTIVE CLASSROOM

Have students use the Quick Write activity and take 30 seconds to write what they know about the reasons for Spanish colonization of North America. Then have students write down an additional question they have about Spanish exploration and settlements that they hope to learn in this lesson.

🖳 ACTIVE CLASSROOM

Have students use a Rank It activity to better understand the class system in New Spain. Ask students to rank the classes according to which had the most significant impact. Ask students to provide a justification for the ranking decisions they made.

ELL Use the ELL activity described in the ELL chart.

INTERACTIVE MAP
Spanish Explorers and Settlements

INTERACTIVE CHART
Social Classes in New Spain

DIGITAL TEXT 5
Transatlantic Slave Trade

Further Instruction

Go through the Interactive Reading Notepad questions for *Discovering Lands to the North, The Colonization of New Spain*, and *Social Order in New Spain* with the class. To extend the lesson, have students go through the primary source *The Destruction of the Indies*, by Las Casas and the additional resource Introducing Physical Geography: Geography.

Be sure students understand the causes and the effects of the Spanish colonization of North America. The Spanish settled in what is now the United States because they wanted to spread Christianity, gain wealth, and satisfy a thirst for adventure. These settlers developed the first colonies in New Spain, with devastating effects on Native American communities.

Draw Conclusions Ask students why they think the Spanish colonies established such a rigid social system. *(To maintain divisions among racial and ethnic groups within the colonies; to ensure the Spanish maintained power over other groups)*

Generate Explanations Most Spanish colonizers were not explorers. What reasons besides adventure prompted Spaniards to settle in the New World? *(Missionaries wanted to convert Native Americans to Christianity; others sought wealth through farming and trade.)*

Objective 3: Explain the causes and effects of the transatlantic slave trade.

Quick Instruction

Project the map of the transatlantic slave trade on the white board to help illustrate the reasons for the development of the transatlantic slave trade. Have students study the map and explain where enslaved Africans were taken. Project the bar graph showing the approximate number of enslaved Africans involved in the transatlantic slave trade. Explain that the number of enslaved Africans necessary to sustain the colonies increased as the Spanish colonies grew. Also, the death toll of Native Americans working to support the colonies continued to rise, which further increased the need for enslaved Africans. Together these factors led to the growth of the transatlantic slave trade.

Summarize Ask students to explain the *transatlantic slave trade* in their own words. *(Africans were captured in Africa, transported across the Atlantic, and sold as slaves in the Americas.)*

Draw Conclusions Why did the deaths of Native Americans to European diseases contribute to the development of the transatlantic slave trade? *(Enslaved Africans were used as a new labor source.)*

ELL Use the ELL activity described in the ELL chart.

Topic ② Lesson 1

Spanish Colonization and New Spain

SYNTHESIZE

DEMONSTRATE

DIGITAL ACTIVITY
Interaction in the Americas

DIGITAL QUIZ
Lesson Quiz and Class Discussion Board

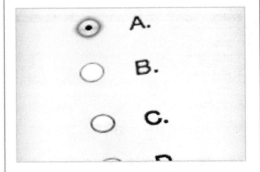

Further Instruction

Go through the Interactive Reading Notepad questions with the class. Review the reasons Las Casas gave for bringing Africans to the Americas. Be sure students understand how the need for labor in European colonies led to the development of the transatlantic slave trade.

Discuss the effects of this development. Emphasize the significant role the development of the transatlantic slave trade played in shaping the early colonies. The slave trade would continue to grow as more Europeans established colonies in North America.

Generate Explanations Explain the reasons for the development of the transatlantic slave trade. *(Because of the high death toll among Native Americans, the Spanish needed new sources of labor for their colonies. They began bringing enslaved Africans to the Americas.)*

Identify Cause and Effect How did the history of slavery in Africa affect the development of the transatlantic slave trade? *(Slavery already existed in Africa. Africans began selling enslaved people to Europeans, who brought them to the Americas.)*

Draw Conclusions How did the growth of European colonization in the Americas contribute to the development of the transatlantic slave trade? *(The growth of colonies increased the need for labor. Europeans relied on slave labor in the colonies, especially on sugar plantations.)*

Have students create a graphic organizer to complete the Interaction in the Americas activity. Ask them to write a few sentences explaining the connections among each group in their graphic organizer, then share their answers with a partner.

Discuss Have partners think about the following question: What were the effects of colonization on Europeans, Native Americans, and Africans? Have students discuss their answers with the class.

Assign the online Lesson Quiz for this lesson if you haven't already done so. Students will be offered automatic remediation or enrichment based on their score.

Pose these questions to the class on the Discussion Board:

In *Spanish Colonization and New Spain*, you read about the beginning of the era of colonization, the causes and effects of the Spanish colonization of North America, the reasons racial and ethnic groups first settled in the present-day United States, and the reasons for the development of the transatlantic slave trade.

Contrast The growth of colonies in the Americas brought different racial and ethnic groups across the Atlantic. Contrast their reasons for settling in the present-day United States. *(The Spanish came voluntarily to convert Native Americans, generate wealth, and expand Spain's empire. Africans were brought against their will to work on plantations as slaves.)*

Make Generalizations Make a generalization about the effect of colonization on Native Americans. *(Colonization had negative effects on most Native Americans. Many people were brutally conquered, forced to work for Europeans, and killed.)*

Topic Inquiry

Have students continue their investigations for the Topic Inquiry.

The First French, Dutch, and English Colonies

Supporting English Language Learners

Use with Digital Text 3, **The Dutch Establish New Netherland.**

Speaking

Have students read the section titled, *European Settlement Affects Native Americans*. Prompt students to express their feelings about the reading that range from communicating single words and short phrases to participating in extended discussions.

Beginning Display a list of feeling words along with this sentence frame: I feel _____. Based on their reading, ask students to choose an appropriate feeling word and to read the completed sentence aloud.

Intermediate In pairs or in groups, ask students to share their feelings about the effects of European settlement on Native Americans, speaking in complete sentences.

Advanced Have students identify the effects of European settlement on North Americans that they feel is most tragic. In pairs or in groups, ask them to share aloud both the effect and how they feel about it, using academic language as appropriate.

Advanced High In pairs or in groups, ask students to engage in an extended discussion, expressing their feelings about the effects of European settlement on Native Americans.

Use with Digital Text 4, **Roanoke and Jamestown.**

Learning

Have students read the text.Use strategic learning techniques such as concept mapping. Display a blank Venn diagram, and explain to students that they will be using it to help them learn new vocabulary.

Beginning Label the Venn diagram circles with the words *Roanoke* and *Jamestown*. Also display new words from the text that fit each part of the diagram. Ask students to match the words to their proper places on the diagram.

Intermediate Have students copy the Venn diagram circles and label them with the words *Roanoke* and *Jamestown*. Invite students to write vocabulary from the text in each part of the diagram. Circulate to check their responses.

Advanced Ask pairs of students to draw, label, and complete a Venn diagram that compares and contrasts the Roanoke and Jamestown colonies. Encourage them to use as much new vocabulary from the text as possible.

Advanced High Have students independently design, draw, label, and complete a Venn diagram that compares and contrasts terms from the reading for each colony. Have them present and explain their diagrams in small groups or in front of the class.

D Differentiate Instruction

Use the Differentiated Instruction notes throughout the lesson plan to support the varied skill sets, levels of readiness, and interests in the mixed-ability classroom.

Challenge These notes include suggestions for expanding the activity for advanced students.

On-Level These notes include suggestions for modifying the activity to address different interests or learning styles.

Extra Support These notes include ideas for providing more scaffolding or reading spuport.

Special Needs These notes provide ideas for adapting instruction to support the needs of various special needs students.

NOTES

Topic ② Lesson 2

The First French, Dutch, and English Colonies

Objectives

Objective 1: Explain why Europeans explored North America's coast.

Objective 2: Identify the reasons for French and Dutch colonization in North America.

Objective 3: Identify the reasons for English colonization.

Objective 4: Explain how Virginia began a tradition of representative government.

Objective 5: Describe how different groups in Jamestown interacted with the environment.

LESSON 2 ORGANIZER		PACING: APPROX. 1 PERIOD, .5 BLOCKS			
				RESOURCES	
		OBJECTIVES	PACING	Online	Print
Connect					
DIGITAL START UP ACTIVITY **How Will You Survive?**			5 min.	●	
Investigate					
DIGITAL TEXT 1 **European Rivalries**		Objective 1	10 min.	●	●
DIGITAL TEXT 2 **New France is Colonized**		Objective 2	10 min.	●	●
DIGITAL TEXT 3 **The Dutch Establish New Netherland**			10 min.	●	●
INTERACTIVE MAP **Lands Controlled by Colonial Powers, 1660**			10 min.	●	
DIGITAL TEXT 4 **Roanoke and Jamestown**		Objective 3	10 min.	●	●
INTERACTIVE GALLERY **Arrival and Early Years at Jamestown**			10 min.	●	
DIGITAL TEXT 5 **An Improved Form of Government**		Objective 4	10 min.	●	●
DIGITAL TEXT 6 **The Jamestown Colony Grows**		Objective 5	10 min.	●	●
Synthesize					
DIGITAL ACTIVITY **Surviving a New World**			5 min.	●	
Demonstrate					
DIGITAL QUIZ **Lesson Quiz and Class Discussion Board**			10 min.	●	

CONNECT

DIGITAL START UP ACTIVITY
How Will You Survive?

Project the Start Up Activity Have students read the scenario and generate their lists as they enter and get settled. Ask students to discuss their choices with a partner. Then poll the class to see what activities appear most on the lists.

Discuss What would you do in this situation? Make a list of the first five things you would do to survive, in the order in which you would do them. *(Answers should include "find food and water" and "build shelter".)*

Tell students that in this lesson they will be learning about the first European colonists in North America.

Aa Vocabulary Development: Use the Interactive Reading Notepad to preview the Key Terms and Academic Vocabulary in this lesson with students.

> **↳ FLIP IT!**
> Assign the Flipped Video for this lesson.

▮ STUDENT EDITION PRINT
PAGES: 56–68

INVESTIGATE

DIGITAL TEXT 1
European Rivalries

Objective 1: **Explain why Europeans explored North America's coast.**

Quick Instruction
Tell the class that they will be identifying reasons for European exploration of North America. Project the map on the whiteboard. Explain that one reason Europeans explored North America was to search for a northwest passage. Europeans hoped to find a waterway through or around North America that would provide a route to Asia.

Analyze Maps Ask students to describe the regions each European powers explored.

Make Predictions How will exploration of North America lead Europeans to establish colonies? *(Explorers will learn about the land and geography of North Americas, which will lead rulers to see the potential for profit in the region.)*

Further Instruction
Go through the Interactive Reading Notepad questions and discuss the answers with the class. To extend the lesson, have students complete the additional resource Geography: Mapping Earth.

Generate Explanations Identify reasons for European exploration of North America. *(European explorers were looking for a northwest passage, or a shorter route to Asia. Also, different European nations were competing to claim and control land in North America.)*

Draw Conclusions What motivated explorers to look for new travel routes around the globe? What does this suggest about the reasons for European colonization of North America? *(Explorers wanted to reach Asia because they wanted wealth from Asian trade. This suggests rulers and colonists were also looking for wealth when they established North American colonies.)*

The First French, Dutch, and English Colonies

DIGITAL TEXT 2
New France is Colonized

DIGITAL TEXT 3
The Dutch Establish New Netherland

INTERACTIVE MAP
Lands Controlled by Colonial Powers, 1660

Objective 2: Identify the reasons for French and Dutch colonization in North America.

Quick Instruction
Interactive Map: Lands Controlled by Colonial Powers, 1660 Project the map on the whiteboard. Click through the layers showing the land controlled by each European power. Identify the reasons for European colonization of North America: spreading Christianity, gaining wealth, and expanding empire.

Analyze Maps Have students review the map and identify European reasons for colonization of North America. Ask how the physical characteristics of the environment influenced the economic activities of the early colonial powers. *(Resources determined exports and trade; waterways impacted how goods and wealth traveled from the colonies to Europe)*

⬛ ACTIVE CLASSROOM
Divide students into groups and use the Walking Tour activity to pick key passages from the lessons that describe the reasons for French and Dutch colonization in North America. Have groups post their passages on individual pages around the room, then tour the passages and then summarize each one.

ELL Use the ELL activity described in the ELL chart.

Further Instruction
Go through the Interactive Reading Notepad questions for *New France is Colonized* and *The Dutch Establish New Netherland* with the class. Have students begin completing the graphic organizer to take notes about the English, Dutch, and French colonies. Be sure students understand the causes of colonization, particularly the reasons for European colonization of North America.

Compare and Contrast French and Dutch immigrants and their reasons for colonization. *(Compare—both sought profit, especially from the fur trade. Contrast—the French also prioritized missionaries; the Dutch established a port colony while the French built smaller settlements inland.)*

Draw Conclusions Describe the effects of colonization, using examples from Dutch and French colonization. *(A fur trade developed and led to a network of trade routes in the interior of North America. French control over the continent's interior gave them a strategic advantage over the Spanish and English. Colonization brought enslaved Africans to North America. Trade rivalries developed between the French and the Dutch over the fur trade. Both sought alliances with Native Americans. The fur trade nearly wiped out beaver populations. European diseases killed thousands of Native Americans. Missionaries brought Christianity to Native Americans.)*

Identify Central Issues Have students describe the places of importance where French and Dutch colonists settled. Ask what geographic factors compelled them to choose these locations. *(French colonists settled along the St. Lawrence and Mississippi Rivers, using the waterways for transportation and trade; they also settled in wooded areas to be close to fishing, trapping, and trade. The Dutch created a port at New Amsterdam in the mouth of the Hudson River. They transported goods along the Hudson and were close to the Atlantic to send furs to the Netherlands.)*

DIGITAL TEXT 4

Roanoke and Jamestown

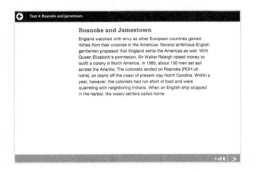

INTERACTIVE GALLERY

Arrival and Early Years at Jamestown

DIGITAL TEXT 5

An Improved Form of Government

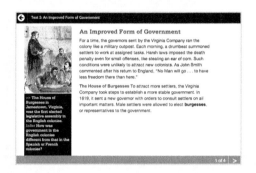

Objective 3: Identify reasons for English colonization.

Quick Instruction

Interactive Gallery: Arrival and Early Years at Jamestown Project the Interactive Gallery on the white board. Look at each image individually and then the collection as a whole. Discuss students' reactions to the images. Ask what they think it would have been like to be part of the Jamestown settlement.

Summarize Ask students to explain why 1607 is a significant year in American history. *(It marks the founding of Jamestown, the first successful English settlement in North America.)*

Identify Central Issues Why did settlers want to build a colony in Jamestown, Virginia? *(They were looking for wealth and a passage to Asia, and wanted to claim the land for England.)*

📓 ACTIVE CLASSROOM

Have students complete a See-Think-Wonder activity using the Interactive Gallery. Ask students to pair with a partner and ask: What do you see? What does that make you think? What are you wondering about now that you've seen this? Once each partner has answered the questions about the images, ask them to share their insights with the class.

ELL Use the ELL activity described in the ELL chart.

Further Instruction

Go through the Interactive Reading Notepad questions with the class and have students continue completing the graphic organizer to take notes about English, Dutch, and French colonies.

Summarize How did the physical characteristics of the environment influence where the Jamestown colonists settled? *(They wanted somewhere secure, and their location in the Chesapeake Bay along the James River made it difficult for the Spanish to find and fire upon them.)*

Identify Cause and Effect How did the physical characteristics of the Chesapeake Bay influence the Jamestown Colony and its economic activities? *(Jamestown was swampy; the unhealthy water and mosquitoes spread disease. However, it had fertile land for growing tobacco, which the colonists sold to England.)*

Compare and Contrast Describe how different immigrant groups, such as the Dutch colonists in New Netherland and the English colonists in Virginia, interacted with the environment in North America during the 17th century. *(The Dutch in New Netherland interacted with the environment mainly through trade. Their fur trade with Native Americans nearly wiped out the beaver population of the Iroquois lands. The English in Virginia interacted with the environment mainly by relying on it for food—first by hunting, fishing, and raiding nearby Indians, later increasingly through farming tobacco and other crops.)*

Objective 4: Explain how Virginia began a tradition of representative government.

Quick Instruction

Project the image of the Magna Carta on the white board. Explain that the Magna Carta, or Great Charter, was a document from 1215 listing the rights of British nobles that couldn't be taken away by the king. Point out its influence on the U.S. system of government. Explain that the Virginia Company established a government in Jamestown that drew on the Magna Carta in order to set up a representative government in the English colonies.

Use Context Clues Ask students to define the term *representative government* and explain why the growth of representative government during the colonial period was an improvement over the colony's previous government. *(In a representative government, voters elect representatives to make laws for them. It was an improvement over Virginia's previous government, which gave people less of a voice.)*

D Differentiate: Challenge Have students read selections from the Magna Carta and identify passages that they think influenced the development of representative government in the United States, citing examples to support their reasoning.

Further Instruction

Go through the Interactive Reading Notepad questions with the class and have students continue completing the graphic organizer to take notes about English, Dutch, and French

The First French, Dutch, and English Colonies

DIGITAL TEXT 6

The Jamestown Colony Grows

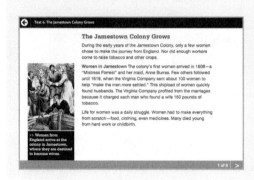

colonies. Be sure that students understand the reasons for the new institution that developed in Virginia during this time: the House of Burgesses.

Generate Explanations Explain the reasons for the growth of representative government during the colonial period. How was the House of Burgesses important to its development? *(The Virginia Company wanted to create a more stable government to attract settlers. It established the House of Burgesses, the first representative government in the colonies.)*

Draw Conclusions How did the Magna Carta influence the development of representative government in Virginia? *(The House of Burgesses called Virginia's charter the "Great Charter" after the Magna Carta. Both documents said that subjects have rights and that all people are subject to the law.)*

Identify Cause and Effect Name an important effect the Jamestown Colony had on the U.S. system of government. *(Established representative government; affirmed that citizens have political rights; said all people are subject to the law)*

Objective 5: **Describe how different groups in Jamestown interacted with the environment.**

Quick Instruction

Project the infographic of the ethnic origins of colonial settlers. Explain that ethnic groups had different reasons for immigrating. Jamestown was initially populated by white men looking to make money in the colonies. Small numbers of women came to the colony to marry and work. Enslaved Africans were brought to work on tobacco plantations.

Analyze Data Ask students how the ethnic origins of colonial settlers changed over time, and why. *(More Africans arrived in the colonies as tobacco plantations grew.)*

Further Instruction

Go through the Interactive Reading Notepad questions with the class and have students finish the graphic organizer to take notes about English, Dutch, and French colonies.

Compare and Contrast Ask students to consider what they have learned in this lesson so far. Have them identify different ethnic groups that settled in the present-day United States and explain their reasons for immigration. *(Dutch settlers came mainly to take advantage of trade opportunities. English settlers in Virginia first came seeking gold and trade routes and later came to profit from raising tobacco. Africans came to Virginia to work on plantations because they were forced to do so by slave traders.)*

Support Ideas with Examples Give examples of how different immigrant groups, such as enslaved Africans and English settlers, interacted with the environment in Jamestown. *(Enslaved Africans had to work on plantations growing tobacco; English women used available resources to make what they needed from scratch; English male settlers worked to establish farms and pushed further inland, taking over more land.)*

SYNTHESIZE

DIGITAL ACTIVITY
Surviving a New World

Ask students to recall the list they made for the Digital Start Up Activity at the beginning of this lesson. Have them write a paragraph evaluating their list in light of what they learned about the early colonists.

Discuss Ask students if they would change any of their responses now that they have learned more about the early colonies.

Have students think about the following question: How did geographic factors and the physical characteristics of the environment affect the growth of the early colonies? Discuss students' answers with the class.

DEMONSTRATE

DIGITAL QUIZ
Lesson Quiz and Class Discussion Board

Assign the online Lesson Quiz for this lesson if you haven't already done so. Students will be offered automatic remediation or enrichment based on their score.

Pose these questions to the class on the Discussion Board:

You have read about the development of early European colonies in the Americas, including the reasons for colonization, the impact of the physical environment on the colonies, the racial and ethnic groups that immigrated, and the growth of new institutions.

Identify Central Issues Name at least one political, social, economic, and religious reason for the establishment of French, Dutch, and English colonies. *(political: expansion of European empires; social: arrival of women in Jamestown made the colony feel settled; economic: wealth from farming and trade; religious: missionaries spread Christianity)*

Compare and Contrast France and England's economic reasons for establishing colonies. *(Compare: Both hoped to gain wealth. Contrast: France gained wealth through the fur trade; England gained wealth through tobacco plantations.)*

Topic Inquiry
Have students continue their investigations for the Topic Inquiry.

The New England Colonies

Supporting English Language Learners

Use with Digital Text 2, **Plymouth Colony.**

Learning
Read with students, or have students read the section titled, *A New Pledge to Govern the Colony*. Then define the term *Mayflower Compact*, modeling nonverbal cues, synonyms, and circumlocution.

Beginning Display this sentence frame: The Mayflower Compact was important because _____. Ask students to complete the sentence aloud. Encourage them to use circumlocution, and to raise their hands to ask for help as needed.

Intermediate Ask students to make a statement about why the Mayflower Compact was important. Encourage them to use synonyms and circumlocution if they cannot think of the precise wording for their ideas.

Advanced Ask students about the Mayflower Compact and its significance. Encourage extended responses that push the limits of students' vocabulary. Remind them to use gestures, synonyms, and circumlocution to help them express their thoughts.

Advanced High Tell students to speak about the Mayflower Compact as if they were addressing students at a lower grade level, using gestures and other nonverbal cues as appropriate. Encourage them to use synonyms and circumlocution in place of vocabulary that students at a lower grade level might not understand.

Use with Digital Text 3, **Overcoming Hardships in Plymouth.**

Speaking
Have students read the text. Explain that this text tells the story of the Pilgrims' first year in Plymouth. Prompt students to narrate with increasing specificity and detail.

Beginning In pairs or in small groups, have students narrate a brief summary of the Pilgrims' first year in their own words.

Intermediate In pairs or in small groups, ask students to tell the story of the Pilgrims' first year in about three sentences (beginning, middle, end). Have students' partners ask questions during their narration in order to elicit further detail.

Advanced In pairs or in small groups, ask students to tell the story of the Pilgrims' first year. Encourage them to include descriptive details in their narrative.

Advanced High In pairs or in small groups, have students suppose they must tell the story of the Pilgrims' first year to someone who knows nothing about it. Encourage them to narrate that story, providing plenty of detail so that their listener fully understands.

D Differentiate Instruction

Use the Differentiated Instruction notes throughout the lesson plan to support the varied skill sets, levels of readiness, and interests in the mixed-ability classroom.

Challenge These notes include suggestions for expanding the activity for advanced students.

On-Level These notes include suggestions for modifying the activity to address different interests or learning styles.

Extra Support These notes include ideas for providing more scaffolding or reading spuport.

Special Needs These notes provide ideas for adapting instruction to support the needs of various special needs students.

◼ NOTES

PEARSON realize.™
www.PearsonRealize.com

▶

Go online to access additional resources including:
Primary Sources • Biographies • Supreme Court cases •
21st Century Skill Tutorials • Maps • Graphic Organizers.

Objectives

Objective 1: Explain how the desire for religious freedom led to the settlement of the New England colonies.

Objective 2: Identify the significance of the Mayflower Compact.

Objective 3: Describe how conflicts over religion and politics were resolved in colonial New England.

Objective 4: Identify reasons for conflict between settlers and Native Americans.

Objective 5: Describe the daily life and the economy in the New England colonies.

LESSON 3 ORGANIZER		OBJECTIVES	PACING	RESOURCES	
				Online	Print
Connect					
DIGITAL START UP ACTIVITY **The First Thanksgiving**			5 min.	●	
Investigate					
DIGITAL TEXT 1 **Seeking Religious Freedom**		Objective 1	10 min.	●	●
DIGITAL TEXT 2; DIGITAL TEXT 3 **The Plymouth Colony; Overcoming Hardships in Plymouth**		Objective 2	20 min.	●	●
3-D MODEL **Plymouth Plantation**			10 min.	●	
DIGITAL TEXT 4; DIGITAL TEXT 5 **Forming Massachusetts Bay Colony; New Colonies Form Over Religious Differences**		Objective 3	20 min.	●	●
INTERACTIVE CHART **Thomas Hooker**			10 min.	●	
DIGITAL TEXT 6 **War Erupts Between Puritans and Native Americans**		Objective 4	10 min.	●	●
DIGITAL TEXT 7 **The Towns of New England**		Objective 5	10 min.	●	●
INTERACTIVE MAP **The New England Colonies**			10 min.	●	
Synthesize					
DIGITAL ACTIVITY **Challenges of Being a Colonist**			5 min.	●	
Demonstrate					
DIGITAL QUIZ **Lesson Quiz and Class Discussion Board**			10 min.	●	

PACING: APPROX. 1 PERIOD, .5 BLOCKS

The New England Colonies

■ CONNECT

DIGITAL START UP ACTIVITY
The First Thanksgiving

Project the Start Up Activity Ask students to answer the questions as they enter and get settled. Then have them share their ideas with another student, either in class or through a chat or blog space.

Discuss Prompt students to consider if this is an accurate image of early Pilgrims' lives. What difficulties might they have had to overcome when they first arrived to North America? *(Building shelter, finding adequate food and water, growing crops, etc.)*

Tell students they will be learning about life in some of the early North American colonies.

Aa Vocabulary Development: Use the Interactive Reading Notepad to preview Key Terms and Academic Vocabulary in the lesson with students.

⇅ FLIP IT!
Assign the Flipped Video for this lesson.

■ STUDENT EDITION PRINT PAGES: 69–82

■ INVESTIGATE

DIGITAL TEXT 1
Seeking Religious Freedom

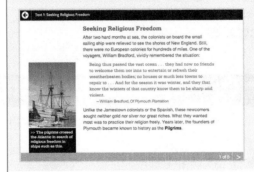

Objective 1: Explain how the desire for religious freedom led to the settlement of the New England Colonies.

Quick Instruction
Project the lesson on the whiteboard. Tell students that Pilgrims and other religious groups were put on trial for violating religious restrictions in England. Explain that Pilgrims were one religious group that settled in the United States. Religion was an important factor in motivating immigration to the colonies.

Use Context Clues Read the section titled "The Pilgrims." Based on context clues in this section, predict how the Pilgrims' circumstances would be a cause of colonization. *(Persecution would cause the Pilgrims to start a new colony to seek religious freedom.)*

Generate Explanations Ask students why they think religion motivated many people to immigrate to the colonies. *(People probably wanted an opportunity to create a new life in which they were free to worship as they pleased.)*

D Differentiate: Extra Support As students discuss the image, have them focus their attention on the individual characters and setting of the image before asking them to discuss the image as a whole.

Further Instruction
Go through the Interactive Reading Notepad questions and discuss the answers with the class.

Identify Central Issues What reasons led the Separatists to establish a colony in North America? *(They wanted to leave the Church of England, escape religious persecution, and preserve their culture.)*

Express Problems Clearly Ask students to describe the problems in Europe that motivated religious groups to immigrate to the colonies. *(European rulers established churches and persecuted people with other beliefs. Those who did not follow the established church had to worship in secret and were imprisoned or even killed if they were caught.)*

Identify Cause and Effect How do you think the arrival of Quakers, Puritans, and other religious groups will affect religious freedom in the colonies? *(There will probably be more religious freedom and a greater openness to different religions in the colonies.)*

DIGITAL TEXT 2

The Plymouth Colony

DIGITAL TEXT 3

Overcoming Hardships in Plymouth

3-D MODEL

Plymouth Plantation

Objective 2: Identify the significance of the Mayflower Compact.

Quick Instruction

The Separatists won a charter from England to set up a colony in Virginia. Describe the Pilgrims' religious motivation for migration to America. *(The Pilgrims migrated to America seeking religious freedom.)* Explain the significance of 1620, the year the Pilgrims arrived in present-day Massachusetts, signed the Mayflower Compact, and established a new colony with its own representative government based on the principle of religious freedom. The Mayflower Compact created a representative government for the colony.

3D Model: Plymouth Plantation Project the 3-D Model on the whiteboard and move the cursor to explore the image of Plymouth Plantation. Discuss how the physical characteristics of the environment influenced the colony.

Express Ideas Clearly How did religion and virtue contribute to the growth of representative government in the North American colonies? *(The Pilgrims expected their elected representatives to show the same religious values and virtue as the citizens they represented and to make decisions for the common good, such as protecting religious freedom. The protection of religious freedom gave the representatives more legitimacy in the eyes of the citizens. This strengthened the institution of representative government.)*

ACTIVE CLASSROOM

Have students use the See-Think-Wonder strategy as they look at the 3-D model of Plymouth Plantation. Ask: What do you see? What does it make you think? What are you wondering about now that you've seen this? Call on students to share their insights with the class.

ELL Use the ELL activity described in the ELL chart.

Further Instruction

Go through the Interactive Reading Notepad questions for *The Plymouth Colony* and *Overcoming Hardships in Plymouth* with the class. Assign the Primary Source: Mayflower Compact.

Interpret Explain how the Mayflower Compact contributed to the growth of representative government in the colonies. *(The Mayflower Compact set a precedent of representative government in the colonies. The people agreed to form a government of elected representatives who would in turn make laws for the greater good.)*

Identify Central Issues Why was the year 1620 significant for the development of religious freedom in the United States? *(1620 was the year the Pilgrims established the Mayflower Compact. The Mayflower Compact established the new representative government's role in protecting religious freedom.)*

The New England Colonies

DIGITAL TEXT 4	DIGITAL TEXT 5	INTERACTIVE CHART
Forming Massachusetts Bay Colony	**New Colonies Form Over Religious Differences**	**Thomas Hooker**

   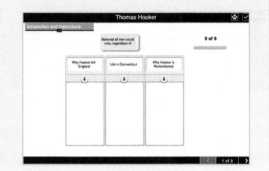

Objective 3: Describe how conflicts over religion and politics were resolved in colonial New England.

Quick Instruction

The Puritans established a new government in Massachusetts that did not tolerate religious dissent. Those who questioned the Puritans' policies or beliefs were forced to leave. As a result, other colonies were formed.

Interactive Chart: Thomas Hooker Project the Interactive Chart on the whiteboard and read through the tiles. Explain that Thomas Hooker was a Puritan who left Massachusetts Bay Colony to found a new colony based on principles of self-government.

Compare and Contrast the reasons for immigration of different religious groups, such as the Pilgrims and Puritans. *(Compare: conflicts with the Church of England; search for religious freedom. Contrast: Puritans wanted to reform the Church instead of separate from it.)*

📷 ACTIVE CLASSROOM

Break students into groups and use Circle Write strategy to answer the question: What influence did Thomas Hooker have on the development of self-government in colonial America? Have students write as much as they can for one minute and then switch with the person on their right. Have the next person improve or elaborate on the response. Continue switching until the paper returns to the first person. Have groups share the best responses with the class.

Further Instruction

Go through the Interactive Reading Notepad questions for *Forming Massachusetts Bay Colony* and *New Colonies Form Over Religious Differences* with the class. Have students complete the graphic organizer to summarize why each group left Massachusetts Bay Colony and what happened as a result.

Generate Explanations What relationship did the Fundamental Orders of Connecticut have with the growth of representative government? *(The Fundamental Orders of Connecticut expanded the vote to include all male property owners, not just church members, and limited the governor's power. The limitations on the governor's power and increased political participation strengthened the idea of representative government in the colonies.)*

Summarize How did the founding a new colony in Rhode Island resolve conflicts between people from various religious groups? *(In Massachusetts, the government supported a particular church and non-Puritans were unable to openly practice their faith. By leaving Massachusetts with his followers, Williams resolved conflicts over religion there. Freedom of religion in Rhode Island allowed for the peaceful resolution of conflicts between people from different religious groups.)*

DIGITAL TEXT 6

War Erupts Between Puritans and Native Americans

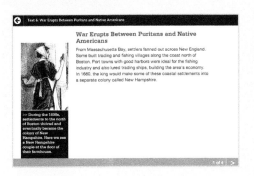

DIGITAL TEXT 7

The Towns of New England

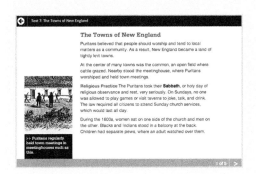

INTERACTIVE MAP

The New England Colonies

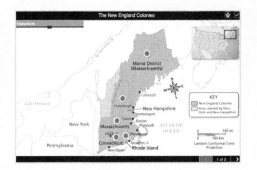

Objective 4: Identify reasons for conflict between settlers and Native Americans.

Quick Instruction

Project the image of colonists and Native Americans fighting on the whiteboard. Explain that conflicts broke out as settlements spread and colonists took over more Native American land. These conflicts would not be resolved for centuries.

Identify Central Issues How did the physical characteristics of the environment contribute to conflict between colonists and Native Americans? *(Population growth strained natural resources. Competition for scarce resources led to hostilities.)*

Further Instruction

Go through the Interactive Reading Notepad questions with the class. Make sure students understand how competition for land and resources led to hostilities between colonists and Native Americans.

Draw Conclusions Ask students how they think the physical characteristics of the environment influenced settlement patterns and economic activity in New England in the 17th century. *(Colonists probably wanted to settle where they had access to natural resources like water and good farmland. These environmental characteristics in turn encouraged specific industries such as farming, fishing, and shipping.)*

Objective 5: Describe the daily life and the economy in the New England Colonies.

Quick Instruction

Puritans established close-knit towns and villages. People gathered together for town meetings and religious services. They modified the environment to cultivate food and resources and to grow their economy. The culture, values, and traditions of this religious group had a lasting impact on American national identity.

Interactive Map: The New England Colonies Project the Interactive Map. Describe how the physical characteristics of the environment influenced economic activities in the colonies: forests for timber and furs; oceans and rivers for fishing and whaling; and land for meat, dairy, and crops. Colonists made a living by farming, fishing, logging, shipbuilding, whaling, and trading.

ACTIVE CLASSROOM

Have students use the Plus/Minus/Interesting strategy to record their reactions to the ways people modified the physical environment for economic purposes in the New England Colonies. Ask: 1. What are the positive ideas about this? 2. What are the negative ideas about this? 3. What is interesting about this? Have students share their responses with the class.

Further Instruction

Go through the Interactive Reading Notepad questions with the class. Be sure students understand the religious practices, form of government, and economic activities of the Puritans.

Compare and Contrast the physical characteristics of the New England Colonies. How did these characteristics contribute to economic differences within the region? *(Connecticut had land for farming and for meat and dairy production. Maine, Massachusetts, and Rhode Island had thick forests and long coastlines with access to the ocean's resources. New Hampshire also had forests and water. These colonies relied on fishing, shipbuilding, and trade.)*

Identify Central Issues What economic factors promoted growth in the New England Colonies? *(Colonists fished and farmed, but they generated the most wealth through shipbuilding, whaling, ironworking, timber exports, and the fur trade.)*

Interpret What were some of the most important effects of colonization in New England? *(Colonization led to the development of representative self-government and religious freedom in New England, and to the development of industries such as shipbuilding and ironworking.)*

The New England Colonies

SYNTHESIZE

DIGITAL ACTIVITY
Challenges of Being a Colonist

Have students complete the Challenges of Being a Colonist activity. Ask students to share their lists with a partner, and then work together to brainstorm parallels between the colonial period and today. Discuss reasons for immigration and the religious, economic, political, and social differences one might encounter in a new land.

Discuss Have students think about the following question. How did physical characteristics of the environment influence where people settled in the New England Colonies and what their lives were like? Discuss students' answers with the class.

DEMONSTRATE

DIGITAL QUIZ
Lesson Quiz and Class Discussion Board

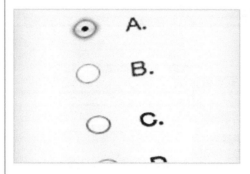

Assign the online Lesson Quiz for this lesson if you haven't already done so. Students will be offered automatic remediation or enrichment based on their score.

Pose these questions to the class on the Discussion Board:

In *The New England Colonies*, you read about the economy, politics, and society of the New England Colonies. Many colonists came to New England seeking religious freedom as well as economic gain. The colonies they established contributed to the rise of representative government and religious freedom in the United States.

Identify Central Issues What new institutions developed in the colonies during this period, and why? *(Representative governments such as the Fundamental Orders of Connecticut and the General Court developed to give colonists a greater say in governance. New religious communities also spread in Massachusetts, Connecticut, and Rhode Island to account for different and dissenting beliefs.)*

Support Ideas with Examples Name three significant individuals who shaped the New England Colonies and explain their impact. *(William Bradford: led Plymouth for 36 years; Squanto: helped the Pilgrims learn to farm and fish; John Winthrop: led Massachusetts Bay Colony; Thomas Hooker: founded Connecticut and the Fundamental Orders of Connecticut; Roger Williams: founded Rhode Island and spread religious tolerance; Anne Hutchinson: became a symbol for religious freedom)*

Topic Inquiry
Have students continue their investigations for the Topic Inquiry.

The Middle Colonies

Supporting English Language Learners

Use with Digital Text 2, **New Jersey Forms Out of New York.**

Learning
Have students read the text. Point out the use of the related words *proprietary* and *proprietors* in the section titled *A Proprietary Colony and Free Enterprise*. Prompt students to internalize new basic language in speaking activities that build concept and language attainment.

Beginning Display this sentence and have students read it after you: The owner of the land was wealthy. Ask students which word is a synonym of *proprietor*. Have students reread the sentence with *proprietor* in place of *owner*. Then have students write a sentence of their own using the word *proprietor*.

Intermediate Discuss the use of *proprietors* in the section. Ask students to use the word (singular or plural form) aloud in an original written sentence about the colonial era. In pairs or in small groups, invite students to use the word *proprietor* in a spoken sentence.

Advanced Have students discuss what makes a colony proprietary. Ask: What other things can be proprietary? Encourage students to use the word *proprietary* in written responses, then have them discuss their responses in pairs or small groups, again using the word *proprietary*.

Advanced High Point out the noun *proprietors* and the adjective *proprietary* in the text. Discuss the words' similarities and differences. Have students use both words to write a paragraph about the colonial era. Then, in pairs or in small groups, have students use the words *proprietors* and *proprietary* to discuss colonial America and the United States today.

Use with Digital Text 3, **Pennsylvania Becomes a Colony.**

Speaking
Have students read the text up to the section titled *Pennsylvania Expands*. Point out the image of William Penn's landing and read the caption. Encourage students to include specificity and detail in their descriptions of the image.

Beginning In pairs or in small groups, have students describe the image in their own words.

Intermediate In pairs or in small groups, ask students to say two sentences describing what they see in the image. The first sentence can be general, but the second should focus on details.

Advanced Ask pairs of students to describe specific parts of the image.

Advanced High In pairs or in small groups, ask students to describe the image in full detail, including all significant parts of the image.

D Differentiate Instruction

Use the Differentiated Instruction notes throughout the lesson plan to support the varied skill sets, levels of readiness, and interests in the mixed-ability classroom.

Challenge These notes include suggestions for expanding the activity for advanced students.

On-Level These notes include suggestions for modifying the activity to address different interests or learning styles.

Extra Support These notes include ideas for providing more scaffolding or reading spuport.

Special Needs These notes provide ideas for adapting instruction to support the needs of various special needs students.

■ NOTES

The Middle Colonies

Objectives

Objective 1: Explain the reasons for the establishment of the colonies of New York and New Jersey.

Objective 2: Explain the reasons for the establishment of the colonies of Pennsylvania and Delaware.

Objective 3: Describe the economy of the Middle Colonies, including the relationship between the economy and the physical environment.

LESSON 4 ORGANIZER		PACING: APPROX. 1 PERIOD, .5 BLOCKS			
				RESOURCES	
		OBJECTIVES	**PACING**	**Online**	**Print**
Connect					
DIGITAL START UP ACTIVITY **Your City**			5 min.	●	
Investigate					
DIGITAL TEXT 1 **A Dutch Colony Becomes English**		Objective 1	10 min.	●	●
DIGITAL TEXT 2 **New Jersey Forms Out of New York**			10 min.	●	●
DIGITAL TEXT 3 **Pennsylvania Becomes a Colony**		Objective 2	10 min.	●	●
INTERACTIVE GALLERY **The Middle Colonies**			10 min.	●	
DIGITAL TEXT 4 **Daily Life in the Middle Colonies**		Objective 3	10 min.	●	●
INTERACTIVE GALLERY **The Economy of the Middle Colonies**			10 min.	●	
Synthesize					
DIGITAL ACTIVITY **Why Do People Move?**			5 min.	●	
Demonstrate					
DIGITAL QUIZ **Lesson Quiz and Class Discussion Board**			10 min.	●	

PEARSON
realize™
www.PearsonRealize.com

Go online to access additional resources including:
Primary Sources • Biographies • Supreme Court cases •
21st Century Skill Tutorials • Maps • Graphic Organizers.

■ CONNECT

DIGITAL START UP ACTIVITY
Your City

Project the Start Up Activity Ask students to fill in their chart as they enter and get settled. Have students share what they know about the history of their city or town's human and physical characteristics, either in class or through a chat or blog space.

Discuss What do you know about the founding of your city or town? Who started it? When? Did its name ever change? What groups of people moved there and what did they do? *(Answers should address what students know about the history of their city or town, including its physical and human characteristics.)*

Aa Vocabulary Development: Use the Interactive Reading Notepad to preview the Key Terms and Academic Vocabulary in the lesson with students.

⇧ FLIP IT!

Assign the Flipped Video for this lesson.

■ STUDENT EDITION PRINT PAGES: 83–91

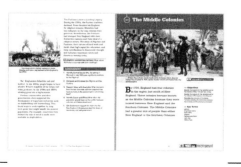

■ INVESTIGATE

DIGITAL TEXT 1
A Dutch Colony Becomes English

Objective 1: **Explain the reasons for the establishment of the colonies of New York and New Jersey.**

Quick Instruction
Project the map of the Middle Colonies on the whiteboard. Dutch Protestants founded New Amsterdam to make money from the fur trade. England then took over the colony and renamed it New York. New York industry and New Jersey farmland attracted immigrants in search of peace, prosperity, and religious freedom.

Identify Central Issues What were the political and economic reasons the Dutch and English colonized North America? *(The Dutch and English colonized North America to expand their empires and to make money, especially from trade.)*

Summarize What were the characteristics and benefits of the free-enterprise system in New Jersey during the 18th century? *(Under the free enterprise system, New Jersey colonists could take advantage of available resources and build businesses with minimal government interference.)*

ELL Use the ELL activity described in the ELL chart.

Further Instruction
Go through the Interactive Reading Notepad questions for *A Dutch Colony Becomes English* and *New Jersey Forms Out of New York* and discuss the answers with the class. Discuss the political, economic, religious, and social reasons for the establishment of New York and New Jersey.

DIGITAL TEXT 2
New Jersey Forms Out of New York

Summarize What ethnic and religious groups settled in New York? Why did many religious groups choose to settle in New York during the 17th century? *(In New Amsterdam and then New York, there were Dutch Protestants, Roman Catholics, French Protestants, Jews, and others. Generally speaking, people enjoyed freedom of worship.)*

Distinguish For what economic reasons was the colony of New Jersey established? *(New Jersey was founded as a proprietary colony, in which economic control was in the hands of a few private individuals who preferred the economy to run with little interference from local government.)*

The Middle Colonies

DIGITAL TEXT 3
Pennsylvania Becomes a Colony

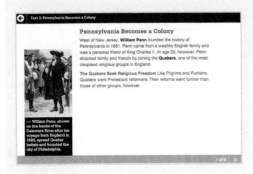

INTERACTIVE GALLERY
The Middle Colonies

Objective 2: **Explain the reasons for the establishment of the colonies of Pennsylvania and Delaware.**

Quick Instruction
A Quaker named William Penn founded Pennsylvania as a haven for people of different religions. Protestants, Catholics, and Jews settled in the colony. Later, immigrants from England, Scotland, the Netherlands, France, and Germany arrived along with persecuted religious groups such as the Amish and Mennonites. Enslaved Africans were also brought to work as laborers.

Interactive Gallery: The Middle Colonies Project the Interactive Gallery and click through the images. Discuss the contributions of different ethnic groups that immigrated to Pennsylvania, including the English, Scotch-Irish, German, and Dutch. Ask how the arrival of these groups have contributed to America's identity.

Compare What ethnic groups settled Pennsylvania in the 17th and 18th centuries, and what were their reasons for immigration? How did these ethnic groups contribute to the development of our national identity? *(English, Scotch-Irish, German, and Dutch immigrants came to escape persecution as well as for economic gain. The ethnically diverse population of Pennsylvania contributed to the development of a national identity based on ethnic diversity.)*

▣ ACTIVE CLASSROOM
Have students use the Conversation strategy and imagine they are having a conversation with William Penn. Have students write down a question they would ask William Penn, what Penn would say to them, and what they would say in response.

D Differentiate: Extra Support Remind students that persecuted means punished for one's beliefs. Have students explain why persecuted religious groups like the Quakers moved to Pennsylvania.

ELL Use the ELL activity described in the ELL chart.

Further Instruction
Go through the Interactive Reading Notepad questions with the class. Be sure students understand how Pennsylvania developed self-government and religious freedom.

Generate Explanations Explain the role of William Penn in the development of self-government in colonial America. *(He proposed a constitution for Pennsylvania and a General Assembly with increased powers.)*

Compare the political, economic, social, and religious reasons for the establishment of Pennsylvania as a colony with the political, economic, and religious reasons for the establishment of other English colonies? *(Like Roger Williams in Rhode Island, William Penn wanted to establish a colony in which religious freedom was encouraged. As in Rhode Island, Penn had a social goal of harmony among people of different faiths. As in New York and New Jersey, Pennsylvania's political roots were as a proprietary, but as in New England and Virginia, Penn established self-government in Pennsylvania. Like other colonies, Pennsylvania's economic reasons for establishment were to generate a profit for its private funders.)*

DIGITAL TEXT 4

Daily Life in the Middle Colonies

INTERACTIVE GALLERY

The Economy of the Middle Colonies

Objective 3: Describe the economy of the Middle Colonies, including the relationship between the economy and the physical environment.

Quick Instruction

Interactive Gallery: The Economy of the Middle Colonies Project the Interactive Map. Explicitly point out the economic reasons for the establishment of the Middle Colonies. Have students identify the major economic activities of the region: farming, trade, textile production, and paper-making. Discuss the aspects of the physical environment that made agriculture and trade central to the economy, emphasizing fertile land for livestock and crops.

📹 ACTIVE CLASSROOM

Have students use the A Closer Look strategy to examine the Interactive Map. Project the map and assign New York, New Jersey, Pennsylvania, and Delaware the numbers 1 through 4. Have students count off one through four and then look closely at the corresponding colony. Have them explain what they see and what they learned as a result from their focus on this part of the map. Collect insights for each colony.

Make Predictions Have students make a prediction about how fertile farmland will impact the Middle Colonies. *(The colonies will do well economically; more immigrants will settle there; the colonies will expand; there may be conflict as settlers encroach on Native American lands.)*

Further Instruction

Go through the Interactive Reading Notepad questions with the class.

Compare and Contrast the physical characteristics of the Middle Colonies and New England. How did differences in the physical environment contribute to economic differences between the two regions? *(Land along the Hudson and Delaware Rivers was fertile. Winters were milder and the growing season longer than in New England. These characteristics made farmland better in the Middle Colonies. Farms were big enough to let colonists develop an economy based on cash crops. They also raised livestock to sell.)*

Identify Patterns How did the physical environment influence population distribution and settlement patterns in the Middle Colonies? *(People settled on fertile land for farming. They also lived in areas along the Delaware River with iron deposits. Many people settled in cities and towns close to harbors and waterways for transportation. Others moved inland to clear forests and settle the backcountry.)*

Cite Evidence How did immigrants interact with the environment when they settled the backcountry in the 18th century? *(They cleared forests and relied on natural resources to survive. They used knots from pine trees as candles, made wooden dishes from logs, gathered honey, and hunted animals for food.)*

The Middle Colonies

SYNTHESIZE

DIGITAL ACTIVITY
Why Do People Move?

Have students complete the Why Do People Move activity. Ask students to answer the questions and then share their lists with a partner. Discuss the religious, social, economic, and political motivations that prompted immigrants to move to the colonies. Ask students which of those motivations apply to immigrants today.

Discuss Have students think about the following question. How did the physical characteristics of the environment influence economic activities in the Middle Colonies? Discuss students' answers with the class.

DEMONSTRATE

DIGITAL QUIZ
Lesson Quiz and Class Discussion Board

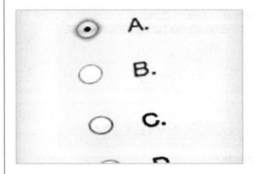

Assign the online Lesson Quiz for this lesson if you haven't already done so. Students will be offered automatic remediation or enrichment based on their score.

Pose these questions to the class on the Discussion Board:

In *The Middle Colonies*, you read about the economy, politics, and society of the Middle Colonies. New York, New Jersey, Pennsylvania, and Delaware were founded by people of different religions and ethnicities seeking economic opportunities and religious freedom. They contributed to the growth of self-government and religious freedom, and to the development of our national identity.

Draw Conclusions What reasons led to the establishment of the Middle Colonies? *New York was founded by the Dutch as New Netherland, mainly to pursue trade. New Jersey was founded by private proprietors to make a profit from its fertile land. Pennsylvania was founded for religious freedom and its fertile land, forests, and minerals. Delaware was founded because its settlers want to be free of the control of Pennsylvania.)*

Identify Cause and Effect How did the desire for religious freedom affect the development of the Middle Colonies? *(Different religious groups settled in the region. Persecuted groups were attracted to Pennsylvania because of its religious freedom, and they contributed to the colony's growth. Later, the English made Pennsylvania turn away Catholics and Jews. New Netherland had freedom of religion as well, before it became New York.)*

Topic Inquiry
Have students continue their investigations for the Topic Inquiry.

The Southern Colonies

Supporting English Language Learners

Use with Digital Text 1, **Lord Baltimore's Colony.**

Learning
Have students read the text. Then point out the term *Act of Toleration* and discuss its meaning. Prompt students to internalize new basic language in writing activities that build concept and language attainment.

Beginning Have students write a sentence using the word *toleration*. Invite them to ask for help if they are having difficulty. After they have written one sentence, ask them to write a second sentence that uses the word.

Intermediate Ask students to write a brief paragraph using the word *toleration* correctly at least twice.

Advanced Display the words *toleration, tolerance,* and *tolerate,* and discuss their meanings. Ask students to use each of the words at least twice to write original paragraphs about religious freedom.

Advanced High Display the words *toleration, tolerance, tolerant,* and *tolerate,* and discuss their meanings. Have students write a brief essay using each of the words at least twice to compare and contrast colonists' tolerance toward people with different religions and their attitudes toward Native Americans.

Use with Digital Text 3, **Two Regions Develop Differently.**

Speaking
Have students read the section titled *Tidewater Plantations on the Coast.* In pairs, ask students to explain how Tidewater plantations operated. Encourage students to use as much specificity and detail and detail as possible.

Beginning Have students explain verbally, in their own words, why plantations tended to develop along the coast.

Intermediate Ask students to use details from the text to explain verbally how Tidewater plantations operated.

Advanced Ask students to provide facts from the text to explain the economy of tidewater plantations in detail and with specificity.

Advanced High Ask students to provide facts from the text to explain the economy of tidewater plantations in detail and with specificity and to provide details of how the economy of these plantations differed from farming in other parts of the colonies.

▣ Differentiate Instruction

Use the Differentiated Instruction notes throughout the lesson plan to support the varied skill sets, levels of readiness, and interests in the mixed-ability classroom.

Challenge These notes include suggestions for expanding the activity for advanced students.

On-Level These notes include suggestions for modifying the activity to address different interests or learning styles.

Extra Support These notes include ideas for providing more scaffolding or reading spuport.

Special Needs These notes provide ideas for adapting instruction to support the needs of various special needs students.

■ NOTES

The Southern Colonies

Objectives

Objective 1: Explain the reasons for the establishment of Maryland.

Objective 2: Explain the reasons for the establishment of the Carolinas and Georgia.

Objective 3: Describe the relationship between different environments, different settlement patterns, and different economic systems in the Southern Colonies.

Objective 4: Explain the development of the slave trade and the spread of slavery in the Southern Colonies.

LESSON 5 ORGANIZER	PACING: APPROX. 1 PERIOD, .5 BLOCKS				
		OBJECTIVES	PACING	RESOURCES	
				Online	Print
Connect					
DIGITAL START UP ACTIVITY **Challenges for Settlers**			5 min.	●	
Investigate					
DIGITAL TEXT 1 **Lord Baltimore's Colony**		Objective 1	10 min.	●	●
DIGITAL TEXT 2 **Settlement in the Carolinas and Georgia**		Objective 2	10 min.	●	●
INTERACTIVE MAP **Comparing the Thirteen Colonies**			10 min.	●	
DIGITAL TEXT 3 **Two Regions Develop Differently**		Objective 3	10 min.	●	●
INTERACTIVE ILLUSTRATION **Plantations of the Southern Colonies**			10 min.	●	
DIGITAL TEXT 4 **The Slave Trade Expands**		Objective 4	10 min.	●	●
Synthesize					
DIGITAL ACTIVITY **The Tidewater and the Backcountry**			5 min.	●	
Demonstrate					
DIGITAL QUIZ **Lesson Quiz and Class Discussion Board**			10 min.	●	

CONNECT

DIGITAL START UP ACTIVITY
Challenges for Settlers

Project the Start Up Activity Ask students to answer the questions as they enter and get settled. Then have them share their ideas with another student, either in class or through a chat or blog space.

Discuss Prompt students to think of some challenges associated with moving over a great distance in the eighteenth century. Encourage them to compare the challenges settlers faced with moving to a new home in a different state today.

Tell students that in this lesson they will be learning about the history of the Southern Colonies.

Aa Vocabulary Development: Use the Interactive Reading Notepad to preview the Key Terms and Academic Vocabulary in this lesson with students.

⇅ FLIP IT!

Assign the Flipped Video for this lesson.

STUDENT EDITION PRINT
PAGES: 92–100

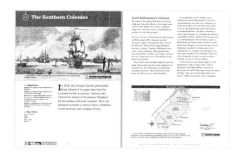

INVESTIGATE

DIGITAL TEXT 1
Lord Baltimore's Colony

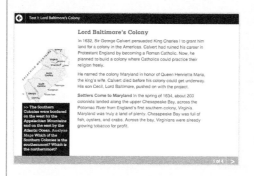

Objective 1: Explain the reasons for the establishment of Maryland.

Quick Instruction

Project the map of the Southern Colonies on the whiteboard. Explain that Maryland was founded by Catholics who wanted to worship freely and hoped to benefit from the fertile land available in the South.

Draw Conclusions Sir George Calvert was a Roman Catholic in Protestant England. Why do you think he requested a land grant to build the colony of Maryland? *(To establish a place where Catholics could worship freely)*

Generate Explanations What were the religious and political reasons for the establishment of Maryland? *(Religious freedom; economic gain from tobacco and natural resources)*

Infer How did Lord Baltimore, proprietor of Maryland, encourage immigrants to settle in the colony? Why do you think he promoted these policies? *(By offering generous land grants and welcoming both Protestants and Catholics; he probably hoped the colony would grow in order to generate wealth)*

ELL Use the ELL activity described in the ELL chart.

Further Instruction

Go through the Interactive Reading Notepad questions and discuss the answers with the class. Be sure students understand the political, social, economic, and religious reasons Maryland was colonized.

Identify Patterns How did the Act of Toleration contribute to the development of religious freedom in the United States? What were the limitations of the act? *(It ensured religious freedom for all Christians, whether Protestant or Catholic; it was limited to Christians and did not grant religious freedom to Jews.)*

Identify Central Issues How did immigrants interact with the environment in Maryland? How did the physical characteristics of the environment influence their settlement patterns and economic activities? *(Immigrants took advantage of the fertile land to build farms and plantations, where they made money from tobacco. They used the Chesapeake Bay for fish, oysters, and crabs, but they avoided building towns in swampy lowlands.)*

Support Ideas with Evidence What evidence suggests that Lord Baltimore contributed to the growth of representative government during the colonial period? *(Although he appointed a governor and a council, he also created an elected assembly. This gave colonists representation in government and a greater say in the colony's affairs.)*

The Southern Colonies

DIGITAL TEXT 2
Settlement in the Carolinas and Georgia

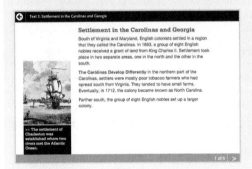

INTERACTIVE MAP
Comparing the Thirteen Colonies

Objective 2: **Explain the reasons for the establishment of the Carolinas and Georgia.**

Quick Instruction

English settlers from the Caribbean and others immigrants from Europe came to in the Carolinas to grow tobacco, rice, and indigo. Further south, Georgia was founded as a colony where debtors who owed money could restart their lives.

Interactive Map: Comparing the Thirteen Colonies Project the interactive map and click through the layers. Have students locate the three important regions: New England, the Middle Colonies, and the Southern Colonies. Prompt students to consider how the physical characteristics of each region influenced economic activity.

Identify Central Issues How did different immigrant groups interact with the environment in the Carolinas? *(Immigrants came to the Carolinas to farm. They built settlements near rivers and used swampy coastal areas to grow rice.)*

D **Differentiate: Extra Support** Remind students of the characteristics that define the U.S. free-enterprise system, such as limited government interference with business. Have students reread the last paragraph in the section on Georgia and explain what government decision enabled the colony to grow.

🎥 ACTIVE CLASSROOM

Have students use the Quick Write strategy and take 30 seconds to write what they know about Georgia and the Carolinas. Have students share their conclusions with partners or with the class.

Further Instruction

Go through the Interactive Reading Notepad questions with the class.

Compare the human characteristics of Georgia and the Carolinas. Ask students who populated these regions and how they used the land. *(Georgia was founded by a social reformer and populated by debtors. Initially, farms were small and slavery was prohibited. The Carolinas were populated by poor tobacco farmers and European immigrants. They had small farms as well as larger rice and indigo plantations.)*

Compare the economic, political, and social reasons for the establishment of the Carolinas and Georgia with the economic, political, and social reasons for the establishment of other English colonies. *(The Carolinas, like other proprietary colonies, were established to make money for their proprietors. Georgia was established as a haven for debtors, while Pennsylvania and the New England colonies were founded as havens for people facing religious persecution. While New York was established to secure English control over a former Dutch colony, Georgia was established to protect other English colonies from Spanish Florida.)*

Identify Cause and Effect Ask students to give an example of how a free-enterprise system caused the colony of Georgia to grow. *(The government's decision not to limit farm size or slavery brought more people to the region.)*

DIGITAL TEXT 3
Two Regions Develop Differently

INTERACTIVE ILLUSTRATION
Plantations of the Southern Colonies

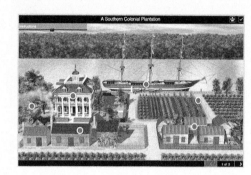

Objective 3: Describe the relationship between different environments, different settlement patterns, and different economic systems in the Southern Colonies.

Quick Instruction
Two regions of the Southern colonies developed different farming systems during the 17th century, or 1600s, and the 18th century, or 1700s. Prompt students to note the relationship between the physical characteristics of the environment of each region and the differences in settlement patterns and population distribution between the two regions. Enslaved Africans labored on plantations in the Tidewater region, clustered near the ocean and rivers. Farther inland, immigrants tended smaller, self-sufficient farms scattered across the backcountry, mainly in valleys.

Interactive Illustration: Plantations of the Southern Colonies Project the interactive illustration and click through the hotspots. Review the reasons for the development of the plantation system and the ways this contributed to the spread of slavery.

Analyze Images What does the image of the Great House suggest about life in some parts of the colonial South? *(Plantation owners were often wealthy and lived in luxurious homes overlooking their property. They were served by enslaved Africans.)*

Generate Explanations Explain why the plantation system and slave labor spread across the Southern Colonies. *(The plantation system and slave labor spread because of the*

headright, or a grant of land for each settler. Wealthy white settlers could gain wealth by purchasing enslaved Africans and thereby gaining more land. They relied on slave labor from Africa because few white settlers were willing to do the heavy work. Colonists found that the most profitable way to raise crops such as tobacco or rice was on large plantations.)*

🎞 ACTIVE CLASSROOM
Have students use the See-Wonder-Think strategy with the images in the interactive gallery. Pair students and have them select an image in the gallery. Ask: What do you see? What does that make you think? What are you wondering about now that you've seen this? Share insights with the class.

ELL Use the ELL activity described in the ELL chart.

Further Instruction
Go through the Interactive Reading Notepad questions with the class and complete the graphic organizer comparing and contrasting the Tidewater and backcountry areas of the Southern Colonies.

Identify Cause and Effect Identify the causes and effects of economic differences between the Tidewater and the backcountry. *(The causes of the differences were that the Tidewater had fertile land and good water transportation access that favored the development of plantation agriculture, while the more remote backcountry was better suited to small farmers raising crops and*

animals for their own needs. The effects of the differences included the spread of slavery and a rich planter class in the Tidewater and greater equality and democracy in the backcountry.)*

Draw Conclusions How did different immigrant groups interact with the environment in the colonies during the 18th century, or 1700s? *(Enslaved Africans used farming skills they had brought from Africa to grow rice on Tidewater plantations. Scotch-Irish immigrants to the backcountry cleared forests and grew crops such as wheat or raised cattle or pigs on the cleared land.)*

The Southern Colonies

DIGITAL TEXT 4

The Slave Trade Expands

Objective 4: Explain the development of the slave trade and the spread of slavery in the Southern Colonies.

Quick Instruction

Project the image of the slave ship. Have students discuss their reactions. Explain that the Middle Passage referred to the journey that slave-trading ships made from Africa to the colonies and identify selected racial groups that subsequently settled in the United States.

Identify Central Issues How did the plantation system relate to the spread of slavery? *(Planters wanted enslaved Africans to work on their plantations, which created demand for the transatlantic slave trade.)*

Further Instruction

Go through the Interactive Reading Notepad questions with the class. Be sure students understand how the development of the plantation system connected to the transatlantic slave trade and the spread of slavery. Explain that Africans were identified by white colonists as a racial group, and that Africans were settled in the English colonies against their will. That is, the reason why Africans immigrated is that they were forced into slavery and brought to the colonies in chains to work on plantations. Assign the primary source *The Interesting Narrative of the Life of Olaudah Equiano*, by Olaudah Equiano.

Generate Explanations Explain the reasons for the spread of slavery. *(As plantations grew, plantation owners brought more enslaved Africans to work their fields. Racism and the demand for free labor enabled this practice to spread.)*

Infer In the early 1600s, some Africans were servants rather than slaves. Others were able to purchase their freedom. Why do you think these policies changed? *(Enslaved Africans became increasingly necessary to the economy. The spread of slavery meant owners did not want Africans to become free.)*

SYNTHESIZE

DIGITAL ACTIVITY

The Tidewater and the Backcountry

Have students complete *The Tidewater and the Backcountry* activity. Ask students to create a chart and then work with a partner to answer the question. Discuss the physical characteristics of both environments, as well as their economies.

Have students think about the following question. How did the physical characteristics of the environment influence economic activities in the Southern Colonies? Discuss students' answers with the class.

DEMONSTRATE

DIGITAL QUIZ

Lesson Quiz and Class Discussion Board

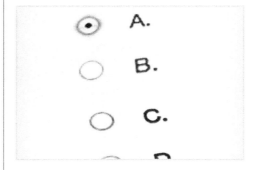

Assign the online Lesson Quiz for this lesson if you haven't already done so. Students will be offered automatic remediation or enrichment based on their score.

Pose these questions to the class on the Discussion Board:

In *The Southern Colonies*, you read about the economy, politics, and society of the Southern Colonies. The growth of the plantation system led to the development of the transatlantic slave trade and the spread of slavery across the South.

Draw Conclusions Why were the Southern Colonies founded? *(Virginia: for gold and trade routes but was later settled mainly to grow tobacco and other crops. Maryland: to promote religious freedom for Catholics and for tobacco cultivation. North Carolina: for profit as a proprietary colony for tobacco farmers spreading south from Virginia. South Carolina: as a proprietary colony for plantation agriculture. Georgia: as a refuge for debtors and to defend the English colonies from Spanish Florida.)*

Compare and Contrast Why did the plantation system develop in the South rather than in the other English colonies? *(The physical environment of the South lent itself to large plantations. Rich soil in low-lying areas was especially ideal for growing rice, which could not grow in the climate or soil further north.)*

Topic Inquiry

Have students continue their investigations for the Topic Inquiry.

Colonial Society

Supporting English Language Learners

Use with Digital Text 3, A New Religious Movement.

Speaking
Have students read the section titled, *Enthusiastic Preachers*. Discuss whether Jonathan Edwards likely used informal (casual, conversational) language or formal (elaborate, complex) language in his sermons.

Beginning Display a list of informal words that describe Jonathan Edwards. Work with students in pairs or small groups to replace each word with a more formal synonym. Have each student use one of the formal words in a spoken sentence.

Intermediate Express a one-sentence informal statement about Jonathan Edwards. Work with students in pairs or small groups to replace each part of the sentence with more formal language. Have students practice saying the formal statement using proper tone of voice. Ask students to add a sentence of their own about Jonathan Edwards using formal language.

Advanced In pairs or in small groups, ask students to make a brief statement, including a few sentences in formal language, about Jonathan Edwards. Remind them to speak as if they were addressing a principal or the president, not a friend, and to use a more formal posture and tone of voice as well.

Advanced High In pairs or in small groups, ask students to give a brief speech, using formal language, about Jonathan Edwards and his influence on colonial society. Review the posture, gestures, and tone of voice appropriate to a speech.

Use with Digital Text 5, A New World of Ideas.

Learning
Read aloud the introduction to the text. Point out the word *logic* and define it. Discuss why it is important. Prompt students to internalize new academic language by using and reusing it in meaningful ways in speaking activities that build concept and language attainment.

Beginning Display the following: logical ≠ illogical. Explain, act out, or show images of situations that are either logical or illogical. Have students identify each situation by completing this sentence aloud: That is not _____; it is _____.

Intermediate Display the following: logical ≠ illogical. Discuss the differences between the words' meanings and spellings. In pairs or in small groups, ask students to make statements using the terms *logical* and *illogical*.

Advanced Place students in pairs. Ask each student to make at least two statements contrasting the terms *logic* and *superstition* from the text.

Advanced High In pairs or in small groups, ask students to use academic language to discuss the differences between logic and superstition.

▣ Differentiate Instruction

Use the Differentiated Instruction notes throughout the lesson plan to support the varied skill sets, levels of readiness, and interests in the mixed-ability classroom.

Challenge These notes include suggestions for expanding the activity for advanced students.

On-Level These notes include suggestions for modifying the activity to address different interests or learning styles.

Extra Support These notes include ideas for providing more scaffolding or reading spuport.

Special Needs These notes provide ideas for adapting instruction to support the needs of various special needs students.

▮ NOTES

Objectives

Objective 1: Outline the structure of colonial society.

Objective 2: Describe colonial art,music, and literature, and the impact of ideas on colonial society.

Objective 3: Describe the causes of the Great Awakening and its effects on colonial society.

Objective 4: Explain the growth of educational institutions.

LESSON 6 ORGANIZER		PACING: APPROX. 1 PERIOD, .5 BLOCKS			
				RESOURCES	
		OBJECTIVES	**PACING**	**Online**	**Print**
Connect					
DIGITAL START UP ACTIVITY **Predictions About Colonial Life**			5 min.	●	
Investigate					
DIGITAL TEXT 1 **Society in Colonial Times**		Objective 1	10 min.	●	●
DIGITAL TEXT 2 **Colonial Art, Literature, and Music**			10 min.	●	●
DIGITAL TEXT 5 **A New World of Ideas**		Objective 2	10 min.	●	●
INTERACTIVE GALLERY **The Arts in Colonial America**			10 min.	●	
DIGITAL TEXT 3 **A New Religious Movement**		Objective 3	10 min.	●	●
DIGITAL TEXT 4 **Colonial Schools and Colleges**		Objective 4	10 min.	●	●
INTERACTIVE CHART **Education in the Colonies**			10 min.	●	
Synthesize					
DIGITAL ACTIVITY **Checking Your Predictions**			5 min.	●	
Demonstrate					
DIGITAL QUIZ **Lesson Quiz and Class Discussion Board**			10 min.	●	

Colonial Society

■ CONNECT

DIGITAL START UP ACTIVITY
Predictions About Colonial Life

Project the Start Up Activity Have students read the questions as they enter and get settled, and then predict what colonial life was like. Have students share their predictions in class or through a chat or blog space.

Discuss What social classes existed in colonial America? What jobs did people hold? What new religious ideas took hold? *(Upper, middle, and lower classes; planters, merchants, ministers, lawyers, officials, craftsworkers, tradespeople, farmhands, servants, maids, cooks, nurses the Great Awakening developed new religious ideas.)*

Tell students that in this lesson they will learn about colonial life, including art, music, and literature, the influence of religions, and the contributions of various groups to American culture and society.

Aa Vocabulary Development: Use the Interactive Reading Notepad to preview the Key Terms and Academic Vocabulary in the lesson with students.

⇅ FLIP IT!

Assign the Flipped Video for this lesson.

■ STUDENT EDITION PRINT PAGES: 101–111

■ INVESTIGATE

DIGITAL TEXT 1
Society in Colonial Times

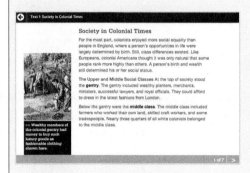

Objective 1: Outline the structure of colonial society.

Quick Instruction
Project the images of the colonial gentry and workers and have students to describe what they see. Discuss the differences between the two images. Ask what evidence suggests one image is of the gentry and one is of the middle class.

Distinguish between the gentry and the middle class. *(Gentry—upper class, including wealthy planters, merchants, ministers, successful lawyers, and royal officials. Middle class—not quite as wealthy, included farmers who owned land, skilled crafts workers, and some tradespeople. Many colonists were middle-class.)*

Support Ideas with Evidence Identify the social and economic contributions of women to colonial society. *(Women ran the home and contributed by cooking, milking cows, watching children, and making necessary goods; they worked in the fields in the backcountry; they got jobs as maids, cooks, nurses, midwives; they learned crafts and trades.)*

Further Instruction
Go through the Interactive Reading Notepad questions with the class and complete the graphic organizer about the various classes that made up colonial society. Discuss how each class contributed to the colonies. Be sure students also understand the contributions of women and African Americans.

Infer Why do you think indentured servants agreed to work without wages? *(They wanted to earn passage to the colonies. They hoped that after their service, they would be able to own land and become more successful.)*

Draw Conclusions Describe the contributions of enslaved Africans to colonial society. *(Enslaved Africans developed new languages such as Gullah, brought their skills to farming, building, and crafts, and contributed to new customs and traditions in the colonies.)*

DIGITAL TEXT 2

Colonial Art, Literature, and Music

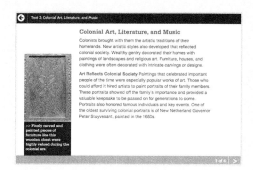

DIGITAL TEXT 5

A New World of Ideas

INTERACTIVE GALLERY

The Arts in Colonial America

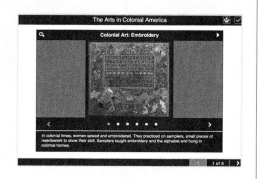

Objective 2: Describe colonial art, music, and literature, and the impact of ideas on colonial society.

Quick Instruction

Project the image of Isaac Newton. Explain that the Enlightenment was a movement of the late 1600s and early 1700s in which European thinkers tried to understand society through reason and science. This movement spread to the colonies to influence daily life in the United States. Colonists also looked to European traditions in art, music, and literature, all of which significantly impacted colonial society. However, certain subsequent developments in those areas were unique to American culture.

Interactive Gallery: Art, Music, and Literature in Colonial America Project the interactive gallery and view the images. Explicitly note the way in which art, music, and literature were reflections of American society in colonial times.

Analyze Images How does the image of Newton illustrate the principles of the Enlightenment? *(Newton is using reason and logic to examine the light, studying the physical laws of the world around him. He is trying to make discoveries based on observation and experimentation.)*

🖳 ACTIVE CLASSROOM

Have students use the Sticky Notes strategy and spend five minutes jotting down their responses to this question on sticky notes: What are examples of American, art, music, and literature that reflected society in the colonial era? Ask students to pair up and share their responses. Then have partners discuss why their examples are significant to the creation of a unique American culture.

Draw Conclusions What were the connections between music and religious life in the colonies? *(Music was played in churches. Spirituals and hymns were popular both in and outside church.)*

D Differentiate: Extra Support Point out that *to enlighten* means to provide greater knowledge or understanding. Ask students what how they think the Enlightenment affected society, based on this definition.

ELL Use the ELL activity described in the ELL chart.

Further Instruction

Go through the Interactive Reading Notepad questions with the class. Discuss the new ideas that developed out of the Enlightenment and how these ideas impacted colonial society.

Draw Conclusions How were miniature paintings an example of American art that reflected colonial society? *(The paintings celebrated people and events important to the colonies, for example the founders of colonies. They also affirmed the importance of the family being painted. This suggested prosperity and permanence in the colonies.)*

Support Ideas with Examples What examples show that Benjamin Franklin's scientific discoveries influenced daily life in the colonies? *(Bifocal glasses helped people see, a new kind of iron stove heated houses better, and lightning rods protected buildings during storms. Paved streets made travel easier, fire companies made communities safer, and lending libraries made books and knowledge more available.)*

Draw Conclusions What factors likely contributed to the growth of colonial newspapers during this period? *(Newspapers developed as the colonies grew. People probably wanted to read about what was happening in their communities. The Enlightenment may have led readers to be more curious about understanding society. The emphasis on learning may have made them interested in reading about important events.)*

Colonial Society

DIGITAL TEXT 3
A New Religious Movement

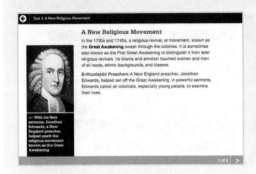

DIGITAL TEXT 4
Colonial Schools and Colleges

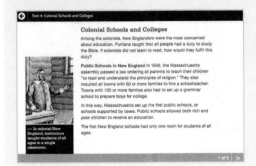

Objective 3: **Describe the impact of the Great Awakening on colonial society.**

Quick Instruction

Project the image of George Whitefield. Explain that Whitefield was an English minister who helped spread a religious movement known as the Great Awakening through the colonies. Point out to students that the Great Awakening was a social movement and discuss its impact on colonial society.

Identify Cause and Effect What were the causes of the Great Awakening? What impact did it have on colonial society? *(Causes— new, powerful preachers inspired colonists. Impact—some religions expanded; new churches grew; people began thinking about religious tolerance and self-rule.)*

Identify Central Issues How did ideas about religion and virtue put forward in the Great Awakening contribute to the growth of representative government in the American colonies? *(Church members controlling their parishes made people think about the importance of self-rule. Preachers also encouraged a spirit of independence. People began believing they could apply the virtues used to run their churches to the running of their government.)*

ELL Use the ELL activity described in the ELL chart.

Further Instruction

Go through the Interactive Reading Notepad questions with the class.

Draw Conclusions How did the Great Awakening contribute to the development of religious freedom in the United States? *(Many new churches sprung up. Colonists had to encounter and become tolerant of people of different faiths.)*

Hypothesize Among the religious influences that led to the Great Awakening as a social movement were the powerful sermons of preachers such as Whitefield and the idea that individuals could shape their own life in parishes without relying on authorities. What impact might this attitude have had on colonists? *(The idea that people could define their own religious life and run their own parishes led to a spirit of independence and a willingness to challenge authorities outside the religious realm.)*

Objective 4: **Explain the growth of educational institutions.**

Quick Instruction

Educational institutions varied by region. New England established the first public schools. The Middle and Southern Colonies had private schools and tutors. Throughout the colonies, boys learned skills through apprenticeships. Enslaved Africans were denied formal educations.

Interactive Chart: Education in the Colonies Project the interactive chart and highlight the regional differences in educational institutions.

Generate Explanations Explain the reasons for the growth of institutions such as public schools during the colonial period. *(Massachusetts Puritans wanted children to learn to read in order to study the Bible. They required towns to hire schoolteachers and set up grammar schools. These were the first public schools that were supported by taxes and open to students regardless of social class.)*

★ ACTIVE CLASSROOM

Have students use the If Images Could Talk strategy and look at the image in the lesson of a woman educating a child. Ask: What do you think the teacher and the pupil would say if they could talk? What's your evidence?

SYNTHESIZE

DEMONSTRATE

INTERACTIVE CHART

Education in the Colonies

DIGITAL ACTIVITY

Checking Your Predictions

DIGITAL QUIZ

Lesson Quiz and Class Discussion Board

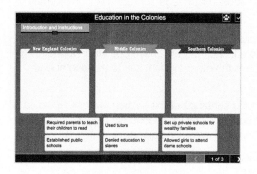

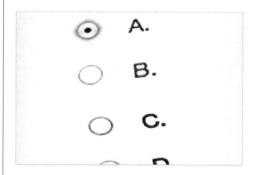

Further Instruction

Go through the Interactive Reading Notepad questions with the class and use the graphic organizer to sum up how formal education developed in different regions of the colonies. Be sure students understand why educational institutions grew during the colonial period.

Generate Explanations Explain the reasons for the growth of colleges and universities during the colonial period. *(To promote European culture and to educate future ministers; colleges later expanded to teach additional areas of study to men)*

Draw Conclusions Why didn't all children go to school in the colonial era? *(Public schools were not widespread and many children could not afford private schools or tutors. Some families lived too far from schools to send their children. Some students worked or served as apprentices instead of attending school. Enslaved African Americans were not allowed to go to school.)*

Cite Evidence How did women contribute to American society through dame schools? *(Women ran dame schools to educate girls, who were not accepted to New England schools. They taught girls reading, writing, and other skills.)*

Have students complete the Checking Your Predictions activity. Have students review the predictions they made at the beginning of the lesson and then answer the questions. Have students discuss the final question with a partner and share their insights with the class.

Discuss Have students think about the following questions. What were unique aspects of American culture during the colonial era? How are these aspects similar to or different from American culture today? Discuss students' answers with the class.

Assign the online Lesson Quiz for this lesson if you haven't already done so. Students will be offered automatic remediation or enrichment based on their score.

Pose these questions to the class on the Discussion Board:

In *Colonial Society*, you read about unique aspects of American society in the colonial era. Colonists developed art, music, and literature that reflected society at the time. Science and religion brought important changes as well.

Identify Cause and Effect How did the Great Awakening impact colonial society? *(New churches developed; ideas about democracy and self-governing spread; people thought about self-improvement and social reform.)*

Summarize What new institutions developed during the colonial era? *(Churches; public schools; colleges and universities; cultural institutions such as theaters and newspapers also developed for entertainment and information)*

Topic Inquiry

Have students continue their investigations for the Topic Inquiry.

Colonial Trade and Government

Supporting English Language Learners

Use with Digital Text 1, **Mercantilism and the English Colonies.**

Learning
Have students read the text. Discuss the meaning of mercantilism. Prompt students to internalize new language in writing activities that build concept and language attainment. Point out the use of *benefit* (first paragraph) and of *benefited* (fourth paragraph), as well as their meanings. Model two or three sentences using the words *benefit* or *benefited*.

Beginning Have students write two sentences about mercantilism using the word *benefit* or *benefited*.

Intermediate Ask students who benefited and who did not benefit from the Navigation Acts. Tell them to use the words *benefited* and *benefit* at least twice each in their written response.

Advanced Display the words *benefited* and *beneficial*, and discuss their similarities and usage. Ask pairs of students to write a paragraph about mercantilism that uses both words at least twice.

Advanced High Display the words *benefited*, *beneficial*, and *beneficiary*, and discuss their similarities and usage. Have students write at least two paragraphs that describe mercantilism and uses each of the three words at least twice.

Use with Digital Text 3, **Foundations of Representative Government.**

Speaking
Have students read the section *William Blackstone and Common Law*. Encourage students to adapt spoken language appropriately for informal purposes.

Beginning Read the second sentence of the section. Ask: How would you describe common law to a friend? In pairs, have one student briefly describe common law and have the other student ask a question about common law.

Intermediate Read the second sentence of the section. Ask: How would you simplify this definition of common law for a friend? In pairs or in small groups, have students offer informal definitions aloud.

Advanced Ask pairs of students to discuss the meaning and use of common law. Encourage them to use informal, everyday language with each other. Ask: How was your language different from that of the text?

Advanced High In pairs, have students give a brief presentation about common law to an imaginary group of younger students. Encourage them to use informal, accessible language during their talk.

◨ Differentiate Instruction

Use the Differentiated Instruction notes throughout the lesson plan to support the varied skill sets, levels of readiness, and interests in the mixed-ability classroom.

Challenge These notes include suggestions for expanding the activity for advanced students.

On-Level These notes include suggestions for modifying the activity to address different interests or learning styles.

Extra Support These notes include ideas for providing more scaffolding or reading spuport.

Special Needs These notes provide ideas for adapting instruction to support the needs of various special needs students.

■ NOTES

Objectives

Objective 1: Explain the development of mercantilism and colonists' response to it.

Objective 2: Outline the relationship of the slave trade to other kinds of trade.

Objective 3: Describe the development of governments and legal systems in the colonies.

LESSON 7 ORGANIZER		PACING: APPROX. 1 PERIOD, .5 BLOCKS		
	OBJECTIVES	**PACING**	**RESOURCES**	
			Online	**Print**
Connect				
DIGITAL START UP ACTIVITY **William Blackstone**		5 min.	●	
Investigate				
DIGITAL TEXT 1 **Mercantilism and the English Colonies**	Objective 1	10 min.	●	●
DIGITAL TEXT 2 **Trading Across the Atlantic**	Objective 2	10 min.	●	●
INTERACTIVE MAP **The Triangular Trade**		10 min.	●	
DIGITAL TEXT 3 **Foundations of Representative Government**	Objective 3	10 min.	●	●
INTERACTIVE CHART **Influences on Colonial Government**		10 min.	●	
Synthesize				
DIGITAL ACTIVITY **Government Traditions**		5 min.	●	
Demonstrate				
DIGITAL QUIZ **Lesson Quiz and Class Discussion Board**		10 min.	●	

Colonial Trade and Government

■ CONNECT

DIGITAL START UP ACTIVITY
William Blackstone

Project the Start Up Activity Have students read the quote and answer the question as they enter and get settled. Ask students to paraphrase Blackstone's main points and discuss their answers with a partner.

Discuss Why do you think Blackstone's ideas became popular in the colonies? *(He emphasized liberty and justice, especially the right to a fair trial. He was critical of unfair and arbitrary government, a feeling colonists also shared.)*

Tell students that in this lesson they will be learning about the government and economy of the 13 English colonies. This period saw the growth of triangular trade and the development of representative government in the colonies.

Aa Vocabulary Development: Use the Interactive Reading Notepad to preview the Key Terms and the Academic Vocabulary in this lesson with students.

🔃 FLIP IT!
Assign the Flipped Video for this lesson.

■ STUDENT EDITION PRINT
PAGES: 112–116

■ INVESTIGATE

DIGITAL TEXT 1
Mercantilism and the English Colonies

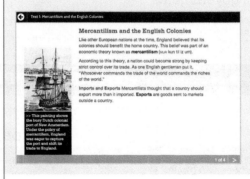

Objective 1: Explain the development of mercantilism and colonists' response to it.

Quick Instruction
Project the image of colonial shipbuilding and discuss industries such as shipbuilding that were strong in the colonies. Explain that mercantilism is an economic theory that says a nation becomes strong by controlling its trade. According to this theory, England believed it should benefit from colonial trade.

Make Predictions Make a prediction about why mercantilism will be one of the causes of the American Revolution. *(Colonists will not want England controlling their trade and making money off their labor.)*

D Differentiate: Extra Support Explain to students that when nations trade, they both buy and sell goods. Exports are goods that are sent out of a country. Imports are goods that are brought into a country. Ask students to come up with an example of an import and an export, from the colonial period or the present day.

ELL Use the ELL activity described in the ELL chart.

Further Instruction
Go through the Interactive Reading Notepad questions with the class and complete the graphic organizer to take notes about the Navigation Acts. Ask students why colonists disliked the Navigation Acts. Be sure students understand why mercantilism and mercantilist policies like the Navigation Acts would become causes of the American Revolution.

Hypothesize Ask students how they think many colonists felt about their trade benefiting England. *(They were probably not happy with this arrangement. They would have wanted to benefit from their trade.)*

Infer What does mercantilism suggest about England's attitude toward its colonies? *(England saw the colonies mainly as a source of wealth for the mother country.)*

DIGITAL TEXT 2

Trading Across the Atlantic

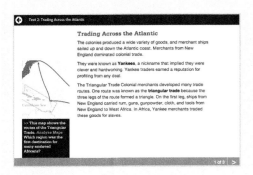

Objective 2: Outline the relationship of the slave trade to other kinds of trade.

Quick Instruction

Colonists in New England, the Middle Colonies, and the Southern Colonies traded with Africa and the Caribbean. These trade routes are known as the triangular trade because together they formed a triangle.

Interactive Map: Triangular Trade Project the map on the whiteboard and explore the regions. Have students use the map to describe the trade routes in their own words.

Identify Patterns How did the triangular trade connect to the development of the transatlantic slave trade? *(The transatlantic slave trade was one leg of the triangular trade. Traders sold rum to buy enslaved Africans, who were brought via the slave trade to work on sugar plantations in the Caribbean. The sugar was sold to the North American colonies and made into rum, which was used to buy more slaves.)*

📖 ACTIVE CLASSROOM

Have students use the Connect Two strategy. List the following words for students to copy: merchants, triangular trade, slaves, molasses, Yankees, gunpowder, profits, Middle Passage, transatlantic slave trade, rum, and Navigation Acts. Read the list of words with students. Ask students to choose two words they think might belong together and state the reason. During the reading, have students look for evidence to support or refute their connections.

INTERACTIVE MAP

The Triangular Trade

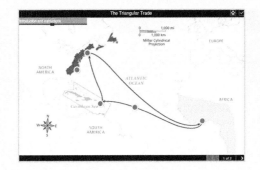

Further Instruction

Go through the Interactive Reading Notepad questions with the class. Be sure students understand the routes of the triangular trade and how it contributed to the development of the transatlantic slave trade.

Identify Central Issues How did the triangular trade benefit both England and the colonies economically? *(The colonies made money from selling rum and enslaved Africans, and from the plantations where enslaved Africans worked. Although traders disregarded the Navigation Acts, England benefited from the economic success of the colonies. England also bought rice, silk, indigo, and tobacco from the Southern Colonies.)*

Identify Cause and Effect Identify an effect of colonization on each group: colonial merchants, the English, and Africans. *(Colonial merchants became wealthy from the triangular trade; the English generated wealth and received new goods such as rice and tobacco; Africans were enslaved and brought to plantations.)*

DIGITAL TEXT 3

Foundations of Representative Government

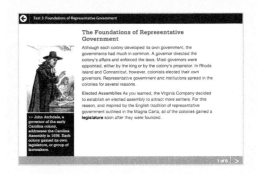

Objective 3: Describe the development of governments and legal systems in the colonies.

Quick Instruction

Interactive Chart: Influences on Colonial Government Project the interactive chart on the whiteboard and have students read through the tiles about the three documents. Explain that historic documents such as the English Bill of Rights strongly influenced the development of representative government during the colonial period.

Summarize What government institutions emerged during the colonial period? *(Colonies legislatures emerged and many had elected assemblies. Colonies also had governors and judges.)*

📖 ACTIVE CLASSROOM

Have students use the Write 1-Get 3 strategy to answer the question: What were four key characteristics of colonial government? Have students take a piece of paper and fold it into quarters. Students write down one response in the first box and then go around the room asking to hear other responses. When students think a response is correct, they write it in their boxes until they have three more responses on the page. Have students share responses with the class.

ELL Use the ELL activity described in the ELL chart.

Colonial Trade and Government

INTERACTIVE CHART
Influences on Colonial Government

DIGITAL ACTIVITY
Government Traditions

DIGITAL QUIZ
Lesson Quiz and Class Discussion Board

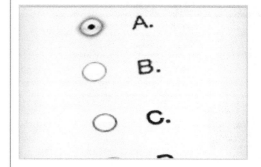

Further Instruction

Go through the Interactive Reading Notepad questions with the class. Review the Commentaries on the Laws of England, the Magna Carta, and the English Bill of Rights. Discuss how and why these documents influenced colonial government. Assign the Primary Source: The English Bill of Rights.

Identify Patterns What ideas from the English Bill of Rights have influenced the U.S. system of government? *(Individuals have rights that the government must protect; those accused of a crime have the right to a trial by jury; rulers cannot raise taxes or an army without approval from a separate legislative body.)*

Draw Conclusions How did William Blackstone contribute to the development of self-government in colonial America? *(Blackstone viewed individuals as free agents capable of controlling themselves, and therefore capable of governing themselves.)*

Cite Evidence Explain the reasons for the growth of representative government and institutions during the colonial period. *(The idea of representative government was enshrined in the Magna Carta, and colonists cherished this and other English democratic traditions. Representative government was strengthened as a result of England's Glorious Revolution in 1688 and its Bill of Rights, which gave more rights and powers to parliament and which also strengthened the position of colonial legislatures.)*

Have students complete the Government Traditions activity. Have students fill in their charts and then answer the questions. Ask students to make a prediction about how the growth of representative government in the colonies will affect relations with England.

Discuss Have students think about the following question: How were the colonies setting themselves up to be economically and politically independent from England? Discuss students' answers with the class.

Assign the online Lesson Quiz for this lesson if you haven't already done so. Students will be offered automatic remediation or enrichment based on their score.

Pose these questions to the class on the Discussion Board:

In *Colonial Trade and Government*, you read about the economy and government of the colonies. Mercantilism led to a brisk trade between the colonies and England, while additional trade routes developed to include Africa and the Caribbean. At the same time, colonial government was laying the foundations for self-rule.

Identify Cause and Effect What economic factors caused the colonies to prosper? How might this prosperity affect relations with England? *(Farming, resources, and the triangular trade generated wealth; England might have expected a greater share of the profits from the colonies than colonists wanted to give.)*

Formulate Questions What is a question you have about the development of self-government in the colonies? *(What factors led the U.S. government to extend greater freedoms to those whose rights were limited in the colonies?)*

Topic Inquiry

Have students continue their investigations for the Topic Inquiry.

European Colonization of North America (1500–1750)

SYNTHESIZE

DIGITAL ACTIVITY
Reflect on the Essential Question and Topic

First ask students to reconsider the Topic Essential Question: Why do people move? Remind students that people move because different political, economic, and social factors "push" them from one place and "pull" them to another.

Have students list the push and pull factors that compelled at least five different groups of people to move to North America. Ask: Do you think colonists who moved to North America were able to build the lives they'd imagined when they decided to move? Ask them to consider different groups of colonists and give evidence for support. Discuss their answers as a class or ask students to post their answers on the Class Discussion board.

Next ask students to reflect on the topic as a whole and think of someone they know, or know of, who moved from one place to another. Have students write down why they think this person moved and three additional questions they have about this person's motivations. Have students consider the following motivators if they need help getting started:

- political reasons
- economic reasons
- social reasons
- personal reasons

You may ask students to share their questions and answers on the Class Discussion Board.

Topic Inquiry
Have students complete Step 3 of the Topic Inquiry.

DEMONSTRATE

DIGITAL TOPIC REVIEW AND ASSESSMENT
European Colonization of North America (1500–1750)

Students can prepare for the Topic Test by answering the questions in the Topic Review and Assessment online or the Assessment questions in the Print Student text. They can also prepare by reviewing their answers to the Interactive Reading Notepad questions or reviewing their notes in the Reading and Notetaking Study Guide.

DIGITAL TOPIC TEST
European Colonization of North America (1500–1750)

TOPIC TEST
Assign the Topic Test to assess students' understanding of topic content.

BENCHMARK TESTS
Assign these benchmark tests as you complete the relevant topics to monitor student progress toward mastering the course content and as preparation for the End-of-Course Test.

Benchmark Test 1: Topics 1–2

Benchmark Test 2: Topics 3–4

Benchmark Test 3: Topics 5–6

Benchmark Test 4: Topics 7–9

Benchmark Test 5: Topics 10–12

Benchmark Test 6: Topics 13–14

Benchmark Test 7: Topics 15–17

Topic ③

The Revolutionary Era (1750–1783)

TOPIC 3 ORGANIZER	PACING: APPROX. 1 PERIOD, .5 BLOCKS
	PACING
Connect	1 period
MY STORY VIDEO **Benjamin Franklin and the Fight for Independence**	10 min.
DIGITAL ESSENTIAL QUESTION ACTIVITY **When is War Justified?**	10 min.
DIGITAL OVERVIEW ACTIVITY **The Revolutionary Era**	10 min.
TOPIC INQUIRY: PROJECT-BASED LEARNING **Write an American Revolution Blog**	20 min.
Investigate	2–5 periods
TOPIC INQUIRY: PROJECT-BASED LEARNING **Write an American Revolution Blog**	Ongoing
LESSON 1 The French and Indian War	30–40 min.
LESSON 2 Tensions with Britain	30–40 min.
LESSON 3 Taking Up Arms	30–40 min.
LESSON 4 Declaring Independence	30–40 min.
LESSON 5 Winning Independence	30–40 min.
Synthesize	1 period
DIGITAL ACTIVITY **Reflect on the Essential Question and Topic**	10 min.
TOPIC INQUIRY: PROJECT-BASED LEARNING **Write an American Revolution Blog**	20 min.
Demonstrate	1–2 periods
DIGITAL TOPIC REVIEW AND ASSESSMENT **The Revolutionary Era**	10 min.
TOPIC INQUIRY: PROJECT-BASED LEARNING **Write an American Revolution Blog**	20 min.

TOPIC INQUIRY: PROJECT-BASED LEARNING

Write an American Revolution Blog

In this Topic Inquiry, students create, publish, and present an American Revolution blog. The blog will document their decision-making process as they consider whether they would have sided with Britain, the Patriots, or remained neutral during the Revolutionary War if they lived in the Chesapeake Bay in 1776. Learning about how colonists decided which side to support will contribute to students' understanding of the Topic Essential Question: When is war justified?

STEP 1: CONNECT
Develop Questions and Plan the Investigation

Read the Project Launch
Explain to students that in this project, they will be deciding whether they would have supported the British, the Patriots, or remained neutral if they lived in the Chesapeake Bay in 1776. Explain that they will need to create a written presentation of social studies material in the form of a blog. Have students read the Project Launch and review the fictional request from Commander George Washington.

Suggestion: To provide extra support, ask students which side Washington chose. Remind them that not all colonists supported the Patriots. Make sure they understand they are being asked to research how Chesapeake Bay colonists chose sides and will use this information to make their own decision.

Plan the Investigation
Form students into groups. Have them sign the *Project Contract*. Ask the groups to discuss the five steps of the decision-making process. Have students begin their *Need to Know Questions* to form a list of research questions. They may want to consider geography, location, economy, religion, political allegiances, and other social and historical factors that impacted colonists' decisions.

Suggestion: You may assign students their groups, or let students choose. Groups may then select their three subgroups, or you can assign them.

Resources
- Project Launch
- Project Contract
- Rubric for a Written Blog and Group Presentation
- Student Instructions

STEP 2: INVESTIGATE
Apply Disciplinary Concepts and Tools

Gathering Sources for Research on the Chesapeake Bay
Groups will work together to identify the information they need to investigate the Chesapeake Bay in 1776.

Suggestion: Students can conduct their research online, but should also remember to consult the readings for this topic.

Investigate Factors Influencing the Decision
Groups will break into three subgroups to address the steps in the decision-making process. Group 1 will identify the situation, Group 2 will identify options, and Group 3 will predict consequences.

Suggestion: If groups get stuck, remind them to review the information they have already gathered from the readings and their research on the region and then generate questions relevant to their step in the decision-making process.

Write and Edit Your Subgroup's Blog Post
Each subgroup will write and edit its own blog post presenting the information gathered as part of the decision-making process. Blog posts should be well organized, stay on topic, and include maps, images, and quotes. Work with students to make sure that they use social studies terminology, standard grammar, spelling, sentence structure, punctuation, and proper citation of sources.

Suggestion: Review how to incorporate research into written material, including proper formatting for citing sources.

Resources
- Work in Teams
- Project Tracker
- Search for Information on the Internet
- Make Decisions
- Information Organizer
- Need to Know Questions
- Model Blog

⏻ PROFESSIONAL DEVELOPMENT

Project-Based Learning
Be sure to view the Project-Based Learning Professional Development resources in the online course.

Topic ③

Write an American Revolution Blog *(continued)*

STEP 3: SYNTHESIZE
Evaluate Sources and Use Evidence to Formulate Conclusions

Build Your Group Blog
Have groups come together to build their blogs. Blogs should incorporate each subgroup's blog post and use both images and text.

Suggestion: If your class has limited access to the Internet, you could supply materials for students to make a physical binder or book to present their posts.

Write Your Conclusions
Have students use their group's blogs to make their own decision about which side they would have taken during the American Revolution. Students should use the prompts to explain the reasons for their decision.

Suggestion: Poll the class to see whether students arrived at different conclusions, and what factors most influenced their decision-making process.

Resources
• Getting Started with WordPress Tutorial

STEP 4: DEMONSTRATE
Communicate Conclusions and Take Informed Action

Present Your Blog
Have students present their blogs to the class or an invited audience. To help students structure their presentations and ensure equal participation, have them divide the presentation among group members.

Suggestion: If your classroom is not equipped to view the blog during the presentation, have students pass around hard copies of their posts for audience members to see.

Reflect on the Project
Have groups meet to go over what went well and what did not so they can be more effective in the future. Students will then complete the Team/Peer Assessment individually.

Suggestion: As an extension, have students use the information they gathered about the Chesapeake Bay to consider how the region was affected by the war.

Heading
• Give an Effective Presentation
• Team/Peer Assessment

INTRODUCTION

The Revolutionary Era (1750–1783)

By the mid-1700s, European powers were fighting to grow their empires in North America. War broke out—the French and Indian War—between Britain, France, and several Native American tribes. The British won, but victory came at a cost. To pay for the war, Parliament imposed new taxes on the colonies, and widespread protests broke out. The American Revolution was not only a fight to break from Britain. It was also a fight for a radically new society and an experimental form of government: democratic republicanism.

■ CONNECT

MY STORY VIDEO
Benjamin Franklin and the Fight for Independence

Watch a video about the life and accomplishments of Benjamin Franklin.

Check Understanding What key role did Benjamin Franklin play during the American Revolution. *(A diplomat to France, he helped persuade the French to support the American side.)*

Draw Conclusions Why has Franklin been called an 18th century version of a Renaissance man? *(Like leading Renaissance thinkers, Franklin was interested in all aspects of human endeavor. He was conducted experiments, he was an inventor and a writer, and he was deeply involved in the intellectual life of the American colonies.)*

⇡ FLIP IT!

Assign the My Story video.

DIGITAL ESSENTIAL QUESTION ACTIVITY
When is War Justified?

Ask students to think about the Essential Question for this topic: When is war justified? Not all colonists supported the American Revolution. Were the colonists right to go to war?

If students have not already done so, ask them to think about the questions in the activity. Then go over the answers as a class.

Generate Explanations Explain why some colonists might not have thought war with Britain was justified. *(They were loyal to Britain; they hoped the conflict could be solved without war; they did not agree with the reasons for the war.)*

Make Predictions What reasons do you think the colonists will give for going to war? *(To stand up for political ideals; to protect their way of life; to reject British policies; to develop their own government)*

DIGITAL OVERVIEW ACTIVITY
The Revolutionary Era

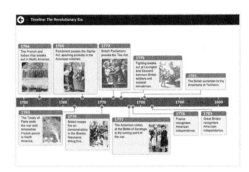

Display the timeline showing key events of the revolutionary era. This timeline will help provide a framework in which students can place the events they learn about during this topic.

Analyze Information Based on the timeline, what major issues between Britain and the colonies were causes of the American Revolution? *(the Stamp Act and the Boston Massacre)*

Identify Cause and Effect How do you think the British victory in the French and Indian War contributed to the causes of the American Revolution? *(Colonists might not have liked Britain gaining power in the region; Britain may have sought money from the colonies to pay for the war; Britain may have imposed policies about land and settlement in new territories that colonists did not like.)*

Topic Inquiry

Launch the Topic Inquiry with students after introducing the topic.

The French and Indian War

Supporting English Language Learners

Use with Digital Text 3, **A Meeting in Albany.**

Learning
Have students read the first paragraph of the text. Use accessible language to help students learn new and essential language. Use accessible language to define the words *delegates*, *cement*, and *alliance*, as used in this paragraph.

Beginning Have students reread the paragraph. Working in groups of three, have each student use his or her own words explain the meaning of one of the three words that you have defined.

Intermediate Have students write their own sentence using each of the three words that you have defined.

Advanced Working in pairs, have students read the second paragraph of this section. Ask students to take turns identifying words in the paragraph that are new to them. Based on the context provided by the more accessible words in the paragraph, have students define in their own words the new words that they have identified.

Advanced High Have students take turns reading sentences in the second and third paragraphs of the reading in small groups or for the whole class. Have each student identify at least one new and challenging word in his or her sentence and define it using accessible language.

Use with Digital Text 5, **Quebec and New France Fall.**

Speaking
Read the text orally, or invite volunteers to do so in order to reinforce concept attainment. Then display the timeline and read its content together, encouraging students to respond orally to the information presented.

Beginning Ask: When does Britain declare war on France? Display this sentence to support their response: Britain declares war in the year _____. As students answer aloud, have them point to the information on the timeline.

Intermediate Ask: What happens in the French and Indian War during the year 1755? Have students read aloud the appropriate entry on the timeline and restate it aloud in their own words.

Advanced Ask: Do the British negotiate with the Iroquois and Ohio Indians before or after more British troops are sent to North America? Have students answer aloud and explain their response by pointing to relevant information on the timeline.

Advanced High Have students read aloud the timeline entries in chronological order and then restate them in their own words. Ask: How does this timeline help you to better understand the war?

▣ Differentiate Instruction

Use the Differentiated Instruction notes throughout the lesson plan to support the varied skill sets, levels of readiness, and interests in the mixed-ability classroom.

Challenge These notes include suggestions for expanding the activity for advanced students.

On-Level These notes include suggestions for modifying the activity to address different interests or learning styles.

Extra Support These notes include ideas for providing more scaffolding or reading spuport.

Special Needs These notes provide ideas for adapting instruction to support the needs of various special needs students.

■ NOTES

Objectives

Objective 1: Explain how the rivalry between Britain and France and conflict over the Ohio Valley led to the French and Indian War in North America.

Objective 2: Identify how mistakes and lack of unity led to British defeats early in the war.

Objective 3: Summarize how the tide of the war turned in Britain's favor.

Objective 4: Explain how the British won the war.

Objective 5: Describe the power shift that occurred after the war.

LESSON 1 ORGANIZER		PACING: APPROX. 1 PERIOD, .5 BLOCKS			
		OBJECTIVES	PACING	RESOURCES Online	Print
Connect					
DIGITAL START UP ACTIVITY **Causes of the French and Indian War**			5 min.	●	
Investigate					
DIGITAL TEXT 1 **Europeans Fight Over North American Land**		Objective 1	10 min.	●	●
DIGITAL TEXT 2 **The French and Indian War Begins in the Ohio Valley**			10 min.	●	●
DIGITAL TEXT 3 **A Meeting in Albany**			10 min.	●	●
DIGITAL TEXT 4 **British Defeats in the Ohio Valley**		Objective 2	10 min.	●	●
INTERACTIVE MAP **Major Battles of the French and Indian War**			10 min.	●	
DIGITAL TEXT 5 **Quebec and New France Fall**		Objectives 3, 4, 5	10 min.	●	●
INTERACTIVE CHART **Effects of the French and Indian War**			10 min.	●	
Synthesize					
DIGITAL ACTIVITY **Effects of the French and Indian War**			5 min.	●	
Demonstrate					
DIGITAL QUIZ **Lesson Quiz and Class Discussion Board**			10 min.	●	

The French and Indian War

DIGITAL START UP ACTIVITY
Causes of the French and Indian War

Project the Start Up Activity As they enter and get settled, ask students to look at the maps. Then have them discuss their answers with another student, either in class or through a chat or blog space.

Locate places of importance on the map with students.

Discuss Based on this map, why do you think war broke out between France and Britain? *(The empires were close to one another and fought over territory.)* What do you predict will happen to the Native American tribes in the region? *(They look like they will be caught in the middle and forced to take sides.)*

Tell students that in this lesson they will learn how physical and human geographic factors affected the French and Indian War.

Aa Vocabulary Development: Use the Interactive Reading Notepad to preview the Key Terms and Academic Vocabulary in the lesson with students.

✂ FLIP IT!
Assign the Flipped Video for this lesson.

■ STUDENT EDITION PRINT PAGES: 122–129

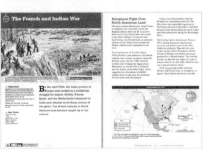

■ INVESTIGATE

DIGITAL TEXT 1
Europeans Fight Over North American Land

Objective 1: Explain how the rivalry between Britain and France and conflict over the Ohio Valley led to the French and Indian War in North America.

Quick Instruction
Project the map of North America. Have students identify the European powers in North America and their territories. Ask students to locate the Ohio River Valley and discuss its strategic importance.

Analyze Maps Why do you think France wanted to maintain its hold over the Ohio River Valley? *(It wanted to control the fur trade in the region. It also used the river to connect settlements in the region.)*

D Differentiate: Extra Support Have students copy the map and highlight the Ohio River. Ask what areas it connects. Discuss the different ways settlers relied on rivers, including for water, fishing, trapping, and transportation.

Further Instruction
Go through the Interactive Reading Notepad questions for *Europeans Fight Over North American Land* and *The French and Indian War Begins in the Ohio Valley* and discuss the answers with the class, including the graphic organizer noting the alliances and reasons they were formed. Be sure students understand how conflicts over land and resources led fighting to break out.

DIGITAL TEXT 2
The French and Indian War Begins in the Ohio Valley

Compare and Contrast French and British settlements in North America. *(France—claimed lands west of the St. Lawrence River; built forts for protection; were mostly trappers and traders; many adopted Native American ways. Britain—settled primarily along the coast; began pushing west of the Appalachian Mountains; cleared forests for farms; many ignored Native American's rights.)*

Draw Conclusions Why did fighting break out in the Ohio Valley? *(Britain wanted to expand westward. France wanted to limit British expansion into its territories. Native Americans did not want to give up their land.)*

Identify Cause and Effect How did the physical geography of the Ohio Valley affect the early stages of the French and Indian War? How did people interact with the environment? *(Both sides could hide in the woods. The woods also made it possible to sneak up on the enemy. This led the British and French to build forts for protection along rivers in the region.)*

DIGITAL TEXT 3

A Meeting in Albany

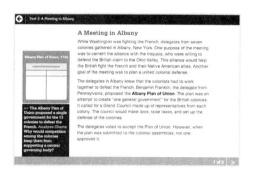

DIGITAL TEXT 4

British Defeats in the Ohio Valley

INTERACTIVE MAP

Major Battles of the French and Indian War

Objective 2: **Identify how mistakes and lack of unity led to British defeats early in the war.**

Quick Instruction

Interactive Map: Major Battles of the French and Indian War Project the map and click through the layers. Ask students how the physical geography of the frontier affected the major battles of the war.

Sequence Events Ask students to give the chronology of events described in the interactive map. *(Washington marched to Great Meadows and was defeated at Fort Necessity; General Braddock was defeated at Fort Duquesne; France captured Fort Oswego; British troops were attacked by Native Americans while fleeing Fort William Henry; Britain captured Louisbourg; France burned Fort Duquesne; Britain captured the fort and renamed it Fort Pitt; Britain captured Quebec; France surrendered.)*

ELL Use the ELL activity described in the ELL chart.

🎬 ACTIVE CLASSROOM

Have students use the Cartoon It strategy to draw one compelling image from the texts on a piece of paper. Have students turn their drawing into a political cartoon that illustrates a key concept or main idea. Students can hang their cartoons in the classroom or scan them to a class blog.

Further Instruction

Go through the Interactive Reading Notepad questions for *A Meeting in Albany* and *British Defeats in the Ohio Valley* with the class.

Be sure students understand the reasons for British defeats early in the war. In addition to addressing the physical geographic factors that shaped the war, remind students of the human geographic factors that contributed to British losses, including the lack of British unity and experience with the land in which they fought.

Generate Explanations Explain why British losses strained Britain's alliance with the Iroquois. *(The Iroquois wanted Britain's protection from France and faced further danger from enemy tribes after Britain's early losses.)*

Draw Conclusions Why were the Great Lakes of strategic importance in the war? *(They provided access to areas for trapping and trading in the frontier, allowed for transportation via ships, and connected to rivers used for travel, transportation, and trade.)*

Cite Evidence What evidence suggests British soldiers were unprepared for fighting in the forests of North America? *(The soldiers moved slowly and noisily through the forests so the enemy could track them. Their bright red uniforms made them clear targets.)*

The French and Indian War

DIGITAL TEXT 5

Quebec and New France Fall

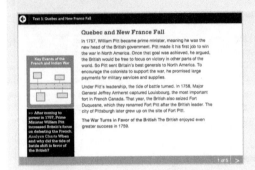

INTERACTIVE CHART

Effects of the French and Indian War

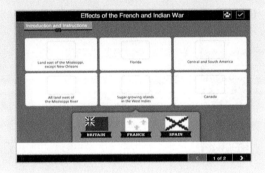

Objectives 3: **Summarize how the tide of the war turned in Britain's favor; 4:** **Explain how the British won the war; 5:** **Describe the power shift that occurred after the war.**

Quick Instruction

Britain won the war when it captured Quebec, a major center of New France. Britain took advantage of the physical geography of the city to launch a surprise attack. Britain's victory shifted the balance of power among European empires in North America.

Interactive Chart: Effects of the French and Indian War Project the interactive chart on the whiteboard and have students read through the table and the flags. Ask students to explain how land in North America was divided after the war.

🎬 ACTIVE CLASSROOM

Have students use the Act It Out strategy to explore the fall of Quebec. Project the image of James Wolfe on the whiteboard. Divide students into two groups representing Montcalm's and Wolfe's soldiers and have them bring to life what happened before, during, and after this image. Have students write a short script describing what the soldiers are thinking. Then have them act out their scene.

Summarize What physical geographic features of Quebec did the British exploit to capture the city? *(They took advantage of the river to approach by water. Then they climbed the steep cliff, which the French were not expecting.)*

ELL Use the ELL activity described in the ELL chart.

Further Instruction

Go through the Interactive Reading Notepad questions with the class.

Evaluate Arguments The author writes, "The fall of Quebec sealed the fate of New France." Do you think this is a reasonable claim? Why or why not? *(Yes; Quebec was important to the defense of New France and supplied forts up the St. Lawrence River. Without control over this area, France could not hope to win.)*

Make Generalizations Make a generalization about the power shift in North America following the French and Indian War. *(Britain increased its power and territory over France and Spain.)*

■ **SYNTHESIZE**

■ **DEMONSTRATE**

DIGITAL ACTIVITY
Effects of the French and Indian War

DIGITAL QUIZ
Lesson Quiz and Class Discussion Board

Have students use the Think-Pair-Share Strategy to make predictions about the effects of the French and Indian War in the digital activity. Allow students to work alone or in groups to complete the chart, and then write down or discuss their answers with the class.

Discuss Have students think about the following question. How will Britain's victory affect the colonization of North America? Have students give examples supporting their claims.

Assign the online Lesson Quiz for this lesson if you haven't already done so. Students will be offered automatic remediation or enrichment based on their score.

Pose these questions to the class on the Discussion Board:

In *The French and Indian War Begins in the Ohio Valley*, you read about the causes, effects, and major events of the French and Indian War, and how these outcomes were influenced by the geography of the region.

Compare and Contrast the physical geographic factors of North America that helped and hindered British soldiers during the war. *(Hindered—soldiers were unfamiliar with fighting in North American forests. They dressed and walked through the woods in ways that made them easy targets. Helped— they used the St. Lawrence River and the cliff on which Quebec is built to their advantage when launching a surprise attack against the city.)*

Identify Central Ideas How did the fighting between Britain and France over the North American frontier impact Native Americans tribes in the region? *(Tribes like the Iroquois were forced to choose sides between the British and the French and became involved in the fighting. The expansion of European colonial powers in the frontier region also threatened Native American lands.)*

Topic Inquiry
Have students continue their investigations for the Topic Inquiry.

Tensions with Britain

Supporting English Language Learners

Use with Digital Text 4, **Causes of the American Revolution: The Stamp Act.**

Learning
Read aloud the section titled, *Resistance to the Stamp Act* or invite volunteers to do so. Point out the section's two quotations (at the end of the first and third paragraphs) to help students distinguish between formal and informal English.

Beginning Read aloud the two quotations, using appropriate gestures and tone of voice. Identify each as formal or informal. Then underline the formal and informal language in each.

Intermediate Read aloud the two quotations, using appropriate gestures and tone of voice. Ask students to identify each as formal or informal, as well as to identify specific words that support their response.

Advanced Ask students to identify each of the two quotations as formal or informal. Then have them read the quotations aloud, using appropriate gestures and tone of voice. Ask how paying attention to gestures and tone can help to identify formal and informal language.

Advanced High Ask students to identify each quotation as formal or informal. Have them read aloud the quotations and then add to them, choosing language that is similar in tone. Ask how they knew whether the language they chose was formal or informal.

Use with Digital Text 7, **The Boston Massacre.**

Speaking
Display the chart titled, *The Rising Tide of Conflict*. Read aloud each of the events, or invite volunteers to do so. Encourage students to respond orally to build and reinforce language attainment.

Beginning Point out how each act caused a result to happen. Display these sentences: The _____ are British laws. The _____ are what happens because of them. Have students complete the sentences and say them aloud.

Intermediate Explain that to proclaim something is to announce it in an official and public way. Ask: What was proclaimed in the Proclamation of 1763? How would you define the word proclamation? Have students give their answers aloud.

Advanced Explain that a tide is the rise or fall of the sea. Ask: What does the title of the chart mean? How else could the same idea be expressed? Have students give their answers aloud.

Advanced High Ask: What did it mean when colonists staged violent protests against the Stamp Act? How is staging a violent protest like and unlike staging a play? Have students give their answers aloud.

◨ Differentiate Instruction

Use the Differentiated Instruction notes throughout the lesson plan to support the varied skill sets, levels of readiness, and interests in the mixed-ability classroom.

Challenge These notes include suggestions for expanding the activity for advanced students.

On-Level These notes include suggestions for modifying the activity to address different interests or learning styles.

Extra Support These notes include ideas for providing more scaffolding or reading spuport.

Special Needs These notes provide ideas for adapting instruction to support the needs of various special needs students.

■ NOTES

PEARSON ....
realize™
www.PearsonRealize.com

Go online to access additional resources including:
Primary Sources • Biographies • Supreme Court cases •
21st Century Skill Tutorials • Maps • Graphic Organizers.

Objectives

Objective 1: Describe conflicts in the west after the French and Indian War.

Objective 2: Explain how Britain attempted to ease tensions with the Proclamation of 1763.

Objective 3: Explain why colonists opposed new British taxes such as the Stamp Act.

Objective 4: Describe new colonial leaders who emerged as conflicts with Britain escalated.

Objective 5: Summarize the significance of the Boston Massacre.

LESSON 2 ORGANIZER		PACING: APPROX. 1 PERIOD, .5 BLOCKS			
				RESOURCES	
		OBJECTIVES	PACING	Online	Print
Connect					
DIGITAL START UP ACTIVITY **The Rights of the Colonists**			5 min.	●	
Investigate					
DIGITAL TEXT 1 **Conflict Over Land**		Objective 1	10 min.	●	●
DIGITAL TEXT 2 **Causes of the American Revolution— The Proclamation of 1763**		Objective 2	10 min.	●	●
DIGITAL TEXT 3 **Causes of the American Revolution—Mercantilism and Taxation**			10 min.	●	●
DIGITAL TEXT 4 **Causes of the American Revolution—The Stamp Act**		Objective 3	10 min.	●	●
DIGITAL TEXT 5 **Causes of the American Revolution— Townshend Acts**			10 min.	●	●
INTERACTIVE CHART **Crisis on the Frontier**			10 min.	●	
DIGITAL TEXT 6 **Significant Individuals Provide Colonial Leadership**		Objective 4	10 min.	●	●
INTERACTIVE GALLERY **Important People of the American Revolution**			10 min.	●	
DIGITAL TEXT 7 **The Boston Massacre**		Objective 5	10 min.	●	●
Synthesize					
DIGITAL ACTIVITY **Causes of the American Revolution**			5 min.	●	
Demonstrate					
DIGITAL QUIZ **Lesson Quiz and Class Discussion Board**			10 min.	●	

Tensions with Britain

DIGITAL START UP ACTIVITY
The Rights of the Colonists

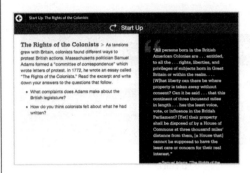

Discuss What complaints does Adams make about the British legislature? *(Property is taken without consent; colonists have no say in British Parliament; Parliament is too removed from the colonies to care about them.)* How do you think colonists felt about what he had written? *(Many colonists probably agreed and felt more strongly anti-British; some colonists probably felt Adams was being disloyal.)*

Tell students that in this lesson they will analyze causes of the American Revolution and learn about the roles significant individuals played during this time.

Aa Vocabulary Development: Use the Interactive Reading Notepad to preview the Key Terms and Academic Vocabulary in this lesson with students.

⇅ FLIP IT!
Assign the Flipped Video for this lesson.

■ STUDENT EDITION PRINT
PAGES: 130–140

■ INVESTIGATE

DIGITAL TEXT 1
Conflict Over Land

Objective 1: Describe conflicts in the West after the French and Indian War.

Quick Instruction
Project the image of Chief Pontiac. After the French and Indian War, British settlers began heading west to the Ohio Valley. This led to clashes with Native American tribes along the frontier. Ask students to locate the Ohio Valley and explain why conflict erupted in this area.

Hypothesize Why do you think British settlers wanted to move west into the Ohio Valley? *(Exploit new resources; claim land that used to belong to the French)*

Compare and Contrast how French and British settlers interacted with Native Americans in the Ohio Valley. *(French traders treated Native Americans as friends. They held feasts and exchanged gifts. British settlers clashed with Native Americans. They raised prices and cleared land.)*

Further Instruction
Go through the Interactive Reading Notepad questions and discuss the answers with the class. Remind students that the British victory in the French and Indian War meant Britain claimed lands along the frontier that used to belong to the French. Conflicts with Native Americans led to the Proclamation of 1763, which was one of the causes of the American Revolution.

Draw Conclusions How did the Treaty of Paris impact Native Americans on the frontier? *(Native Americans could not turn to the French for help against the encroaching British, because the French no longer had power in the region.)*

Make Predictions Make a prediction about how Pontiac's War and other conflicts between colonists and Native Americans will contribute to the Revolutionary War. *(Colonists may not like British policies regarding Native American tribes and land claims. They may want to make their own decisions about settlements.)*

DIGITAL TEXT 2

Causes of the American Revolution—The Proclamation of 1763

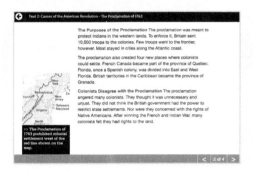

DIGITAL TEXT 3

Causes of the American Revolution— Mercantilism and Taxation

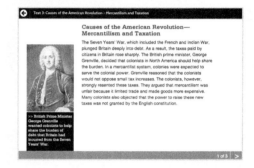

Objective 2: Explain how Britain attempted to ease tensions with the Proclamation of 1763.

Quick Instruction

Project the map showing migration west of the Proclamation Line. Explain that colonists were not allowed to settle west of this line.

Sequence Events Explain why Pontiac's War led to the Proclamation of 1763. *(British officials were worried about the safety of settlers and the protection of Native Americans. Pontiac's War led the government to decide that settlers should not provoke conflicts by moving too far west.)*

Analyze Information How did the Proclamation of 1763 contribute to the outbreak of the American Revolution? *(It made colonists angry with the British government for restricting their settlements and keeping land from them. It also made them not want to pay for British policies they had not approved.)*

D Differentiate: Extra Support Explain that a proclamation is an official announcement. The Proclamation of 1763 was an official announcement that created a new rule for settlers.

Further Instruction

Go through the Interactive Reading Notepad questions and discuss the answers with the class. Be sure students analyze how the Proclamation of 1763 was one of the causes of the American Revolution.

Summarize What did the Proclamation of 1763 declare? *(It made an imaginary line along the Appalachian Mountains beyond which colonists could not settle; it created four new spaces for colonists to settle in what used to be Spanish and French territories. These four spaces included Quebec, East Florida, West Florida, and Granada.)*

Determine Point of View What did many colonists think of the Proclamation of 1763, and why? *(They were angered by the Proclamation. They didn't think the British government had the power to tell them where to settle. They thought they had a right to the land and weren't concerned about Native American's rights. They also did not want to pay for the British troops brought over to enforce the rule.)*

Objective 3: Explain why colonists opposed new British taxes such as the Stamp Act.

Quick Instruction

Interactive Chart: Crisis on the Frontier Project the interactive chart and have students read through the tiles. Explain that there were other causes of the American Revolution in addition to the Proclamation of 1763. Economic policies following the French and Indian War, mercantilism, the Stamp Act, and the lack of representation in Parliament all led to unrest.

Generate Explanations Explain how British economic policies following the French and Indian War were among the causes of the American Revolution. *(Britain raised taxes to pay for its troops and debts from the French and Indian War. Colonists resented paying new taxes without their consent or representation in Parliament.)*

ACTIVE CLASSROOM

List the following policies on the board: Proclamation of 1763, Sugar Act, Stamp Act, Townshend Acts. Have students use the Rank It strategy to rank the policies from most to least influential in causing the American Revolution, providing justifications for their decisions. Poll the class to see if students agree.

ELL Use the ELL activity described in the ELL chart.

Tensions with Britain

DIGITAL TEXT 4

Causes of the American Revolution—The Stamp Act

DIGITAL TEXT 5

Causes of the American Revolution—Townshend Acts

INTERACTIVE CHART

Crisis on the Frontier

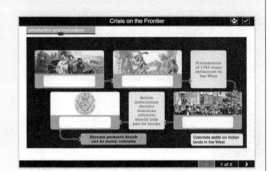

Further Instruction

Go through the Interactive Reading Notepad questions with the class. Assign the additional resource Economics Basics: Core Concepts.

Support Ideas with Evidence What evidence suggests that a free-enterprise system of economics will develop in the new nation? Why did colonists want minimal government intrusion? *(The colonists wanted a free-enterprise system to contribute to economic growth. They hoped to limit government intrusion so that the market, not the government, would determine costs. They looked to a different economic model because they thought British taxes were overly restrictive and limited growth.)*

Cite Evidence that the Stamp Act was an important cause of the American Revolution. *(It united colonists, prompted colonists to send petitions to King George III and Parliament, and led colonists to boycott British goods.)*

Draw Conclusions Why was the lack of representation in Parliament one of the causes of the American Revolution? *(Colonists thought only they or their representatives should be able to impose taxes. They fought to not pay taxes with which they disagreed.)*

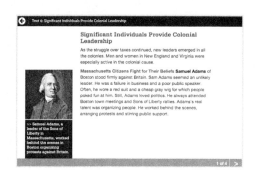

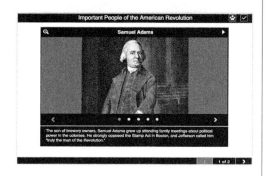

DIGITAL TEXT 6

Significant Individuals Provide Colonial Leadership

INTERACTIVE GALLERY

Important People of the American Revolution

DIGITAL TEXT 7

The Boston Massacre

Objective 4: Describe new colonial leaders who emerged as conflicts with Britain escalated.

Quick Instruction

Interactive Gallery: Important People of the American Revolution Project the interactive gallery and have students look at the images individually and as a whole. Explain that new leaders emerged to fight for colonists' rights.

Draw Conclusions Ask students how they think significant individuals like those discussed in the gallery shaped colonists' attitudes toward Britain. *(The individuals probably led colonists to feel more strongly against the British and to take action against the crown.)*

📷 ACTIVE CLASSROOM

Have students use the Conversations with History Strategy and suppose they are having a conversation with one of the people in the interactive gallery. Have students select one of the significant individuals and write down a question they would like to ask, what that person would say to them, and what they would say in response.

Further Instruction

Go through the Interactive Reading Notepad questions with the class, including the graphic organizer that sums up the contributions of each colonial leader and how he or she helped the American cause. Be sure students

understand the roles played by Mercy Otis Warren, Abigail Adams, Samuel Adams, John Adams, and Patrick Henry in the early stages of the American Revolution. To extend the lesson, assign the primary source readings *Remember the Ladies* (Abigail Adams) and *Give Me Liberty or Give Me Death* (Patrick Henry).

Compare the roles played by Mercy Otis Warren and Abigail Adams leading up to the American Revolution. *(Both used writing to rally colonists against the British and called for women's rights.)*

Summarize How did Samuel Adams contribute to the revolutionary cause? *(He attended meetings and rallies, organized colonists, arranged protests, and generated support for the colonists' cause.)*

Evaluate Arguments What did Patrick Henry mean when he cried, "If this be treason, make the most of it"? What do you think listeners thought of this speech? *(If the colonists were going to be treasonous, they should commit to it and turn against Britain. His comments probably shocked some but encouraged others to fight.)*

Objective 5: Summarize the significance of the Boston Massacre.

Quick Instruction

Project the engraving of the Boston Massacre by Paul Revere on the whiteboard. Explain that the Boston Massacre was a violent attack that took place when British soldiers fired into a crowd outside the Boston customs house.

Analyze Images How does Revere's engraving present the events of the massacre? How might this have influenced popular opinion? *(The engraving shows well-organized British soldiers firing into an unarmed crowd. This probably made colonists feel the British were violent, tyrannical, and treating them unfairly.)*

Identify Cause and Effect Name one cause and one effect of the Boston Massacre. *(Cause—colonists were angered by the presence of British soldiers; Effect— anti-British feeling spread among the colonies)*

ELL Use the ELL activity described in the ELL chart.

Further Instruction

Go through the Interactive Reading Notepad questions and discuss the answers with the class. Ask students why the Boston Massacre was an important event in the steps leading up to the American Revolution.

Draw Conclusions Why do you think Crispus Attucks's death played such a significant role in the American Revolution? *(Attucks was one of the first to die in the Boston Massacre. This probably made him an important symbol of the American cause.)*

Tensions with Britain

SYNTHESIZE

DEMONSTRATE

DIGITAL ACTIVITY

Causes of the American Revolution

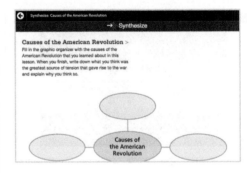

DIGITAL QUIZ

Lesson Quiz and Class Discussion Board

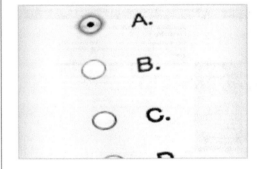

Identify Patterns How did the actions of King George III shape relations between Britain and the colonies following the massacre? *(Many acts that angered the colonists were ended, including the Townshend Acts and the Quartering Act, but the king still kept the tax on tea. Although relations improved, the change was not permanent.)*

Have students fill in the graphic organizer with the causes of the American Revolution. Then have students write down or discuss with a partner the greatest sources of tension, explaining their reasoning.

Have students think about the following question: What were the colonists' political, economic, and social grievances against Britain, and why did these grievances ultimately lead to war? Have students give examples from the text.

Assign the online Lesson Quiz for this lesson if you haven't already done so. Students will be offered automatic remediation or enrichment based on their score.

Pose these questions to the class on the Discussion Board:

In *Tensions with Britain*, you read about the multiple causes leading to conflicts between the colonists and Britain as well as the significant individuals who led the colonists' cause.

Hypothesize Explain how colonists' anger over the lack of representation may have been expressed in the Declaration of Independence. *(The Declaration of Independence expressed the colonists' desire for a representative government that would defend their rights.)*

Compare and Contrast mercantilism and a free-enterprise system. Which economic policy did colonists favor, and why? *(Mercantilism says that colonies exist to generate wealth for the colonial power. A free-enterprise system is based on minimal government intrusion and lets the market, not the government, set prices. Colonists felt that Britain's mercantilist policies were unfair because they limited trade, increased prices, and led to excessive taxes. Colonists favored a free-enterprise system because it led to economic growth.)*

Topic Inquiry

Have students continue their investigations for the Topic Inquiry.

Taking Up Arms

Supporting English Language Learners

Use with Digital Text 3, **The Battles of Lexington and Concord.**

Reading
Read aloud the first paragraph of the section's introduction, or invite volunteers to do so. Prompt students to focus on the specific sounds they hear as the introduction is read aloud. Then direct students' attention to specific words and focus on both the relationship between the sounds and corresponding letters in given words.

Beginning Display the word *Massachusetts*. Sound out the syllables, highlighting the corresponding letters as you do so. Then have students sound out the syllables as you highlight the corresponding letters.

Intermediate Display the word *Massachusetts*. As you sound out the word's syllables, have students identify the corresponding groups of letters.

Advanced Display the word *massacre*. As you sound out the word's syllables, have students identify the corresponding groups of letters. Discuss the relationship between the letters *cre* and the sound they represent. Challenge pairs of students to find other words ending with *-cre*.

Advanced High Display the words *minutemen* and *minute*. As you sound out the word's syllables, have students identify the corresponding groups of letters. Ask: In what other way can minute be pronounced? How do you know which way to pronounce it?

Use with Digital Text 4, **The Fighting Continues.**

Learning
Read aloud the section titled, *Vermont Rebels Gain a Route to Canada*, or invite volunteers to do so. Point out the quotation, "Come out, you old rat!" Identify the speaker and his intended audience in order for students to demonstrate increasing knowledge of when to use formal or informal English.

Beginning Explain the meaning of the words *old rat*. Ask: Is this informal or formal language? Help students complete this sentence with a word or phrase: Allen called the commander "old rat" because _____.

Intermediate Ask students to explain the meaning of the quotation and identify it as formal or informal English. Then have them state why Allen would have used such language to call the British commander.

Advanced Have students explain the meaning of the quotation and identify it as formal or informal English. Ask: How do you think the British commander's soldiers addressed him? His wife? His children? Why?

Advanced High Have students identify the quotation as formal or informal English. Then ask them to list other people who might have addressed the British commander and to rank them according to how formally they might have spoken with him. Have pairs of students compare their lists.

▣ Differentiate Instruction

Use the Differentiated Instruction notes throughout the lesson plan to support the varied skill sets, levels of readiness, and interests in the mixed-ability classroom.

Challenge These notes include suggestions for expanding the activity for advanced students.

On-Level These notes include suggestions for modifying the activity to address different interests or learning styles.

Extra Support These notes include ideas for providing more scaffolding or reading spuport.

Special Needs These notes provide ideas for adapting instruction to support the needs of various special needs students.

■ NOTES

Taking Up Arms

Objectives

Objective 1: Explain how a dispute over tea led to further tension between the colonists and Great Britain.

Objective 2: Describe ways that the British Parliament punished the colonists for the Boston Tea Party.

Objective 3: Explain how fighting broke out in Massachusetts, including battles in Lexington and Concord and Bunker Hill.

Objective 4: Explain actions the First and Second Continental Congress enacted to address the crisis with Britain.

Objective 5: Describe the advantages and disadvantages of Britain and the colonists as the war began.

LESSON 3 ORGANIZER	PACING: APPROX. 1 PERIOD, .5 BLOCKS				
				RESOURCES	
		OBJECTIVES	PACING	Online	Print
Connect					
DIGITAL START UP ACTIVITY **Civil Disobedience in the Colonies**			5 min.	●	
Investigate					
DIGITAL TEXT 1 **The Boston Tea Party**		Objective 1	10 min.	●	●
DIGITAL TEXT 2 **King George III Strikes Back at Boston**		Objective 2	10 min.	●	●
DIGITAL TEXT 3 **The Battles of Lexington and Concord**		Objective 3	10 min.	●	●
DIGITAL TEXT 4 **The Fighting Continues**		Objective 4	10 min.	●	●
DIGITAL TEXT 5 **Opposing Sides at War**			10 min.	●	●
DIGITAL TEXT 6 **The War Comes to Boston**		Objective 5	10 min.	●	●
INTERACTIVE CHART **Advantages and Disadvantages of the British and Colonists**			10 min.	●	
Synthesize					
DIGITAL ACTIVITY **From Protests to War**			5 min.	●	
Demonstrate					
DIGITAL QUIZ **Lesson Quiz and Class Discussion Board**			10 min.	●	

■ CONNECT

DIGITAL START UP ACTIVITY
Civil Disobedience in the Colonies

Project the Start Up Activity Ask students to read the definition of civil disobedience as they enter and get settled. Then have them write down their answers and share them with another student, either in class or through a chat or blog space.

Discuss Were the colonists right to practice acts of civil disobedience against the British? Why or why not? *(Answers will vary but should explain why students do or do not think the colonists were right.)*

Tell students that in this lesson they will learn about the causes of the American Revolution, the outbreak of war at the Battles of Lexington and Concord, and the roles of significant individuals who advanced the American cause.

Aa Vocabulary Development: Use the Interactive Reading Notepad to preview the Key Terms and Academic Vocabulary in this lesson with students.

⇅ FLIP IT!
Assign the Flipped Video for this lesson.

■ STUDENT EDITION PRINT PAGES: 141–152

■ INVESTIGATE

DIGITAL TEXT 1
The Boston Tea Party

Objective 1: Explain how a dispute over tea led to further tension between the colonists and Great Britain.

Quick Instruction
Colonists opposed taxes on tea because they did not think Britain had the right to tax them. They launched a protest in Boston Harbor known as the Boston Tea Party.

Interactive Illustration: Boston Tea Party Project the interactive illustration and click through the images. Have students explain in their own words the sequence of events leading up to the Boston Tea Party, identifying the location of each incident.

Express Problems Clearly What were the reasons for the civil disobedience of the Boston Tea Party? What might be the impact of the Tea Party? *(Colonists objected to British taxes on tea and the Tea Act. They dumped tea into the harbor when British ships carrying the tea would not leave the harbor without unloading it. The colonists may end up being punished for their actions.)*

📷 ACTIVE CLASSROOM
Have students use the Graffiti Concepts Strategy to create a visual image and/or phrase that represents the concept of civil disobedience. Ask students to post their "graffiti" on the board or on chart paper. Have students look at the visuals and discuss similarities and differences in the responses as a group.

D Differentiate: Extra Support Review the definition of civil disobedience: the nonviolent refusal to obey laws. Explain that boycotting British tea and dumping it into the harbor were acts of civil disobedience. Ask students to come up with other examples of civil disobedience.

Further Instruction
Go through the Interactive Reading Notepad questions and discuss the answers with the class. Review the reasons for and impact of the Boston Tea Party.

Support Ideas with Examples What examples show that Samuel Adams played a significant role in instigating the Boston Tea Party? *(Adams organized the gathering at the Old South Meeting House. He wanted the governor to allow ships in the harbor to leave without unloading their tea. When the governor refused, Adams declared the meeting could do no more. This seemed to be a signal for colonists to go to the harbor, suggesting he had a role in planning what was going to happen.)*

Identify Central Issues How did British economic policies following the French and Indian War, such as mercantilism, contribute to the Boston Tea Party? *(Due to mercantilist policies that generated wealth for Britain, colonists paid taxes on tea and were cut out of the tea trade. Colonists resisted these policies, and this resistance led to the Boston Tea Party.)*

Taking Up Arms

DIGITAL TEXT 2

King George III Strikes Back at Boston

DIGITAL TEXT 3

The Battles of Lexington and Concord

Objective 2: Describe ways that the British Parliament punished the colonists for the Boston Tea Party.

Quick Instruction

Project the image of the British warships in Boston Harbor. Explain that King George III of England was outraged by the Boston Tea Party and acted with Parliament to punish the colonists.

Summarize What were the Intolerable Acts, and why were they a cause of the American Revolution? *(The Intolerable Acts closed Boston's port, limited Massachusetts town meetings, allowed officials to be tried outside the state, and imposed a new Quartering Act. These laws angered the colonists, furthering their desire for independence.)*

Further Instruction

Go through the Interactive Reading Notepad questions with the class, including the graphic organizer on the Intolerable Acts. As students read, have them take notes about each act and why the colonists opposed it. Be sure students understand how the Intolerable Acts contributed to the Revolution.

Cite Evidence that Thomas Jefferson strongly opposed the Intolerable Acts. (See the heading *The Intolerable Acts Draw Other Colonies into the Struggle* for assistance with this answer.) *(Thomas Jefferson suggested that a day be set aside to mark the shame of the Intolerable Acts.)*

Draw Conclusions How did the physical geography of Boston lead the city to suffer as a result of the Intolerable Acts? *(Boston was a port city. When Parliament shut down the port, the city's economy declined.)*

Generate Explanations Explain why the extension of Quebec strained relations between the colonists and Parliament. *(Parliament gave land that some American colonists had already claimed to French Canada. These colonists did not want Parliament making decisions about their settlements.)*

Objective 3: Explain how fighting broke out in Massachusetts, including the Battles of Lexington and Concord and Bunker Hill.

Quick Instruction

Analyze Maps Project the map showing the initial battles of the American Revolution. Have students locate Lexington and Concord and explain their importance. *(They were where the first battles of the American Revolution occurred.)*

Sequence Events leading up to the Battles of Lexington and Concord. *(Minutemen collected weapons; British troops marched to Concord to get the weapons; colonists signaled the arrival of the British; the minutemen confronted the British in Lexington; a shot was fired; the British advanced to Concord where colonial troops met them; more fighting broke out.)*

ELL Use the ELL activity described in the ELL chart.

Further Instruction

Go through the Interactive Reading Notepad questions with the class. Discuss the issues surrounding the important early events of the American Revolution, including the Battles of Lexington and Concord. Be sure students understand why the war began.

DIGITAL TEXT 4

The Fighting Continues

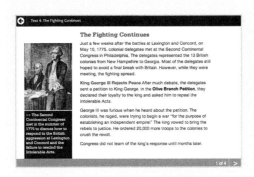

Text 4. The Fighting Continues

The Fighting Continues

Just a few weeks after the battles at Lexington and Concord, on May 10, 1775, colonial delegates met at the Second Continental Congress in Philadelphia. The delegates represented the 13 British colonies from New Hampshire to Georgia. Most of the delegates still hoped to avoid a final break with Britain. However, while they were meeting, the fighting spread.

King George III Rejects Peace After much debate, the delegates sent a petition to King George. In the **Olive Branch Petition**, they declared their loyalty to the king and asked him to repeal the Intolerable Acts.

George III was furious when he heard about the petition. The colonists, he raged, were trying to begin a war "for the purpose of establishing an independent empire!" The king vowed to bring the rebels to justice. He ordered 20,000 more troops to the colonies to crush the revolt.

Congress did not learn of the king's response until months later.

>> The Second Continental Congress met in the summer of 1775 to discuss how to respond to the British aggression at Lexington and Concord and the failure to rescind the Intolerable Acts.

1 of 4 >

Infer What can you infer about the minutemen based on the fighting at Lexington and Concord? *(They were organized, because they were able to signal each other using lamps hung from the Old North Church. That they had been collecting weapons and were prepared to fight suggests they expected a battle to break out.)*

Draw Conclusions How did the physical geography of New England affect the Battles of Lexington and Concord? Why did the colonists have an advantage in this location? *(Colonists could signal each other across the river in Boston and prepare to meet the British in Lexington. At Concord, colonists hid in the woods to fire at the British and then took cover behind the trees.)*

Objective 4: Explain actions the First and Second Continental Congress enacted to address the crisis with Britain.

Quick Instruction
Project the image of George Washington. Explain that Washington played an important role by leading the Continental Army. Washington was appointed by the Second Continental Congress, which formed to address the growing crisis.

Draw Conclusions What do you think the appointment of Washington as commander of the Continental Army signaled to Britain? *(The colonists were putting together an army and were serious about seeking independence.)*

ELL Use the ELL activity described in the ELL chart.

Further Instruction
Go through the Interactive Reading Notepad questions with the class. Be sure students understand the significant roles King George III and George Washington played in the early stages of the war.

Determine Point of View What did King George III think about the colonists' desire for independence? How do you know? *(He thought the rebellion was unacceptable. He was angry that the colonists were trying to establish independence. This is evident by his rejection of the Olive Branch Petition and his decision to send troops to end the revolt.)*

Summarize Why was Vermont so important in the early battles of the war? *(The seizure of Fort Ticonderoga in Vermont gave the Green Mountain Boys a supply of cannons and gunpowder as well as strategic access to routes into Canada.)*

Evaluate Arguments Do you agree with John Adams and Samuel Adams that war could not be avoided? Explain your reasoning. *(Yes; since the king rejected the Olive Branch Petition and sent more troops to the colonies, there was nothing the colonists could do to maintain the peace.)*

Taking Up Arms

DIGITAL TEXT 5

Opposing Sides at War

INTERACTIVE CHART

Advantages and Disadvantages of the British and Colonists

DIGITAL TEXT 6

The War Comes to Boston

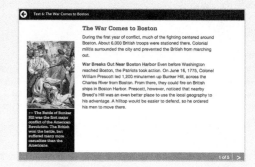

Objective 5: Describe the advantages and disadvantages of Britain and the colonists as the war began.

Quick Instruction

Not all colonists wanted independence. Patriots favored war. Loyalists supported Britain. Other colonists did not take sides. There were more Patriots in the New England colonies, which was where most of the fighting centered in the first year of the war.

Interactive Chart: Advantages and Disadvantages of the British and Colonists Project the interactive chart and have students read through the possible answers. Ask students which side they think had the greatest advantages going into the war, using the chart to support their reasoning.

Identify Cause and Effect How did the physical geography of Boston impact the Battle of Bunker Hill? *(Patriots used the high elevation of the hill to fire down on British ships in the harbor. The British traveled by river and then pushed up the hills. Although the British won, this vulnerable approach left many of their soldiers wounded or dead.)*

Identify Central Issues What factors caused Patriots to fight for independence? *(They opposed British policies; they thought British rule was harsh and unjust; they wanted to defend their homes and properties.)*

🖳 ACTIVE CLASSROOM

Divide students into groups and have them use the PMI Strategy to consider the importance of the Battle of Bunker Hill. Have groups create a three-column organizer with the headings Plus/Minus/ Interesting. Have groups use the organizer to record their responses to the questions: What were the positive outcomes of the Battle of Bunker Hill for the Patriots? What were the negative outcomes? What is interesting about this battle?

Further Instruction

Go through the Interactive Reading Notepad questions and discuss the answers with the class.

Draw Conclusions How did Washington serve to unite the colonists following the Battle of Bunker Hill? *(He got soldiers from different colonies to work together and form a trained army.)*

Make a Prediction about how colonists will respond to King George III's blockade. *(They will probably be even more angered. They may have to find ways around the blockade. This could help them come together and form a more organized army.)*

SYNTHESIZE

DIGITAL ACTIVITY
From Protests to War

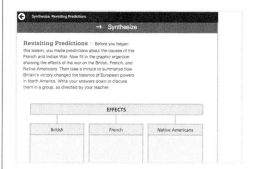

Have students create a timeline of dates, people, and events from the lesson, using the sample timeline to get started. Have students choose one event on their timeline and write down its significance. Discuss with the class what events students chose.

Discuss Have students think about the following question: What were the major causes of the American Revolution? Have students consider the political, economic, and social reasons the colonists went to war.

DEMONSTRATE

DIGITAL QUIZ
Lesson Quiz and Class Discussion Board

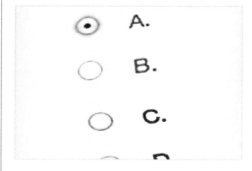

Assign the online Lesson Quiz for this lesson if you haven't already done so. Students will be offered automatic remediation or enrichment based on their score.

Pose these questions to the class on the Discussion Board:

In *Taking Up Arms*, you read about the causes of the American Revolution, the location and importance of major early battles, and the roles of significant individuals as fighting broke out.

Identify Patterns Why do you think King George III and Parliament passed increasingly strict measures against the colonists? Do you think this approach was successful, from the point of view of the British? *(They wanted the colonists to serve Britain and hoped stronger punishments would end the revolt; this approach was not successful because it led many colonists to favor independence.)*

Support a Point of View with Evidence The Declaration of Independence details why the colonists chose to "dissolve the political bands" that tied them to Britain. Name one British political or economic policy and explain why it caused the colonists to make this declaration. *(The Quartering Act—colonists resented having troops in the colonies during peacetime, did not want the troops enforcing British taxes, and felt that hosting the troops was an imposition and another tax.)*

Topic Inquiry
Have students continue their investigations for the Topic Inquiry.

Declaring Independence

Supporting English Language Learners

Use with Digital Text 2, **Choosing Independence.**

Learning
Read aloud the first paragraph of the section titled, *Drafting the Declaration of Independence*. Explain the terms *literal* and *figurative* in order to help students add the ability to analyze sayings and expressions in context to their repertoire of learning strategies.

Beginning Have students act out the verb *face* and complete this sentence: I face the _____. Then display the paragraph's first sentence. Have students face a sign with the question "What will we do?" Ask: Did the delegates really do this? Guide students to a figurative meaning for *faced*.

Intermediate Display the paragraph's first sentence and highlight the word *faced*. Ask: Are the delegates physically facing the decision? If not, what are they doing? Have students write new sentences that replace the word *faced* with a synonymous word or phrase.

Advanced Display the paragraph, and highlight the phrase *no turning back*. Ask students to explain the phrase and determine whether it is literal or figurative. Have them communicate the same idea using other language.

Advanced High Display the paragraph, and highlight the phrases *no turning back* and *fell into British hands*. Discuss the literal and figurative meanings of these expressions. Ask: Which meanings are appropriate for this paragraph? Why do you think figurative expressions were used?

Use with Digital Text 3, **The Declaration of Independence.**

Reading
Read aloud the first page of the text, or invite volunteers to do so. Review the concept of decoding, or sounding out, unknown words when reading.

Beginning Display the words *birth* and *with*. Have students underline the final consonant blend in each. Together, practice the *th* sound and then sound out the words.

Intermediate Display the words *followed* and *endowed*. Ask students to draw a line separating each verb's root from its suffix. Review the pronunciation of the suffix, and have students practice sounding out the words.

Advanced Display the words *happiness* and *government*. Ask students to draw a line separating each word's root from its suffix and to sound out the words. Have pairs of students think of other words with these same suffixes and practice pronouncing them.

Advanced High Display the words *inalienable* and *independence*. Ask students to draw lines separating each word's prefix, root, and suffix. Have them sound out the words. Then ask: What other words share these word parts? How can your prior knowledge help you pronounce them?

▷ Differentiate Instruction

Use the Differentiated Instruction notes throughout the lesson plan to support the varied skill sets, levels of readiness, and interests in the mixed-ability classroom.

Challenge These notes include suggestions for expanding the activity for advanced students.

On-Level These notes include suggestions for modifying the activity to address different interests or learning styles.

Extra Support These notes include ideas for providing more scaffolding or reading spuport.

Special Needs These notes provide ideas for adapting instruction to support the needs of various special needs students.

▮ NOTES

Objectives

Objective 1: Describe the impact of Thomas Paine's pamphlet, *Common Sense*.

Objective 2: Explain the steps Congress took to declare independence.

Objective 3: Summarize the main ideas of the Declaration of Independence.

LESSON 4 ORGANIZER		PACING: APPROX. 1 PERIOD, .5 BLOCKS			
				RESOURCES	
		OBJECTIVES	**PACING**	**Online**	**Print**
Connect					
DIGITAL START UP ACTIVITY **Why He Fought**			5 min.	●	
Investigate					
DIGITAL TEXT 1 **Thomas Paine's *Common Sense***		Objective 1	10 min.	●	●
INTERACTIVE GALLERY **Thomas Paine's *Common Sense***			10 min.	●	
DIGITAL TEXT 2 **Choosing Independence**		Objective 2	10 min.	●	●
DIGITAL TEXT 3 **The Declaration of Independence**		Objective 3	10 min.	●	●
INTERACTIVE GALLERY **Interactive Declaration of Independence**			10 min.	●	
Synthesize					
DIGITAL ACTIVITY **Reasons for Going to War**			5 min.	●	
Demonstrate					
DIGITAL QUIZ **Lesson Quiz and Class Discussion Board**			10 min.	●	

Declaring Independence

◼ CONNECT

DIGITAL START UP ACTIVITY
Why He Fought

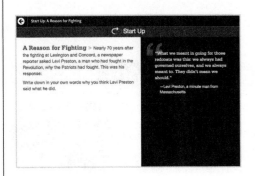

Project the Start Up Activity Ask students to read the quote as they enter and get settled. Have them discuss with partners what Preston said and then write down in their own words why they think he said it.

Discuss Write down in your own words why you think Levi Preston said what he did. *(Answers should address Preston's desire for self-government.)*

Tell students that in this lesson they will be learning about the roles significant individuals played during the American Revolution, the contributions of the Founding Fathers, and the drafting and adoption of the Declaration of Independence.

Aa Vocabulary Development: Use the Interactive Reading Notepad to preview the Key Terms and Academic Vocabulary in this lesson with students.

↻ FLIP IT!
Assign the Flipped Video for this lesson.

◼ STUDENT EDITION PRINT
PAGES: 153–157

◼ INVESTIGATE

DIGITAL TEXT 1
Thomas Paine's Common Sense

Objective 1: Describe the impact of Thomas Paine's pamphlet *Common Sense*.

Quick Instruction
Born in England, Thomas Paine moved to the colonies in 1774. He played a significant role in inspiring the American Revolution. His influential pamphlet *Common Sense* encouraged the colonists to declare independence.

Interactive Gallery: Thomas Paine's Common Sense Project the interactive gallery and click through the images. Ask students to explain Paine's vision of government. Discuss why it seemed radical at the time.

Paraphrase Have students read the quote from *Common Sense* in the lesson and restate it in their own words. *(The king does little, and most of what he does do makes the nation worse. An honest man is worth more than a king.)*

👥 ACTIVE CLASSROOM
Have students use the Make Headlines Strategy to write a headline that captures the most important aspect of Paine's *Common Sense* that should be remembered. Have students share their headlines with a partner to review.

INTERACTIVE GALLERY
Thomas Paine's Common Sense

Further Instruction
Go through the Interactive Reading Notepad questions and discuss the answers with the class. To extend the lesson, assign the primary source *Common Sense* (Thomas Paine) and the biography of Thomas Paine.

Be sure students understand the main ideas put forth in *Common Sense* and the important role Paine played in the American Revolution. Paine's assertions that the colonists did not owe loyalty to Britain and could form their own representative government prompted many to consider independence.

Draw Conclusions How did Thomas Paine influence the Declaration of Independence? *(Paine helped inspire the change from monarchy to a new, independent government. His pamphlets compelled the colonists to identify natural rights held by all people and to list their grievances against the king.)*

Determine Point of View Why did Paine think the colonists should declare independence? *(Britain wasn't looking out for the colonists' best interests; Parliament didn't have the right to make laws for the colonies; colonists didn't owe allegiance to the crown.)*

DIGITAL TEXT 2

Choosing Independence

Choosing Independence

Common Sense caused many colonial leaders to move toward declaring independence from Britain. It also deeply impressed many members of the Continental Congress. **Richard Henry Lee** of Virginia wrote to Washington, "I am now convinced . . . of the necessity for separation." In June 1776, Lee rose to his feet in Congress to introduce a resolution in favor of independence:

Resolved, That these United Colonies are and of right ought to be, free and independent States, that they are absolved from all allegiance to the British Crown, and that all political connection between them and the State of Great Britain is, and ought to be, totally dissolved.

—Richard Henry Lee, Resolution at the Second Continental Congress, June 7, 1776

>> Thomas Jefferson labored several days writing the Declaration of Independence. In this painting, Jefferson and other committee members present the Declaration to the Continental Congress.

1 of 5 >

DIGITAL TEXT 3

The Declaration of Independence

The Declaration of Independence

The Declaration of Independence consists of a **preamble**, or introduction, followed by three main parts.

Unalienable Rights The first section of the Declaration stresses the idea of **natural rights**, or rights that belong to all people from birth. In bold, ringing words, Jefferson wrote:

We hold these truths to be self-evident, that all men are created equal, that they are endowed by their Creator with certain unalienable rights, that among these are life, liberty, and the pursuit of happiness.

— The Declaration of Independence

According to the Declaration of Independence, people form governments in order to protect their natural rights and liberties.

>> The Declaration emphasized that natural rights belong to all people from birth. Colonists, such as this family, wanted to protect what they saw as their natural right to pursue life, liberty, and happiness.

1 of 5 >

Objective 2: **Explain the steps the Congress took to declare independence.**

Quick Instruction

Project the image of the Declaration of Independence. Explain the significance of 1776, the year when the declaration was adopted, and the year some consider to be the birth of the United States. Review the factors that caused the colonies to declare independence from Britain.

Identify Steps in a Process Why was the adoption of the Declaration of Independence an important event in the American Revolution and a necessary step in the process of achieving independence? *(It made the separation from Britain public and official.)*

Determine Point of View How do you think Loyalists and those who did not take sides in the war felt about the decision to declare independence? *(They probably opposed the declaration. Loyalists may have been afraid of being targeted by Patriots and concerned about the direction the country was headed. Some may have fled the colonies.)*

D **Differentiate: Challenge** Have students select one of the founders such as John Adams, Benjamin Franklin, or Thomas Jefferson and research his contributions to the Declaration of Independence. Have students use the information they gather to write a short speech from that person's perspective convincing other colonists to support independence. Students may deliver their speeches to the class.

ELL Use the ELL activity described in the ELL chart.

Further Instruction

Go through the Interactive Reading Notepad questions and discuss the answers with the class. To extend the lesson, assign the primary sources *Virginia Declaration of Rights* and *Virginia Statute for Religious Freedom* (Thomas Jefferson) as well as the biography of Benjamin Franklin.

Generate Explanations Why was it risky for the colonies to declare independence? Why do you think the Continental Congress decided to take this risk? *(Britain would consider the colonists traitors and punish them if they lost the war. The Congress felt independence was worth the potential costs.)*

Identify Steps in a Process How did Thomas Jefferson, John Adams, and Benjamin Franklin contribute to the process of separating from Britain? *(They served on the committee charged with telling the world the colonies were separating from Britain. Jefferson drafted the Declaration of Independence, which the other delegates then approved.)*

Predict Consequences Make a prediction about what the effects of signing the Declaration of Independence will be. *(Both sides will intensify the war effort. Other countries will decide whether to recognize the new nation or side with Britain.)*

Objective 3: **Summarize the main ideas of the Declaration of Independence.**

Quick Instruction

Interactive Gallery: Interactive Declaration of Independence Project the interactive gallery and click through the hotspots. Review the sections of the Declaration: the Preamble, the discussion of natural rights, the list of grievances, and the assertion of independence.

Identify Central Issues Why was it so radical for the Declaration of Independence to assert that government requires the "consent of the governed"? *(This was a new idea. It asserted the right of the people to protect their rights and freedoms by overthrowing unjust governments.)*

Generate Explanations Define unalienable rights, give an example of one, and explain what makes it unalienable. *(Unalienable rights are rights that cannot be taken away, such as life, liberty, and the pursuit of happiness. They are unalienable because these rights cannot be taken away by governments.)*

Declaring Independence

INTERACTIVE GALLERY

Interactive Declaration of Independence

▶ ACTIVE CLASSROOM

Have students use the Walking Tour Strategy to consider the issues surrounding the Declaration of Independence. Divide students into three groups and assign each group a section from the text: *Unalienable Rights*, *Colonial Grievances*, and *Independence*. Have groups post passages from their section around the room. Have students tour the room and discuss each passage, then summarize what they learned.

ELL Use the ELL activity described in the ELL chart.

Further Instruction

Go through the Interactive Reading Notepad questions with the class, including the graphic organizer on the content of the three main parts of the Declaration, and discuss the answers. Assign the primary source The U.S. Declaration of Independence.

Evaluate Arguments What grievances does the Declaration list against Britain? Do you think this list makes a compelling case for independence? Explain your reasoning. *(King George III disbanded colonial legislatures, sent troops to the colonies in peacetime, limited trade, imposed taxes without the people's consent, and did not correct these injustices after the colonists expressed their discontent. Yes; the colonists had many legitimate complaints and sufficiently showed the king's rule to be unfair.)*

Support Ideas with Examples Give one example of how the founders modeled civic virtue for the nation. Why was this an important contribution to the early United States? *(They put forward ideas about natural rights, liberty, and democracy that are foundational to the U.S. government. They modeled how leadership derived from the consent of the governed. They worked to protect rights and meet people's needs.)*

■ **SYNTHESIZE**

DIGITAL ACTIVITY
Reasons for Going to War

Have students work alone or in groups to list the grievances American leaders used to justify declaring independence. Ask students to explain which grievance they think most justified going to war. Have students write their answers or discuss them with the class.

Have students think about the following question: How did significant individuals advance the cause of freedom during the American Revolution? Ask students to consider what central ideas these individuals imparted.

■ **DEMONSTRATE**

DIGITAL QUIZ
Lesson Quiz and Class Discussion Board

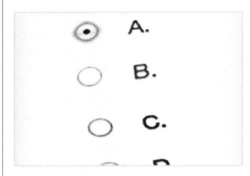

Assign the online Lesson Quiz for this lesson if you haven't already done so. Students will be offered automatic remediation or enrichment based on their score.

Pose these questions to the class on the Discussion Board:

In *Declaring Independence*, you read about the issues surrounding the Declaration of Independence, the significant individuals who shaped the document, and the main ideas it imparts.

Identify Author's Purpose What was the purpose for writing the Declaration of Independence? Did it fulfill what its authors set out to achieve? *(The authors wanted to write a formal declaration asserting independence from Britain. They listed their reasons for independence and put forward new ideas about government. This fulfilled their intention to justify their decision and tell other nations of their plan.)*

Summarize What ideas about government and rights were expressed in the Declaration of Independence? *(People have unalienable rights; government comes from the consent of the governed; people have the right to overthrow a government and create a new one if it fails to protect their rights.)*

Identify Patterns How did important historical documents like the Magna Carta, English Bill of Rights, and *Common Sense* lead the colonists to choose independence? *(These documents put forward ideas about natural rights that led colonists to seek a new government to better protect their liberties.)*

Topic Inquiry
Have students continue their investigations for the Topic Inquiry.

Winning Independence

Supporting English Language Learners

Use with Digital Text 1, **Early Challenges for the Continental Army.**

Reading

Display the chart titled, *Continental vs. British forces*, and explain its purpose in order for students to better recognize directionality of English reading both left-to-right and top-to-bottom.

Beginning Read the chart's title and the content of various cells. As you do so, have students underline the text with their fingers to emphasize the left-to-right aspect of reading English. Have them repeat after you.

Intermediate Discuss the structure of the chart. Ask: To find out whether the forces' supplies are compared, what steps would you take? Guide students to read down the first column until they arrive at *Supplies*.

Advanced Discuss the structure of the chart. Ask: How would you find out about the quality of American forces? Guide students to move down the *Continental* column, to move across the *Quality of forces* row, and to read the information in the intersecting cell.

Advanced High Ask: What is a common-sense way of reading this chart? Once students come up with a logical order (e.g., title, row and column headings, factual content), have them read the chart aloud in this way.

Use with Digital Text 9, **Explaining the American Victory.**

Listening

Read aloud the section titled, *Assistance from Allies*, enunciating each word. Encourage students to focus their attention on specific sounds in order to more easily distinguish between them.

Beginning Display the words *and, along,* and *aid*. Sound out each word, emphasizing the beginning *a* sound. Have students repeat after you. Then make an *a* sound and have students identify which of the words begins with that sound.

Intermediate Display the seven words from the section that begin with the letter *a*. As students sound out each word, reinforce its beginning *a* sound. Then guide students in sorting the words according to their beginning sound.

Advanced Ask pairs of students to locate and list seven different words from the section that begin with the letter *a*. Have them sound out the words together and then sort them according to their beginning sound.

Advanced High Ask students to locate and list words from the section that contain the letter *a* (in any position). Have them sound out the words and then sort them according to their *a* sound (words with more than one *a* may sort into more than one category).

◧ Differentiate Instruction

Use the Differentiated Instruction notes throughout the lesson plan to support the varied skill sets, levels of readiness, and interests in the mixed-ability classroom.

Challenge These notes include suggestions for expanding the activity for advanced students.

On-Level These notes include suggestions for modifying the activity to address different interests or learning styles.

Extra Support These notes include ideas for providing more scaffolding or reading spuport.

Special Needs These notes provide ideas for adapting instruction to support the needs of various special needs students.

■ NOTES

Objectives

Objective 1: Describe the war in the middle states, including how the battles at Trenton and Saratoga marked turning points.

Objective 2: Describe the roles of women and African Americans in the war.

Objective 3: Explain how the war was fought on the western frontier and at sea.

Objective 4: Describe the war in the south, including the American victory at Yorktown.

Objective 5: Summarize the reasons why the Americans won the war.

LESSON 5 ORGANIZER	PACING: APPROX. 1 PERIOD, .5 BLOCKS			
	OBJECTIVES	PACING	RESOURCES Online	Print
Connect				
DIGITAL START UP ACTIVITY **Young People in the War**		5 min.	●	
Investigate				
DIGITAL TEXT 1; DIGITAL TEXT 2; DIGITAL TEXT 3 **Early Challenges for the Continental Army;** **The Tide Turns for the Americans; Winter at Valley Forge**	Objective 1	30 min.	●	●
DIGITAL TEXT 4; DIGITAL TEXT 5 **Women Contribute to the War Effort; African Americans in the War**	Objective 2	20 min.	●	●
INTERACTIVE GALLERY **Notable People of the American Revolution**	Objective 2	10 min.	●	
DIGITAL TEXT 6 **Native Americans and the Spanish Choose Sides**	Objective 3	10 min.	●	●
DIGITAL TEXT 7; DIGITAL TEXT 8 **Fighting for Independence in the Southern Colonies and at Sea;** **A Decisive Win Brings the War to a Close**	Objectives 3, 4	20 min.	●	●
DIGITAL TEXT 9 **Explaining the American Victory**	Objective 5	10 min.	●	●
INTERACTIVE TIMELINE **Foreign Aid Plays a Role**		10 min.	●	
Synthesize				
DIGITAL ACTIVITY **Choosing Sides in Time of War**		5 min.	●	
Demonstrate				
DIGITAL QUIZ **Lesson Quiz and Class Discussion Board**		10 min.	●	

Topic ③ Lesson 5

Winning Independence

■ CONNECT

DIGITAL START UP ACTIVITY
Young People in the War

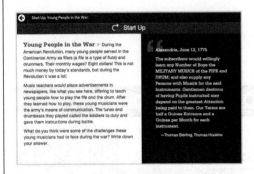

Project the Start Up Activity. Ask students to read the quote as they enter and get settled and then write down their answers to the question. Have them share their thoughts with another student, either in class or through a chat or blog space.

Discuss What do you think were some of the challenges these young musicians had to face during the war? *(Traveling long distances; missing home; hunger and fatigue; danger from battle)*

Tell students that in this lesson they will be learning about the important events of the American Revolution and the contributions of significant individuals to the war.

Aa Vocabulary Development: Use the Interactive Reading Notepad to preview the Key Terms and Academic Vocabulary in the lesson with students.

↴ FLIP IT!

Assign the Flipped Video for this lesson.

■ STUDENT EDITION PRINT PAGES: 158–172

■ INVESTIGATE

DIGITAL TEXT 1
Early Challenges for the Continental Army

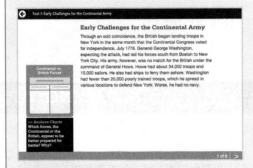

DIGITAL TEXT 2
The Tide Turns for the Americans

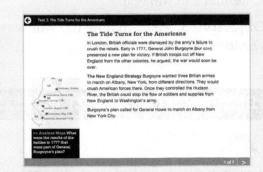

Objective 1: Describe the war in the Middle States, including how the Battles of Trenton and Saratoga marked turning points.

Quick Instruction
Project the chart comparing Continental and British forces. Explain that while the British were more prepared for battle, General George Washington led the Continental Army to surprising victories in the Middle States.

Identify Patterns Describe the effects of physical geographic factors on the Battles of Long Island, Trenton, and Saratoga. *(Battle of Long Island—the water surrounding New York was a disadvantage to the Americans. Howe used ships to ferry soldiers to New York, but Washington had no navy; Battle of Trenton—the British did not expect Washington to cross the Delaware River at night, which let the Americans make a surprise attack; Battle of Saratoga— Patriots used the woods to slow the British by cutting down trees to block the route.)*

Test Conclusions What evidence will you look for to help you conclude that the Battles of Trenton and Saratoga marked turning points in the war? *(Evidence that the Americans struggled, won these battles, and then met with more success)*

ELL Use the ELL activity described in the ELL chart.

Further Instruction
Go through the Interactive Reading Notepad questions and discuss the answers with the class. To extend the lesson, assign the biographies of Haym Salomon and the Marquis de Lafayette.

Generate Explanations What important role did Haym Salomon play in the revolution? Why do you think he is still remembered today? *(He is remembered for his loyalty and sacrifice. He helped the government get loans to pay for the war and donated money to the military. He was captured by the British but escaped and continued supporting the American cause.)*

Infer What inferences can you make about the Continental Army based on the events at Valley Forge? Give evidence supporting your claims. *(The army did not have enough money or supplies, as soldiers did not have enough warm clothes or even shoes to survive the winter. The army was well supported by many in the nation, as Patriots sent needed supplies.)*

DIGITAL TEXT 3

Winter at Valley Forge

Winter at Valley Forge

The victory at Saratoga and the promise of help from Europe boosted American morale. Washington's Continental Army began preparing for the winter of 1777–1778 by building a makeshift camp at **Valley Forge**.

Conditions at Valley Forge were difficult, but the soldiers endured. About 2,000 huts were built as shelter. Several soldiers were improperly dressed, although many did have proper uniforms. As the winter wore on, soldiers also suffered from disease, a common problem in military camps. An army surgeon from Connecticut wrote about his hardships:

>> The Marquis de Lafayette, George Washington, and their troops spent the winter at Valley Forge. They spent much of their days training for upcoming battles.

1 of 3 >

DIGITAL TEXT 4

Women Contribute to the War Effort

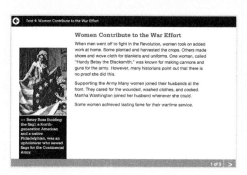

Women Contribute to the War Effort

When men went off to fight in the Revolution, women took on added work at home. Some planted and harvested the crops. Others made shoes and wove cloth for blankets and uniforms. One woman, called "Handy Betsy the Blacksmith," was known for making cannons and guns for the army. However, many historians point out that there is no proof she did this.

Supporting the Army Many women joined their husbands at the front. They cared for the wounded, washed clothes, and cooked. Martha Washington joined her husband whenever she could.

Some women achieved lasting fame for their wartime service.

>> Betsy Ross (holding the flag), a fourth-generation American and a native Philadelphian, was an upholsterer who sewed flags for the Continental Army.

1 of 3 >

Objective 2: Describe the roles of women and African Americans in the war.

Quick Instruction

Interactive Gallery: Notable People of the American Revolution Project the interactive gallery and click through the images. Explain that women and people of various racial groups made important contributions during the revolution.

Draw Conclusions Based on the experiences of Deborah Sampson, Sybil Ludington, and Mary Ludwig Hays, how do you think the American Revolution changed life for women in America? *(Women faced many dangers. Some took on roles that were previously held by men.)*

ACTIVE CLASSROOM

Have students use the Sticky Notes Strategy and take 3 minutes to jot down their ideas about how the contributions of women, African Americans, and other racial groups to the war effort shaped the nation's early identity. Have students post their stickies on a wall. Sort and discuss their observations as a group.

D Differentiate: **Extra Support** Have students write the contributions that women and African Americans made during the war on their stickies. Ask students to pick one contribution and consider an effect it had on American society.

DIGITAL TEXT 5

African Americans in the War

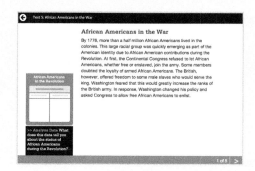

African Americans in the War

By 1776, more than a half million African Americans lived in the colonies. This large racial group was quickly emerging as part of the American identity due to African American contributions during the Revolution. At first, the Continental Congress refused to let African Americans, whether free or enslaved, join the army. Some members doubted the loyalty of armed African Americans. The British, however, offered freedom to some male slaves who would serve the king. Washington feared that this would greatly increase the ranks of the British army. In response, Washington changed his policy and asked Congress to allow free African Americans to enlist.

African Americans in the Revolution

>> Analyze Data What does this data tell you about the status of African Americans during the Revolution?

1 of 5 >

Further Instruction

Go through the Interactive Reading Notepad questions and discuss the answers with the class. To extend the lesson, assign the biographies of Wentworth Cheswell and James Armistead.

Compare and Contrast the reasons some African Americans supported the British and others supported the Patriots. *(Compare—both sides hoped the war would result in their freedom. Contrast—Britain offered freedom to some African American soldiers. Other African Americans hoped a Patriot victory would end slavery.)*

Compare the contributions of James Armistead and Wentworth Cheswell to the American Revolution. *(Armistead—Patriot spy who helped achieve an American victory at Yorktown; Cheswell—issued warnings when the British were advancing toward Lexington and Concord and enlisted to fight at Saratoga)*

Summarize What economic and social contributions did women make to the war effort? *(Economic—planting and harvesting; making supplies like shoes, blankets, and uniforms; making cannons; Social—caring for wounded soldiers; demonstrating patriotism by sewing flags; speaking out about women's rights)*

Winning Independence

Notable People of the American Revolution

Native Americans and the Spanish Choose Sides

Objective 3: Explain how the war was fought on the western frontier and at sea.

Quick Instruction

Project the map titled, *The War in the West*. Explain that many Native American tribes such as the Iroquois hoped a British victory would keep colonists from spreading west. Other tribes in the Ohio Valley sided with the Patriots.

Draw Conclusions Why were the West and Southwest important regions during the American Revolution, even though the British colonies were in the East? *(The fighting spread from the eastern colonies. Major battles took place along the frontier and in Native American territories.)*

Further Instruction

Go through the Interactive Reading Notepad questions with the class. Be sure students understand that some Native American tribes and Spanish officials contributed to American independence by providing the Patriots with soldiers and supplies. To extend the lesson, assign the biography of Bernardo de Gálvez.

Generate Explanations How did George Rogers Clark use the physical geography of the frontier to help defeat the British? *(He spread his troops through the woods to make it look like there were more Americans than there really were. Without the trees, the British commander would have known Clark's numbers were small. Instead, the commander surrendered.)*

Summarize How did Bernardo de Gálvez help the Patriots in the Southwest? *(He supplied medicine, cloth, muskets, and gunpowder to the Americans, seized British forts, and drove the British from West Florida.)*

DIGITAL TEXT 7

Fighting for Independence in the Southern Colonies and at Sea

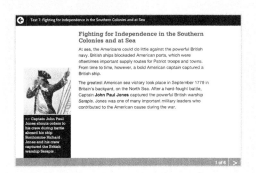

DIGITAL TEXT 8

A Decisive Win Brings the War to a Close

DIGITAL TEXT 9

Explaining the American Victory

Objectives 3: **Explain how the war was fought on the western frontier and at sea; 4: Describe the war in the South, including the American victory at Yorktown.**

Quick Instruction
Project the map of the Battle of Yorktown. Ask students how the physical geography of the bay led to an American victory at Yorktown. Explain that American victories in the South led to the British defeat and the Treaty of Paris.

Draw Conclusions How did American military leaders use their knowledge of the physical geography of the southern region to defeat the British there? *(They knew where to advance and how to seize advantageous locations, putting the British at a disadvantage. They also knew how to use different geographic features, like woods or swamps, to hide from the enemy.)*

Further Instruction
Go through the Interactive Reading Notepad questions with the class, including the graphic organizer on the tactics used by commanders to win victories against the British in the South. Be sure students understand how the physical geography of the region affected the outcome of the war.

Generate Explanations Explain the events surrounding the Battle of Yorktown. How did the Americans win? What was the effect of this victory? *(Cornwallis had been raiding American towns in an effort to capture Virginia and cut off supply routes to the South. Then Cornwallis retreated to the Yorktown peninsula, mistakenly thinking he could receive supplies from the British there. Washington's soldiers, Lafayette's soldiers, and the French naval fleet trapped Cornwallis on the peninsula, where he could not escape or get supplies. Cornwallis was under siege until he surrendered. The defeat led to the Treaty of Paris.)*

Identify Cause and Effect What was the result of the Treaty of Paris? *(Britain recognized the United States as an independent nation.)*

Objective 5: **Summarize the reasons why the Americans won the war.**

Quick Instruction
Remind students of the advantages Britain held at the outset of war, which they learned about in the *Continental vs. British forces* chart from earlier in the lesson. Explain that there are several reasons Americans won: the physical geography of the North American region, assistance from allies, the contributions of people of various racial groups, and the efforts of General Washington and other significant military leaders.

Interactive Timeline: Foreign Aid Plays a Role Project the interactive chart and click through the tiles. Discuss the ways that aid from France helped the Patriots win the war.

Draw Conclusions What effect do you think foreign aid had on the way Americans felt about the war, and why? *(It probably improved morale and inspired Americans to keep fighting because other nations believed in their cause and recognized their autonomy.)*

📹 ACTIVE CLASSROOM

Have students use the Conversation with History Strategy to suppose they are having a conversation with George Washington after the American victory. Have students write down a question they would ask about the war or its immediate aftermath, then what Washington would say to them, and what they would say in response.

Winning Independence

SYNTHESIZE

DEMONSTRATE

INTERACTIVE TIMELINE
Foreign Aid Plays a Role

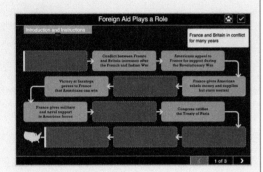

ELL Use the ELL activity described in the ELL chart.

Further Instruction
Go through the Interactive Reading Notepad questions and discuss the answers with the class. Be sure students can explain the reasons America won the war.

Hypothesize Why was George Washington such an important figure in the American Revolution? What do you think might have happened in the war had he not been in command? *(He trained troops to fight and led the Americans to victory with his skilled leadership. Without his leadership, the Patriots might not have been as successful against the British.)*

Summarize How did people of various racial and social groups contribute to American independence and the American identity? *(People of different racial and social groups fought together for the common cause of freedom and independence. This sense of unity became part of the national identity.)*

Identify Cause and Effect What physical geographic factors of the United States impacted the war? What was their effect? *(Distance across the Atlantic—made it hard for Britain to send troops and supplies; large and spread out area—made it difficult for Britain to target soldiers; rivers, woods, and hills—Americans knew the terrain and could use these features to sneak up on, hide from, or attack the enemy.)*

DIGITAL ACTIVITY
Choosing Sides in Time of War

Have students work alone or in groups to create the chart with columns labeled *Patriots* and *Loyalists*. Have students write down which position they think is most valid and why, or have students discuss their views as a class.

Discuss Have students think about the following question: What difficulties do you think Patriots and Loyalists faced working together in the new nation following the war? Have students discuss their views as a class.

DIGITAL QUIZ
Lesson Quiz and Class Discussion Board

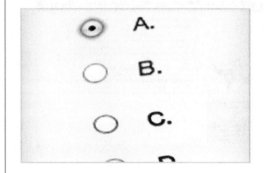

Assign the online Lesson Quiz for this lesson if you haven't already done so. Students will be offered automatic remediation or enrichment based on their score.

Pose these questions to the class on the Discussion Board:

In *Winning Independence*, you read about how both military leaders and ordinary people won the war for the Americans.

Draw Conclusions How was the Continental Army able to overcome its disadvantages in order to win the war? *(Strong leadership from figures like General Washington; the help of many Patriots, including women, African Americans, and other racial groups; help from allies such as the French, Spanish, and some Native American tribes; knowledge of local geography, which helped Americans against a larger and better trained army)*

Make Predictions What do you think is going to be the first major task the new country will have to take on? *(Developing a federal government)*

Topic Inquiry
Have students continue their investigations for the Topic Inquiry.

The Revolutionary Era (1750–1783)

■ SYNTHESIZE

DIGITAL ACTIVITY

Reflect on the Essential Question and Topic

First ask students to reconsider the Essential Question for the topic: When is war justified? Remind students of the lists they made at the beginning of the lesson. For example, justifications may include:

- to secure land or gain resources
- to stand up for ideas
- to defend against aggressors
- to help other allies
- to protect a way of life

Ask students: Do you think the colonists were justified in going to war against Britain? Ask them to give at least three reasons to support their position. Discuss their answers as a class or ask students to post their answers on the Class Discussion Board.

Next ask students to reflect on the topic as a whole and consider why the Patriots went to war. Ask students to write down the three most important principles for which the Patriots were fighting, and how these principles continue to shape our national identity today. Ask these questions if students need help getting started:

- Why were the Patriots angry with Britain?
- Why did the colonists want to form their own nation?
- How did colonists want the government and society of the United States to differ from Britain?

You may ask students to share their questions and answers on the Class Discussion Board.

Topic Inquiry

Have students complete Step 3 of the Topic Inquiry.

■ DEMONSTRATE

DIGITAL TOPIC REVIEW AND ASSESSMENT

The Revolutionary Era (1750–1783)

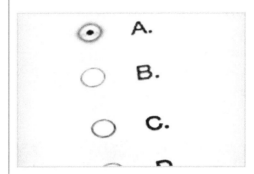

Students can prepare for the Topic Test by answering the questions in the Topic Review and Assessment online or the Assessment questions in the Print Student text. They can also prepare by reviewing their answers to the Interactive Reading Notepad questions or reviewing their notes in the Reading and Notetaking Study Guide.

DIGITAL TOPIC TEST

The Revolutionary Era (1750–1783)

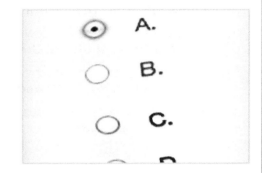

TOPIC TEST

Assign the Topic Test to assess students' understanding of topic content.

BENCHMARK TESTS

Assign these benchmark tests as you complete the relevant topics to monitor student progress toward mastering the course content and as preparation for the End-of-Course Test.

Benchmark Test 1: Topics 1–2

Benchmark Test 2: Topics 3–4

Benchmark Test 3: Topics 5–6

Benchmark Test 4: Topics 7–9

Benchmark Test 5: Topics 10–12

Benchmark Test 6: Topics 13–14

Benchmark Test 7: Topics 15–17

A Constitution for the United States (1776–Present)

TOPIC 4 ORGANIZER	PACING: APPROX. 1 PERIOD,. 5 BLOCKS
	PACING
Connect	1 period
MY STORY VIDEO **James Madison, The Federalist Papers**	10 min.
DIGITAL ESSENTIAL QUESTION ACTIVITY **How Much Power Should Government Have?**	10 min.
DIGITAL TIMELINE ACTIVITY **A Constitution for the United States**	10 min.
TOPIC INQUIRY: CIVIC DISCUSSION **Senate Representation**	20 min.
Investigate	3–7 periods
TOPIC INQUIRY: CIVIC DISCUSSION **Senate Representation**	Ongoing
LESSON 1 A Weak Confederation	30–40 min.
LESSON 2 Drafting a Constitution	30–40 min.
LESSON 3 Ideas That Influenced the Constitution	30–40 min.
LESSON 4 Federalists, Antifederalists and the Bill of Rights	30–40 min.
LESSON 5 Understanding the Constitution	30–40 min.
LESSON 6 Amending the Constitution	30–40 min.
LESSON 7 Citizens' Rights and Responsibilities	30–40 min.
Synthesize	1 period
DIGITAL ACTIVITY **Reflect on the Essential Question and Topic**	10 min.
TOPIC INQUIRY: CIVIC DISCUSSION **Senate Representation**	20 min.
Demonstrate	1–2 periods
DIGITAL TOPIC REVIEW AND ASSESSMENT **A Constitution for the United States**	10 min.
TOPIC INQUIRY: CIVIC DISCUSSION **Senate Representation**	20 min.

TOPIC INQUIRY: CIVIC DISCUSSION

Senate Representation

In this Topic Inquiry, students work in teams to examine different perspectives on this issue by analyzing several sources, arguing both sides of a Yes/No question, then developing and discussing their own point of view on the question: **Should representation in the United States Senate be based on population?**

STEP 1: CONNECT
Develop Questions and Plan the Investigation

Launch the Civic Discussion

Divide the class into groups of four students. Students can access the materials they'll need in the online course or you can distribute copies to each student. Read the main question and introduction with the students.

Have students complete Step 1 by reading the Discussion Launch and filling in Step 1 of the Information Organizer. The Discussion Launch provides YES and NO arguments on the main question. Students should extract and paraphrase the arguments from the reading in Step 1 of their Information Organizers.

Next, students share within their groups the arguments and evidence they found to support the YES and NO positions. The group needs to agree on the major YES and NO points and each student should note those points in their Information Organizer.

Resources
- Student Instructions
- Information Organizer
- Discussion Launch

STEP 2: INVESTIGATE
Apply Disciplinary Concepts and Tools

Examine Sources and Perspectives

Students will examine sources with the goal of extracting information and perspectives on the main question. They analyze each source and describe the author's perspective on the main question and key evidence the author provides to support that viewpoint in Information Organizer Step 2.

Ask students to keep in mind:

- **Author/Creator:** Who created the source? An individual? Group? Government agency?
- **Audience:** For whom was the source created?
- **Date/Place:** Is there any information that reveals where and when the source was created?
- **Purpose:** Why was the source created? Discuss with students the importance of this question in identifying bias.
- **Relevance:** How does the source support one argument or another?

Suggestion: Reading the source documents and filling in Step 2 of the Information Organizer could be assigned as homework.

Resources
- Student Instructions
- Information Organizer
- Source documents

⏻ PROFESSIONAL DEVELOPMENT

Civic Discussion
Be sure to view the Civic Discussion Professional Development resources in the online course.

 TOPIC INQUIRY: CIVIC DISCUSSION

Senate Representation *(continued)*

STEP 3: SYNTHESIZE
Use Evidence to Formulate Conclusions

Formulate Compelling Arguments with Evidence
Now students will apply perspectives and evidence they extracted from the sources to think more deeply about the main question by first arguing one side of the issue, then the other. In this way students become more prepared to formulate an evidence-based conclusion on their own.

Within each student group, assign half of the students to take the position of YES on the main question and the others to take the position of NO. Students will work with their partners to identify the strongest arguments and evidence to support their assigned YES or NO position.

Present Yes/No Positions
Within each group, those assigned the YES position share arguments and evidence first. As the YES students speak, those assigned NO should listen carefully, take notes to fill in the rest of the Compelling Arguments Chart (Step 3 in Information Organizer) and ask clarifying questions.

When the YES side is finished, students assigned the NO position present while those assigned YES should listen, take notes, and ask clarifying questions. Examples of clarifyin questions are:

- I think you just said [x]. Am I understanding you correctly?
- Can you tell me more about [x]?
- Can you repeat [x]? I am not sure I understand, yet.

Suggestion: You may want to set a 5 minute time limit for each side to present. Provide a two-minute warning so that students make their most compelling arguments within the time frame.

Switch Sides
The students will switch sides to argue the opposite point of view. To prepare to present the other position, partners who first argued YES will use the notes they took during the NO side's presentation, plus add any additional arguments and evidence from the reading and sources. The same for students who first argued the NO position.

STEP 4: DEMONSTRATE
Communicate Conclusions and Take Informed Action

Individual Points of View
Now the students will have the opportunity to discuss the main question from their own points of view. To help students prepare for this discussion, have them reflect on the YES/NO discussions they have participated in thus far and fill in Step 4 of their Information Organizers.

After all of the students have shared their points of view, each group should list points of agreement, filling the last portion of Step 4 on their Information Organizers.

Reflect on the Discussion
Ask students to reflect on the civic discussion thinking about:

- The value of having to argue both the YES and NO positions.
- If their individual views changed over the course of the discussion and why.
- What they learned from participating in the discussion.

Resources
- Student Instructions
- Information Organizer

INTRODUCTION

A Constitution for the United States (1776–Present)

After the Revolutionary War, Americans began the hard work of constructing a new government. First, they needed a new constitution. Drafting the United States Constitution was a challenging task. There were disagreements over the size and scope of the new federal government relative to the individual states in the republic. There were also debates over the best ways to safeguard the liberties for which Americans had fought so dearly. However, after continued debate and compromises, a new, politically united nation took form.

CONNECT

MY STORY VIDEO

James Madison, The Federalist Papers

Watch a video that introduces students to one of the most important political thinkers in U.S. history.

Identify Central Issues Why did Madison, Hamilton, and Jay write the Federalist Papers? (To explain political ideas and promote the ratification of the new Constitution.)

Cite Evidence Explain why Madison was so important in creating the new U.S. government. (Possible answers: He explained political ideas such as checks and balances, was important in debate at Constitutional Convention, helped ensure ratification, served as Secretary of State and then President.)

DIGITAL ESSENTIAL QUESTION ACTIVITY

How Much Power Should Government Have?

Ask students to think about the Essential Question for this Topic: How much power should government have? Americans disagreed about how much power the federal government of the new nation should have and how that power should be shared with the states.

If students have not already done so, ask them to read the list of government powers and decide which ones they think governments should claim. Have students share their reasoning with the class.

Hypothesize Why do you think Americans disagreed about how much power the government should have following the American Revolution? (Americans had just fought a war against a government they thought was too powerful. Many people worried about tyranny. Others argued that the government needed enough powers to function effectively.)

Identify Central issues What powers from the list do you think are the most important for a government to have? Why? (Answers will vary.)

Evaluate Arguments Give an argument for limiting government powers. (Preventing tyranny; protecting individual rights and freedoms; creating a balance of power)

DIGITAL TIMELINE ACTIVITY

A Constitution for the United States

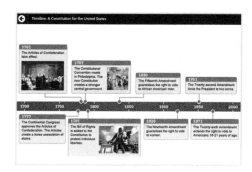

Display the timeline showing the major events surrounding the creation and ratification of the United States Constitution. During this Topic students will learn about these events and many more, but this timeline will provide a framework for placing the events about which they will learn.

Identify Steps in a Process What document came before the United States Constitution? (The Articles of Confederation)

Draw Conclusions How has the United States Constitution changed since its ratification in 1787, and why? (New amendments have been added to expand individual rights and protect liberties.)

Topic Inquiry

Launch the Topic Inquiry with students after introducing the Topic.

A Weak Confederation

Supporting English Language Learners

Use with Digital Text 2, **The Articles of Confederation.**

Reading
Before they begin reading, have students make a list of words in a selection of the text that the recognize by sight. Then have them read a selection from the text and list new words that they have learned to recognize to develop basic sight vocabulary used routinely in written classroom materials.

Beginning Have each student make a list of words that he or she recognizes by sight in the first two paragraphs. Then have students read those paragraphs, helping them as needed with words they do not recognize. Finally, have them add new words to their list of words that they will recognize by sight in the future.

Intermediate Have each student make a list of words that he or she recognizes by sight in the first four paragraphs. Then have students read those paragraphs. Finally, have them list new words that are more familiar to them after reading that they will recognize by sight in the future.

Advanced Have students list examples of words that they recognize by sight after a brief scan of the entire text. Then have them read the text and list words that are more familiar to them after reading that they will recognize by sight in the future.

Advanced High Have students list examples of words that they recognize by sight after a brief scan of the entire text. Then have them read the text and list words that are more familiar to them after reading that they will recognize by sight in the future. Have them write brief definitions of each.

Use with Digital Text 4, **An Orderly Expansion.**

Listening
Read aloud the text using proper intonation. Explain that people tend to stress certain words and syllables when speaking or reading aloud.

Beginning Display these words from the text: *important, govern, established*. Say each word with correct intonation, and have students repeat after you. Ask students to underline each word's stressed syllable.

Intermediate Display these words from the text: *important, govern, established*. Say each word with correct intonation, and have students repeat after you. Ask students to underline each word's stressed syllable. Then, in pairs or small groups, have them read the first paragraph, paying special attention to their intonation of these words.

Advanced Read aloud the first sentence of the text, emphasizing the word *did*. Have students identify the stressed word. Ask: Why did I emphasize the word did? What extra meaning did I give the sentence?

Advanced High Read aloud the first sentence of the text twice: emphasize *did* the first time, and *important* the second time. Have students identify the stressed word in each version. Ask: How does changing which word is emphasized affect the sentence's meaning?

▶ Differentiate Instruction

Use the Differentiated Instruction notes throughout the lesson plan to support the varied skill sets, levels of readiness, and interests in the mixed-ability classroom.

Challenge These notes include suggestions for expanding the activity for advanced students.

On-Level These notes include suggestions for modifying the activity to address different interests or learning styles.

Extra Support These notes include ideas for providing more scaffolding or reading spuport.

Special Needs These notes provide ideas for adapting instruction to support the needs of various special needs students.

■ NOTES

PEARSON
realize™
www.PearsonRealize.com

Go online to access additional resources including:
Primary Sources • Biographies • Supreme Court cases •
21st Century Skill Tutorials • Maps • Graphic Organizers.

Objectives

Objective 1: Explain why state governments wrote constitutions.

Objective 2: Identify the strengths and weaknesses of the Articles of Confederation.

Objective 3: Describe the process the Articles created for admitting new states.

Objective 4: Explain why many Americans called for changes to the Articles.

Objective 5: Summarize Shays' Rebellion and how it influenced leaders to change the Articles of Confederation.

LESSON 1 ORGANIZER		PACING: APPROX. 1 PERIOD,.5 BLOCKS			
				RESOURCES	
		OBJECTIVES	**PACING**	**Online**	**Print**
Connect					
DIGITAL START UP ACTIVITY **Thinking About Government Power**			5 min.	●	
Investigate					
DIGITAL TEXT 1 **Each State Creates a Constitution**		Objective 1	10 min.	●	●
DIGITAL TEXT 2 **The Articles of Confederation**			10 min.	●	●
INTERACTIVE MAP **Claims to Western Lands**			10 min.	●	
DIGITAL TEXT 3 **Weaknesses of the Confederation**		Objectives 2, 3	10 min.	●	●
INTERACTIVE CHART **Problems and Effects of the Articles of Confederation**			10 min.	●	
DIGITAL TEXT 4 **An Orderly Expansion**		Objective 3	10 min.	●	●
DIGITAL TEXT 5 **Economic Problems Lead to Change**		Objectives 4, 5	10 min.	●	●
Synthesize					
DIGITAL ACTIVITY **Debating the Power of a Government**			5 min.	●	
Demonstrate					
DIGITAL QUIZ **Lesson Quiz and Class Discussion Board**			10 min.	●	

A Weak Confederation

■ CONNECT

DIGITAL START UP ACTIVITY

Thinking About Government Power

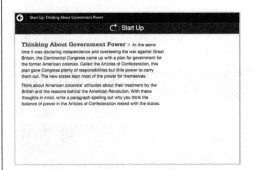

Project the Start Up Activity Ask students to read the instructions and write a brief paragraph about why the balance of power in the Articles of Confederation rested with the states.

Discuss Think about the reasons for the American Revolution. Why were many people reluctant to give up the powers of the states? *(They had just fought a war against a government they thought was tyrannical. They did not want the federal government to be too strong.)*

Tell students that in this lesson they will be learning about the issues surrounding the writing of the Articles of Confederation.

Aa Vocabulary Development: Use the Interactive Reading Notepad to preview the Key Terms and Academic Vocabulary in this lesson with students.

> **⚡ FLIP IT!**
> Assign the Flipped Video for this lesson.

■ STUDENT EDITION PRINT PAGES: 178–184

■ INVESTIGATE

DIGITAL TEXT 1

Each State Creates a Constitution

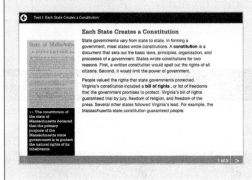

Objective 1: Explain why state governments wrote constitutions.

Quick Instruction

Display the image of the Massachusetts state constitution. States wrote constitutions to enumerate citizens' rights and limit government powers. Discuss why the creation of state constitutions was an important issue surrounding the American Revolution.

Generate Explanations Explain why states needed to create their own constitutions. *(To establish their own governments and protect citizens' rights)*

Further Instruction

Go through the Interactive Reading Notepad questions and discuss the answers with the class. Be sure students understand how state constitutions were structured.

As each state wrote its own constitution, the Continental Congress wrote a constitution for the national government, which they called the Articles of Confederation.

Summarize Reread the excerpt from the Massachusetts Constitution of 1780. What rights did the state guarantee? *(Life, liberty, property, safety, and happiness)*

Hypothesize Why do you think the new nation will decide to draft a national constitution in addition to each state constitution? *(There will need to be a federal government to unite and oversee the different states. That government will require its own written constitution.)*

Identify Patterns How do you think state constitutions will influence the Articles of Confederation drafted by the Continental Congress? *(They may establish some of the rights and liberties discussed in the Articles; the Articles will have to discuss how to balance federal and state power, as laid out in the state constitutions.)*

DIGITAL TEXT 2

The Articles of Confederation

INTERACTIVE MAP

Claims to Western Lands

DIGITAL TEXT 3

Weaknesses of the Confederation

Objectives 2: Identify the strengths and weaknesses of the Articles of Confederation; 3: Describe the process the Articles created for admitting new states.

Quick Instruction

Generate Explanations Why was writing the Articles of Confederation an important event of the American Revolution? *(The Articles of Confederation formalized a loose alliance of states in order for them to act together to win independence.)*

Interactive Chart: Problems and Effects of the Articles of Confederation Next, project the interactive chart on the whiteboard. Explain that the procedure for expanding the United States was just one problem the Articles had to address. Have students read through the problems of the Articles and summarize the weaknesses of the document.

Interactive Map: Claims to Western Lands Project the interactive map on the whiteboard and move the slider. One issue surrounding the Articles of Confederation was who controlled western lands. Why do you think state claims to western lands created a problem for the Articles of Confederation? *(The Articles did not have the authority to resolve disputes between states over land ownership.)*

📷 ACTIVE CLASSROOM

Have students use the PMI Strategy to summarize the strengths and weaknesses of the Articles of Confederation. Divide students into groups and have them create a three-column organizer with headings Plus/Minus/Interesting to record their answers to the following questions: What are the positive aspects about the Articles of Confederation? What are its negative aspects? What is interesting about this document?

📷 ACTIVE CLASSROOM

Using the map as their reference, ask students to Make Headlines that summarizes what the map shows about the resolution of disputes among the states over claims to lands west of the Appalachian Mountains, and how those resolutions led to the passage of the Articles of Confederation.

ELL Use the ELL activity described in the ELL chart.

Further Instruction

Go through the Interactive Reading Notepad questions and discuss the answers with the class. Assign the Primary Source: Articles of Confederation.

Summarize the strengths of the Articles of Confederation. *(It let states make their own decisions, limited federal power, granted the states equal representation, and gave the government necessary powers to declare war, coin money, operate post offices, and sign treaties.)*

Summarize the weaknesses of the Articles of Confederation. *(The Congress's powers were limited; laws had to be approved and enforced by the states; there was no president; the Congress couldn't regulate trade or issue taxes; there was no court system; central government couldn't resolve disputes between states.)*

A Weak Confederation

INTERACTIVE CHART
Problems and Effects of the Articles of Confederation

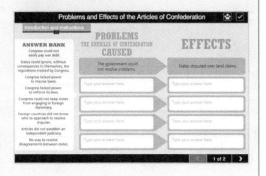

DIGITAL TEXT 4
An Orderly Expansion

Identify Central Issues Why was the value of U.S. currency so low following the Revolution? How did the weaknesses of the Articles of Confederation contribute to this issue? *(During the Revolution, the Congress printed paper money that wasn't backed by silver or gold, which made the currency almost worthless. States therefore began printing their own money. There was not a strong central government to establish a valuable currency consistent across states.)*

Objective 3: Describe the process the Articles created for admitting new states.

Quick Instruction
Project the chart on the whiteboard. Remind students that one weakness of the Articles of Confederation was that it didn't grant the federal government enough authority to regulate disputes between states over land. Explain how the Northwest Ordinance established principles and procedures for the orderly expansion of the United States.

Draw Conclusions Why did the nation need a land ordinance for the Northwest Territory? Why weren't the Articles of Confederation sufficient to oversee the orderly expansion of the United States? *(The Articles of Confederation didn't account for how to resolve disputes among states over land in the territories. The nation needed to establish rules for expansion and settlement of new areas.)*

ELL Use the ELL activity described in the ELL chart.

D Differentiate: Extra Support Explain that an ordinance is an authoritative order. Have students locate the Northwest Territory on a map and state in their own words what authoritative order the Northwest Ordinance made.

Further Instruction
Go through the Interactive Reading Notepad questions and discuss the answers with the class. Assign the Primary Source: Northwest Ordinance. Be sure students can explain how the Northwest Ordinance established

principles and procedures for the orderly the expansion of the United States.

Generate Explanations Explain how the Northwest Ordinance established principles and procedures for the orderly expansion of the United States. *(It established a government in the Northwest Territory and allowed the region to be further divided into separate territories. It established the principle that settlers in U.S. territories had basic rights, including the rights to freedom of religion, trial by jury, and basic government functions. It also established the principle and procedures by which new territories could become states. These regulations allowed for orderly expansion.)*

Identify Steps in a Process List the procedures territories had to undergo to become states, as established by the Land Ordinance of 1785 and the Northwest Ordinance. *(Territories were surveyed, then divided into townships. Townships were divided into smaller sections and sold to settlers. Territories had to amass a population over 60,000. Then territories could ask Congress to be admitted as a state.)*

Contrast Why was the Northwest Ordinance more successful than the Articles of Confederation in establishing principles for orderly expansion? *(It established the principle that new territories could become states and set up procedures territories could follow to become states, which the Articles otherwise did not have the authority to direct.)*

DIGITAL TEXT 5

Economic Problems Lead to Change

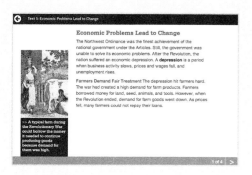

Economic Problems Lead to Change

The Northwest Ordinance was the finest achievement of the national government under the Articles. Still, the government was unable to solve its economic problems. After the Revolution, the nation suffered an economic depression. A **depression** is a period when business activity slows, prices and wages fall, and unemployment rises.

Farmers Demand Fair Treatment The depression hit farmers hard. The war had created a high demand for farm products. Farmers borrowed money for land, seed, animals, and tools. However, when the Revolution ended, demand for farm goods went down. As prices fell, many farmers could not repay their loans.

>> A typical farm during the Revolutionary War could borrow the money it needed to continue producing goods because demand for them was high.

1 of 4 >

Objectives 4: **Explain why many Americans called for changes in the Articles;** 5: **Summarize Shays' Rebellion and how it influenced leaders to change the Articles of Confederation.**

Quick Instruction

Project the image of the Massachusetts state militia on the whiteboard. Remind students that the country was in serious debt following the American Revolution. Economic problems caused anger in the new nation and convinced leaders the Articles of Confederation were too weak to provide useful governance. These problems were some of the causes of the creation of the Constitution.

Identify Central Issues How did the weakness of the federal government under the Articles of Confederation impact the economy of the new nation? *(The weaknesses of the Articles meant the federal government did not have the authority to tax. The nation also lacked a strong and stable single currency. This made it difficult to pay off debt and revive the economy.)*

Further Instruction

Go through the Interactive Reading Notepad questions and discuss the answers with the class. Be sure students understand why the Articles of Confederation needed to be replaced.

Recognizing the weaknesses of the Articles of Confederation, the nation's leaders met in Philadelphia in 1787 to begin drafting the United States Constitution. These weaknesses were the main causes for the creation of the Constitution.

Identify Cause and Effect Identify the causes and effects of Shay's Rebellion. *(Causes—A depression following the war meant farmers could not repay their debts. Effects—Leaders decided the Articles of Confederation had to be revised.)*

Evaluate Arguments Why did Washington call the new government "limping?" What does this quote suggest about the Articles of Confederation? *(He is describing the inability of the government to take strong steps to move the country forward. He therefore suggests the Articles of Confederation are too weak.)*

A Weak Confederation

DIGITAL ACTIVITY

Debating the Power of a Government

Have students make a list of five ways the early nation could have strengthened the central government without leading to abuses of power. Poll the class to see if students agree on possible solutions.

Have the class consider the following questions: What powers should the federal government have? What federal powers should be limited? Have students generate two lists.

Discuss Have students review their paragraphs from the beginning of the lesson. Ask if they would change anything now that they have learned more about the Articles of Confederation.

DIGITAL QUIZ

Lesson Quiz and Class Discussion Board

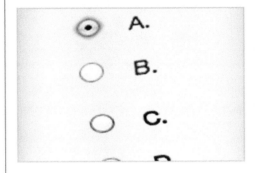

Assign the online Lesson Quiz for this lesson if you haven't already done so. Students will be offered automatic remediation or enrichment based on their score.

Pose these questions to the class on the Discussion Board:

In *A Weak Confederation* you read about the strengths and weaknesses of the Articles of Confederation and how the Northwest Ordinance contributed to the orderly expansion of the United States.

Draw Conclusions Why do you think many colonists wanted a weak federal government, as evidenced by the Articles of Confederation? *(They were wary of centralized power after the Revolution.)*

Make Predictions Name one change you think the United States Constitution would make to strengthen the federal government following the Articles of Confederation, and why. *(It would give the federal government the power to levy taxes in order to generate revenue for the nation to pay off its debts.)*

Topic Inquiry

Have students continue their investigations for the Topic Inquiry.

Drafting a Constitution

Supporting English Language Learners

Use with Digital Text 1, **A Historic Convention.**

Listening
Read aloud the text, or invite volunteers to do so. As you read, have students follow along and pay special attention to your pronunciation. Prompt students to recognize elements in newly acquired vocabulary, such as long and short vowels.

Beginning Display these words from the text: *revise, describe, debate.* Point out the "long vowel-consonant-silent e" pattern. Then say each word on the list, emphasizing the long vowel sound, and have students repeat after you.

Intermediate Review the "long vowel-consonant-silent e" pattern, and display examples from the text. Then create another list of words from the text that have the spelling but not the sound pattern (e.g., *private, representative, delegate*). Have students practice reading both lists of words.

Advanced Display a list of words from the text that mixes "long vowel-consonant-silent e" words and exceptions to that rule. Ask students to pronounce the words and sort them into a two-column chart based on their sound pattern.

Advanced High Review that some words have a long vowel while others do not. Have students search the text for words of both types, sort them into a two-column chart, and compare their chart with a partner's.

Use with Digital Text 5, **The Convention Comes to a Conclusion.**

Reading
Distribute the following linguistically accommodated version of the quote from Benjamin Franklin to students, as appropriate according to their level:

"I don't know if any other meeting could make a better Constitution. . . . I wish that every member of this meeting who has problems with this Constitution would do the same as I am doing. That is to see that you might be wrong this time and . . . vote for this Constitution."

Beginning Have students read the linguistically accommodated version of the quote and help them understand words and phrases in this version that are too difficult for them. Have them look at the version of the quote in the student text. Ask them to briefly state the meaning of the quote.

Intermediate Have students read the linguistically accommodated version of the quote and then the version of the quote in the student text, helping them with words and phrases they do not understand. Ask them to explain the meaning of the quote.

Advanced Have students read the version of the quote in the student text, helping them with words and phrases they do not understand. Have them explain the meaning of the quote.

Advanced High Pre-teach a few challenging words from the text as a whole (e.g., *infallibility, instrument, endorsed*). Have students read the version of the quote in the student text, then have them briefly explain their understanding of its meaning and Franklin's reasons for making this statement in writing or in a class discussion.

▣ Differentiate Instruction

Use the Differentiated Instruction notes throughout the lesson plan to support the varied skill sets, levels of readiness, and interests in the mixed-ability classroom.

Challenge These notes include suggestions for expanding the activity for advanced students.

On-Level These notes include suggestions for modifying the activity to address different interests or learning styles.

Extra Support These notes include ideas for providing more scaffolding or reading spuport.

Special Needs These notes provide ideas for adapting instruction to support the needs of various special needs students.

▮ NOTES

Drafting a Constitution

Objectives

Objective 1: Identify the leaders of the Constitutional Convention.

Objective 2: Compare the main differences between the two rival plans for the new Constitution.

Objective 3: Summarize compromises the delegates had to reach before the Constitution could be signed.

LESSON 2 ORGANIZER		PACING: APPROX. 1 PERIOD, .5 BLOCKS			
				RESOURCES	
		OBJECTIVES	**PACING**	**Online**	**Print**
Connect					
DIGITAL START UP ACTIVITY **Compromise in Government**			5 min.	●	
Investigate					
DIGITAL TEXT 1 **A Historic Convention**		Objective 1	10 min.	●	●
DIGITAL TEXT 2 **Disagreements Over a New Government**		Objective 2	10 min.	●	●
INTERACTIVE GALLERY **Delegates of the Constitutional Convention**			10 min.	●	
DIGITAL TEXT 3 **The Great Compromise**		Objective 3	10 min.	●	●
INTERACTIVE CHART **The Great Compromise**			10 min.	●	
DIGITAL TEXT 4 **The Three-Fifths Compromise**			10 min.	●	●
DIGITAL TEXT 5 **The Convention Comes to a Conclusion**			10 min.	●	●
Synthesize					
DIGITAL ACTIVITY **Compromise in Government**			5 min.	●	
Demonstrate					
DIGITAL QUIZ **Lesson Quiz and Class Discussion Board**			10 min.	●	

Go online to access additional resources including:
Primary Sources • Biographies • Supreme Court cases •
21st Century Skill Tutorials • Maps • Graphic Organizers.

CONNECT

DIGITAL START UP ACTIVITY

Compromise in Government

Project the Start Up Activity Ask students to review the activity as they enter and get settled. Then have students write their paragraphs and share them with each other either in class or through a blog space.

Discuss Prompt students to think about the primary need for compromise during the Convention, especially in regards to the question of the size and scope of a new federal government relative to the states.

Tell students that in this lesson they will be learning about the issues of the Constitutional Convention and the writing of the United States Constitution.

Aa Vocabulary Development: Use the Interactive Reading Notepad to preview the Key Terms and Academic Vocabulary in this lesson with students.

> **⇅ FLIP IT!**
>
> Assign the Flipped Video for this lesson.

■ STUDENT EDITION PRINT PAGES: 185–190

INVESTIGATE

DIGITAL TEXT 1

A Historic Convention

Objective 1: Identify the leaders of the Constitutional Convention.

Quick Instruction

Project the image of Franklin and Washington at the Constitutional Convention. Explain that 1787 is a significant date in U.S. history. It is the year delegates gathered in Philadelphia to write the United States Constitution.

Make Predictions Name one issue you predict will come up in the Constitutional Convention as delegates meet to revise the Articles of Confederation. *(State vs. federal power; the structure of the new government; balance of power among states)*

ELL Use the ELL activity described in the ELL chart.

Further Instruction

Go through the Interactive Reading Notepad questions and discuss the answers with the class. Be sure students can identify key leaders of the Constitutional Convention, including Washington, Franklin, and Madison. These leaders are some of the nation's founders. They will help negotiate important compromises at the Convention to bring about peaceful solutions.

Summarize What was the significance of the year 1787 and the location Philadelphia, Pennsylvania? *(Delegates met at the Constitutional Convention in Philadelphia in 1787 to write the Untied States Constitution.)*

Compare and Contrast Benjamin Franklin and James Madison. How did both of these founders contribute to the convention? *(Contrast—Franklin was 81 and Madison only 36; Franklin had more experience in government while Madison was quiet and shy. Compare—Both had ideas about how to structure the new government; both modeled civic virtue for the new nation.)*

Identify Cause and Effect How did the weaknesses of the Articles of Confederation cause the Constitution to be created? *(The nation needed a new federal government stronger than the one under the Articles.)*

Drafting a Constitution

DIGITAL TEXT 2

Disagreements Over a New Government

INTERACTIVE GALLERY

Delegates of the Constitutional Convention

DIGITAL TEXT 3

The Great Compromise

Objective 2: **Compare the main differences between two rival plans for the new Constitution.**

Quick Instruction

Interactive Gallery: Delegates of the Constitutional Convention Project the interactive gallery on the whiteboard and click through the images.

Analyze Images Look at the image of George Washington. How did Washington model civic virtue at the Constitutional Convention? *(He continued to serve the nation instead of retiring; he was a respected leader; he served as president of the Convention.)*

Summarize As you look through the gallery, name one issue that came up for the delegates during the creation of the Constitution. *(How much power small versus large states should have; how the federal government should be structured; how the states should be represented in the federal government.)*

ACTIVE CLASSROOM

Have students use the Walking Tour Strategy to analyze the issues of the Constitutional Convention of 1787. Divide the class into two groups. Have one group post passages from *Virginia Proposes a Plan* on one side of the room. Have the other group post passages from *New Jersey Disagrees* on the other side of the room. Have groups tour the room and discuss the passages, summarizing the different plans.

Further Instruction

Go through the Interactive Reading Notepad questions and discuss the answers with the class. Be sure students can summarize the Virginia and New Jersey plans and understand why the delegates disagreed.

Evaluate Arguments Why did the delegates decide they needed to create a new constitution? *(They didn't think the Articles of Confederation could be sufficiently revised.)*

Compare Points of View How did small states view the Virginia Plan, and why? Why was this difference of opinion such an important issue facing the Convention? *(Small states opposed the Virginia Plan because it awarded delegates to the legislature based on population, giving more power to larger states. The issue needed to be solved because delegates would not be able to create a new government without agreeing on representation.)*

Make Predictions How do you think the delegates would compromise on the Virginia and New Jersey plans to arrive at a peaceful solution? *(They would create two legislative branches, one with seats awarded by population and one with equal representation.)*

Objective 3: **Summarize compromises the delegates had to reach before the Constitution could be signed.**

Quick Instruction

Interactive Chart: The Great Compromise Project the interactive chart on the whiteboard and read through the columns. Review the opposing views put forth in the Virginia and New Jersey plans. Discuss why representation was an issue at the Constitutional Convention of 1787.

Analyze Information Analyze the issues that led to the Great Compromise, and explain how the Great Compromise resulted in a peaceful solution. *(Small states did not want to be outvoted by large states, and large states wanted representation proportional to their population. The Great Compromise resolved this issue by creating a bicameral legislature, with seats in the House of Representatives awarded by population and seats in the Senate set at two per state. This compromise satisfied both larger and smaller states.)*

D Differentiate: Extra Support Explain that *bi-* means two and *cameral* refers to judicial or legislative chambers. Have students use these definitions to explain the meaning of *bicameral legislature.*

ELL Use the ELL activity described in the ELL chart.

INTERACTIVE CHART

The Great Compromise

DIGITAL TEXT 4

The Three-Fifths Compromise

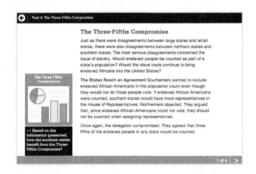

DIGITAL TEXT 5

The Convention Comes to a Conclusion

Further Instruction

Go through the Interactive Reading Notepad questions and discuss the answers with the class. Be sure students can analyze the issues of the Constitutional Convention, including the Great Compromise and the Three-Fifths Compromise, and can summarize how these compromises resulted in a peaceful solution. After the delegates sign the Constitution, it will still need to be ratified by the states.

Interpret Analyze the issues surrounding the Three-Fifths Compromise. *(Northern and southern states disagreed over how to count enslaved African Americans when calculating the number of representatives to the House. Northern states did not think enslaved African Americans should be counted, while southern states wanted them counted. The compromise counted three-fifths of the enslaved population.)*

Identify Cause and Effect What was the main effect of the creation of the Constitution? *(It led to a process by which states had to decide whether to approve it.)*

Drafting a Constitution

■ SYNTHESIZE

DIGITAL ACTIVITY
Compromise in Government

Discuss with students their definitions of power. Then have them write down their thoughts about where legitimate government gets its authority. Have students share their ideas with a a partner.

Have partners consider the following question. According to the United States Constitution, where does the federal government get its authority? Have pairs share their answers with the class.

Discuss Ask students why they think the founders divided the government into different branches. Discuss how the structure they came up with affects the power of the government.

■ DEMONSTRATE

DIGITAL QUIZ
Lesson Quiz and Class Discussion Board

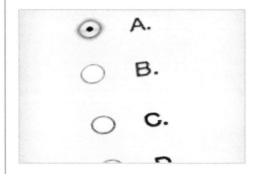

Assign the online Lesson Quiz for this lesson if you haven't already done so. Students will be offered automatic remediation or enrichment based on their score.

Pose these questions to the class on the Discussion Board:

In *Drafting a Constitution* you read about the issues surrounding the Constitutional Convention of 1787 and the compromises delegates made in writing the United States Constitution.

Draw Conclusions Why was compromise necessary for the creation of the Constitution? *(States disagreed over representation in the new government. Delegates needed to compromise over how to represent both large and small states in the legislature.)*

Hypothesize Do you think the Three-Fifths Compromise offered a genuine solution to the issue of representation? Did it result in a peaceful resolution? Explain your reasoning. *(No, it was not a solution because slavery continued to be an issue in the nation. The peaceful resolution was temporary, as the issue eventually led to the Civil War.)*

Topic Inquiry
Have students continue their investigations for the Topic Inquiry.

Ideas That Influenced the Constitution

Supporting English Language Learners

Use with Digital Text 2, **English Influences.**

Reading

Have students read the first two paragraphs of the text. Explain that students will be learning vocabulary used routinely in written classroom materials.

Beginning Display the first sentence, and underline the word *examples*. Demonstrate its meaning by naming familiar categories and showing examples of them (e.g., books, pencils). Ask: What are some examples of rights included in the Constitution? Have them use the word *examples* in a sentence.

Intermediate Help students find the meanings of the words *examples*, *valued*, and *consulting* using context clues. Have use each of these words in a sentence.

Advanced Have students read the entire text under this heading. Then have them write an original paragraph that uses the words *examples*, *extended*, *influenced*, and *affirmed*.

Advanced High Display the first sentence of the text's last paragraph, and underline the word *further*. Explain that *farther* refers to physical distance, while *further* usually refers to something abstract. Discuss how this meaning is exemplified in the text.

Use with Digital Text 3, **America Draws on Its Own Traditions.**

Listening

Read the following instructions to students: "Listen to my instructions not only so that you know what to do, but also so that you learn new language structures. Not only does this text review material you learned earlier, but it also introduces new material. While reading the text, note both the colonial traditions and the other influences that shaped the thinking of the Constitutions framers." Help students learn new language structuresby focusing on the "not only . . . but also" structure and the "both . . . and" structure in your instructions.

Beginning Make sure that students understand these two structures. Ask them what it means when you say not only to do this but also to do that, or when you say "both this and that."

Intermediate Make sure students understand the two structures in your instructions. Working in pairs or in small groups, have each student create a sentence using one of these structures and take turns listening to one another's sentences.

Advanced Have students, in pairs or small groups, create their own sentences using the "not only . . . but also" and the "both . . . and" structures and take turns listening to one another's sentences.

Advanced High Explain to students the concept of the compound sentence, and that the "not only . . . but also" structure can be used to write a compound sentence, as in your instructions. Working in pairs, have students create their own compound sentences and take turns listening to one another's sentences.

▶ Differentiate Instruction

Use the Differentiated Instruction notes throughout the lesson plan to support the varied skill sets, levels of readiness, and interests in the mixed-ability classroom.

Challenge These notes include suggestions for expanding the activity for advanced students.

On-Level These notes include suggestions for modifying the activity to address different interests or learning styles.

Extra Support These notes include ideas for providing more scaffolding or reading spuport.

Special Needs These notes provide ideas for adapting instruction to support the needs of various special needs students.

■ NOTES

Ideas That Influenced the Constitution

Objectives

Objective 1: Identify what American leaders learned about government from studying ancient Rome.

Objective 2: Summarize the traditions of freedom that Americans inherited from England and from their own colonial past.

Objective 3: Describe how the Enlightenment ideas shaped the development of the Constitution.

LESSON 3 ORGANIZER		PACING: APPROX. 1 PERIOD, .5 BLOCKS			
				RESOURCES	
		OBJECTIVES	PACING	Online	Print
Connect					
	DIGITAL START UP ACTIVITY **How to Form a Government**		5 min.	●	
Investigate					
	DIGITAL TEXT 1 **Principles from the Roman Republic**	Objective 1	10 min.	●	●
	DIGITAL TEXT 2 **English Influences**		10 min.	●	●
	DIGITAL TEXT 3 **America Draws on its Own Traditions**	Objectives 2, 3	10 min.	●	●
	INTERACTIVE TIMELINE **Influences on the Constitution**		10 min.	●	
	INTERACTIVE GALLERY **Two Treatises of Government**		10 min.	●	
Synthesize					
	DIGITAL ACTIVITY **Ideas That Influenced the Constitution**		5 min.	●	
Demonstrate					
	DIGITAL QUIZ **Lesson Quiz and Class Discussion Board**		10 min.	●	

PEARSON realize™
www.PearsonRealize.com

Go online to access additional resources including:
Primary Sources • Biographies • Supreme Court cases •
21st Century Skill Tutorials • Maps • Graphic Organizers.

■ CONNECT

DIGITAL START UP ACTIVITY
How to Form a Government

Project the Start Up Activity Ask students to read about Madison and Jefferson as they enter and get settled. Have each student brainstorm topics and then share ideas with another student, either in class or through a blog space.

Discuss If you were James Madison, what topics do you think you would want to read about before you formed a new government? *(Different structures of government; forms of government throughout history; liberty and natural rights) Why? (I would want to learn about other models of government that could provide useful examples and think about the values and principles I wanted the new government to uphold.)*

Aa Vocabulary Development: Use the Interactive Reading Notepad to preview the Key Terms and Academic Vocabulary in this lesson with students.

⇅ FLIP IT!
Assign the Flipped Video for this lesson.

■ STUDENT EDITION PRINT
PAGES: 168–171

■ INVESTIGATE

DIGITAL TEXT 1
Principles from the Roman Republic

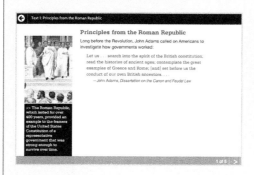

Objective 1: Identify what American leaders learned about government from studying ancient Rome.

Quick Instruction
Project the image of the Roman Republic. Define republic as a government in which citizens rule themselves through elected representatives. Explain that the founders looked to ancient Rome as an example for how to create a lasting republic.

Draw Conclusions How did the formation of a republic stand to address colonial grievances? *(The colonists objected to the king's tyranny. The founders sought to limit tyranny by having citizens rule through elected representatives.)*

Further Instruction
Go through the Interactive Reading Notepad questions and discuss the answers with the class. Be sure students understand how the founders drew on the principles and civic virtues of the Roman Republic when creating the United States Constitution. To extend the lesson, assign Government and Civics: Democracy, Monarchy, and Republic.

Identify Patterns Identify two civic virtues of Rome that the founders drew on and evaluate how they impacted the creation of the United States Constitution. *(Independence and public service: both virtues are found in the Constitution. In order for self-government to work, citizens must be independent-minded and serve the country for the greater good.)*

Evaluate Arguments How did John Adams propose to address colonial grievances in the United States Constitution? Why do you think this was a successful approach? *(He suggested looking to previous examples from ancient civilizations and the British. This was successful because it gave the founders ideas for how to structure the new government and let them learn from history the shortcomings they hoped to avoid.)*

Identify Bias What evidence from the texts shows the founders had a biased view of Rome as a model of civic virtue? *("Historians today admit that the founders somewhat exaggerated the virtues of Rome's republic.")*

Ideas That Influenced the Constitution

DIGITAL TEXT 2
English Influences

DIGITAL TEXT 3
America Draws on its Own Traditions

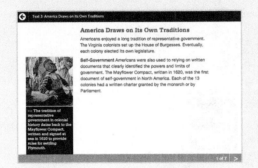

INTERACTIVE TIMELINE
Influences on the Constitution

Objectives 2: Summarize the traditions of freedom that Americans inherited from England and from their own colonial past; 3: Describe how Enlightenment ideas shaped the development of the Constitution.

Quick Instruction

The U.S. system of government was influenced by ideas from historic documents including the Magna Carta and English Bill of Rights. It was also influenced by colonial history. Virginia's House of Burgesses and the Mayflower Compact were important to the growth of representative self-government in the early United States.

Interactive Timeline: Influences on the Constitution Project the interactive timeline and discuss each point on the timeline with students. What ideas did the Magna Carta give the founders about how to set up the U.S. system of government? *(The rule of law and the idea that citizens have the right to fair treatment under the law)*

Interactive Gallery: Two Treatises of Government Project the interactive gallery and click through the images. Discuss the example and how it reflects a free-enterprise system.

Identify Central Issues What views of property rights are reflected in Locke's treatise? *(Property is private and acquired through labor; people can use their property but not hoard it.)* How did those views in turn contribute to the development of a free-enterprise system in the new nation? *(The idea of private property was equated with the rights of private business owners to run their businesses with as little interference from the government as possible, which is essential to the development of a free-enterprise system.)*

🖼 ACTIVE CLASSROOM

Have students use the Sticky Notes Strategy and spend 3 minutes jotting down their response to the following questions: "What ideas from historic documents influenced the United States Constitution? How did these ideas address colonial grievances listed in the Declaration of Independence?" Ask students to share their responses with a partner.

🖼 ACTIVE CLASSROOM

Have students use the Wallpaper Strategy to review the passages on Locke and Montesquieu. Have students design a piece of "wallpaper" that encapsulates an idea from those thinkers that influenced the development of self-government in America. Have students post their wallpaper around the classroom and walk through the gallery, jotting down ideas.

D Differentiate: Challenge Challenge students to select an Enlightenment thinker not discussed in the lesson whose ideas influenced the U.S. system of government, such as Voltaire, Beccaria, or Wollstonecraft. Have students compile a list of important quotes from their thinker and write a few sentences explaining each quote and its impact on the United States.

ELL Use the ELL activity described in the ELL chart.

Further Instruction

Go through the Interactive Reading Notepad questions and discuss the answers with the class. Assign the Primary Sources: Iroquois Confederation and Magna Carta. Be sure students can identify the influence of ideas from the Magna Carta on the U.S. system of government.

■ **SYNTHESIZE**

■ **DEMONSTRATE**

INTERACTIVE GALLERY

Two Treatises of Government

DIGITAL ACTIVITY

Ideas That Influenced the Constitution

DIGITAL QUIZ

Lesson Quiz and Class Discussion Board

Draw Conclusions How did the Virginia House of Burgesses contribute to the growth of representative government? *(It was the first elected legislative assembly and established the tradition of representative government in America.)*

Identify Patterns What ideas from the Mayflower Compact influenced the U.S. system of government? How did these ideas contribute to the growth of representative government in the United States? *(It showed that people could rule themselves. It was also an example of how to write out the powers and limits of government. It established the tradition of self-government in the United States.)*

Cite Evidence that the United States Constitution explicitly addressed colonial grievances listed in the Declaration of Independence. *(The colonists felt the king put military power above civilians, so they made an elected leader, the President, head of the military. The colonists also felt the judges followed the king, so they established an independent court system.)*

Have students generate a list of influential Enlightenment ideas and then pick the one they think was the most important in influencing the Constitution. Poll the class to see whether students agree. Call on students to support their ideas with evidence.

Have students consider the following question. Why did the Framers of the United States Constitution look to models from the past when creating a new government? Have students give examples for support.

Discuss Have students review the topics they came up with at the beginning of the lesson that they thought James Madison would want to consider. Ask if they would change or add to their response now that they have learned more about the ideas that influenced the Constitution.

Assign the online Lesson Quiz for this lesson if you haven't already done so. Students will be offered automatic remediation or enrichment based on their score.

Pose these questions to the class on the Discussion Board:

In *Ideas that Influenced the Constitution* you read about the ideas from historic documents, significant individuals, and the colonies that influenced the U.S. system of government.

Identify Patterns What colonial grievances do you think the Framers most wanted to address in the Constitution? What ideas did they draw on to find a solution? *(They wanted government to protect people's rights without becoming too powerful. They drew on Enlightenment thinkers to come up with a separation of powers to guard against tyranny. They also learned from historic documents to write out citizens' rights and government powers.)*

Draw Conclusions How did the Constitution build upon on a tradition of self-government in the colonies? *(The Constitution extended the scope and reach of the representative governments established in the colonies, for example the House of Burgesses and the Mayflower Compact, to apply to the nation.)*

Topic Inquiry

Have students continue their investigations for the Topic Inquiry.

Federalists, Antifederalists and the Bill of Rights

Supporting English Language Learners

Use with Digital Text 3, **The Ratification Process.**

Listening
Working in groups of three, have students take turns reading aloud the paragraphs in the section titled *The Debate in New England*. Point out the sayings used in the quotation by the Federalist farmer as you prompt students to learn these new expressions.

Beginning Display this phrase from the quotation: *Don't be in a hurry.* Also display other ways it might be heard in a classroom (e.g., "Don't rush." "Slow down."). Have students interact with another using these expressions.

Intermediate Display this phrase from the quotation: *Don't take a leap in the dark*. Help students think of other ways of expressing the same idea in a classroom (e.g., "Don't take risks." "Don't do something dangerous."). Have students interact with one another using one of the expressions.

Advanced Display this phrase from the quotation: *Gather fruit when it is ripe.* Ask students, working in pairs, to take turns stating the meaning of this expression in their own words. Have students interact with one another using one of the expressions.

Advanced High Display this phrase from the quotation: *Don't take a leap in the dark*. Also display this phrase: *Don't take a leap in the dark*. Have pairs of students explain the meanings of these expressions and how they contrast with one another. Then have students interact with one another using these expressions.

Use with Digital Text 4, **New Amendments.**

Reading
Read aloud the text, or invite volunteers to do so. Prompt students to comprehend English language structures used routinely in written classroom materials.

Beginning Display these phrases from the text: *10 amendments, 12 amendments*. Explain that a cardinal, or simple, number shows the quantity of a noun and comes before it. Have students complete and read this sentence: The Bill of Rights has _____ amendments, but _____ were proposed.

Intermediate Display these phrases from the text: *first election, Third Amendment*. Explain that ordinal numbers show the order of nouns and come before them. Display the ordinal numbers through tenth, placing each before *amendment*. Have students read the list.

Advanced Make sure that students understand how cardinal and ordinal numbers work with nouns. Then draw their attention to the last sentence in the second-to-last paragraph in this text, beginning "It was only after . . ." Explain that the first phrase in the sentence sets a condition related to timing. The second phrase in the sentence, beginning "that . . ." is true only if the condition set in the first phrase is true.

Advanced High Make sure that students understand how cardinal and ordinal numbers work with nouns. Then draw their attention to the last sentence in the second-to-last paragraph in this text, beginning "It was only after . . ." Explain that the first phrase in the sentence sets a condition related to timing. The second phrase in the sentence, beginning "that . . ." is true only if the condition set in the first phrase is true. Have students create their own complex sentences using this structure.

▣ Differentiate Instruction

Use the Differentiated Instruction notes throughout the lesson plan to support the varied skill sets, levels of readiness, and interests in the mixed-ability classroom.

Challenge These notes include suggestions for expanding the activity for advanced students.

On-Level These notes include suggestions for modifying the activity to address different interests or learning styles.

Extra Support These notes include ideas for providing more scaffolding or reading spuport.

Special Needs These notes provide ideas for adapting instruction to support the needs of various special needs students.

■ NOTES

PEARSON
realize
www.PearsonRealize.com

Go online to access additional resources including:
Primary Sources • Biographies • Supreme Court cases •
21st Century Skill Tutorials • Maps • Graphic Organizers.

Objectives

Objective 1: Identify the key issues in the constitutional debate.

Objective 2: Explain how the Constitution was finally ratified.

Objective 3: Describe how the Bill of Rights was added to the Constitution.

LESSON 4 ORGANIZER	PACING: APPROX. 1 PERIOD, .5 BLOCKS			
			RESOURCES	
	OBJECTIVES	PACING	Online	Print
Connect				
DIGITAL START UP ACTIVITY **List Your Rights**		5 min.	●	
Investigate				
DIGITAL TEXT 1 **The Federalists and the Antifederalists**		10 min.	●	●
INTERACTIVE CHART **Federalists Versus Antifederalists**	Objective 1	10 min.	●	
DIGITAL TEXT 2 **A Bill of Rights**		10 min.	●	●
DIGITAL TEXT 3 **The Ratification Process**	Objective 2	10 min.	●	●
DIGITAL TEXT 4 **New Amendments**	Objective 3	10 min.	●	●
INTERACTIVE MAP **Ratification of the Constitution**		10 min.	●	
Synthesize				
DIGITAL ACTIVITY **List Your Rights**		5 min.	●	
Demonstrate				
DIGITAL QUIZ **Lesson Quiz and Class Discussion Board**		10 min.	●	

Federalists, Antifederalists and the Bill of Rights

▉ CONNECT

DIGITAL START UP ACTIVITY
List Your Rights

Project the Start Up Activity Ask students to read about the rights listed in the Declaration of Independence and then make a list of the rights they have, or feel they should have. Have students share their lists with another student, either in class or through a blog space.

Discuss Make a list of the rights you have, or that you feel you should have. *(Life, liberty, property, safety, free speech, freedom of movement)* Do you think you could list every single right? Why or why not? *(I probably couldn't list every right because there are so many; I could because rights can be clearly spelled out.)*

Aa **Vocabulary Development:** Use the Interactive Reading Notepad to preview the Key Terms and Academic Vocabulary in this lesson with students.

⇅ FLIP IT!
Assign the Flipped Video for this lesson.

▉ STUDENT EDITION PRINT
PAGES: 197–202

▉ INVESTIGATE

DIGITAL TEXT 1
The Federalists and the Antifederalists

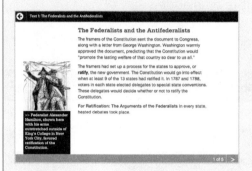

Objective 1: **Identify the key issues in the constitutional debate.**

Quick Instruction
Interactive Chart: Federalists Versus Antifederalists Project the interactive chart and read through the columns. Remind students that after the Framers signed the Constitution, it had to be ratified by at least nine states to take effect. Supporters of the Constitution called themselves Federalists. Opponents were Antifederalists.

Analyze Information Analyze the arguments of the Federalists and Antifederalists for and against ratification. *(Federalists argued that the Constitution gives the federal government the authority necessary to govern while protecting states' rights. Federalists believed that a strong federal government was needed to perform crucial functions, and that the Constitution provided this while preserving the rights of the states. Antifederalists argued that the Constitution makes the federal government too strong compared to the states and gives the President too much power. Antifederalists were opposed to a strong federal government and believed that most functions of government could best be handled by the states.)*

INTERACTIVE CHART
Federalists Versus Antifederalists

▶ ACTIVE CLASSROOM
Have students Take a Stand on the balance of power between the federal government and the states. Ask: Who was right, the Federalists or the Antifederalists? Have students move to opposite sides of the room according to their views. Each group writes a justification of their opinion and presents its statement to the other side. Groups may then craft rebuttals.

D **Differentiate: Extra Support** The word federal refers to the national government. It describes a government formed by the union of states. This should help students remember that Federalists supported the Constitution because they supported the federal government. Antifederalists were against (anti–) a strong federal government.

Further Instruction
Go through the Interactive Reading Notepad questions and discuss the answers with the class. Assign the Primary Sources: Antifederalist positions/papers and *The Federalist* (#1, 9, 10, 14, 39, 51, 78). Be sure students are able to analyze the arguments for and against ratification.

Evaluate Arguments Analyze the arguments of Patrick Henry against ratification. What is he arguing in his speech, and why? *(He is arguing the Constitution gives too much power to the President. After fighting for independence, he is worried the President could become tyrannical, like a king.)*

DIGITAL TEXT 2
A Bill of Rights

DIGITAL TEXT 3
The Ratification Process

Draw Conclusions How have ideas from the *Federalist Papers* influenced the U.S. system of government? *(The papers defend the Constitution and discuss the benefits of and reasons for the U.S. system of government.)* How did Antifederalist writings influence the U.S. system of government? *(Writings such as George Mason's "Objections to This Constitution of Government" supported the Bill of Rights.)*

Contrast Analyze the Antifederalist arguments of George Mason and the arguments of Federalists like Alexander Hamilton and James Madison regarding ratification. Contrast the Antifederalist arguments with the arguments of the Federalists. *(Mason supported a bill of rights to protect citizens from presidential power. Hamilton and Madison thought people's natural rights were too many to list. They argued the Constitution protected citizens without the need for a bill.)*

Objective 2: Explain how the Constitution was finally ratified.

Quick Instruction

Project the political cartoon and ask students to describe the image. Identify the creation and ratification of the Constitution as a major event in U.S. history. Explain that debates occurred between Federalists and Antifederalists throughout all 13 states. Discuss the causes and effects of the creation and ratification of the Constitution, including how disagreements over whether or not to ratify the Constitution threatened the unity of the new nation.

Identify Central Issues Why did Patrick Henry and George Mason oppose ratification? *(They thought the Constitution gave the federal government too much power. Mason wanted to include a bill of rights to protect citizens.)*

ELL Use the ELL activity described in the ELL chart.

Further Instruction

Go through the Interactive Reading Notepad questions and discuss the answers with the class. To extend the lesson, assign the biographies of Alexander Hamilton, James Madison, and George Mason. Discuss the opposing viewpoints of these prominent Federalists and Antifederalists and their reasons for and against ratification.

Determine Point of View What did Federalists mean by the saying "gather fruit when it is ripe"? What does this phrase suggest about their view of the Constitution? How was it an argument for ratification? *(They meant the Constitution was ready to be passed, or "ripe." The country wouldn't benefit from waiting. This suggests they thought the Constitution, while not necessarily perfect, was the best government for the nation and should pass without delay.)*

Support Ideas with Evidence What major change finally convinced many states to vote for ratification? How do you know? *(Federalists promised to include a bill of rights. Virginia then ratified the Constitution, followed by New York, North Carolina, and Rhode Island. This suggests it was the Bill of Rights that finally swayed public opinion.)*

Generate Explanations Explain how the Bill of Rights addressed the grievances the colonists had fought for in the American Revolution. *(It safeguarded rights that colonists felt had been trampled on by the British monarchy.)*

Federalists, Antifederalists and the Bill of Rights

DIGITAL TEXT 4
New Amendments

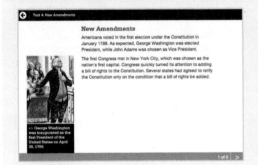

INTERACTIVE MAP
Ratification of the Constitution

Objective 3: Describe how the Bill of Rights was added to the Constitution.

Quick Instruction

Interactive Map: Ratification of the Constitution Project the interactive map and click through the layers to see the ratification process. Remind students that Virginia and New York, two large and influential states, did not ratify the Constitution until the Federalists promised to include a bill of rights.

Analyze Maps Look at the map and compare the sizes of different states. Why do you think Rhode Island ratified the Constitution by such a narrow margin? What arguments do you think Rhode Island Antifederalists may have made against ratification? *(Rhode Island is a small state. Antifederalists may have worried that the power the Constitution gives the federal government would allow large states to dominate smaller states.)*

📹 ACTIVE CLASSROOM

Have groups of two or three students write three newspaper headlines that track the ratification process for the nation's new Constitution. Each headline should summarize a key event in the ratification process. Have students share their headlines and ask for feedback.

ELL Use the ELL activity described in the ELL chart.

Further Instruction

Go through the Interactive Reading Notepad questions and discuss the answers with the class. Be sure students understand how the Bill of Rights addressed colonists' grievances listed in the Declaration of Independence and caused states to ratify the Constitution.

Cite Evidence Name an amendment included in the Bill of Rights that reflects individual rights and explain how it addressed colonial grievances. *(Third Amendment— government cannot quarter troops in citizens' homes without their consent. This addressed the colonists' grievance in the Declaration of Independence that the king forced them to quarter troops in their homes. The Sixth and Seventh Amendments guarantee trial by jury, a right the king suspended.)*

Support Ideas with Examples Give an example of how the United States Constitution reflects the principle of individual rights. *(It gives every citizen equal rights under the law; the Bill of Rights lists rights all people have.)*

Determine Point of View Do you think the inclusion of the Bill of Rights satisfied the concerns of Antifederalists like George Mason and Patrick Henry? Explain your reasoning. *(Mason had called for a bill of rights, so was probably satisfied with the inclusion. Other Antifederalists may have been glad to see a bill of rights but still might have had reservations about federal power.)*

○ A.
○ B.
○ C.

■ SYNTHESIZE

DIGITAL ACTIVITY

List Your Rights

Have students review the lists they made at the beginning of the lesson and their thoughts about the possibility of listing all their natural rights. Ask whether they would like to revise their answers based on what they have learned. Discuss whether they agree with the Federalists or Antifederalists regarding the necessity of a bill of rights.

Have students consider the following question. How have both Federalist and Antifederalist ideas continued to influence the U.S. system of government today? Have students discuss their answers with the class.

Discuss Ask students whose arguments they agree with more, those of the Federalists or Antifederalists. Ask them to provide examples for support.

■ DEMONSTRATE

DIGITAL QUIZ

Lesson Quiz and Class Discussion Board

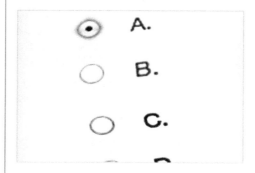

Assign the online Lesson Quiz for this lesson if you haven't already done so. Students will be offered automatic remediation or enrichment based on their score.

Pose these questions to the class on the Discussion Board:

In *Federalists, Antifederalists, and the Bill of Rights* you read about the arguments of Federalists and Antifederalists surrounding ratification and the ways the Bill of Rights addressed colonial grievances.

Evaluate Arguments Do you agree with the Federalists that the United States Constitution reflects the principle of limited government, or do you side with Antifederalist arguments that the Constitution gives federal government dangerous power? Explain your reasoning. *(I think the Constitution reflects the principles of limited government because it creates separate branches of government to limit the power of each branch, and because it lists citizen's rights to prevent government from becoming tyrannical.)*

Topic Inquiry

Have students continue their investigations for the Topic Inquiry.

Understanding the Constitution

Use with Digital Text 1, **The Preamble, the Articles, and the Amendments.**

Reading

Use prereading supports such as pretaught topic-related vocabulary, graphic organizers, and other activities to enhance comprehension of written text. Explain to students that before reading the text, they will learn some new vocabulary and create graphic organizers to help them comprehend the material. Display the text's title and first two subheadings. Explain both using simpler vocabulary. Have students create concept web graphic organizers, with the word *preamble* at the center of the web. Have them write words and phrases from the preamble in other cells in the web, along with definitions of those terms in their own words.

Beginning Have students read the introduction and first two sections and fill in their graphic organizers. Ask: What is the Preamble of the Constitution?

Intermediate Have students read the text and fill in their graphic organizers. Ask: What is domestic tranquillity?

Advanced Have students read the text, fill in their graphic organizers, and look up in a dictionary any words that are unfamiliar and not clear from the context. Ask: What is the purpose of the Preamble?

Advanced High Have students read the text and fill in their graphic organizers. In pairs or for the whole class, have them take turns explaining the different terms in the Preamble, and the relationship of the Preamble to the rest of the Constitution.

Use with Digital Text 2, **Seven Basic Principles.**

Listening

Have students read the introduction and the first two subheads of the text. Circulate to make sure that they understand key terms such as *popular sovereignty*, and *limited government*. Prompt students to learn basic vocabulary heard by listening during classroom instruction and interactions. Explain that students will learn basic vocabulary to help them talk about the text.

Beginning Display the words *believe* and *don't believe*, and explain their meanings. Then ask: Do you believe that a governments powers should be limited? Have students answer by saying, "I believe they should" or "I don't believe they should." In pairs, have students take turns listening to one another use the expressions *believe* and *don't believe* in sentences about the text.

Intermediate Display these terms: *agree, disagree*. Explain the meanings of these terms and model sentences using them. Ask: Popular sovereignty is not really important. Do you agree or disagree? Then have each student respond with a sentence of his or her own using one of these terms. Have them take turns, working in pairs, listening to each other's sentences.

Advanced Display these terms: *fact, opinion*. Explain the meanings of these terms and model sentences using them. Then have each student create two sentences of his or her own, each one of these terms. Have them take turns, working in pairs, listening to each other's sentences.

Advanced High Display these terms: *suppose, supposing, assume, assuming*. Explain the meanings of these terms.Then ask questions that use these terms, such as: Assuming a government has no separation of powers, can it have a system of checks and balances? Suppose you had to get rid of one of the seven principles. Which would it be, and why? Working in pairs, have students take turns listening to each other's responses to your questions, which should use these terms.

▣ Differentiate Instruction

Use the Differentiated Instruction notes throughout the lesson plan to support the varied skill sets, levels of readiness, and interests in the mixed-ability classroom.

Challenge These notes include suggestions for expanding the activity for advanced students.

On-Level These notes include suggestions for modifying the activity to address different interests or learning styles.

Extra Support These notes include ideas for providing more scaffolding or reading spuport.

Special Needs These notes provide ideas for adapting instruction to support the needs of various special needs students.

▮ NOTES

Objectives

Objective 1: Explain the basic goals of the Constitution as defined by the Preamble.

Objective 2: Identify the framework of government that the Constitution established.

Objective 3: Summarize the seven basic principles of American government.

Objective 4: Identify the powers and duties of the legislative branch, executive branch, and judicial branch of the American government.

Objective 5: Describe the services that state and local governments provide.

LESSON 5 ORGANIZER	PACING: APPROX. 1 PERIOD, .5 BLOCKS				
				RESOURCES	
		OBJECTIVES	PACING	Online	Print
Connect					
DIGITAL START UP ACTIVITY **Your Government, Your Welfare**			5 min.	●	
Investigate					
DIGITAL TEXT 1 **The Preamble, the Articles, and the Amendments**		Objective 1	10 min.	●	●
DIGITAL TEXT 6 **Preventing Abuse of Power**		Objective 2	10 min.	●	●
DIGITAL TEXT 2 **Seven Basic Principles**		Objective 3	10 min.	●	●
INTERACTIVE CHART **The Federal System**			10 min.	●	
DIGITAL TEXTS 3, 4, 5 **The Legislative Branch: Congress; The Executive Branch: the President; the Judicial Branch: the Courts**		Objective 4	30 min.	●	●
INTERACTIVE GALLERY **The U.S. Congress**			10 min.	●	
DIGITAL TEXT 7 **State Government**		Objective 5	10 min.	●	●
DIGITAL TEXT 8 **The Responsibilities of Local Government**			10 min.	●	●
Synthesize					
DIGITAL ACTIVITY **Goals and Principles of the Constitution**			5 min.	●	
Demonstrate					
DIGITAL QUIZ **Lesson Quiz and Class Discussion Board**			10 min.	●	

Understanding the Constitution

■ CONNECT

DIGITAL START UP ACTIVITY
Your Government, Your Welfare

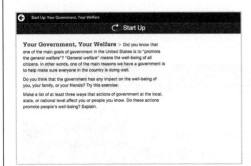

Project the Start Up Activity Ask students to read the definition of "general welfare" and list at least three actions the government takes. Have each student share his or her list with another student, either in class or through a blog space, and have them discuss how these actions affect their lives.

Discuss Do these actions promote people's well-being? *(Answers will vary; students should explain how the actions they listed affect themselves or people they know.)*

Tell students that in this lesson they will be learning about the principles reflected in the United States Constitution.

Aa Vocabulary Development: Use the Interactive Reading Notepad to preview the Key Terms and Academic Vocabulary in this lesson with students.

⇅ FLIP IT!
Assign the Flipped Video for this lesson.

■ STUDENT EDITION PRINT
PAGES: 203–218

■ INVESTIGATE

DIGITAL TEXT 1
The Preamble, the Articles, and the Amendments

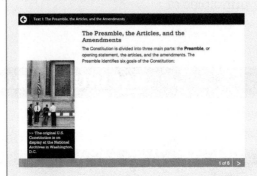

Objective 1: **Explain the basic goals of the Constitution as defined by the Preamble.**

Quick Instruction
Project the image of the Constitution on the whiteboard. The Constitution begins with an introductory Preamble. It is followed by 7 sections, or articles, and 27 amendments. Read the Preamble aloud with the class.

Draw Conclusions How does the Constitution's intention to form "a more perfect union"reflect the principle of federalism? *(The intention is to join the states into a union in which power is shared between the federal government and the states.)*

D Differentiate: Extra Support Review the definition of federalism, a system government in which power is shared between the federal government and the states. Remind students of the reasons Federalists supported federalism. Why did they think this system would make a more perfect union?

ELL Use the ELL activity described in the ELL chart.

Further Instruction
Go through the Interactive Reading Notepad questions and discuss the answers with the class. Assign the Primary Source: The United States Constitution.

The Constitution reflects a number of principles that are central to democracy and balance the power of the government with the rights of individuals.

Cite Evidence that the American justice system is based on the principle of individual rights. *(T"he American justice system requires that the law be applied fairly to every American.")*

Analyze Information How does Article VI of the United States Constitution reflect the principle of federalism? *(It addresses how power is shared between the federal government and the states. State laws may not conflict with federal laws.)*

Hypothesize Review the goals of the Constitution. Name one way you think adopting the Constitution affected the early republic. *(It made the republic more stable and united; it gave the federal government more power to lead the nation.)*

DIGITAL TEXT 6
Preventing Abuse of Power

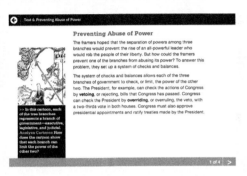

DIGITAL TEXT 2
Seven Basic Principles

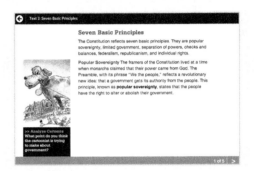

Objective 2: Identify the framework of government that the Constitution established.

Quick Instruction
Project the image of Governor Jan Brewer on the whiteboard. Explain that the separation of powers and system of checks and balances are principles designed to prevent abuse of power. They reflect the principle of limited government put forth in the United States Constitution.

Evaluate Arguments How does the Constitution reflect the principle of separation of powers? What are the reasons for this system? *(The Constitution divides the government into three branches: legislative, executive, and judicial. Each branch can limit the power over the others so that the government does not become too powerful.)*

Further Instruction
Go through the Interactive Reading Notepad questions and discuss the answers with the class. Discuss how the system of checks and balances prevents abuses of power.

Support an Idea with Examples Give an example of how the system of checks and balances reflects the principle of limited government. *(Examples—the President can veto Congress's bills; Congress can override the President's veto; the Supreme Court can declare laws unconstitutional. Each example provides a limit to restrict the power of one branch of government.)*

Draw Conclusions How does the principle of limited government reflected in the Constitution show how the Constitution supports individual rights? *(The Constitution limits government power to ensure the government does not trample individual rights.)*

Objective 3: Summarize the seven basic principles of American government.

Quick Instruction
Interactive Chart: The Federal System
Project the interactive chart and read through the state, national, and concurrent powers outlined in the Constitution. Analyze and discuss how these powers reflect the principle of federalism in the Constitution. To extend the lesson, assign Government and Civics: Rights of the Individual, Process of Naturalization, and Freedom.

Analyze Information Name the seven principles reflected in the United States Constitution and analyze how the Constitution reflects each of them. *(Popular sovereignty: The Constitution's language and content reflect the principle that the government gets its power from the people. Limited government: The Constitution states that government has only the powers granted by the Constitution. Separation of powers: the Constitution divides government into three branches. Checks and balances: The Constitution gives each branch the power to limit the others. Federalism: The Constitution divides power between the federal government and the states. Republicanism: The Constitution creates a system in which citizens elect representatives. Individual rights: The Constitution's Bill of Rights protects the individual rights of citizens.)*

Understanding the Constitution

INTERACTIVE CHART

The Federal System

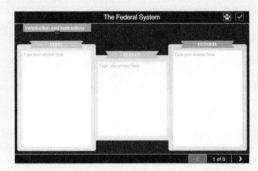

DIGITAL TEXT 3

The Legislative Branch: Congress

ELL Use the ELL activity described in the ELL chart.

▶ ACTIVE CLASSROOM

Have students select one of the seven principles reflected in the United States Constitution and use the Word Wall Strategy to create a visual image of their principle along with with a definition. Ask students to post their words on the board and look at the various responses. Discuss similarities and differences in the responses as a group.

Further Instruction

Go through the Interactive Reading Notepad questions and discuss the answers with the class. Be sure students understand the principles reflected in the United States Constitution.

Identify Central Issues Why was the principle of popular sovereignty reflected in the United States Constitution such a revolutionary idea at the time? *(Under the principle of popular sovereignty, government gets its authority from the people and can be changed or overthrown. This was a new idea at a time when governments were led by monarchs who claimed that their power came from God, not from citizens.)*

Generate Explanations What caused the Framers to create a Constitution that reflected the principle of limited government? *(They wanted to place limits on the government because the Framers felt the British monarchy had too much power over them when they were colonies.)*

Identify Cause and Effect How does the separation of powers affect the principle of checks and balances reflected in the United States Constitution? *(The separation of powers makes it possible to have a system of checks and balances. The government is divided into three branches. Each has the power to limit the actions of the others.)*

Objective 4: **Identify the powers and duties of the legislative branch, executive branch, and judicial branch of the U.S. government.**

Quick Instruction

Interactive Gallery: the U.S. Congress Project the interactive gallery on the whiteboard and click through the images. Remind students that the Great Compromise divided Congress into two parts: the House of Representatives and the Senate.

Analyze Information How does the Seventeenth Amendment reflect the principle of popular sovereignty? *(It lets people elect senators directly.)*

▶ ACTIVE CLASSROOM

Have students break into groups and use the Circle Write Strategy to answer the question: How does the United States Constitution reflect the principle of republicanism? Have students write as much as they can for 1 minute, then switch with the person on their right. The next person tries to improve or elaborate on the response. Continue to switch until the paper comes back to the first person. The group then shares the best response with the class.

INTERACTIVE GALLERY
The U.S. Congress

DIGITAL TEXT 4
The Executive Branch: the President

DIGITAL TEXT 5
The Judicial Branch: the Courts

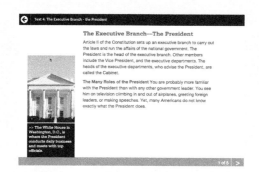

The Executive Branch—The President

Article II of the Constitution sets up an executive branch to carry out the laws and run the affairs of the national government. The President is the head of the executive branch. Other members include the Vice President, and the executive departments. The heads of the executive departments, who advise the President, are called the Cabinet.

The Many Roles of the President You are probably more familiar with the President than with any other government leader. You see him on television climbing in and out of airplanes, greeting foreign leaders, or making speeches. Yet, many Americans do not know exactly what the President does.

>> The White House in Washington, D.C., is where the President conducts daily business and meets with top officials.

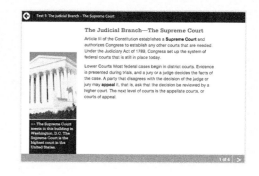

The Judicial Branch—The Supreme Court

Article III of the Constitution establishes a **Supreme Court** and authorizes Congress to establish any other courts that are needed. Under the Judiciary Act of 1789, Congress set up the system of federal courts that is still in place today.

Lower Courts Most federal cases begin in district courts. Evidence is presented during trials, and a jury or a judge decides the facts of the case. A party that disagrees with the decision of the judge or jury may **appeal** it, that is, ask that the decision be reviewed by a higher court. The next level of courts is the appellate courts, or courts of appeal.

>> The Supreme Court meets in this building in Washington, D.C. The Supreme Court is the highest court in the United States.

Further Instruction

Go through the Interactive Reading Notepad questions and discuss the answers with the class. Be sure students understand how the separation of powers creates a system of checks and balances to limit government power and protect individual rights.

Compare and Contrast What is the elastic clause and why is this an issue over which political parties have differing points of view to this day? *(The elastic clause gives Congress the power to make laws that are "necessary and proper." Parties disagree*

over how broadly or narrowly the clause should be interpreted and how much it should limit government power. Some think the clause gives Congress powers not explicitly mentioned in the Constitution. Others think the clause should not stretch government powers too greatly.)

Evaluate Arguments Do you think the electoral college reflects the principle of popular sovereignty? Explain your reasoning. *(No, because it doesn't put the power for electing the President directly in the hands of the people. It gives that authority to electorates instead.)*

Identify Central Issues Identify the origin of judicial review. How does this power reflect the principle of checks and balances? *(The Supreme Court has argued that this power is implicit in the Constitution. It was first asserted in the Supreme Court case* Marbury v. Madison *(1803). It grants the Court authority to declare acts of Congress or the President unconstitutional. This puts a check on the powers of the legislative and executive branches.)*

Understanding the Constitution

DIGITAL TEXT 7
State Government

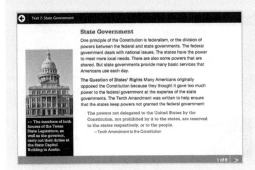

State Government

One principle of the Constitution is federalism, or the division of powers between the federal and state governments. The federal government deals with national issues. The states have the power to meet more local needs. There are also some powers that are shared. But state governments provide many basic services that Americans use each day.

The Question of States' Rights Many Americans originally opposed the Constitution because they thought it gave too much power to the federal government at the expense of the state governments. The Tenth Amendment was written to help ensure that the states keep powers not granted the federal government:

The powers not delegated to the United States by the Constitution, nor prohibited by it to the states, are reserved to the states respectively, or to the people.
-- Tenth Amendment to the Constitution

>> The members of both houses of the Texas State Legislature, as well as the governor, carry out their duties at the State Capitol Building in Austin.

DIGITAL TEXT 8
The Responsibilities of Local Government

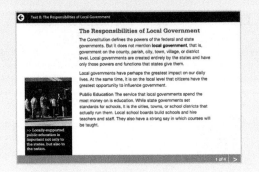

The Responsibilities of Local Government

The Constitution defines the powers of the federal and state governments. But it does not mention **local government**, that is, government on the county, parish, city, town, village, or district level. Local governments are created entirely by the states and have only those powers and functions that states give them.

Local governments have perhaps the greatest impact on our daily lives. At the same time, it is on the local level that citizens have the greatest opportunity to influence government.

Public Education The service that local governments spend the most money on is education. While state governments set standards for schools, it is the cities, towns, or school districts that actually run them. Local school boards build schools and hire teachers and staff. They also have a strong say in which courses will be taught.

>> Locally-supported public education is important not only to the states, but also to the nation.

Objective 5: Describe the services that state and local governments provide.

Quick Instruction
Project the image of the Texas State Capitol on the whiteboard. Remind students that the United States Constitution reflects the principle of federalism, in which power is shared between the national and state governments. States create local governments to serve cities, towns, and other local communities.

Hypothesize How do you think the principle of federalism serves the general welfare of the states? *(It lets state governments retain the power to meet their citizens' needs.)*

Generate Explanations Explain how local governments reflect the principle of popular sovereignty. *(Citizens have the opportunity to influence their local government.)*

Further Instruction
Go through the Interactive Reading Notepad questions and discuss the answers with the class. Discuss the services both state and local governments provide. Be sure students understand how power is shared on the national, state, and local level, and how this division reflects the principles of federalism and republicanism described in the United States Constitution.

Support Ideas With Examples Use the example of public education to explain how, in a federalist system, power is shared among national, state, and local governments. *(Because states have certain powers under federalism, education is primarily a state concern rather than a federal one. States set school standards, and local governments run the schools.)*

Identify Patterns How do state and local governments reflect the principle of limited government? *(State governments have their own constitutions, which limit the powers of state government and protect individual liberties. Local governments have only the power granted them by the states and must conform to state constitutions.)*

Draw Conclusions How do state and local governments reflect the principle of republicanism? *(The people have popular sovereignty and elect legislators and council or board members to represent them in state and local governments.)*

○ A.
○ B.
○ C.

SYNTHESIZE

DIGITAL ACTIVITY
Goals and Principles of the Constitution

Have students review the lists of goals and principles. Explain how the goal of securing the blessings of liberty is supported by the principle of individual rights. Have students choose one item from each list and explain how they relate. Call on students to share their explanations, making sure to cover a variety of items on the lists.

Have students consider the following question. How do the goals and principles reflected in the Constitution promote their general welfare and well-being? Have students discuss their answers with the class, providing examples to support their reasoning.

Discuss Ask students which goals and principles reflected in the Constitution they think have the greatest impact on their daily lives and why, providing examples for support.

DEMONSTRATE

DIGITAL QUIZ
Lesson Quiz and Class Discussion Board

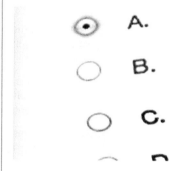

Assign the online Lesson Quiz for this lesson if you haven't already done so. Students will be offered automatic remediation or enrichment based on their score.

Pose these questions to the class on the Discussion Board:

In *Understanding the Constitution,*you read about the principles reflected in the United States Constitution and the powers granted to national, state, and local governments.

Evaluate Arguments Explain the debate over the Tenth Amendment and the elastic clause. What are the different points of view of policial parties on contemporary issues connected with the elastic clause? With whom do you agree, and why? *(The Tenth Amendment grants states rights not explicitly granted to the national government. The elastic clause gives the federal government powers not explicitly stated in the Constitution. Some people think powers not given to the federal government belong to the states, while others think the federal government can assume those powers based on the elastic clause. Student answers should give reasons for their point of view.)*

Identify Central Issues The United States Constitution has endured for hundreds of years. What aspects of the document do you think have enabled it to last? *(The Constitution promotes stability and continuity by sharing power among different branches and levels of government. It is also clear about what powers government has and what individual rights belong to the people, while remaining flexible enough to allow for interpretation and historical change.)*

Topic Inquiry
Have students continue their investigations for the Topic Inquiry Discussion.

Amending the Constitution

Supporting English Language Learners

Use with Digital Text 1, **Constitutional Amendment.**

Listening
Have students read the text. Circulate to make sure that they understand difficult passages. Tell them that they willl earn academic vocabulary heard during classroom instruction. Summarize the main ideas together to encourage students to learn academic vocabulary during interactions with others.

Beginning Display the academic vocabulary *identify*, and demonstrate its meaning by identifying objects in the classroom. Use the word in classroom instruction, saying: Identify the two ways to propose an amendment. Have students, working in pairs, take turns listening to each other's responses to your prompt.

Intermediate Display the academic vocabulary *consist of*, and explain its meaning. Have students, working in pairs, take turns listening to each other tell what everyday items consist of. Then use the term during classroom instruction by saying: What steps does the amendment process consist of? Have students take turns listening to each other use the words *consist of* in their responses.

Advanced Display the academic vocabulary *evaluate*. Discuss its meaning and identify synonyms for it. Use the word in classroom instruction by saying: Evaluate how well the amendment process works. Encourage students, working in pairs, take turns listening to their partner evaluate the ease of amending the Constitution when necessary, as well as protection against too much change.

Advanced High Display the academic vocabulary *draw conclusions*, and discuss its meaning. Demonstrate how the word order changes in a question by asking: What conclusions can you draw about the amendment process? After students, working in pairs, take turns listening to a partner's response, have them use the term in classroom interaction by creating an additional question for a partner to answer.

Use with Digital Text 2, **The Bill of Rights.**

Reading
Have students circulate around the classroom in pairs to look at labels and other forms of writing on objects around the room. Have students derive the meaning of this environmental print.

Beginning Have members of each pair of students take turns pointing out a word in a label or a classroom object and stating the meaning of that word.

Intermediate Have members of each pair of students take turns pointing out a sentence or phrase in a label or a classroom object and stating the meaning of that sentence or phrase.

Advanced Have members of each pair of students take turns pointing out a sentence or phrase in a label or a classroom object and stating the meaning of that sentence or phrase and also explaining the purpose or significance of the label or object.

Advanced High Have pairs of students discuss the meaning and significance of labels and objects in the classroom with writing, and have them compare and contrast those objects.

Differentiate Instruction

Use the Differentiated Instruction notes throughout the lesson plan to support the varied skill sets, levels of readiness, and interests in the mixed-ability classroom.

Challenge These notes include suggestions for expanding the activity for advanced students.

On-Level These notes include suggestions for modifying the activity to address different interests or learning styles.

Extra Support These notes include ideas for providing more scaffolding or reading spuport.

Special Needs These notes provide ideas for adapting instruction to support the needs of various special needs students.

NOTES

PEARSON
realize™
www.PearsonRealize.com

Go online to access additional resources including:
Primary Sources • Biographies • Supreme Court cases •
21st Century Skill Tutorials • Maps • Graphic Organizers.

Objectives

Objective 1: Explain how the Constitution can be amended.

Objective 2: Identify the rights that the Bill of Rights protects.

Objective 3: Summarize how later amendments expanded democratic rights.

LESSON 6 ORGANIZER		PACING: APPROX. 1 PERIOD, .5 BLOCKS		RESOURCES	
	OBJECTIVES	PACING	Online	Print
Connect					
DIGITAL START UP ACTIVITY **First Amendment Rights**		5 min.	●	
Investigate					
DIGITAL TEXT 1 **Constitutional Amendment**	Objective 1	10 min.	●	●
INTERACTIVE CHART **Methods of Amending the Constitution**		10 min.	●	
DIGITAL TEXT 2 **The Bill of Rights**	Objective 2	10 min.	●	●
INTERACTIVE GALLERY **The First Amendment**		10 min.	●	
DIGITAL TEXT 3 **Additional Amendments**	Objective 3	10 min.	●	●
Synthesize					
DIGITAL ACTIVITY **Understanding the Bill of Rights**		5 min.	●	
Demonstrate					
DIGITAL QUIZ **Lesson Quiz and Class Discussion Board**		10 min.	●	

Amending the Constitution

CONNECT

DIGITAL START UP ACTIVITY
First Amendment Rights

Project the Start Up Activity Ask students to read the First Amendment as they enter and get settled and then write a paragraph about how one of the rights listed in the amendment affects their everyday lives.

Discuss Summarize the amendment in your own words. (*Congress cannot make laws that keep people from practicing their religion, speaking freely, assembling, or petitioning the government.*) Pick one of the rights that the First Amendment protects and write one paragraph about how this right affects you in your everyday life. (*Answers will vary but should focus on freedom of religion, freedom of speech, the right to assembly, or the right to petition.*)

Aa Vocabulary Development: Use the Interactive Reading Notepad to preview the Key Terms and Academic Vocabulary in this lesson with students.

𝕹 FLIP IT!
Assign the Flipped Video for this lesson.

◼ STUDENT EDITION PRINT PAGES: 219–223

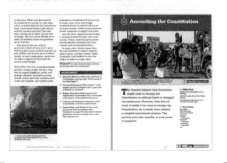

INVESTIGATE

DIGITAL TEXT 1
Constitutional Amendment

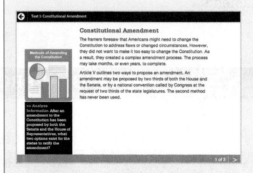

Objective 1: Explain how to amend the Constitution.

Quick Instruction
Interactive Chart: Methods of Amending the Constitution Project the interactive chart on the whiteboard and have students read through the graphic. Walk through the process for proposing and ratifying amendments to the United States Constitution.

Summarize the process for amending the United States Constitution. (*Amendments can be proposed by two thirds of the House and Senate, or by national convention. Amendments can be ratified by three fourths of the state legislatures or by special conventions in three fourths of the states.*)

🎥 ACTIVE CLASSROOM
Have students divide into groups and use the Sequence It Strategy to explore the process of amending the Constitution. Give each student a piece of paper with a single step in the amendment process. Have students form lines showing the correct order for proposing and ratifying amendments.

ELL Use the ELL activity described in the ELL chart.

Further Instruction
Go through the Interactive Reading Notepad questions and discuss the answers with the class. Be sure students can summarize the purposes and process of amending the United States Constitution.

INTERACTIVE CHART
Methods of Amending the Constitution

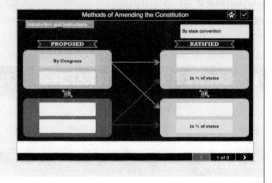

Identify Central Issues What is the purpose of amending the United States Constitution? (*To change the Constitution to address flaws or new circumstances*)

Determine Point of View Why did the Framers make the process of amending the United States Constitution so involved? (*They wanted to make it difficult to change the Constitution to ensure the document would endure regardless of who was in power.*)

Identify Steps in a Process Summarize the process taken to ratify most of the amendments to the United States Constitution. (*The amendment is passed by two thirds of both the House and Senate and ratified by three fourths of the state legislatures.*)

DIGITAL TEXT 2

The Bill of Rights

INTERACTIVE GALLERY

The First Amendment

Objective 2: Identify the rights that the Bill of Rights protects.

Quick Instruction

The first 10 amendments are called the Bill of Rights. These amendments protect important rights and freedoms that continue to shape the American way of life.

Interactive Gallery: the First Amendment
Project the interactive gallery and click through the images. Have students read through the rights guaranteed by the First Amendment.

Summarize the rights guaranteed in the Bill of Rights. *(Free speech, freedom of the press, religious freedom, right to bear arms, freedom from the requirement to house troops, protection against unlawful searches, rights to a fair trial and trial by jury, protection against self-incrimination, protection from cruel or unusual punishment, rights not specifically listed in the Constitution, states' rights not granted to the federal government)*

Make Generalizations Make a generalization about how the passage of the First Amendment shaped the development of religious freedom in the United States. *(It built on colonial traditions of religious freedom and guaranteed religious freedom by law throughout the United States.)*

ACTIVE CLASSROOM

Have students use the Sticky Notes Strategy and spend 3 minutes jotting down their response to the following questions: "Why is free speech important in a constitutional republic?" Have students post their Sticky Notes on the board or on chart paper. Ask them to look at the various responses and then discuss the similarities and differences in the responses as a group. *(Responses should state that free speech is important to a republic because it allows citizens to take part freely in political life.)*

ELL Use the ELL activity described in the ELL chart.

Further Instruction

Go through the Interactive Reading Notepad questions and discuss the answers with the class.

Identify Central Issues Describe the importance of a free press, or free media, in a constitutional republic. *(Free press and media help citizens remain informed and able to make decisions about government.)*

Compare Points of View Identify different points of view on the Second Amendment. Why does this amendment remain controversial today? *(People disagree over how to interpret the wording of the amendment. Some think it guarantees individuals the right to bear arms. Others think it means states have the right to maintain militias.)*

Draw Conclusions Analyze the impact that the guarantee of religious freedom in the First Amendment has had on the American way of life. *(It has led to religious diversity and allowed Americans to worship as they choose.)*

Amending the Constitution

DIGITAL TEXT 3
Additional Amendments

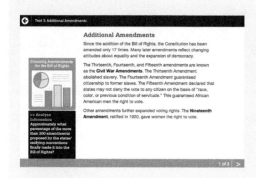

Objective 3: Summarize how later amendments expanded democratic rights.

Quick Instruction

Project the graph on the whiteboard and remind students of the process for ratifying an amendment. Discuss how the ratification of amendments in addition to the Bill of Rights has affected the United States Constitution and the American way of life.

Cite Evidence from the text that summarizes the purpose for amending the Constitution beyond the Bill of Rights. *("Many later amendments reflect changing attitudes about equality and the expansion of democracy.")*

D **Differentiate: Challenge** students to select one of the amendments discussed in this lesson and research its ratification process. Have students prepare a short report in which they present the purpose of the amendment, the process of ratification, and the debates surrounding its approval.

Further Instruction

Go through the Interactive Reading Notepad questions and discuss the answers with the class. Be sure students understand the purposes of the amendments listed and how they changed the Constitution.

Make Generalizations Make a generalization about the purpose for the Thirteenth, Fourteenth, and Fifteenth Amendments of the United States Constitution. *(These amendments expanded rights for African Americans following the Civil War.)*

Support Ideas With Examples Give an example that shows how amending the United States Constitution has made the country more equal. *(The Nineteenth Amendment gave women the right to vote.)*

SYNTHESIZE

DIGITAL ACTIVITY

Understanding the Bill of Rights

Have students fill in the chart with each amendment they learned about the lesson, the protection(s) it offers, and its purpose(s). Have students share their charts with a partner to compare responses.

Have partners review their charts and consider the following questions: Why have these amendments been added to the Constitution? How have they expanded rights and freedoms in the United States? Have partners share their answers with the class.

Discuss Have students review the paragraphs they wrote about the First Amendment. Ask students to pick a different amendment from their chart and write a paragraph explaining how it affects them in their everyday lives. Ask why they think the amendment they chose is important to the American way of life.

DEMONSTRATE

DIGITAL QUIZ

Lesson Quiz and Class Discussion Board

Assign the online Lesson Quiz for this lesson if you haven't already done so. Students will be offered automatic remediation or enrichment based on their score.

Pose these questions to the class on the Discussion Board:

In *Amending the Constitution* you read about the purposes and process of amending the United States Constitution and the rights guaranteed by important amendments.

Draw Conclusions How does the process of amending the United States Constitution affect the balance of power between the federal government and the states? *(The states serve as a check on federal power by limiting Congress's ability to change the Constitution at will.)*

Identify Central Issues How does the Bill of Rights reflect the principle of individual rights in the United States Constitution? *(Nearly all of the rights guaranteed in the Bill of Rights, such as the right to free speech, freedom of religion, and the right to a fair trial, are all rights held by individuals. They apply equally to all Americans.)*

Topic Inquiry

Have students continue their investigations for the Topic Inquiry Discussion.

Citizens' Rights and Responsibilities

Supporting English Language Learners

Use with Digital Text 2, **The Importance of Civic Virtue.**

Reading
Display the two images that accompany the text as visual support as students read grade-appropriate content area text. Ask students to describe what they see. Explain that they will also be using contextual support to read the text

Beginning Use the definition of *civic virtue* and the example of Cincinnatus as contextual support for the ideas in the first two sentences of the text. Use the community projects image as visual support for the ideas presented in the text. Then have students read the sentences, relying on the visual and contextual support you have provided.

Intermediate Point out the boldface terms *civic virtue* and *patriotism* in the text. Discuss how the images illustrate the meanings of these terms and how the surrounding sentences provide contextual support. Provide time for students to read the text in light of this visual and contextual support.

Advanced Display key terms from the text, such as *sacrifice*, *responsibility*, *civic virtue*, and *patriotism*. Ask pairs of students to explore their meanings using the visual support of the photographs and the contextual support of the surrounding text. Then have students read the text, referencing the images and context as needed for further visual support.

Advanced High Display key terms from the text, such as *sacrifice*, *responsibility*, *civic virtue*, and *patriotism*. Ask students to read the text independently and use the visual support of the images and the contextual support of the surrounding text to understand these terms as they are encountered.

Use with Digital Text 3, **Responsible Citizenship.**

Listening
Tell students that you will be instructing them in the key concepts of this text and asking them to work with one another on these concepts. Tell students that they should monitor their understanding of spoken language during this classroom discussion and interaction. Review the meaning of *citizen*. Introduce the concept *responsible.* Remind them to monitor their understanding of your instruction and to ask for help as needed.

Beginning Have students, working in small groups, listen to one another discussing what it could mean to be a responsible citizen. Remind them to monitor their understanding of their partners' language and to ask for help as needed.

Intermediate Have students. working in small groups, listen to one another discussing examples of responsible citizenship. Remind them to monitor their understanding of their partners' language and to ask for help as needed.

Advanced Have students. working in small groups, listen to one another's response to the question, "Why are responsible citizens important in a democracy?" Remind them to monitor their understanding of their partners' language and to ask for help as needed.

Advanced High Have students. working in small groups, listen to one another's response to the question, "What are the dangers to a democracy if citizens are not responsible?" Remind them to monitor their understanding of their partners' language and to ask for help as needed.

▣ Differentiate Instruction

Use the Differentiated Instruction notes throughout the lesson plan to support the varied skill sets, levels of readiness, and interests in the mixed-ability classroom.

Challenge These notes include suggestions for expanding the activity for advanced students.

On-Level These notes include suggestions for modifying the activity to address different interests or learning styles.

Extra Support These notes include ideas for providing more scaffolding or reading spuport.

Special Needs These notes provide ideas for adapting instruction to support the needs of various special needs students.

▮ NOTES

Objectives

Objective 1: Summarize what makes a person a citizen of the United States.

Objective 2: Identify how Americans can develop democratic values.

Objective 3: Describe the responsibilities of citizenship.

LESSON 7 ORGANIZER		PACING: APPROX. 1 PERIOD, .5 BLOCKS			
				RESOURCES	
		OBJECTIVES	PACING	Online	Print
Connect					
DIGITAL START UP ACTIVITY **How to Be a Responsible Citizen**			5 min.	●	
Investigate					
DIGITAL TEXT 1 **American Citizenship**		Objective 1	10 min.	●	●
DIGITAL TEXT 2 **The Importance of Civic Virtue**		Objective 2	10 min.	●	●
INTERACTIVE CHART **Civic Responsibility**			10 min.	●	
DIGITAL TEXT 3 **Responsible Citizenship**		Objective 3	10 min.	●	●
INTERACTIVE CHART **Voting Responsibly**			10 min.	●	
Synthesize					
DIGITAL ACTIVITY **Are You a Responsible Citizen?**			5 min.	●	
Demonstrate					
DIGITAL QUIZ **Lesson Quiz and Class Discussion Board**			10 min.	●	

Citizens' Rights and Responsibilities

■ CONNECT

DIGITAL START UP ACTIVITY

How to Be a Responsible Citizen

Project the Start Up Activity Ask students to make a list of citizens' rights and responsibilities and then write a paragraph on what it means to be a responsible citizen.

Discuss What do citizens do to support the nation? *(Vote, accept responsibility for their behavior, support their families, obey rules, obey laws, stay informed on public issues, serve on juries)* What protections do citizens' have? *(Rights guaranteed by the Constitution)* What happens if citizens do not uphold their responsibilities? *(Democracy may suffer if citizens do not take responsibility, stay informed, vote, and serve their communities. Citizens may also be fined or imprisoned for disobeying laws.)*

Aa Vocabulary Development Use the Interactive Reading Notepad to preview the Key Terms and Academic Vocabulary in this lesson with students.

⇅ FLIP IT!

Assign the Flipped Video for this lesson.

■ STUDENT EDITION PRINT PAGES: 224–229

■ INVESTIGATE

DIGITAL TEXT 1

American Citizenship

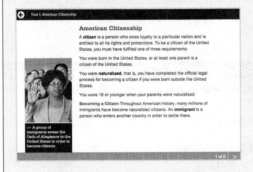

Objective 1: Summarize what makes a person a citizen of the United States.

Quick Instruction

Project the photo of American immigrants taking the oath of citizenship on the whiteboard and define the term *citizen*: a person who owes loyalty to a particular nation and is entitled to all of its rights and protections. Explain that some citizens are born in the United States and others are naturalized, or are born elsewhere and later admitted as citizens.

Summarize some of the rights of citizens of the United States. *(Citizens of the United States enjoy rights to free speech, free worship, and the freedom to vote.)*

D Differentiate: Extra Support Review the three different ways people can become American citizens. Ask students to think of a citizen they know and explain how that person became a citizen.

Further Instruction

Go through the Interactive Reading Notepad questions and discuss the answers with the class. To extend the lesson, assign Government and Civics: U.S. Citizenship According to the Constitution. Make sure students understand the criteria and process by which immigrants become naturalized citizens of the United States.

Identify Steps in a Process Explain the process for becoming a naturalized citizen of the United States. *(Immigrants submit paperwork and attend interviews to become resident aliens. After five years, applicants take a test to show they meet the criteria. They are interviewed about their reasons for wanting to become a citizen. Lastly, they appear before a judge to take an oath.)*

Support Ideas with Examples Give an example of how the rights and responsibilities of U.S. citizens reflect our national identify. *(The right and the responsibility to vote reflect American values such as independence, liberty, and self-governance.)*

DIGITAL TEXT 2

The Importance of Civic Virtue

INTERACTIVE CHART

Civic Responsibility

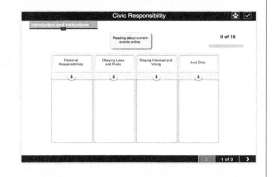

DIGITAL TEXT 3

Responsible Citizenship

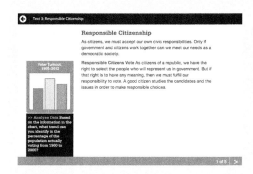

Objective 2: Identify how Americans can develop democratic values.

Quick Instruction

Examples of responsible citizenship are both public and private. Being a responsible citizen involves taking responsibility for yourself and thinking about the needs of others.

Interactive Chart: Civic Responsibility
Project the interactive chart on the whiteboard and read through the tiles. Ask students to think of additional examples of responsible citizenship that they practice in their everyday lives.

Support Ideas With Examples Give an example of when you have accepted responsibility for your behavior. Explain why accepting personal responsibility for one's behavior is important in a democracy. *(Example—drinking a soft drink and recycling the can instead of littering. It is important to take personal responsibility because, in a democracy, individuals are expected to look out for themselves and one another.)*

🗣 ACTIVE CLASSROOM

Have students use the Write 1-Get 3 Strategy to answer the question: What are four key characteristics of responsible citizenship? Have students fold a piece of paper into quarters and write down one response. Ask students to go around the room asking to hear other responses. When they think an answer is correct, they write it in their boxes until they have three more responses on their page. Have students share responses with the class.

ELL Use the ELL activity described in the ELL chart.

Further Instruction

Go through the Interactive Reading Notepad questions and discuss the answers with the class. To extend the lesson, assign Government and Civics: Respect for the Rights of Others. Be sure students can explain the importance of personal responsibilities, such as accepting responsibility for one's behavior and supporting one's family. Ask why it is important for people to take responsibility for supporting their families. *(Families depend on one another.)*

Generate Explanations Identify at least three characteristics of responsible citizenship and explain why these qualities are necessary in a democracy. *(Honesty, compassion, patriotism, courage, responsibility, respect; serving others and working for the good of the community are neccessary for citizens to help make a democracy run.)*

Summarize What is civic virtue, and how did the founders model this behavior for the nation? *(Willingness to work for the greater good; the founders put the good of the country ahead of their own personal wishes.)*

Objective 3: Describe the responsibilities of citizenship.

Quick Instruction

Citizens have responsibilities to help democracy work. Citizens serve the nation, help others, follow laws, and participate in self-government.

Interactive Chart: Civic Responsibility: Voting Project the interactive chart and have students read through the tiles. Discuss why voting is an example of responsible citizenship.

Apply Concepts Identify the examples of responsible citizenship described in the text and explain how you fulfill at least one of these responsibilities. *(Voting, obeying laws, obeying rules, defending the nation, serving on juries, participating in one's community, staying informed on public issues. Sample answers may include following rules at home and at school, volunteering, or reading the news.)*

🗣 ACTIVE CLASSROOM

Post passages from the reading around the room. Have students use the Walking Tour Strategy to tour the room and discuss each passage. Have students identify examples of responsible citizenship and summarize their importance. Ask what examples of responsible citizenship students practice in their own lives.

ELL Use the ELL activity described in the ELL chart.

Citizens' Rights and Responsibilities

SYNTHESIZE

DEMONSTRATE

A.
B.
C.

INTERACTIVE CHART
Voting Responsibly

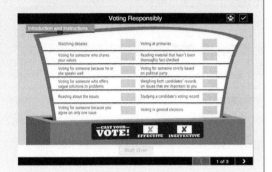

DIGITAL ACTIVITY
Are You a Responsible Citizen?

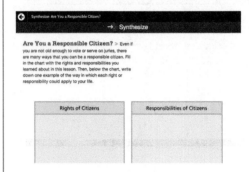

DIGITAL QUIZ
Lesson Quiz and Class Discussion Board

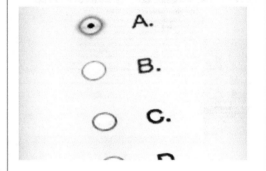

Further Instruction

Go through the Interactive Reading Notepad questions and discuss the answers with the class. Ask students to identify examples of responsible citizenship. Be sure they understand why civic responsibility is necessary in a democratic society.

Generate Explanations Why is staying informed on public issues an important part of responsible citizenship? *(Citizens must be educated about society, political candidates, and political issues in order to make good decisions about whom to vote for and what government policies to support.)*

Compare and Contrast What is the difference between a rule and a law? Why is it important to obey both? *(Contrast—A law is a rule imposed by the nation. A rule is not enforced by the government. Compare—Both keep people safe, help communities live together, and keep people accountable.)*

Summarize What is jury duty, and how does this service help the nation? *(Jury duty is the responsibility to serve on juries. Defendants have the right to a trial by jury. Responsible citizens must serve on juries to ensure that defendants have their rights fulfilled.)*

Have students fill in the chart with the rights and responsibilities they learned about in this lesson. Then have them write down an example of how each right or responsibility applies to their lives. Have students share their lists with the class and generate ideas for how to practice responsible citizenship.

Have students review their charts and consider the following question: How do the rights and responsibilities they listed reflect our national identity? Discuss answers with the class.

Discuss Have students consider examples of responsible citizenship and come up with one additional way they can exercise civic responsibility in their everyday lives. Ask how their additional example can improve their lives or their communities.

Assign the online Lesson Quiz for this lesson if you haven't already done so. Students will be offered automatic remediation or enrichment based on their score.

Pose these questions to the class on the Discussion Board:

In *Citizens' Rights and Responsibilities* you read about examples of responsible citizenship that reflect our national identity.

Support Ideas With Examples Give an example of how education can help you become a responsible citizen. *(It can teach me to obey rules and help me stay informed on public issues.)*

Draw Conclusions In what ways does democracy depend on responsible citizens? *(Democracy requires that citizens work together to govern themselves. Citizens must stay informed, vote for representatives, and serve the public good.)*

Have students continue their investigations for the Topic Inquiry Discussion.

PEARSON
realize.™
www.PearsonRealize.com
Access your Digital Lesson

A Constitution for the United States (1776–Present)

■ SYNTHESIZE

DIGITAL ACTIVITY
Reflect on the Essential Question and Topic

First ask students to reconsider the Essential Question for this Topic: How much power should the government have? Remind students of the government powers they considered at the start of this Topic, for example:

- declare war
- build and maintain roads
- help people meet basic needs
- regulate corporations
- impose taxes
- make and enforce laws
- fund schools, libraries, and research centers
- control natural resources
- control the economy
- maintain relations with other nations

Ask students, "Do you think the United States Constitution gives the government the right amount of power?" Ask them to list one area in which they think the government has too much power, one area in which it has too little, and one area in which they think the balance of power is correct. Discuss their answers as a class or ask students to post their answers on the Class Discussion Board.

Next ask students to reflect on the Topic as a whole and write down three ways their lives are impacted by the Constitution and its amendments. Have students consider the following questions to help them get started:

1. What freedoms do you have that the Constitution guarantees?

2. What government resources or public facilities do you regularly use?

3. How might life be different without the protections of the Constitution?

Have students complete Step 3 of the Topic Inquiry.

■ DEMONSTRATE

DIGITAL TOPIC REVIEW AND ASSESSMENT
A Constitution for the United States (1776–Present)

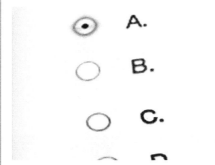

Students can prepare for the Topic Test by answering the questions in the Topic Review and Assessment online or the Assessment questions in the Print Student text. They can also prepare by reviewing their answers to the Interactive Reading Notepad questions or reviewing their notes in the Reading and Notetaking Study Guide.

DIGITAL TOPIC TEST
A Constitution for the United States (1776–Present)

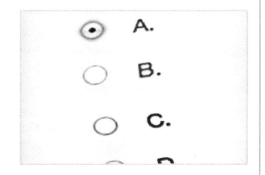

TOPIC TEST
Assign the Topic Test to assess students' understanding of topic content.

BENCHMARK TESTS
Assign these benchmark tests as you complete the relevant topics to monitor student progress toward mastering the course content and as preparation for the End-of-Course Test.

Benchmark Test 1: Topics 1–2

Benchmark Test 2: Topics 3–4

Benchmark Test 3: Topics 5–6

Benchmark Test 4: Topics 7–9

Benchmark Test 5: Topics 10–12

Benchmark Test 6: Topics 13–14

Benchmark Test 7: Topics 15–17

Topic 5

The Early Republic (1789–1825)

TOPIC 5 ORGANIZER	PACING: APPROX. 1 PERIOD, .5 BLOCKS
	PACING
Connect	1 period
MY STORY VIDEO **William Clark, Mapping the American Frontier**	10 min.
DIGITAL ESSENTIAL QUESTION ACTIVITY **What should governments do?**	10 min.
DIGITAL TIMELINE ACTIVITY **The Early Republic**	10 min.
TOPIC INQUIRY: PROJECT-BASED LEARNING **Hold a Mock Cabinet Meeting**	
Investigate	3–6 periods
TOPIC INQUIRY: PROJECT-BASED LEARNING **Hold a Mock Cabinet Meeting**	Ongoing
LESSON 1 Washington's Presidency	30–40 min.
LESSON 2 The Origin of Political Parties	30–40 min.
LESSON 3 John Adams's Presidency	30–40 min.
LESSON 4 Jefferson's Presidency	30–40 min.
LESSON 5 Madison and the War of 1812	30–40 min.
LESSON 6 Monroe's Presidency	30–40 min.
Synthesize	1 period
DIGITAL ACTIVITY **Reflect on the Essential Question and Topic**	10 min.
TOPIC INQUIRY: PROJECT-BASED LEARNING **Hold a Mock Cabinet Meeting**	20 min.
Demonstrate	1–2 periods
DIGITAL TOPIC REVIEW AND ASSESSMENT **The Early Republic (1789–1825)**	10 min.
TOPIC INQUIRY: PROJECT-BASED LEARNING **Hold a Mock Cabinet Meeting**	20 min.

TOPIC INQUIRY: PROJECT-BASED LEARNING

Hold a Mock Cabinet Meeting

In this Topic Inquiry, students work in teams to research the relationships between the United States, Britain, and France in the late eighteenth century. Each student will then solve the problem of how best to respond to the war between Britain and France in 1793 as if he or she were an advisor to one of President Washington's Cabinet members. Solving this problem will contribute to students' understanding of the Topic Essential Question: What should governments do?

STEP 1: CONNECT
Develop Questions and Plan the Investigation

Launch the Project and Generate Questions
Display the request for a Cabinet meeting from President Washington. Tell students they will need to research, write, and perform a mock Cabinet meeting to decide what position the United States should take in the war between Britain and France.

Plan the Investigation
Form students into teams. Have each team review the Skills Tutorials, *Work in Teams* and *Solve Problems*, read and sign the *Project Contract*, and complete the *Need-to-Know Questions* document.

Suggestion: Include students with varied skill levels on each team and ensure the group's responsibilities are evenly distributed.

Walk students through the problem-solving process:

1. Identifying the problem that requires a solution
2. Gathering information to help them decide how to solve it
3. Identifying the available options
4. Predicting the consequences of each option and weighing the advantages and disadvantages of each
5. Choosing and implementing a solution
6. Evaluating the effectiveness of the solution

Resources
- Project Launch
- Student Instructions
- Skills Tutorial, *Work in Teams*
- Project Contract
- Need-to-Know Questions
- Skills Tutorial, *Solve Problems*

STEP 2: INVESTIGATE
Apply Disciplinary Concepts and Tools

Gathering Sources for Research on the American Response to the War Between Britain and France
Groups should document the responsibilities of each member and the overall work of the team on the Project Tracker. To guide their research, each subgroup has been provided with a list of viable sources from which to choose as they answer the questions they've created and complete the Information Organizer.

Investigate Factors Influencing the Solution to the Problem
Each subgroup will then research political, economic, and social issues from the late eighteenth century that must influence their decision on a solution to the problem and identify the best options available given that information.

Write and Edit Your Subgroup's Position Paper
Each subgroup should now write the position paper they will use defend their position during the cabinet meeting. Remind students to provide supporting evidence for their position, and encourage them to offer positive, constructive feedback of each other's work.

- Project Tracker
- Information Organizer

⏻ PROFESSIONAL DEVELOPMENT

Project-Based Learning
Be sure to view the Project-Based Learning Professional Development resources in the online course.

TOPIC INQUIRY: PROJECT-BASED LEARNING

Hold a Mock Cabinet Meeting *(continued)*

STEP 3: SYNTHESIZE
Evaluate Sources and Use Evidence to Formulate Conclusions

Hold the Mock Cabinet Meeting to Solve the Problem
Have subgroups come back together to present their position in the mock cabinet meeting. Encourage students to follow the problem-solving process outlined above and in the Student Instructions.

STEP 4: DEMONSTRATE
Communicate Conclusions and Take Informed Action

Summarize the Cabinet's Solution
Have students write an individual summary of the group's solution.

Reflect on the Project
Have students hold a team meeting to reflect on what they have learned and what, if anything, they would have done differently. Each group member should complete a Team/Peer Assessment.

- Team/Peer Assessment

INTRODUCTION

The Early Republic (1789–1825)

After the War of Independence was finally over, Americans debated the role government should play in the life of its citizens. The new government found itself challenged by foreign affairs and another war with Britain, even as the country expanded in size following the Louisiana Purchase. The United States strengthened its presence on the world stage and expanded its influence in newly independent Latin American countries with the Monroe Doctrine.

■ CONNECT

MY STORY VIDEO
William Clark, Mapping the American Frontier

DIGITAL ESSENTIAL QUESTION ACTIVITY
What should governments do?

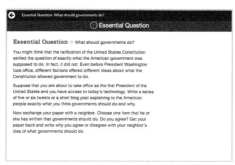

DIGITAL TIMELINE ACTIVITY
The Early Republic

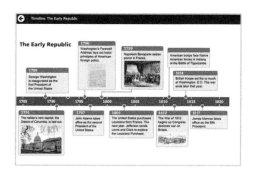

Watch a video about the Lewis and Clark expedition.

Check Understanding What did President Jefferson ask Lewis and Clark to do? *(explore and map the lands west of the Mississippi that had been purchased in 1803 from France)*

Support a Point of View with Evidence Why was the help provided by Native Americans essential to Lewis and Clark? *(The Native Americans knew the lands that Lewis and Clark wanted to explore. They provided them with information about the terrain and supplied guides to lead them on their journey west.)*

Ask students to think about the Essential Question for this Topic: What should governments do? Americans disagreed over what the Constitution allowed federal and state governments to do.

If students have not already done so, ask them to write five or six tweets or a blog post explaining what they think governments should do and why. Have students share their ideas with a partner and discuss whether they agree or disagree.

Evaluate Arguments Give an argument for and an argument against a strong central government that can perform many functions. *(For—government needs the authority to regulate the economy, make and enforce laws, and keep the country running. Against—a strong government that can do many things can also take power away from the people and interfere with individual rights.)*

Identify Central Issues Select an example from your tweets or blog post and explain why it is necessary for government to do. Suppose you are trying to convince someone who disagrees. *(Answers will vary.)*

Display the timeline showing the major events of the early Republic. During this Topic students will learn about all of these events and many more, but this timeline will provide a framework into which they can place the events they learn about.

Summarize Identify two major events that happened in the early Republic. *(The Louisiana Purchase; the War of 1812)*

Draw Conclusions How do you think the presidencies of Washington and Adams shaped the authority of the central government? Explain your reasoning. *(The authority probably expanded, because Jefferson wanted to reduce the power of the federal government when he came into office.)*

Launch the Topic Inquiry with students after introducing the Topic.

Washington's Presidency

Supporting English Language Learners

Use with Digital Text 3, **Creating a Stable Economy.**

Listening
Put students in groups of varied English language proficiency levels to provide support as they seek clarification of spoken language during classroom instruction and interactions. Explain that many northerners supported Hamilton's planned tariff, since there were many manufacturers in the North who would benefit if the tariff raised the prices of imported goods. These might otherwise be cheaper than their own products. Explain that many southerners opposed the tariff because for them it would mean higher prices.

Beginning Next, display these sentence frames: *I do not understand ___* and *Can you explain ___ again?* Encourage students to seek clarification using these frames.

Intermediate Have pairs of students form questions that they could ask to seek clarification about what they hear.

Advanced Have students ask a question to clarify an unclear concept. When they receive an answer, have them seek further clarification on the same topic.

Advanced High Have each student write three questions about Hamilton's planned tariff. Offer help if group members cannot answer one another's questions.

Use with Digital Text 5, **Americans React to the French Revolution.**

Reading
Have students read the introduction and the content under the first two sub-headings. Offer support as needed. Now, remind them of the historical context. Americans had recently won independence from Britain during their own revolution. Direct their attention to the painting of the fire in the streets of Paris. Tell them that they will be using this visual and contextual support to enhance and confirm their understanding.

Beginning Ask students how the American Revolution might affect how Americans viewed the French Revolution. Then ask students to look at the painting and state how American's recent past and events like the one shown in the painting might result in the different reactions mentioned in the text.

Intermediate Look at the painting and ask students to describe what they see. Then ask how the painting and the information you've provided add to what they learned when they read the text.

Advanced Have students explain how the painting and the information you've provided affect their understanding of the content of the text.

Advanced High Have students describe what they see in the painting and describe the conflicting feelings that many Americans may have felt based on the information you've provided and the visual evidence from the painting.

▣ Differentiate Instruction

Use the Differentiated Instruction notes throughout the lesson plan to support the varied skill sets, levels of readiness, and interests in the mixed-ability classroom.

Challenge These notes include suggestions for expanding the activity for advanced students.

On-Level These notes include suggestions for modifying the activity to address different interests or learning styles.

Extra Support These notes include ideas for providing more scaffolding or reading spuport.

Special Needs These notes provide ideas for adapting instruction to support the needs of various special needs students.

▮ NOTES

Objectives

Objective 1: Describe the steps Washington took to set up the government of the new republic.

Objective 2: Explain how Hamilton aimed to create a stable economic system.

Objective 3: Describe arguments around Hamilton's tax plan and the causes and effects of the Whiskey Rebellion.

Objective 4: Explain Washington's foreign policy, including the goal of neutrality and the impact of his Farewell Address.

LESSON 1 ORGANIZER		PACING: APPROX. 1 PERIOD .5 BLOCKS			
		OBJECTIVES	PACING	Online	Print
Connect					
DIGITAL START UP ACTIVITY **A President Takes Office**			5 min.	●	
Investigate					
DIGITAL TEXT 1 **The First American Presidency**		Objective 1	10 min.	●	●
DIGITAL TEXT 2 **Alexander Hamilton and the National Debt**		Objective 2	10 min.	●	●
DIGITAL TEXT 3 **Creating a Stable Economy**			10 min.	●	●
DIGITAL TEXT 4 **Taxation Sparks the Whiskey Rebellion**		Objective 3	10 min.	●	●
INTERACTIVE CHART **A Controversial Tax**			10 min.	●	
DIGITAL TEXT 5 **Americans React to the French Revolution**			10 min.	●	●
DIGITAL TEXT 6 **Washington Defends Neutrality**		Objective 4	10 min.	●	●
INTERACTIVE MAP **Foreign Affairs Under Washington**			10 min.	●	
Synthesize					
DIGITAL ACTIVITY **The Challenge of Neutrality**			5 min.	●	
Demonstrate					
DIGITAL QUIZ **Lesson Quiz and Class Discussion Board**			10 min.	●	

Washington's Presidency

■ CONNECT

DIGITAL START UP ACTIVITY
A President Takes Office

Project the Start Up Activity Ask students to read the quote by Washington and write about his reasons for anxiety as they enter and get settled. Have students share their paragraphs with a partner, either in class or through a blog space.

Discuss If you had seen the new President tremble upon taking office, what would you have thought about him? *(I might have thought he was nervous and wondered about his preparedness to lead the new nation.)* What reasons do you think he had for anxiety? *(As the first President of the United States, he knew there would be difficulties upholding the new government.)*

Aa Vocabulary Development: Use the Interactive Reading Notepad to preview the Key Terms and Academic Vocabulary in this lesson with students.

⚑ FLIP IT!

Assign the Flipped Video for this lesson.

■ STUDENT EDITION PRINT PAGES: 234–244

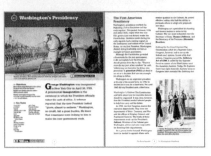

■ INVESTIGATE

DIGITAL TEXT 1
The First American Presidency

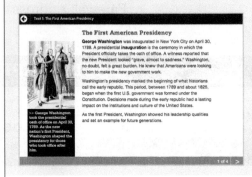

Objective 1: Describe the steps Washington took to set up the government of the new Republic.

Quick Instruction

Project the image of George Washington on the whiteboard. Point out to students that the Constitution was a direct cause of the early Republic's formation. Identify the early Republic as a major era in U.S. history between 1789 and about 1825. Note that the causes of this period were the adoption of the U.S. Constitution and that its effects included the moulding of democratic institutions and practices that have had a lasting impact on the United States. Washington's leadership qualities would set the tone for future presidencies in the early Republic. His important political contributions included choosing strong leaders for his Cabinet and naming the first Chief Justice of the Supreme Court.

Analyze Information How did Washington's actions reflect his leadership qualities? *(Washington was a smart leader who chose well-known, influential, and effective Cabinet members to advise him. The actions that he took set precedents for the federal government. These precedents created a framework for a stable system of government that has lasted to this day.)*

Further Instruction

Go through the Interactive Reading Notepad questions and discuss the answers with the class. Be sure students understand how the leadership qualities of George Washington affected the early Republic and continue to impact the nation today. Explain that one effect of the early Republic on subsequent American history was the establishment of the Supreme Court as outlined in the Constitution.

Summarize Note that one of the major domestic problems the new nation faced was setting up a court system. Describe how Congress addressed this problem. *(Congress passed the Judiciary Act of 1789, which called for the Supreme Court to have one Chief Justice and five Associate Justices. It also created a system of district and circuit courts.)*

Draw Conclusions What precedents did Washington set during his presidency? How did these actions help define the authority of the central government? *(He did not run for three terms and appointed well-known leaders to his Cabinet. These actions limited the power of the President, helped establish a structure for the executive branch, and ensured multiple perspectives would be heard within the government.)*

DIGITAL TEXT 2

Alexander Hamilton and the National Debt

Objective 2: Explain how Hamilton aimed to create a stable economic system.

Quick Instruction
Project the image of the chart on the whiteboard and discuss the major economic problems facing the early Republic. Ask students what factors they think caused the early Republic to be in debt.

Support Ideas With Examples Describe how Alexander Hamilton's helped resolve one of the major domestic problems faced by the leaders of the new Republic: creating a stable economy. *(He created a plan to repay debts by passing a tariff and issuing bonds.)*

D Differentiate: Extra Support To help students understand the economic problems facing the new republic, such as creating a stable economic system, review the definitions of the following terms: national debt, bond, loan, interest, and tariff.

Further Instruction
Go through the Interactive Reading Notepad questions and discuss the answers with the class. Be sure students understand how leaders of the United States proposed to solve the economic problems facing the new nation.

Although southern and northern states compromised on repaying state debts, arguments regarding taxation continued. Alexander Hamilton for example argued in favor of a tax on imports that would raise money to pay off the government's debts.

Compare Points of View Compare the views of political leaders Hamilton and

Madison on how to stabilize the economy. *(Hamilton thought the United States should repay its debts in full by passing a tariff, buying up bonds, and issuing new bonds. Madison opposed paying off the government's old bonds because it rewarded speculators.)*

Infer Describe the contributions of Alexander Hamilton's that show his leadership qualities as an appointed leader. *(He convinced Congress to support much of his plan to pay off the national debt and was also willing to compromise with those who disagreed with him.)*

Draw Conclusions Why was repaying state debts a major domestic problem facing leaders of the new nation? *(The states disagreed over the repayment of state debts. Most southern states had already paid off their debts. They argued that repaying state debts unfairly helped northern states that hadn't repaid what they owed.)*

DIGITAL TEXT 3

Creating a Stable Economy

Objective 3: Describe arguments around Hamilton's tax plan and the causes and effects of the Whiskey Rebellion.

Quick Instruction
Interactive Chart: A Controversial Tax Project the interactive chart on the whiteboard and have students read through the barrels. Summarize the arguments for and against taxation.

Summarize the arguments regarding taxation. Why did northerners and southerners disagree over Hamilton's proposal to impose a protective tariff? *(For—the tariff would increase support for domestic goods. Against—people would have to pay more for imported goods. Northerners supported the tariff to protect their factories. Southerners opposed it because they bought more imported goods.)*

ELL Use the ELL activity described in the ELL chart.

🗪 ACTIVE CLASSROOM

Group students to use the PMI Strategy and create a three-column chart with headings Plus/Minus/Interesting to record responses to the following questions: What are the positive ideas about taxation in the new Republic? What are the negative ideas about this? What is interesting about this issue? Have groups compare responses.

Washington's Presidency

DIGITAL TEXT 4

Taxation Sparks the Whiskey Rebellion

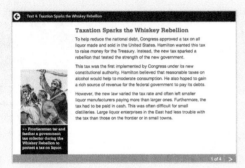

INTERACTIVE CHART

A Controversial Tax

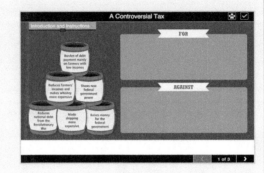

DIGITAL TEXT 5

Americans React to the French Revolution

Further Instruction

Go through the Interactive Reading Notepad questions and discuss the answers with the class. Review the arguments regarding the creation of a banking system. Be sure students understand how disagreements over taxation led to rebellion.

Generate Explanations What major domestic problem did Hamilton's tax proposals address, and how did taxation contribute to the development of a free-enterprise system of economics? *(The government faced a debt crisis and needed to find a form of taxation that allowed it to pay off lenders, because attracting lenders is key to financing government in a free-enterprise system.)*

Draw Conclusions What arguments against taxation emerged during the Whiskey Rebellion? *(Taxes on alcohol that were unequal and had to be paid in cash unfairly burdened small distilleries, farmers, and those in frontier towns.)*

Identify Patterns How did Washington's contribution as a military leader during the Whiskey Rebellion address the early Republic's need to define the authority of the central government? *(Washington was swift to call up the militia to end the rebellion, but he showed mercy against protestors. This helped establish the government's authority to enforce laws prevent violence in the new nation without becoming tyrannical.)*

Objective 4: Explain Washington's foreign policy, including the goal of neutrality and the impact of his Farewell Address.

Quick Instruction

Interactive Map: Foreign Affairs Under Washington Project the interactive map on the whiteboard and click through the icons. In what areas was U.S. national security threatened by conflicts between Britain and France? *(The West Indies, the Great Lakes, the eastern coast)* Point out to students that one important effect of the formation of the early Republic was the ability of the United States to have a single, coherent foreign policy.

Hypothesize Identify the foreign policies of President Washington. What do you think was one effect of Washington's foreign policy? *(Washington aimed to maintain American neutrality in the face of European conflicts. His policies enabled the United States to stay out of foreign wars.)*

Generate Explanations Explain the impact of Washington's Farewell Address. *(Washington urged the country to stay away from foreign alliances that would lead America to become involved in European issues. His advice guided American foreign policy for many years.)*

DIGITAL TEXT 6

Washington Defends Neutrality

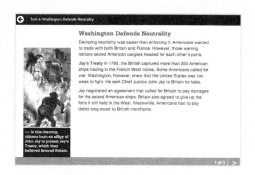

INTERACTIVE MAP

Foreign Affairs Under Washington

🗣 ACTIVE CLASSROOM

Have students Take a Stand on whether or not they agree with Washington's position of neutrality. Ask students to divide into two groups based on their answer and move to separate areas of the classroom. Have students compare their reasons for answering yes or no. Then have a representative present and defend each group's point of view.

ELL Use the ELL activity described in the ELL chart.

Further Instruction

Go through the Interactive Reading Notepad questions and discuss the answers with the class. Be sure students understand how Washington's leadership and his foreign policy helped the United States overcome domestic problems, including national security.

Evaluate Arguments Do you think Washington's foreign policy regarding the French Revolution was effective? Why or why not? *(Yes; in choosing not to take sides in the European wars following the Revolution, he kept the United States from being attacked by Britain and drawn into another war.)*

Identify Central Issues What difficulties did Washington face maintaining national security in his second term? Describe the foreign policy that he developed in response to these problems. *(Washington's foreign policy was to maintain American neutrality in the conflict between Britain and France. However, American trading ships were caught in the middle of this conflict. After Britain seized ships trading with France, Washington had John Jay negotiate a treaty with Britain to pay for damages and give up its forts. In exchange, America paid off its debts to Britain.)*

Washington's Presidency

■ SYNTHESIZE

■ DEMONSTRATE

DIGITAL ACTIVITY
The Challenge of Neutrality

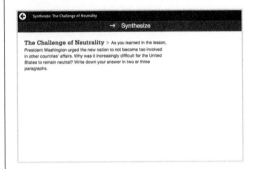

DIGITAL QUIZ
Lesson Quiz and Class Discussion Board

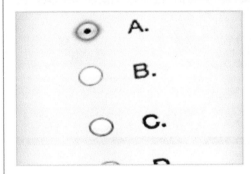

Have students write two to three paragraphs answering the questions about U.S. neutrality during George Washington's presidency and today. Discuss the answers as a class.

Have students review their answers and consider the following question. How did U.S. foreign policy under George Washington respond to issues facing the new Republic? Have students share their answers with the class.

Discuss Have students review the quote by Washington they read at the beginning of the lesson. Ask students to describe the major domestic problems Washington faced during his presidency and explain how he addressed these issues. Ask if they would revise their answers now that they have learned more about his leadership qualities.

Assign the online Lesson Quiz for this lesson if you haven't already done so. Students will be offered automatic remediation or enrichment based on their score.

Pose these questions to the class on the Discussion Board:

In *Washington's Presidency* you read about George Washington's leadership and the major foreign and domestic problems he faced during his presidency.

Identify Patterns Describe how George Washington helped define the authority of the central government during his presidency. *(He limited his presidency to twp terms, appointed well-known leaders to Cabinet positions, and appointed the first Chief Justice of the Supreme Court. He also showed that the government was prepared to enforce laws during the Whiskey Rebellion.)*

Identify Central Issues Describe one of the major problems Washington faced as president and explain how it was addressed. *(Answers will vary but should explain responses to economic instability; the uncertain authority of the central government; foreign challenges; the need for taxation and creation of a banking system; the creation of a Cabinet and court system;or the difficulty of maintaining neutrality following the French Revolution)*

Topic Inquiry
Have students continue their investigations for the Topic Inquiry.

The Origin of Political Parties

Supporting English Language Learners

Use with Digital Text 1, **Americans Divide Over Politics.**

Listening
Read aloud the first page of the text or invite volunteers to do so. Display the accompanying image of George Washington on horseback as a means of using visual support to enhance and confirm understanding of increasingly complex and elaborated spoken language.

Beginning Ask students to describe the image using words or phrases. Use the visual support of the image to enhance and confirm students' understanding of the text. Ask: Do the Americans seem united or divided? Who are they all looking at?

Intermediate Ask students to describe the image. Use the visual support of the image to enhance and confirm students' understanding of the text. Ask: Did Washington want Americans to be united or divided? How does the image show national unity?

Advanced Ask students to describe the image. Have pairs of students use the visual support of the image to enhance and confirm their understanding of the text by answering this question: How does the image reflect the beginning of Washington's presidency when there were no political parties?

Advanced High Have pairs of students describe the image. Then have them use the visual support of the image to enhance and confirm their understanding of the text. Ask them to discuss how this image reflects Washington's ideas, as well as how another image reflecting the emergence of political parties might look.

Use with Digital Text 3, **The Origin of American Political Parties.**

Reading
Have students read the section titled *Newspapers Influence Public Opinion* and view the print of men reading newspapers. Have them use visual and contextual support to develop vocabulary needed to comprehend increasingly challenging language. You may wish to organize the class into groups by reading level.

Beginning Display basic words from the section (e.g., *newspapers, common people, read*). When students have read the section and viewed the print, help them find visual and context clues that suggest the meanings of these words.

Intermediate Display high-frequency academic vocabulary from the section (e.g., *demand, influence*). When students have read the section and viewed the print, help them find visual and context clues that suggest the meanings of these words.

Advanced Display more challenging academic vocabulary from the section (e.g., *rivalry, counterattacks*). When students have read the section and viewed the print, help them find visual and context clues that suggest the meanings of these words.

Advanced High Display more challenging academic vocabulary from the section (e.g., *rivalry, counterattacks*). Using visual and context clues, have students write their own sentences using these words to show their comprehension.

D Differentiate Instruction

Use the Differentiated Instruction notes throughout the lesson plan to support the varied skill sets, levels of readiness, and interests in the mixed-ability classroom.

Challenge These notes include suggestions for expanding the activity for advanced students.

On-Level These notes include suggestions for modifying the activity to address different interests or learning styles.

Extra Support These notes include ideas for providing more scaffolding or reading spuport.

Special Needs These notes provide ideas for adapting instruction to support the needs of various special needs students.

■ NOTES

The Origin of Political Parties

Objectives

Objective 1: Contrast the views of Hamilton and Jefferson.

Objective 2: Explain the origin of political parties in the early republic.

Objective 3: Describe how the election of 1796 increased political tensions.

LESSON 2 ORGANIZER		PACING: APPROX. 1 PERIOD .5 BLOCKS			
				RESOURCES	
		OBJECTIVES	PACING	Online	Print
Connect					
DIGITAL START UP ACTIVITY **New Political Parties**			5 min.	●	
Investigate					
DIGITAL TEXT 1 **Americans Divide Over Politics**		Objective 1	10 min.	●	●
DIGITAL TEXT 2 **Disagreements on Important Issues**		Objective 2	10 min.	●	●
INTERACTIVE GALLERY **Early American Leaders**			10 min.	●	
DIGITAL TEXT 3 **The Origin of American Political Parties**		Objective 3	10 min.	●	●
YOU DECIDE INTERACTIVE CHART **Federalists Versus Republicans**			10 min.	●	
Synthesize					
DIGITAL ACTIVITY **Reasons for Political Parties**			5 min.	●	
Demonstrate					
DIGITAL QUIZ **Lesson Quiz and Class Discussion Board**			10 min.	●	

PEARSON
realize™
www.PearsonRealize.com

Go online to access additional resources including:
Primary Sources • Biographies • Supreme Court cases •
21st Century Skill Tutorials • Maps • Graphic Organizers.

■ CONNECT

DIGITAL START UP ACTIVITY
New Political Parties

Project the Start Up Activity As students enter and get settled, ask them to read the activity and make a prediction about the political parties that would develop in the 1790s. Have students share their predictions with a partner, either in class or through a blog space.

Discuss Given what you know about the Federalists and Antifederalists, make predictions about the two parties that came into existence. What do you think were their main beliefs or arguments about government? *(Federalists and Antifederalists disagreed over how much power the federal government should have. One political party will favor a stronger central government and the other will favor more power for the states.)*

Aa Vocabulary Development: Use the Interactive Reading Notepad to preview the Key Terms and Academic Vocabulary in this lesson with students.

↑↓ FLIP IT!

Assign the Flipped Video for this lesson.

■ STUDENT EDITION PRINT
Pages: 245–250

■ INVESTIGATE

DIGITAL TEXT 1
Americans Divide Over Politics

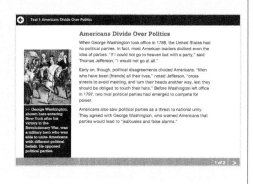

Objective 1: Contrast the views of Hamilton and Jefferson.

Quick Instruction
Project the image of Washington with his supporters on the whiteboard. Explain that when Washington was elected, America had no political parties. By the time he left office, two rival parties had emerged.

Make Predictions Why do you think American political parties would originate during the 1790s? *(Leaders would disagree over political issues. Opposing groups would seek to organize support, creating party divisions.)*

ELL Use the ELL activity described in the ELL chart.

Further Instruction
Go through the Interactive Reading Notepad questions and discuss the answers with the class. To extend the lesson, assign the Primary Source: Declaration of the Rights of Man. Be sure students understand how disagreements between Hamilton and Jefferson contributed to the origin of American political parties.

Evaluate Arguments Why did George Washington oppose the development of American political parties? Do you agree? Explain your reasoning. *(Washington saw political parties as a threat to national unity; answers should explain whether students agree or disagree.)*

Identify Cause and Effect What issues caused factions to develop in the early Republic? *(Hamilton and Jefferson disagreed over how to improve the nation's economy, who should control government, and whether to support Britain or France.)*

DIGITAL TEXT 2
Disagreements on Important Issues

Objective 2: Explain the origin of political parties in the early Republic.

Quick Instruction
Early American leaders disagreed over domestic problems and foreign policy. These disagreements contributed to the development of American political parties in the 1790s.

Interactive Gallery: Early American Leaders Project the image of the interactive gallery on the whiteboard and click through the images. Briefly summarize the political views of each.

Evaluate Arguments How would James Madison explain the origin of American political parties? Explain whether you agree with his reasoning. *(Madison thought parties arose naturally out of political differences. Sample Answer—agree; when people disagree over political issues, they group together with those who share their views in order to work together toward their common goal.)*

👥 ACTIVE CLASSROOM

Pair students to use the Conversations With History Strategy to imagine a conversation between two early American leaders covered in the lesson. The leaders should be from two different political parties. Write down what one of the leaders would say about an important historical issue facing the nation, whether domestic or foreign. Then write down what the other leader would say in response. Have pairs share their dialogues for the class.

Topic (5) Lesson 2

The Origin of Political Parties

INTERACTIVE GALLERY

Early American Leaders

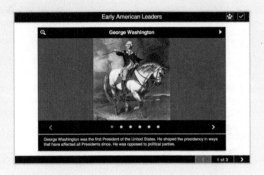

DIGITAL TEXT 3

The Origin of American Political Parties

D **Differentiate: Extra Support** Help students complete the Conversations With History activity by having them write down the contrasting views of Hamilton and Jefferson on the power of the federal government. Ask why these two leaders disagreed over how strong central government should be.

Further Instruction

Go through the Interactive Reading Notepad questions and discuss the answers with the class. Be sure students understand the differences of opinion that led to the development of American political parties.

Compare and Contrast the views of the Federalist Party and the Democratic Republican Party on at least three different historical issues. *(Federalist Party—supported manufacturing and trade, a strong federal government, and favored Britain; Democratic Republican Party—supported small farmers, limited federal government, and favored France.)*

Summarize the arguments for and against the Bank of the United States. *(For—the Constitution gave Congress the power to carry out its duties in the elastic clause. The government needed a bank to collect taxes and pay bills. Against—the Constitution did not explicitly give Congress the power to create a bank, and the elastic clause should not be extended to include powers not explicitly mentioned elsewhere. A national bank gave the government too much power.)*

Draw Conclusions How do you think disagreements between Jefferson and Hamilton on historical issues contributed to the origin of American political parties? *(Politicians and the American public divided according to the leader with whom they most agreed. Political parties arose out of these divisions.)*

Objective 3: **Describe how the election of 1796 increased political tensions.**

Quick Instruction

Interactive Chart: Federalists Versus Republicans Project the interactive chart on the whiteboard and read through the tiles. Discuss how the two political parties originated and their different points of view regarding important historical issues. Tell students that by the end of this lesson they should be able to explain the origin of American political parties.

Summarize How did the Democratic Republican Party originate? *(In 1791, Jefferson and Madison met with New York politicians to organize on behalf of Jefferson and his supporters. They hoped to defeat Hamilton's programs.)*

Summarize How did the Federalist Party originate? *(Alexander Hamilton attracted like-minded supporters, such as northern merchants and manufacturers, who believed in a strong Federal government.)*

ACTIVE CLASSROOM

Have students pretend they are starting a newspaper during the election of 1796 and pick which political party their newspaper will support. Have students use the Make Headlines Strategy to write a headline that capture their party's perspective on an important historical issue and convinces readers to support their view. Have students share their headlines with the class.

SYNTHESIZE

DEMONSTRATE

INTERACTIVE CHART

Federalists Versus Republicans

DIGITAL ACTIVITY

Reasons for Political Parties

DIGITAL QUIZ

Lesson Quiz and Class Discussion Board

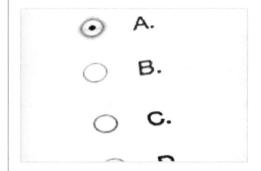

ELL Use the ELL activity described in the ELL chart.

Further Instruction
Go through the Interactive Reading Notepad questions and discuss the answers with the class.

Generate Explanations Explain the role newspapers played in the origin of American political parties. *(Newspapers sided with different parties, influencing public opinion and convincing people to side with one party or the other.)*

Hypothesize How do you think the election of 1796 contributed to the development of American political parties? *(A Federalist, John Adams, became President. A Democratic Republican, Jefferson, became Vice President. Divisions between the two men probably increased political rivalries, causing each party to strengthen its position.)*

Have students write two to three paragraphs explaining the origin of American political parties and whether they think it was right for parties to form. Discuss the answers as a class.

Have students review their answers and consider the following question. How have American political parties developed and changed since their origin in the 1790s? Have students share their answers with the class.

Discuss Have students review the predictions they made at the beginning of the lesson. Ask students whether they would change their predictions about the two political parties and their points of view now that they have learned more about the origin and development of the party system.

Assign the online Lesson Quiz for this lesson if you haven't already done so. Students will be offered automatic remediation or enrichment based on their score.

Pose these questions to the class on the Discussion Board:

In *The Origin of Political Parties*, you read about the origin and development of American political parties and their different points of view on historical issues.

Identify Central Issues How did the disagreement between political parties over a national banking system reflect a deeper disagreement over federal power? *(The parties disagreed over how much power the federal government should have. The controversy over a national bank was part of this deeper disagreement.)*

Make Predictions What do you think would be an effect of the development of American political parties in the early Republic? *(Sample response: Parties would come to dominate politics in the republic.)*

Topic Inquiry
Have students continue their investigations for the Topic Inquiry.

John Adams's Presidency

Supporting English Language Learners

Use with Digital Text 2, **The Alien and Sedition Acts.**

Listening
Display the word *sedition*, and have students practice its spelling and pronunciation. Then use the word with contextual support in order to enhance and confirm student understanding.

Beginning Define the word *sedition* using familiar spoken language and relying mostly on contextual support. Act out a physical act of rebellion against government using props to represent government, your complaint, and so on.

Intermediate Explain the word *sedition* using spoken language and contextual support. To enhance and confirm students' understanding, use props and physical gestures as you speak.

Advanced Explain the word *sedition* using a more complex spoken language that could be understood without contextual support. To enhance and confirm students' understanding, accompany your words with appropriate gestures and facial expressions.

Advanced High Explain the word *sedition* using a more complex and elaborate spoken language that is not linguistically accommodated in any way. Encourage students to ask questions in order to enhance and confirm their understanding of the topic.

Use with Digital Text 3, **An Important Presidential Election.**

Reading
Display the image of the Hamilton-Burr duel on the second screen. If necessary, explain what a duel is. Use visual and contextual support to develop grasp of language structures needed to comprehend increasingly challenging language

Beginning Read this sentence aloud: Alexander Hamilton was killed in a duel. Use the visual support of the image to explain the passive language structure of *was killed*. Guide students to complete this passive sentence: The gun _____ by Aaron Burr.

Intermediate Display this sentence: Alexander Hamilton was killed in a duel. Use the visual support of the image to explain the passive language structure of *was killed*. Then have students construct an original passive sentence based on the image.

Advanced Point out the passive language structure of *was killed* in the first paragraph of the section *The Federalist Era Comes to a Close*. With students, rewrite the sentence with an active construction. Then ask pairs of students to write an original passive sentence based on the image.

Advanced High Point out the passive language structure of *was killed* in the first paragraph of the section *The Federalist Era Comes to a Close*. Ask pairs of students to rewrite the sentence with an active construction, and then to write an original set of active and passive sentences based on the image.

▣ Differentiate Instruction

Use the Differentiated Instruction notes throughout the lesson plan to support the varied skill sets, levels of readiness, and interests in the mixed-ability classroom.

Challenge These notes include suggestions for expanding the activity for advanced students.

On-Level These notes include suggestions for modifying the activity to address different interests or learning styles.

Extra Support These notes include ideas for providing more scaffolding or reading spuport.

Special Needs These notes provide ideas for adapting instruction to support the needs of various special needs students.

■ NOTES

Objectives

Objective 1: Explain Adams's foreign policy.

Objective 2: Describe the controversy over the Alien and Sedition Acts.

Objective 3: Explain why Congress decided the election of 1800 and how that election set a precedent.

LESSON 3 ORGANIZER		PACING: APPROX. 1 PERIOD, .5 BLOCKS			
				RESOURCES	
		OBJECTIVES	**PACING**	**Online**	**Print**
Connect					
DIGITAL START UP ACTIVITY **The Nation's Second President**			5 min.	●	
Investigate					
DIGITAL TEXT 1 **Escalating Conflict With France**		Objective 1	10 min.	●	●
INTERACTIVE TIMELINE **Relations With France**			10 min.	●	
DIGITAL TEXT 2 **The Alien and Sedition Acts**		Objective 2	10 min.	●	●
INTERACTIVE CHART **Hamilton, Adams, or Jefferson?**			10 min.	●	
DIGITAL TEXT 3 **An Important Presidential Election**		Objective 3	10 min.	●	●
Synthesize					
DIGITAL ACTIVITY **An Elected President's Decision**			5 min.	●	
Demonstrate					
DIGITAL QUIZ **Lesson Quiz and Class Discussion Board**			10 min.	●	

John Adams's Presidency

■ CONNECT

DIGITAL START UP ACTIVITY
The Nation's Second President

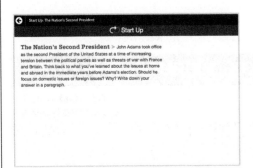

Project the Start Up Activity Have students read the activity and write their paragraphs as they enter and get settled. Have students share their arguments with a partner, either in class or through a blog space.

Discuss Think back to what you've learned about the issues at home and abroad in the immediate years before Adams's election. Should Adams focus on domestic issues or foreign issues? Why? *(If domestic, should mention: the economy, national security, and defining the authority of the central government; if foreign, should mention: the French Revolution, wars between Britain and France, and the Jay Treaty.)*

Aa Vocabulary Development: Use the Interactive Reading Notepad to preview the Key Terms and Academic Vocabulary in this lesson with students.

N FLIP IT!
Assign the Flipped Video for this lesson.

■ STUDENT EDITION PRINT
PAGES: 251–255

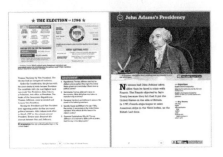

■ INVESTIGATE

DIGITAL TEXT 1
Escalating Conflict With France

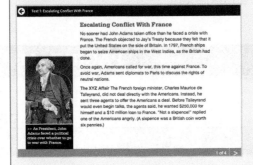

INTERACTIVE TIMELINE
Relations With France

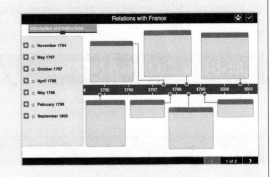

Objective 1: Explain Adams's foreign policy.

Quick Instruction

Interactive Timeline: Relations With France Project the interactive timeline and click through the events. Discuss why relations with France deteriorated as a result of the Jay Treaty and the XYZ affair. Ask how the Treaty of Mortefontaine affected the two nations.

Support Ideas With Evidence Describe Adam's foreign policy and explain what it revealed about his leadership qualities. *(Adams's policy was to maintain American neutrality and to avoid war with France both by strengthening the American military to make the country less of an easy target and by pursuing negotiations for peace with France. This policy showed leadership because it kept the United States out of a dangerous war even though public opinion, especially within Adam's party, supported war with France.)*

⌨ ACTIVE CLASSROOM

Pair students to use the See-Wonder-Think Strategy to analyze the political cartoon. Ask: What do you see? What does that make you think? What are you wondering about now that you've seen this? Then ask students what they think about Adams's foreign policy in light of public opinion toward the French. Have students share their insights with the class.

Further Instruction
Go through the Interactive Reading Notepad questions and discuss the answers with the class.

Compare Points of View Identify the different points of view of the Federalists and the Democratic Republicans regarding Adams's foreign policy with France. *(Federalists—wanted war with France to weaken the Democratic Republicans and strengthen the military; they supported Britain. Democratic Republicans—did not want war with France because they saw France as an ally.)*

Cite Evidence Cite evidence that shows how Adams's decision to strengthen the navy helped define the authority of the central government. *(Adam's actions helped confirm the role of the federal government as the guardian of national security.)*

Identify Cause and Effect Identify one cause and one effect of the XYZ affair on domestic or foreign policy. *(Cause—Adams sent diplomats to France because French ships had seized American ships in the West Indies, even though the United States had declared neutrality. Effects—Americans called for war against France; Adams strengthened the navy; Adams again sent diplomats to negotiate with France to end the conflict with the United States)*

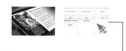

DIGITAL TEXT 2

The Alien and Sedition Acts

INTERACTIVE CHART

Hamilton, Adams, or Jefferson?

Objective 2: Describe the controversy over the Alien and Sedition Acts.

Quick Instruction

Interactive Chart: Hamilton, Adams, or Jefferson? Project the image of the interactive chart and click through the tiles. Identify the views on domestic and foreign policies held by Hamilton, Adams, and Jefferson.

Compare and Contrast How did Adams's foreign policy differ from the approaches favored by Hamilton and Jefferson? *(Adams— did not want war with France or Britain and sent diplomats to negotiate with France. Hamilton—pressured Adams to go to war with France. Jefferson—supported France against Britain.)*

ACTIVE CLASSROOM

Have students use the Sticky Notes Strategy and take 3 minutes to compare and contrast the different points of view of the Federalists and the Democratic Republicans on the Alien and Sedition Acts, citing evidence for support. Have students share their responses with a partner.

D **Differentiate: Extra Support** Review the definitions of alien—foreigner—and sedition—stirring up rebellion against a government. Have students summarize both the Alien Acts and the Sedition Act in their own words.

ELL Use the ELL activity described in the ELL chart.

Further Instruction

Go through the Interactive Reading Notepad questions and discuss the answers with the class. Be sure students understand the causes of the Alien and Sedition Acts and their effects on the early Republic.

Draw Conclusions Describe how the Kentucky and Virginia resolutions challenged the authority of the central government. *(The resolutions said the states had the right to judge whether laws were constitutional and disobey federal laws they deemed unconstitutional. This gave states powers not listed in Constitution.)*

Evaluate Arguments How might Federalists have argued that the Alien and Sedition Acts were necessary for maintaining national security? Do you agree? Explain. *(In order to keep the nation safe, any immigrants thought to be dangerous had to be expelled. It was also a matter of security to keep citizens from causing rebellion. Students should give reasons why they agree or disagree.)*

Identify Cause and Effect How did the Alien and Sedition Acts affect the development of political parties in the late 1700s and early 1800s? *(The acts were aimed to weaken the Democratic Republican Party. They made it harder for immigrants, many of whom supported the Democratic Republicans, to become voting citizens. They also caused Democratic Republicans to be fined or jailed for expression opinions against the government.)*

John Adams's Presidency

DIGITAL TEXT 3

An Important Presidential Election

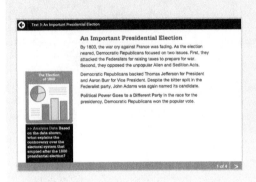

Objective 3: **Explain why Congress decided the election of 1800 and how that election set a precedent.**

Quick Instruction

Project the graphs on the whiteboard and review how the electoral college votes for president. Explain that at the time, the college did not vote separately for President and Vice President.

Identify Central Issues Why did Adams's foreign policy cause a split in the Federalist Party? *(Many Federalists such as Hamilton wanted war with France. They opposed Adams's position of neutrality.)*

ELL Use the ELL activity described in the ELL chart.

Further Instruction

Go through the Interactive Reading Notepad questions and discuss the answers with the class.

Generate Explanations Explain how the election of 1800 affected the development of American political parties. *(The Federalists lost the election as well as several seats in Congress, weakening the party. Democratic Republicans came into power, although many Federalist economic programs remained in place.)*

Make Predictions Name one change you think will result from the election of 1800. Explain your reasoning. *(With Jefferson and the Democratic Republican Party in power, economic policies would be more likely to favor agriculture and the common people over manufacturing and the elite.)*

Draw Conclusions How did the 1800 election set a precedent? *(The election set the precedent that Presidents who failed to win reelection would peacefully and willingly leave office and that the office would pass in an orderly way to the new President.)*

SYNTHESIZE

DIGITAL ACTIVITY
An Elected President's Decision

Have students write two to three paragraphs explaining whether they agree or disagree with Adams's decision to avoid war when many Americans wanted to fight. Discuss the answers as a class.

Have students review their answers and consider the following question. How did John Adams's foreign policy affect the early Republic? Have students share their answers in small groups or with the class.

Discuss Have students review the paragraphs they wrote at the beginning of the lesson about whether they thought Adams should focus on domestic or foreign issues during his presidency. Ask students whether they would change their answer now that they have learned about the domestic and foreign problems he faced.

DEMONSTRATE

DIGITAL QUIZ
Lesson Quiz and Class Discussion Board

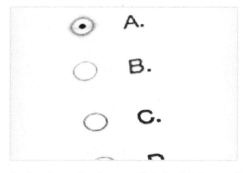

Assign the online Lesson Quiz for this lesson if you haven't already done so. Students will be offered automatic remediation or enrichment based on their score.

Pose these questions to the class on the Discussion Board:

In *John Adams's Presidency*, you read about Adams's leadership, the foreign and domestic problems he faced, and the development of political parties during his presidency.

Identify Patterns How did Adams's foreign policy show continuity and change compared to Washington's foreign policy? *(His foreign policy showed continuity in his effort to maintain U.S. neutrality toward both Britain and France. His foreign policy showed change in his effort to strengthen the nation's defenses and to fight off French attacks.)*

Support Ideas With Examples Why do you think Adams failed to win reelection in 1800? Explain your reasoning. *(Answers should mention Adams's policies that alienated members of both parties.)*

Topic Inquiry
Have students continue their investigations for the Topic Inquiry.

Topic 5 Lesson 4

Jefferson's Presidency

Supporting English Language Learners

Use with Digital Text 1, **Jefferson's Leadership Redefines Government.**

Listening

Use linguistic support to enhance and confirm student understanding of increasingly complex and elaborated spoken language. You may want to group students by language level. Ask students to listen carefully to the following statement about the content in this text, then circulate to the different groups:

"Jefferson brought change to government. He wanted to free the economy from government intrusion. Although his changes alarmed Federalists, he left many Federalist policies in place."

Beginning Repeat the first sentence of your statement. Point out that *brought* is the past tense of *bring*, or a way to say that someone was bringing something in the past. Make sure that students understand each part of the sentence, and the sentence as a whole.

Intermediate Repeat the second sentence of your statement. Point out that to free one thing from a second thing means to take the second thing away so that the first thing is free, or able to do what it wants. Make sure that students understand each part of the sentence, and the sentence as a whole.

Advanced Repeat the third sentence of your statement. Point out that the clause beginning with *although* is a dependent clause, and that a dependent clause beginning with *although* suggests that the idea in the dependent clause is one that would not lead you to expect the idea in the independent clause. Make sure that students understand each part of the sentence, and the sentence as a whole.

Advanced High Repeat the third sentence of your statement. Point out that the clause beginning with *although* is a dependent clause. Have students create their own sentences with dependent clauses and take turns listening to one another's sentences.

Use with Digital Text 5, **American Shipping Faces Challenges.**

Reading

Use the image depicting impressment at the end of the text as a form of visual and contextual support to develop the background knowledge to comprehend the text. Ask students to describe what they see.

Beginning Use the visual support of the image to provide background knowledge about impressment. Explain the meaningof the word *impressment* by describing the image, using physical gestures as needed. Then have students read the final paragraph of the text, providing contextual support as needed.

Intermediate Use the visual support of the image to provide background knowledge about impressment. Identify the various persons in the image and what they are doing.E xplain how the concept of impressment differs from enlistment and the draft. Then have students read the final paragraph of the text, providing contextual support as needed.

Advanced Develop background knowledge by asking students to share what they know about enlisting in and being drafted into the military. Use the visual support of the image to help students understand how the process of impressment is different. Have students read the section titled "Caught Between Britain and France," providing contextual support as needed.

Advanced High Develop background knowledge by asking students how the image might remind them of kidnapping, slavery, or an arrest. Have students read the section titled "Caught Between Britain and France," relying on context as needed to clarify meanings. Then ask students to explain why impressment posed such a challenge to the United States.

D Differentiate Instruction

Use the Differentiated Instruction notes throughout the lesson plan to support the varied skill sets, levels of readiness, and interests in the mixed-ability classroom.

Challenge These notes include suggestions for expanding the activity for advanced students.

On-Level These notes include suggestions for modifying the activity to address different interests or learning styles.

Extra Support These notes include ideas for providing more scaffolding or reading spuport.

Special Needs These notes provide ideas for adapting instruction to support the needs of various special needs students.

NOTES

PEARSON
realize™
www.PearsonRealize.com

Go online to access additional resources including:
Primary Sources • Biographies • Supreme Court cases •
21st Century Skill Tutorials • Maps • Graphic Organizers.

Objectives

Objective 1: Explain why Jefferson acted to limit the size of the federal government.

Objective 2: Describe the significance and effects of *Marbury* v. *Madison*.

Objective 3: Identify the causes and effects of the Louisiana Purchase.

Objective 4: Describe the discoveries of Lewis, Clark, and Pike.

Objective 5: Explain Jefferson's foreign policy, including conflict with the Barbary States, threats to U.S.neutrality, and the Embargo Act.

LESSON 4 ORGANIZER		PACING: APPROX. 1 PERIOD, .5 BLOCKS		
	OBJECTIVES	**PACING**	**RESOURCES**	
			Online	**Print**
Connect				
DIGITAL START UP ACTIVITY **Understanding Judicial Review**		5 min.	●	
Investigate				
DIGITAL TEXT 1 **Jefferson's Leadership Redefines Government**	Objective 1	10 min.	●	●
DIGITAL TEXT 2 **Landmark Supreme Court Cases**	Objective 2	10 min.	●	●
DIGITAL TEXT 3 **The Louisiana Purchase**	Objective 3	10 min.	●	●
DIGITAL TEXT 4 **Exploring the Louisiana Territory**	Objective 4	10 min.	●	●
INTERACTIVE MAP **Expansion and Exploration**		10 min.	●	
DIGITAL TEXT 5 **American Shipping Faces Challenges**		10 min.	●	●
DIGITAL TEXT 6 **A Painful Embargo**	Objective 5	10 min.	●	●
INTERACTIVE CHART **Jefferson's Goals and Policies**		10 min.	●	
Synthesize				
DIGITAL ACTIVITY **The Impact of Judicial Review**		5 min.	●	
Demonstrate				
DIGITAL QUIZ **Lesson Quiz and Class Discussion Board**		10 min.	●	

Jefferson's Presidency

■ CONNECT

DIGITAL START UP ACTIVITY
Understanding Judicial Review

Project the Start Up Activity Have students read the definition of judicial review and answer the question as they enter and get settled. Have students share their answers with a partner, either in class or through a blog space.

Discuss How do you think judicial review would affect the relationship between Congress, the President, and the Court? *(Allowing the Court to strike down laws and actions as unconstitutional would give the Court more authority to check the power of Congress and the President.)*

Tell students that in this lesson they will be learning about the Louisiana Purchase of 1803 and the landmark Supreme Court case *Marbury v. Madison*.

Aa Vocabulary Development: Use the Interactive Reading Notepad to preview the Key Terms and Academic Vocabulary in this lesson with students.

▶ FLIP IT!
Assign the Flipped Video for this lesson.

■ STUDENT EDITION PRINT PAGES: 256–269

■ INVESTIGATE

DIGITAL TEXT 1
Jefferson's Leadership Redefines Government

Objective 1: Explain why Jefferson acted to limit the size of the federal government.

Quick Instruction
Project the image of Thomas Jefferson on the whiteboard and remind students of his political views as a Democratic Republican. Explain that a free-enterprise system is an economic system in which goods and services are exchanged with minimal government interference.

Draw Conclusions How did Jefferson's policies contribute to the development of a free-enterprise system in the new nation? *(Jefferson's policies limited the economic role of the central government. This promoted a free-enterprise system, which involves minimal government intrusion in the economy.)*

D Differentiate: Extra Support Explain that an enterprise is a business or company. Ask students to recall the mercantilist economic system exercised by the British to gain wealth from the American colonies. Discuss how a free-enterprise system differs.

ELL Use the ELL activity described in the ELL chart.

Further Instruction
Go through the Interactive Reading Notepad questions and discuss the answers with the class. Be sure students can explain why a free-enterprise system of economics with minimal government intrusion developed in the new nation.

Support Ideas with Examples Give at least three examples of how Jefferson redefined the authority of the central government following Adams's presidency. *(To reduce the authority of the central government, Jefferson cut the federal budget, decreased the size of government departments, reduced the army and navy, repealed the Whiskey Tax, allowed the Sedition Act to expire, overturned the Alien Act, and promoted a free-enterprise system of economics.)*

Compare and Contrast a free-enterprise system with the economic system favored by Federalists. Why did Jefferson favor a laissez-faire policy? *(A free-enterprise system involves minimal government intrusion. The Federalists wanted a stronger central government that promoted trade and manufacturing. Jefferson favored a laissez-faire approach to reduce government interference.)*

Draw Conclusions How did Jefferson try create a stable economic system in the new Republic? *(He reduced the federal budget and the federal debt and continued to pay off state debts. He also promoted economic competition through a free-enterprise system.)*

DIGITAL TEXT 2

Landmark Supreme Court Cases

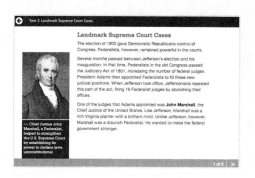

Landmark Supreme Court Cases

The election of 1800 gave Democratic Republicans control of Congress. Federalists, however, remained powerful in the courts.

Several months passed between Jefferson's election and his inauguration. In that time, Federalists in the old Congress passed the Judiciary Act of 1801, increasing the number of federal judges. President Adams then appointed Federalists to fill these new judicial positions. When Jefferson took office, Jeffersonians repealed this part of the act, firing 16 Federalist judges by abolishing their offices.

One of the judges that Adams appointed was **John Marshall**, the Chief Justice of the United States. Like Jefferson, Marshall was a rich Virginia planter with a brilliant mind. Unlike Jefferson, however, Marshall was a staunch Federalist. He wanted to make the federal government stronger.

>> Chief Justice John Marshall, a Federalist, helped to strengthen the U.S. Supreme Court by establishing its power to declare laws unconstitutional.

1 of 5 >

Objective 2: Describe the significance and effects of *Marbury* v. *Madison*.

Quick Instruction

Project the image of Chief Justice John Marshall on the whiteboard. Marshall was an appointed official who showed leadership by strengthening the powers of the Supreme Court.

Summarize the issues, the decision, and the significance of *Marbury* v. *Madison*. (*Chief Justice John Marshall ruled that the Judiciary Act was unconstitutional because it gave the Supreme Court power that had not been granted by the Constitution. Congress had to amend the act. This established the principle of judicial review and strengthened the power of the Court'.)*

Further Instruction

Go through the Interactive Reading Notepad questions and discuss the answers with the class. Assign the Supreme Court Case: *Marbury* v. *Madison*. Have students summarize the issues, decisions, and significance of this landmark case.

Support Ideas With Evidence Describe the leadership qualities of John Marshall as an appointed leader, providing evidence for support. (*Marshall was a savvy leader who found a way to strengthen the Supreme Court, and therefore constitutional checks and balances, by declaring the law that required the Court to hear Marbury's case as unconstitutional.)*

Identify Central Issues Identify the origin of judicial review. *(In Marbury v. Madison, the Supreme Court rejected a law that it considered unconstitutional.)*

Identify Cause and Effect What were the congressional and presidential responses to judicial review during Jefferson's presidency and how did they affect the court's power? *(Congress amended the part of the Judiciary Act ruled unconstitutional. By accepting the Court's ruling and changing the law, Congress affirmed and upheld the Court's power. Jefferson asserted the power of the President to resist some court orders, but he ultimately accepted the process of judicial review.)*

DIGITAL TEXT 3

The Louisiana Purchase

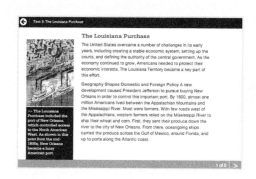

The Louisiana Purchase

The United States overcame a number of challenges in its early years, including creating a stable economic system, setting up the courts, and defining the authority of the central government. As the economy continued to grow, Americans needed to protect their economic interests. The Louisiana Territory became a key part of this effort.

Geography Shapes Domestic and Foreign Policy A new development caused President Jefferson to pursue buying New Orleans in order to control this important port. By 1800, almost one million Americans lived between the Appalachian Mountains and the Mississippi River. Most were farmers. With few roads west of the Appalachians, western farmers relied on the Mississippi River to ship their wheat and corn. First, they sent their produce down the river to the city of New Orleans. From there, oceangoing ships carried the produce across the Gulf of Mexico, around Florida, and up to ports along the Atlantic coast.

>> The Louisiana Purchase included the port of New Orleans, which controlled access to the North American West. As shown in this print from the mid-1800s, New Orleans became a busy American port.

1 of 8 >

Objective 3: Identify the causes and effects of the Louisiana Purchase.

Quick Instruction

Project the map of the Louisiana Purchase on the whiteboard. Identify the areas acquired through the Louisiana Purchase.

Generate Explanations Explain the significance of the following date: 1803. *(In the year 1803, the United States acquired the Louisiana Purchase, which doubled the size of the United States.)*

Analyze Maps How did the physical geography of the United States affect the decision to purchase the Louisiana Territory? *(Farmers between the Appalachian Mountains and the Mississippi River shipped wheat and corn down the Mississippi to New Orleans and then to Atlantic ports. Purchasing the territory allowed the United States to control this shipping route.)*

Further Instruction

Go through the Interactive Reading Notepad questions and discuss the answers with the class. Be sure students can explain the significance of the Louisiana Purchase and identify the areas acquired to form the United States.

Summarize Describe the contributions of James Monroe to the expansion of the United States *(Along with Robert Livingston, he negotiated with the French to buy Louisiana.)*

Jefferson's Presidency

DIGITAL TEXT 4

Exploring the Louisiana Territory

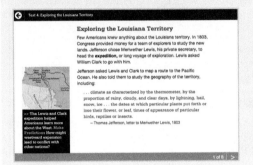

INTERACTIVE MAP

Expansion and Exploration

Draw Conclusions How did the Louisiana Purchase enable leaders of the new Republic to maintain national security? *(The purchase allowed the United States to control the Mississippi, keeping France from building an empire in North America.)*

Identify Cause and Effect What factors caused Jefferson to purchase the Louisiana Territory? What were the effects of this purchase on the early Republic? *(Causes— Napoleon wanted to sell North American territory; Jefferson wanted to control the Mississippi and the port at New Orleans. Effects—the United States doubled its area and controlled lands west of the Mississippi.)*

Objective 4: **Describe the discoveries of Lewis, Clark, and Pike.**

Quick Instruction

Interactive Map: Expansion and Exploration Project the interactive map on the whiteboard and click through the layers. Identify the areas of the Louisiana Purchase explored by Lewis, Clark, and Pike.

Draw Conclusions How did Lewis and Clark's expedition impact U.S. expansion? *(They traveled through areas such as Oregon that were later acquired to form the United States.)*

📷 ACTIVE CLASSROOM

Pair students to use the Audio Tour Strategy to locate places of importance in the United States during the 19th century. Have the first student give the second a verbal tour of the interactive map and the routes it shows. Have the second student explain the significance of the routes and what the map means.

Further Instruction
Go through the Interactive Reading Notepad questions and discuss the answers with the class.

Identify Cause and Effect Identify the effects of Lewis, Clark, and Pike's expeditions on the early Republic. *(Lewis and Clark brought back useful information about the geography of the Louisiana Territory, met Native American groups, and claimed the Oregon Country for the United States. Pike expanded American knowledge about the Southwest.)*

Identify Steps in a Process How did Louisiana gain statehood? *(Settlers moved to the region around the Mississippi River and New Orleans. When the territory had enough U.S. citizens, settlers applied for statehood.)*

DIGITAL TEXT 5

American Shipping Faces Challenges

DIGITAL TEXT 6

A Painful Embargo

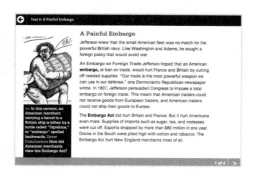

INTERACTIVE CHART

Jefferson's Goals and Policies

Objective 5: Explain Jefferson's foreign policy, including conflict with the Barbary States, threats to U.S. neutrality, and the Embargo Act.

Quick Instruction

Interactive Chart: Jefferson's Goals and Policies Project the interactive chart on the whiteboard and read through Jefferson's goals and policies. Ask students to describe how Jefferson addressed domestic problems such as creating a stable economic system, maintaining national security, and defining the authority of the central government.

Identify Cause and Effect Give an example of how the acquisition of new areas through the Louisiana Purchase affected the U.S. economy. *(Traders bought and sold furs from Native Americans in the region.)*

> ### 👥 ACTIVE CLASSROOM
>
> Have students Take a Stand on the following question: Were Jefferson's efforts to maintain national security and create a stable economic system during his presidency successful? Ask students to talk with each other to compare their reasons for answering yes or no, providing examples for support.

ELL Use the ELL activity described in the ELL chart.

Further Instruction

Go through the Interactive Reading Notepad questions and discuss the answers with the class.

The United States would not be able to remain neutral in the conflict between Britain and France. Fighting with Native Americans in the Ohio Valley eventually drew the Untied States into war with Britain.

Summarize Describe Jefferson's foreign policy. *(Jefferson tried to avoid war and protect American shipping abroad. He ordered the navy to blockade the port of Tripoli and launched a surprise attack to keep Tripoli from interfering with American ships. Rather than go to war with Britain and France, he imposed an embargo on trade.)*

Evaluate Arguments Do you think Jefferson's Embargo Act reflected a free-enterprise system of economics? Why or why not? *(No; the Embargo Act reflected government intervention rather than a free-enterprise system.)*

Compare Points of View Identify the different points of view of both Democratic Republicans and Federalists toward the Embargo Act. *(Democratic Republicans generally supported the Embargo as a means to punish Britain and France. Federalists were generally against the Embargo, because they felt it would hurt the American economy to not trade with two significant countries.)*

Jefferson's Presidency

■ SYNTHESIZE

■ DEMONSTRATE

DIGITAL ACTIVITY

The Impact of Judicial Review

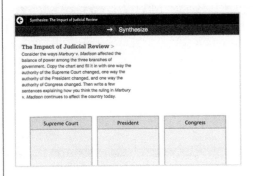

Have students fill in the chart with the ways *Marbury* v. *Madison* affected the three branches of government and explain how the ruling affects the country today. Have students compare their charts with a partner.

Have partners review their charts and consider the following question. How did the landmark case *Marbury* v. *Madison* reflect the principle of checks and balances? Have partners share their answers with the class.

Discuss Have students review the predictions they made at the beginning of the lesson about how judicial review would affect the relationship between Congress, the President, and the Court. Ask students whether they would change their answer now that they have learned more about the significance of judicial review and the responses of Congress and the President.

DIGITAL QUIZ

Lesson Quiz and Class Discussion Board

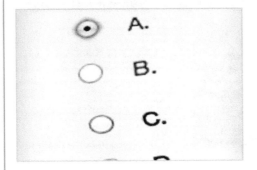

Assign the online Lesson Quiz for this lesson if you haven't already done so. Students will be offered automatic remediation or enrichment based on their score.

Pose these questions to the class on the Discussion Board:

In *Jefferson's Presidency*, you read about the significance of the Louisiana Purchase and the landmark Supreme Court case *Marbury* v. *Madison*.

Identify Central Issues What areas acquired through the Louisiana Purchase allowed the United States to better maintain its national security, and why? *(Control of the Mississippi River and its mouth, including the port of New Orleans, gave the United States better control of its national security since these waterways were vital for settlers in the lands west of the Appalachian Mountains, and any foreign power controlling them could threaten those settlers.)*

Draw Conclusions Why is *Marbury* v. *Madison* considered such a significant Supreme Court case? *(The case established the power of judicial review for the Supreme Court, that is the power to review the constitutionality of laws passed by Congress.)*

Support Ideas with Examples Give an example of Jefferson's use of the authority of the central government during his presidency. *(Possible responses include the Louisiana Purchase and the Embargo Act.)*

Topic Inquiry
Have students continue their investigations for the Topic Inquiry.

Madison and the War of 1812

Supporting English Language Learners

Use with Digital Text 2, **The Causes of the War of 1812.**

Reading
Introduce the text by reading and discussing the title and subheadings in order to model using support from peers and teachers to read grade-appropriate content area text and to develop vocabulary needed to comprehend increasingly challenging language.

Beginning Pre-teach key words from the introductory paragraphs to help students read grade-appropriate content area text and develop vocabulary needed to read and comprehend increasingly challenging language. Then echo read the paragraphs under "War Is Declared" with students. Encourage them to ask you the meanings of additional words after the reading.

Intermediate Pre-teach key words from the text to help students read grade-appropriate content area text and develop vocabulary needed to comprehend increasingly challenging language. Then have students read the text in small groups, assisting one another with additional word meanings and pronunciation as needed.

Advanced Have pairs of students read the text, paragraph by paragraph. Encourage them to develop vocabulary needed to comprehend increasingly challenging language by asking each other to clarify word meanings as they read, as well as asking you or their partner for help with pronunciation.

Advanced High Have students read grade-appropriate content area text independently. As they read, encourage them to make note of unfamiliar words. Then they can develop vocabulary needed to comprehend increasingly challenging language.Encourage students who have mastered vocaulary to help their peers.

Use with Digital Text 5, **The War's Conclusion.**

Listening
Reference the last paragraph of the section titled *Untrained Armies Fall in Washington.* Have students listen to a recording of "The Star-Spangled Banner" to build and reinforce concept attainment. Remind students that "The Star-Spangled Banner"is the U.S. national anthem and was inspired by the War of 1812.

Beginning Play a recording of "The Star-Spangled Banner."Then display key vocabulary from the anthem (e.g., *star-spangled banner, land of the free, home of the brave*) Explain their meanings in order to build and reinforce concept and language attainment.

Intermediate Play a recording of "The Star-Spangled Banner." Then display the lyrics. Explain the meanings of key words and phrases, and encourage students to ask for additional clarification in order to build and reinforce concept and language attainment.

Advanced Play a recording of "The Star-Spangled Banner." Then assign one or two different lines from the anthem to pairs of students. Ask them to restate the lines in their own words and explain the lines' significance in order to build and reinforce concept and language attainment. Have pairs share their work.

Advanced High Play a recording of "The Star-Spangled Banner." Then assign one or two different lines from the anthem to pairs of students. Ask them to restate the lines in their own words and explain the lines' significance in order to build and reinforce concept and language attainment. Have pairs share their work.

▶ Differentiate Instruction

Use the Differentiated Instruction notes throughout the lesson plan to support the varied skill sets, levels of readiness, and interests in the mixed-ability classroom.

Challenge These notes include suggestions for expanding the activity for advanced students.

On-Level These notes include suggestions for modifying the activity to address different interests or learning styles.

Extra Support These notes include ideas for providing more scaffolding or reading spuport.

Special Needs These notes provide ideas for adapting instruction to support the needs of various special needs students.

◼ NOTES

Madison and the War of 1812

Objectives

Objective 1: Explain the reasons for conflict between white settlers and Native Americans during the early 1800s.

Objective 2: Identify the causes of the War of 1812.

Objective 3: Explain the challenges that the United States faced in preparing for war.

Objective 4: Describe the important events and effects of the War of 1812.

LESSON 5 ORGANIZER		OBJECTIVES	PACING	RESOURCES Online	Print
Connect					
DIGITAL START UP ACTIVITY **Making Predictions About the War of 1812**			5 min.	●	
Investigate					
DIGITAL TEXT 1 **Conflict in Ohio**		Objective 1	10 min.	●	●
INTERACTIVE MAP **Indian Lands Lost by 1810**			10 min.	●	
DIGITAL TEXT 2 **The Causes of the War of 1812**		Objective 2	10 min.	●	●
DIGITAL TEXT 3 **Early Events in the War of 1812**		Objective 3	10 min.	●	●
DIGITAL TEXT 4 **The War in Canada**			10 min.	●	●
DIGITAL TEXT 5 **The War's Conclusion**		Objective 4	10 min.	●	●
INTERACTIVE MAP **The War of 1812**			10 min.	●	
DIGITAL TEXT 6 **The Effects of the War of 1812**			10 min.	●	●
Synthesize					
DIGITAL ACTIVITY **Causes and Effects of the War of 1812**			5 min.	●	
Demonstrate					
DIGITAL QUIZ **Lesson Quiz and Class Discussion Board**			10 min.	●	

PACING: APPROX. 1 PERIOD, .5 BLOCKS

PEARSON
realize™
www.PearsonRealize.com

Go online to access additional resources including:
Primary Sources • Biographies • Supreme Court cases •
21st Century Skill Tutorials • Maps • Graphic Organizers.

CONNECT

DIGITAL START UP ACTIVITY
Making Predictions About the War of 1812

Project the Start Up Activity Have students read the activity and predict who supported the war, who was against war, and why the pro-war faction won out. Have students share their predictions with a partner, either in class or through a blog space.

Discuss Write why some people might have been in favor of the war. *(Nationalism; anger toward the British)* Write down why others might have been against the war. *(Favored neutrality; disagreed with the reasons for fighting; feared the war's impact on the economy; questioned whether the U.S. military was strong enough to win)* Predict the pro-war faction won out in the end. *(More Americans favored war.)*

Aa Vocabulary Development: Use the Interactive Reading Notepad to preview the Key Terms and Academic Vocabulary in this lesson with students.

🔃 FLIP IT!
Assign the Flipped Video for this lesson.

STUDENT EDITION PRINT PAGES 270–281

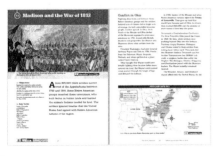

INVESTIGATE

DIGITAL TEXT 1
Conflict in Ohio

Objective 1: Explain the reasons for conflict between white settlers and Native Americans during the early 1800s.

Quick Instruction

Interactive Map: Indian Lands Lost by 1810 Project the interactive map and click through the squares. Have students locate the area of Ohio on the map and discuss its importance.

Make Predictions How will conflicts in Ohio help to causes of the War of 1812? *(The British will fuel Native American attacks on U.S. settlements, drawing the United States into war with Britain.)*

🎦 ACTIVE CLASSROOM

Divide students into groups and give them pieces of paper listing important events from the lesson, including: settlers move past the Appalachians, Little Turtle and Blue Jacket organize a resistance movement, Battle of Fallen Timbers, Treaty of Greenville, Tecumseh forms a confederation, Prophetstown is built, Battle of Tippecanoe. You may use more or fewer events depending on the size of the groups. Have groups use the Sequence It Strategy to put the lists in order.

INTERACTIVE MAP
Indian Lands Lost by 1810

Further Instruction

Go through the Interactive Reading Notepad questions and discuss the answers with the class. Be sure students understand why fighting broke out in Ohio and why this was a cause of the War of 1812.

Identify Central Issues Why did leaders of the new Republic have difficulty maintaining national security along the frontier? *(Fighting broke out when white settlers moved west of the Appalachian Mountains, taking over land where Native American groups lived.)*

Infer How do you think human geographic factors contributed to the fighting between Native American groups and white settlers along the frontier? *(The white settlers and Native American groups had different cultures and ways of life. They were competing over land and resources.)*

Madison and the War of 1812

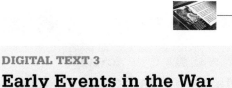

DIGITAL TEXT 2

The Causes of the War of 1812

DIGITAL TEXT 3

Early Events in the War of 1812

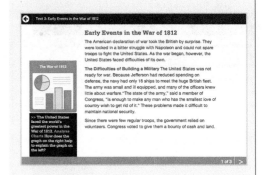

Objective 2: Identify the causes of the War of 1812.

Quick Instruction

Project the image of Henry Clay on the whiteboard. Define the War Hawks as southern and western members of Congress who pushed for war with Britain.

Compare Points of View What were the causes the War Hawks gave for engaging in the War of 1812? Why did some Americans not think these causes justified going to war? *(Nationalism and defending American rights; punishing Britain for seizing American ships; conquering Canada and Florida; bringing safety to the frontier. New Englanders feared the British would attack their seaports. Others thought the war was only to increase U.S. territory and power.)*

D Differentiate: Extra Support Explain that a hawk is a large bird of prey. Ask students why they think a hawk also refers to a person who aggressively pushes for war.

ELL Use the ELL activity described in the ELL chart.

Further Instruction

Go through the Interactive Reading Notepad questions and discuss the answers with the class. Be sure students can explain the causes of the War of 1812.

Cite Evidence from the text to explain the causes of the War of 1812? *(Britain was seizing American ships, blockading ports, and arming Native Americans to fight white settlers on the frontier.)*

Identify Steps in a Process Identify James Madison's foreign policy and how it was connected to the causes of the War of 1812. *(Madison offered to reopen trade with Britain if Britain stopped seizing ships. When Britain refused, he continued to ban shipments to and from Britain. After the British blockaded American ports and continued to impress American sailors, Madison declared war.)*

Objective 3: Explain the challenges the United States faced in preparing for war.

Quick Instruction

Project the image of the U.S.S. *Constitution* and the HMS *Guerriere*. Explain that Britain had a much stronger navy than the United States. The major domestic problems faced by the new Republic included building a military and maintaining national security.

Identify Cause and Effect Why didn't the new Republic have a strong military? *(Jefferson had reduced defense spending. As a result the army was small, ill-equipped, and untrained.)*

Further Instruction

Go through the Interactive Reading Notepad questions and discuss the answers with the class. Be sure students understand why building a military and maintaining national security were major domestic problems for the new Republic.

Summarize How did the United States go about building a military at the start of the War of 1812? *(Congress paid volunteers in cash and land.)*

Generate Explanations Explain the importance of the battle between the U.S.S. *Constitution* and the HMS *Guerriere*. *(The United States did not have a strong navy. Nevertheless, the* Constitution *was able to defeat the British ship.)*

DIGITAL TEXT 4

The War in Canada

>> Present-day Toronto, then called York, was captured by U.S. forces on April 27, 1813.

Objective 4: Describe the important events and effects of the War of 1812.

Quick Instruction

Interactive Map: The War of 1812 Project the interactive map on the whiteboard and click through the red circles.

Analyze Maps Why was the Battle of Lake Erie such an important event in the War of 1812? *(It ensured that the United States would retain its lands along the Great Lakes, letting the Americans use the waterways for transportation and to control surrounding lands.)*

DIGITAL TEXT 5

The War's Conclusion

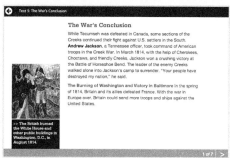

>> The British burned the White House and other public buildings in Washington, D.C., in August 1814.

🗣 ACTIVE CLASSROOM

Divide the interactive map into four numbered quadrants. Have students count off one to four and then use the A Closer Look Strategy to look at the part of the image in their quadrant. Have them tell you what they see and what they learned about the important events of the War of 1812 as a result of their focus. Have students share their insights with the class.

ELL Use the ELL activity described in the ELL chart.

INTERACTIVE MAP

The War of 1812

Further Instruction

Go through the Interactive Reading Notepad questions and discuss the answers with the class. Be sure students can explain the important events of the War of 1812, such as the Battle of Lake Erie, the burning of Washington, victory in Baltimore, and the Battle of New Orleans, as well as the war's effects on the early Republic.

Identify Cause and Effect Explain the effects of the War of 1812. *(The war hurt the economy of New England and led to opposition to the war by Federalists there. U.S. success in the war in turn permanently weakened the Federalist Party. The ability to resist Britain at war may have earned the United States greater respect. Another effect of the war was to strengthen the American national identity.)*

Madison and the War of 1812

 SYNTHESIZE

DIGITAL TEXT 6
The Effects of the War of 1812

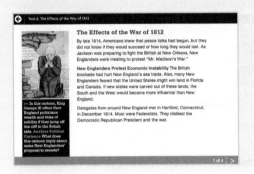

Identify Cause and Effect What was the effect of the War of 1812 on Native Americans? How did the war resolve the conflicts between white settlers and Native American groups? *(The war was devastating for Native American groups. With Tecumseh's defeat, the Indian confederation fell apart. The Creeks also lost to Jackson in the Battle of Horseshoe Bend.)*

DIGITAL ACTIVITY
Causes and Effects of the War of 1812

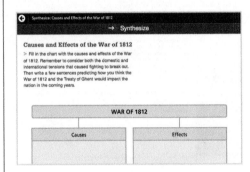

Have students fill in the chart with the causes and effects of the War of 1812 and make a prediction about how the war and the Treaty of Ghent would affect the nation. Have students compare their charts with a partner.

Have partners review their charts and consider the following question. What were the benefits and drawbacks of Madison's foreign policy with regard to Britain? Have partners share their answers with the class.

Discuss Have students review the predictions they made at the beginning of the lesson about why the pro-war faction would win out and consider whether they agree with faction's arguments for war. Ask students whether they would change their answer now that they have learned more about the causes and effects of the War of 1812.

DEMONSTRATE

DIGITAL QUIZ
Lesson Quiz and Class Discussion Board

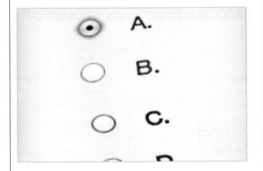

Assign the online Lesson Quiz for this lesson if you haven't already done so. Students will be offered automatic remediation or enrichment based on their score.

Pose these questions to the class on the Discussion Board:

In *Madison and the War of 1812*, you read about the causes, effects, and important events of Madison's foreign policy and the War of 1812.

Evaluate Arguments Based on the effects of the War of 1812, do you think it was worth it for the United States to go to war? Explain your reasoning. *(Sample answers: Yes, the war forced Britain to respect the sovereignty of the United States. No, nothing significant was gained, and it would have been better to negotiate over the issues.)*

Generate Explanations Why did the United States and Britain go to war in 1812? *(Britain was attacking American shipping and kidnapping American sailors. Meanwhile, American War Hawks wanted to punish Britain and conquer its colony, Canada. In response, President Madison asked Congress to declare war.)*

Topic Inquiry
Have students continue their investigations for the Topic Inquiry.

Monroe's Presidency

Supporting English Language Learners

Use with Digital Text 4, **Latin America Wins Independence.**

Listening
Orally highlight language used in the text that pertains to Mexico's relationship with and struggle for independence from Spain in order to prompt students to understand the general meaning of spoken language in which topics are unfamiliar.

Beginning Using basic spoken language, tell students about the relative locations of Spain and Mexico. Then have students show that they understand the general meaning of your words in a phrase or sentence.

Intermediate Using spoken language, summarize the section titled *Mexico Gains Independence*. Then ask students to show that they understand the general meaning of your words by restating your main idea.

Advanced Using spoken language, paraphrase the section titled *Mexico Gains Independence*. Then ask students to show that they understand the general meaning of your words by summarizing what you said.

Advanced High Using spoken language, describe the life of Miguel Hidalgo (using details that are unfamiliar to students and not provided in the text). Ask students to show that they understand the general meaning of your words by summarizing what you said.

Use with Digital Text 6, **The Monroe Doctrine.**

Reading
Review the word *doctrine* to prepare students for reading and comprehending the text. Prompt students to use support from peers and teachers to enhance and confirm understanding.

Beginning Echo read the paragraph that defines the Monroe Doctrine and have students complete this sentence: The Monroe Doctrine said that the United States would not _____. Add details to, or ask questions about, students' responses in order to enhance and confirm their understanding of the paragraph.

Intermediate Read aloud the paragraph that defines the Monroe Doctrine and the following paragraph, or invite volunteers to do so. Ask students to define the Monroe Doctrine. Add details to, or ask questions about, students' responses in order to enhance and confirm their understanding of the paragraphs.

Advanced Have pairs of students read the paragraph that defines the Monroe Doctrine and the following paragraph, and discuss the meaning of the Monroe Doctrine. Encourage them to respond to, add to, and ask questions about each other's statements in order to enhance and confirm their understanding of the paragraphs.

Advanced High Have students independently read the text. With a partner, have them define the Monroe Doctrine and describe its influence on world events. Encourage students to ask questions and build on each other's statements in order to enhance and confirm their understanding of the text.

◨ Differentiate Instruction

Use the Differentiated Instruction notes throughout the lesson plan to support the varied skill sets, levels of readiness, and interests in the mixed-ability classroom.

Challenge These notes include suggestions for expanding the activity for advanced students.

On-Level These notes include suggestions for modifying the activity to address different interests or learning styles.

Extra Support These notes include ideas for providing more scaffolding or reading spuport.

Special Needs These notes provide ideas for adapting instruction to support the needs of various special needs students.

▮ NOTES

Monroe's Presidency

Objectives

Objective 1: Explain the significance of regional differences during the Era of Good Feelings.

Objective 2: Identify different points of view on tariffs.

Objective 3: Explain how the Supreme Court under John Marshall expanded federal power.

Objective 4: Describe the impact of revolution in Latin America.

Objective 5: Explain U.S. foreign policy under Monroe, including the Monroe Doctrine and policies toward Florida.

LESSON 6 ORGANIZER		PACING: APPROX. 1 PERIOD, .5 BLOCKS			
				RESOURCES	
		OBJECTIVES	**PACING**	**Online**	**Print**
Connect					
DIGITAL START UP ACTIVITY **The Era of Good Feelings**			5 min.	●	
Investigate					
DIGITAL TEXT 1 **Sectionalism in the Era of Good Feelings**		Objective 1	10 min.	●	●
DIGITAL TEXT 2 **Creating a Stable Economy After the War**		Objective 2	10 min.	●	●
INTERACTIVE CHART **The Beginnings of Sectionalism**			10 min.	●	
DIGITAL TEXT 3 **Supreme Court Decisions Expand Federal Power**		Objective 3	10 min.	●	●
INTERACTIVE GALLERY **The Expansion of Federal Power**			10 min.	●	
DIGITAL TEXT 4 **Latin America Wins Independence**		Objective 4	10 min.	●	●
DIGITAL TEXT 5 **Gaining Florida**		Objective 5	10 min.	●	●
DIGITAL TEXT 6 **The Monroe Doctrine**			10 min.	●	●
Synthesize					
DIGITAL ACTIVITY **The Legacy of President Monroe**			5 min.	●	
Demonstrate					
DIGITAL QUIZ **Lesson Quiz and Class Discussion Board**			10 min.	●	

Go online to access additional resources including:
Primary Sources • Biographies • Supreme Court cases •
21st Century Skill Tutorials • Maps • Graphic Organizers.

CONNECT

DIGITAL START UP ACTIVITY

The Era of Good Feelings

Project the Start Up Activity Have students read the questions and make a list of why they think people felt optimistic about the country following the War of 1812.

Discuss How did America fare at the end of the War of 1812? *(Americans were patriotic. Its borders were preserved. Industry grew as a result of the war.)* What political and economic changes were underway at this time? *(Decline of the Federalists; feelings of national unity; economic growth followed by instability)* What challenges do you think the country still faced? *(Divisions between North and South; the unresolved question of slavery; economic instabilities)*

Aa Vocabulary Development: Use the Interactive Reading Notepad to preview the Key Terms and Academic Vocabulary in this lesson with students.

⮌ FLIP IT!
Assign the Flipped Video for this lesson.

■ STUDENT EDITION PRINT PAGES: 282–294

■ INVESTIGATE

DIGITAL TEXT 1

Sectionalism in the Era of Good Feelings

Objective 1: Explain the significance of regional differences during the Era of Good Feelings.

Quick Instruction
Project the image of James Monroe. Monroe was a Democratic Republican who hoped to create a sense of national unity after the war.

Identify Central issues How did James Monroe contribute to feelings of national unity after the war? What caused a rift in this harmony? *(Monroe was popular and completed a goodwill tour after his election. However, the rise of sectionalism sharpened divisions within the country.)*

D Differentiate: Extra Support Help students understand the causes of sectionalism by having them locate the different regions of the early Republic on a map: North (the present-day Northeast), South, and West (the present-day Midwest). Explain that each of these regions was known as a section. Ask students to identify at least one way in which the sections differed.

Further Instruction
Go through the Interactive Reading Notepad questions and discuss the answers with the class.

Identify Cause and Effect Explain what sectionalism is and identify its causes. *(Sectionalism is loyalty to one's region or section rather than to the nation. The causes of sectionalism include differences in the culture and economies of the regions. These*

differencs led people to emphasize differences between the regions and identify with their sections.)

Compare and Contrast the leadership qualities of Calhoun, Webster, and Clay. On what points did they disagree? *(Calhoun — energetic and intense speaker from the South; supported slavery and states' rights. Webster — skilled public speaker from the North; against the War of 1812 and slavery, favored more powerful federal government. Clay — known as a charming speaker from the West; favored war and an active federal government.)*

Make Generalizations Identify the economic differences between the North and South. *(The North's economy was based on manufacturing and trade. The southern economy was agrarian.)*

Monroe's Presidency

DIGITAL TEXT 2

Creating a Stable Economy After the War

INTERACTIVE CHART

The Beginnings of Sectionalism

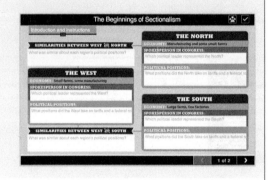

DIGITAL TEXT 3

Supreme Court Decisions Expand Federal Power

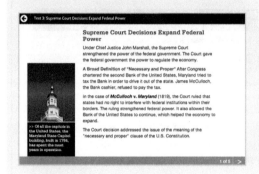

Objective 2: **Identify different points of view on tariffs.**

Quick Instruction

Interactive Chart: The Beginnings of Sectionalism Project the interactive chart and read through the tiles. Have students describe how each leader wanted to approach the major domestic problems faced by the new Republic, including creating a stable economic system and defining the authority of the central government.

Compare and Contrast Analyze the impact of the Tariff of 1816 on sections of the United States, that is, on the North, West, and South. *(North—benefited from the tariff as goods produced by northern factories became cheaper than imported goods. The North could sell more. South and West—had to pay more for imported goods or buy more expensive northern goods.)*

📖 ACTIVE CLASSROOM

Have students use the Write 1-Get 3 Strategy to answer the question: What are four key areas in which sectional leaders disagreed? Have students take a piece of paper and fold it into quarters. Students write down one response in the first box and then go around the room asking to hear other responses. When students think a response is correct, they write it in one of their boxes until they have three more responses on their pages. Have students share their responses with the class.

Further Instruction

Go through the Interactive Reading Notepad questions and discuss the answers with the class.

Summarize Summarize Henry Clay's arguments for protective tariffs. Why did he think tariffs were a good compromise to appeal to different sections of the United States? *(Clay believed tariffs would help the economies of the North, South, and West. He argued that high tariffs would give northerners the money to buy farm products from the South and West. In addition, Congress could use money raised from tariffs for internal improvements to help farmers in these regions.)*

Compare Points of View Explain the arguments for and against the banking system. Why did Democratic Republicans change their point of view on the Bank of the United States? *(For—A central bank could lend money and regulate the money supply to keep prices from rising. Against—Democratic Republicans initially argued a national bank was unconstitutional and gave the federal government too much power. Later they decided a central bank was necessary to create a stable economy.)*

Objective 3: **Explain how the Supreme Court under John Marshall expanded federal power.**

Quick Instruction

Interactive Gallery: The Expansion of Federal Power Project the interactive gallery and click through the images.

Generate Explanations Summarize the decision of the Supreme Court in *McCulloch v. Maryland* as well as the issues behind the decision and its significance. *(The issues were whether a national bank was constitutional and whether a state could regulate an arm of the federal government. The Court interpreted the necessary and proper clause of the Constitution to mean Congress had the power to charter a national bank. This increased the authority of the federal government.)*

Summarize the issues behind the landmark case *Gibbons v. Ogden*. What was the court's decision and the significance of this decision? *(A steamboat company wanted to retain a monopoly on interstate travel granted by New York State. The Court ruled that only the federal government has the power to regulate interstate commerce. This increased federal power over the states and helped the economy by creating a unified nationwide market.)*

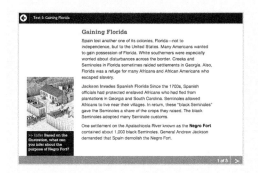

INTERACTIVE GALLERY

The Expansion of Federal Power

DIGITAL TEXT 4

Latin America Wins Independence

DIGITAL TEXT 5

Gaining Florida

ACTIVE CLASSROOM

Have students Take a Stand on the significance of *McCulloch* v. *Maryland*. Was this expansion of federal power relative to the states constitutional? Have students divide into two groups based on their answer and move to separate areas of the classroom. Have students compare their reasons for answering yes or no. Then ask a representative from each side to share and defend the group's point of view.

Further Instruction

Go through the Interactive Reading Notepad questions and discuss the answers with the class. To extend the lesson, assign the Supreme Court cases *McCulloch* v. *Maryland* and *Gibbons* v. *Ogden*. Be sure students can summarize the issues, decisions, and significance of both landmark cases.

Draw Conclusions Why was the Court's ruling in *McCulloch* v. *Maryland* controversial? *(The Court took a loose-constructionist view of the Constitution, deciding the necessary and proper clause gave Congress the power to charter the Bank. Some people argued the Court should take a strict-constructionist view and grant Congress only those powers stated in the Constitution.)*

Support Ideas With Examples Give an example of how John Marshall's leadership defined the authority of the central government. *(Granting Congress powers through the necessary and proper clause and giving the federal government sole power to regulate interstate commerce strengthened the central government. Government could take actions not stated in the Constitution and oversee state activities.)*

Objective 4: Identify the impact of revolution in Latin America.

Quick Instruction
Project the map of new nations in Latin America. Have students identify the new nations formed by revolutions.

Make Predictions How do you think revolutions in Latin America would impact Monroe's foreign policy? *(He would have to decide on a foreign policy toward the new nations.)*

ELL Use the ELL activity described in the ELL chart.

Further Instruction
Go through the Interactive Reading Notepad questions and discuss the answers with the class. Discuss the impact of revolutions in Latin American on U.S. foreign policy.

Compare and Contrast America's Revolutionary War to the revolutionary movements in Latin America. *(Compare— As in the United States, colonies fought for independence from European powers. Contrast—The U.S. colonies united to form a single country; the United States adopted and maintained a democratic government while many Latin American countries did not; not all of the revolutions in Latin America were violent.)*

Hypothesize How do you think revolutions in Latin American affected the United States? *(Monroe had to develop his foreign policy toward the new nations; Americans may have been glad to see other colonies rebelling against European powers and establishing their own governments.)*

Objective 5: Explain U.S. foreign policy under Monroe, including policies toward Florida and the Monroe Doctrine.

Quick Instruction
Project the image of Monroe with his cabinet. Explain that Monroe created a new foreign policy regarding Latin America that has affected that region ever since.

Generate Explanations Explain the Monroe Doctrine and its impact. *(The Doctrine stated that the United States would not interfere with European nations or their colonies, but that the United States would oppose new European attempts to colonize the Americas. The Doctrine kept Europe from intervening in the newly independent republics in the Americas, affirming their independence.)*

ELL Use the ELL activity described in the ELL chart.

Further Instruction
Go through the Interactive Reading Notepad questions and discuss the answers with the class. Be sure students can identify Monroe's foreign policy, including the Monroe Doctrine.

Identify Cause and Effect How did Monroe's foreign policy toward Spain lead to the acquisition of new territory? *(The United States invaded Florida and then negotiated its purchase from Spain.)*

Monroe's Presidency

SYNTHESIZE

DEMONSTRATE

DIGITAL TEXT 6
The Monroe Doctrine

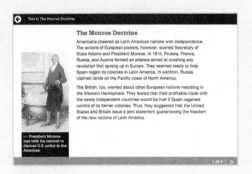

DIGITAL ACTIVITY
The Legacy of President Monroe

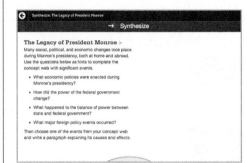

DIGITAL QUIZ
Lesson Quiz and Class Discussion Board

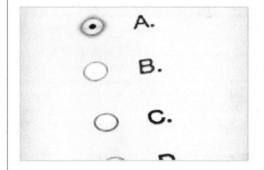

Determine Point of View Why was Monroe's statement about foreign policy toward Latin America an important historical contribution? *(European powers were crushing revolutions and seemed intent on claiming land in the Americas. Monroe aimed to keep European powers from reclaiming the former colonies. The Monroe Doctrine helped achieve this goal. It was also an important contribution because it helped shape U.S. foreign policy for more than 100 years.)*

Determine Author's Purpose Why do you think the author calls the Monroe Doctrine "bold"? Explain your reasoning. *(The author sees the doctrine as bold because the United States was still young and small in population compared to the European powers. Defying those powers was a bold step.)*

Have students complete the concept web with the significant events that took place during Monroe's presidency. Have students compare their concept webs with a partner.

Have partners review their webs and consider the following question. What domestic and foreign problems did Monroe face during his presidency, and how did he address them? Have partners share their answers with the class.

Discuss Have students review the lists they made at the beginning of the lesson about the Era of Good Feelings. Ask students whether they think this era persisted throughout Monroe's presidency, explaining why or why not.

Assign the online Lesson Quiz for this lesson if you haven't already done so. Students will be offered automatic remediation or enrichment based on their score.

Pose these questions to the class on the Discussion Board:

In *Monroe's Presidency*, you read about major domestic problems and foreign policies during Monroe's presidency.

Identify Cause and Effect In what ways did the War of 1812 cause economic change in the nation? *(The war kept British goods out of the country, which contributed to the growth of American industry until the war's end, when cheaper British goods flooded the market. Foreign competition caused New England businesses to fail. This led Congress to pass protective tariffs, which angered southerners and westerners. Economic problems convinced leaders who had initially opposed a national bank that a bank was necessary.)*

Draw Conclusions How did events during Monroe's presidency define the authority of the central government? Give examples for support. *(The central government strengthened through the Supreme Court's rulings in McCulloch v. Maryland and Gibbons v. Ogden and the creation of a national bank.)*

Topic Inquiry
Have students continue their investigations for the Topic Inquiry.

The Early Republic (1789–1825)

SYNTHESIZE

DIGITAL ACTIVITY
Reflect on the Essential Question and Topic

First ask students to reconsider the Essential Question for this Topic: What should governments do? Have students read the quote by Lincoln and consider whether they agree or disagree. Have students edit, rewrite, or completely rework his statement in their own words to provide their own view of what governments should do.

Ask students, "Do you think the U.S. government does what governments should do?" Have students review their statements about what governments should do and give an example of how the U.S. government does or does not fulfill this obligation. Discuss their statements and examples as a class or ask students to post their answers on the Class Discussion Board.

Next ask students to reflect on the Topic as a whole and write down three major events that shaped the early nation and a question about each. Have students consider the following event and question to help them get started:

1. Washington's Proclamation of Neutrality

2. Does Washington's proclamation still make sense in today's world?

Topic Inquiry
Have students complete Step 3 of the Topic Inquiry.

DEMONSTRATE

DIGITAL TOPIC REVIEW AND ASSESSMENT
The Early Republic (1789–1825)

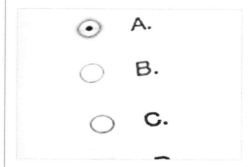

Students can prepare for the Topic Test by answering the questions in the Topic Review and Assessment online or the Assessment questions in the Print Student text. They can also prepare by reviewing their answers to the Interactive Reading Notepad questions or reviewing their notes in the Reading and Notetaking Study Guide.

DIGITAL TOPIC TEST
The Early Republic (1789–1825)

TOPIC TEST
Assign the Topic Test to assess students' understanding of topic content.

BENCHMARK TESTS
Assign these benchmark tests as you complete the relevant topics to monitor student progress toward mastering the course content and as preparation for the End-of-Course Test.

Benchmark Test 1: Topics 1–2

Benchmark Test 2: Topics 3–4

Benchmark Test 3: Topics 5–6

Benchmark Test 4: Topics 7–9

Benchmark Test 5: Topics 10–12

Benchmark Test 6: Topics 13–14

Benchmark Test 7: Topics 15–17

Topic 6

The Age of Jackson and Westward Expansion (1824–1860)

TOPIC 6 ORGANIZER	PACING: APPROX. 1 PERIOD, .5 BLOCKS	
		PACING
Connect		1 period
MY STORY VIDEO **Narcissa Whitman, Pioneer**		10 min.
DIGITAL ESSENTIAL QUESTION ACTIVITY **Why Do People Move?**		10 min.
DIGITAL OVERVIEW ACTIVITY **The Age of Jackson and Westward Expansion**		10 min.
TOPIC INQUIRY: CIVIC DISCUSSION **The U.S.-Mexican-War**		20 min.
Investigate		3–7 periods
TOPIC INQUIRY: CIVIC DISCUSSION **The U.S.-Mexican-War**		Ongoing
LESSON 1 Jackson Wins the Presidency		30–40 min.
LESSON 2 Political Conflict and Economic Crisis		30–40 min.
LESSON 3 Native Americans on the Frontier		30–40 min.
LESSON 4 Westward Movement		30–40 min.
LESSON 5 Settling Oregon Country		30–40 min.
LESSON 6 Independence for Texas		30–40 min.
LESSON 7 Manifest Destiny in California and the Southwest		30–40 min.
Synthesize		1 period
DIGITAL ESSENTIAL QUESTION ACTIVITY **Why do people move?**		10 min.
TOPIC INQUIRY: CIVIC DISCUSSION **The U.S.-Mexican-War**		20 min.
Demonstrate		1–2 periods
DIGITAL TOPIC REVIEW AND ASSESSMENT **The Age of Jackson and Westward Expansion (1824–1860)**		10 min.
TOPIC INQUIRY: CIVIC DISCUSSION **The U.S.-Mexican-War**		20 min.

TOPIC INQUIRY: CIVIC DISCUSSION

The U.S.-Mexican-War

In this Topic Inquiry, students work in teams to examine different perspectives on this issue by analyzing several sources, arguing both sides of a Yes/No question, then developing and discussing their own point of view on the question: **Was the U.S.-Mexican War justified?**

STEP 1: CONNECT
Develop Questions and Plan the Investigation

Launch the Civic Discussion

Divide the class into groups of four students. Students can access the materials they'll need in the online course or you can distribute copies to each student. Read the main question and introduction with the students.

Have students complete Step 1 by reading the Discussion Launch and filling in Step 1 of the Information Organizer. The Discussion Launch provides YES and NO arguments on the main question. Students should extract and paraphrase the arguments from the reading in Step 1 of their Information Organizers.

Next, students share within their groups the arguments and evidence they found to support the YES and NO positions. The group needs to agree on the major YES and NO points and each student should note those points in their Information Organizer.

Resources

• Student Instructions • Information Organizer • Discussion Launch

---

⏻ PROFESSIONAL DEVELOPMENT

Civic Discussion

Be sure to view the Civic Discussion Professional Development resources in the online course.

STEP 2: INVESTIGATE
Apply Disciplinary Concepts and Tools

Examine Sources and Perspectives

Students will examine sources with the goal of extracting information and perspectives on the main question. They analyze each source and describe the author's perspective on the main question and key evidence the author provides to support that viewpoint in Information Organizer Step 2.

Ask students to keep in mind:

• **Author/Creator:** Who created the source? An individual? Group? Government agency?
• **Audience:** For whom was the source created?
• **Date/Place:** Is there any information that reveals where and when the source was created?
• **Purpose:** Why was the source created? Discuss with students the importance of this question in identifying bias.
• **Relevance:** How does the source support one argument or another?

Suggestion: Reading the source documents and filling in Step 2 of the Information Organizer could be assigned as homework.

Resources

• Student Instructions • Information Organizer • Source documents

TOPIC INQUIRY: CIVIC DISCUSSION

The U.S.-Mexican-War *(continued)*

STEP 3: SYNTHESIZE
Use Evidence to Formulate Conclusions

Formulate Compelling Arguments with Evidence
Now students will apply perspectives and evidence they extracted from the sources to think more deeply about the main question by first arguing one side of the issue, then the other. In this way students become more prepared to formulate an evidence-based conclusion on their own.

Within each student group, assign half of the students to take the position of YES on the main question and the others to take the position of NO. Students will work with their partners to identify the strongest arguments and evidence to support their assigned YES or NO position.

Present Yes/No Positions
Within each group, those assigned the YES position share arguments and evidence first. As the YES students speak, those assigned NO should listen carefully, take notes to fill in the rest of the Compelling Arguments Chart (Step 3 in Information Organizer) and ask clarifying questions.

When the YES side is finished, students assigned the NO position present while those assigned YES should listen, take notes, and ask clarifying questions. Examples of clarifyin questions are:

- I think you just said [x]. Am I understanding you correctly?
- Can you tell me more about [x]?
- Can you repeat [x]? I am not sure I understand, yet.

Suggestion: You may want to set a 5 minute time limit for each side to present. Provide a two-minute warning so that students make their most compelling arguments within the time frame.

Switch Sides
The students will switch sides to argue the opposite point of view. To prepare to present the other position, partners who first argued YES will use the notes they took during the NO side's presentation, plus add any additional arguments and evidence from the reading and sources. The same for students who first argued the NO position.

STEP 4: DEMONSTRATE
Communicate Conclusions and Take Informed Action

Individual Points of View
Now the students will have the opportunity to discuss the main question from their own points of view. To help students prepare for this discussion, have them reflect on the YES/NO discussions they have participated in thus far and fill in Step 4 of their Information Organizers.

After all of the students have shared their points of view, each group should list points of agreement, filling the last portion of Step 4 on their Information Organizers.

Reflect on the Discussion
Ask students to reflect on the civic discussion thinking about:

- The value of having to argue both the YES and NO positions.
- If their individual views changed over the course of the discussion and why.
- What they learned from participating in the discussion.

Resources
- Student Instructions
- Information Organizer

INTRODUCTION

The Age of Jackson and Westward Expansion (1824–1860)

The early 1800s was an era of growth for the United States. As the United States grew in size, so too did the number of people who could participate in government.

- As more states were added to the Union, changes were made to the voting process and many more Americans could vote than ever before.
- Although democratization was beneficial to some Americans, others remained without a voice in government.
- While westward expansion was a boon for the American economy and a great opportunity for pioneers, the process was devastating to Native Americans whose homeland was being encroached upon.

■ CONNECT

MY STORY VIDEO

Narcissa Whitman, Pioneer

Now let's watch a video that tells the story of one pioneer who took part in westward expansion. It begins to explore what life was like during their journeys and reasons why Americans began moving westward.

Infer What type of person do you think would have been willing to move to the frontier in the 1800s? *(Adventurous, daring, brave, bold, courageous, fearless, a loner, gutsy)*

Identify Central Issues What kind of difficulties do you think were encountered by pioneers as they traveled West? *(Dangerous river crossings, animal attacks, diseases, hunger/thirst, broken wagons, uncomfortable sleeping arrangements, untrustworthy travel companions, uncertain encounters with Native Americans, inclement weather, desert crossings, runaway horses)*

Hypothesize Would you have been willing to make the trek? Why or why not? *(Although it sounds like it would be a very exciting experience, I don't enjoy camping or living in the outdoors and would be unwilling to travel in this manner.)*

DIGITAL ESSENTIAL QUESTION ACTIVITY

Why Do People Move?

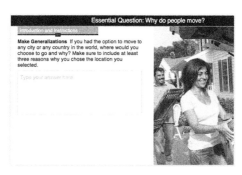

Look at the Essential Question for this Topic: Why do people move? People have moved from place to place since the dawn of time for economic, social, political, or environmental reasons.

Ask students to complete the short answer question for the Essential Question activity. Then review their responses.

Categorize Which of the reasons would be categorized as push factors and which as pull factors? *(Push: few job opportunities, overcrowding, insufficient housing, desire to live in a foreign country; Pull: a specific job opportunity, warm climate, family/friends live there)*

Identify Central Issues Why might someone move to the United States from another country? *(Political persecution/unrest, lack of jobs, better education, democratic freedom, family, better climate)*

D Differentiate: Challenge Which factor—economic, social, political, or environmental—do you think most often causes someone to move? Why do you think this is the case? *(Economic, because people move for a job or better financial opportunities. Or: Political, because many people move due to political unrest in their homeland.)*

DIGITAL OVERVIEW ACTIVITY

The Age of Jackson and Westward Expansion

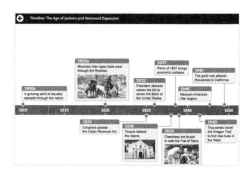

Let's look at a timeline showing the major turning points in *The Age of Jackson and Westward Expansion*. During this Topic, we'll learn about all of these events and many more. This timeline will provide a framework to place the events about which we will learn.

Use Context Clues Which items in the timeline give examples of the Topic title, *Westward Expansion*? *(Mountain men open trails west through the Rockies, the gold rush attracts thousands to California, thousands travel the Oregon Trail to find new lives in the West.)*

Identify Cause and Effect What two events do you think are linked? *(President Jackson vetoes the bill to renew the Bank of the United States and the Panic of 1837 brings economic collapse; Congress passes the Indian Removal Act and Cherokees are forced to walk the Trail of Tears.)*

Topic Inquiry

Launch the Topic Inquiry with students after introducing the topic.

Jackson Wins the Presidency

Supporting English Language Learners

Use with Digital Text 1, **Democracy Expands.**

Listening
Recall the meaning of the term *social class* with students. Prompt students to understand the meaning of spoken language in a range of situations.

Beginning Use familiar vocabulary and language structures to speak about power and voting rights in America and Europe. Have students express the general meaning of what you said by completing this sentence: White men had _____ power and voting rights in America than in Europe.

Intermediate Use familiar vocabulary and language structures to speak about the differences in social class between America and Europe. Have students express the general meaning of what you said in a sentence.

Advanced Use familiar, yet challenging, vocabulary and language structures to speak about the differences in social class between America and Europe. Ask: What is the general meaning of what I said?

Advanced High Combine challenging and unfamiliar vocabulary and language structures to speak about the differences in social class between America and Europe. Ask: What is the general meaning of what I said?

Use with Digital Text 5, **The Spoils System.**

Reading
Review the purpose of before-noun placement of an adjective in English. Support students and encourage them to use support from peers to identify when nouns can be used as adjectives. Recognizing this will prevent confusion while reading and develop their grasp of this and other language structures.

Beginning Have pairs of students work together to determine definitions for noun and adjective. Then display the phrase *government jobs*. Explain how the noun *government* acts as an adjective. Support students in grasping the noun-as-adjective language structure by helping them complete this sentence: Government jobs are jobs in _____.

Intermediate Have pairs of students work together to determine definitions for noun and adjective. Then display the phrases *government employees* and *government jobs*. Explain how the noun *government* acts as an adjective. Support students in grasping the noun-as-adjective language structure by helping them to form other phrases using *government* as an adjective.

Advanced Display the phrase *spoils system*. Explain how the noun *spoils* acts as an adjective. Then have pairs of students support each other as they search the text for three other examples of the noun-as-adjective language structure and explain their meanings.

Advanced High Display the phrases *spoils system* and *government jobs*. Explain how the nouns *spoils* and *government* act as adjectives. Then have students support each other as they write original sentences about the spoils system or Andrew Jackson that include the noun-as-adjective language structure.

▣ Differentiate Instruction

Use the Differentiated Instruction notes throughout the lesson plan to support the varied skill sets, levels of readiness, and interests in the mixed-ability classroom.

Challenge These notes include suggestions for expanding the activity for advanced students.

On-Level These notes include suggestions for modifying the activity to address different interests or learning styles.

Extra Support These notes include ideas for providing more scaffolding or reading spuport.

Special Needs These notes provide ideas for adapting instruction to support the needs of various special needs students.

▮ NOTES

PEARSON
realize™
www.PearsonRealize.com

Go online to access additional resources including:
Primary Sources • Biographies • Supreme Court cases •
21st Century Skill Tutorials • Maps • Graphic Organizers.

Objectives

Objective 1: Describe who gained suffrage by the 1820s.

Objective 2: Identify compromises made after the 1824 election, including the roles of Henry Clay and John Quincy Adams.

Objective 3: Explain the origin and development of new political parties under John Quincy Adams.

Objective 4: Describe the causes and effects of Jacksonian democracy and the impact of the election of Andrew Jackson.

Objective 5: Explain the spoils system.

LESSON 1 ORGANIZER		PACING: APPROX. 1 PERIOD, .5 BLOCKS		
	OBJECTIVES	**PACING**	**RESOURCES**	
			Online	**Print**
Connect				
DIGITAL START UP ACTIVITY **Jackson's Story**		5 min.	●	
Investigate				
DIGITAL TEXT 1 **Democracy Expands**	Objective 1	10 min.	●	●
INTERACTIVE TIMELINE **Changing Voting Rights in Early America**		10 min.	●	
DIGITAL TEXT 2 **The Election of 1824 Leads to a "Bargain"**	Objective 2	10 min.	●	●
DIGITAL TEXT 3 **The Presidency of John Quincy Adams**	Objective 3	10 min.	●	●
INTERACTIVE CHART **Political Parties in the Age of Jackson**		10 min.	●	
DIGITAL TEXT 4 **Jacksonian Democracy**	Objective 4	10 min.	●	●
INTERACTIVE CHART **Causes and Effects of Jacksonian Democracy**		10 min.	●	
DIGITAL TEXT 5 **The Spoils System**	Objective 5	10 min.	●	●
Synthesize				
DIGITAL ACTIVITY **Americans and Their Government**		5 min.	●	
Demonstrate				
DIGITAL QUIZ **Lesson Quiz and Class Discussion Board**		10 min.	●	

Jackson Wins the Presidency

■ CONNECT

DIGITAL START UP ACTIVITY
Jackson's Story

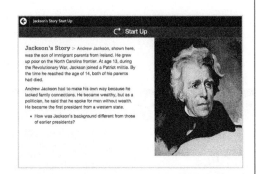

Project the Start Up Activity Ask students to answer the questions as they enter and get settled. You may have them share their ideas with another student or post them to the class discussion board.

Discuss What does Andrew Jackson's life suggest about America during the Age of Jackson? *(It suggests that people could get ahead without money or family connections; or it suggests that white people enjoyed advantages while people from other races suffered.)* How did Jackson's background influence his political positions? *(He spoke out for white men who were, like himself, from poor backgrounds.)*

Aa Vocabulary Development: Use the Interactive Reading Notepad to preview the Key Terms and Academic Vocabulary in this lesson with students.

⚡ FLIP IT!
Assign the Flipped Video for this lesson.

■ STUDENT EDITION PRINT
PAGES: 302–312

■ INVESTIGATE

DIGITAL TEXT 1
Democracy Expands

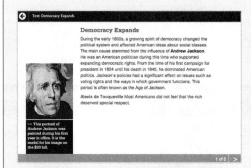

Objective 1: Describe who gained suffrage by the 1820s.

Quick Instruction
Interactive Timeline: Changing Voting Rights in America Project the interactive timeline. Discuss changes in voting rights and percentages of the population who were qualified to vote with students. During the age of Jackson, did the number of states with property qualifications for voting increase or decrease? Why? *(The number of states with property qualifications decreased. Some states removed the property qualifications and new states without property qualifications joined the United States.)*

Compare and Contrast How did the change in voting rights affect poor white men compared to free African American men? How did this change affect enslaved African Americans compared to free African Americans? *(Even though most white men had won suffrage, free African American men lost the right to vote in many states. Enslaved African Americans were not affected by this change because they had no political rights and could not vote in any state.)*

📷 ACTIVE CLASSROOM
Have students Make Headlines. Ask students to suppose they are investigative journalists who have uncovered information about voting rights over the previous few decades. Ask: If you were to write a headline about voting rights in this time frame, what would that headline be? Have students pass their headlines to a partner for revision suggestions.

INTERACTIVE TIMELINE
Changing Voting Rights in Early America

ELL Use the ELL activity described in the ELL chart.

D Differentiate: Extra Support Ask students to think carefully about what the bars above the timeline represent. Ask them to explain this relationship in their own words. Then ask them to think of ways that changes listed below the timeline could lead to changes in the height of the bars above the timeline.

Further Instruction
Integrate Information What concern does de Tocqueville suggest when he writes "It remains to be shown. . .," and how do these concerns reflect de Tocqueville's frame of reference? Cite evidence to support your response. *(His use of expressions such as "superior to the laws," "passions," and "unbounded authority" suggest that unlimited democracy could result in arbitrary or unjust government.)*

DIGITAL TEXT 2

The Election of 1824 Leads to a "Bargain"

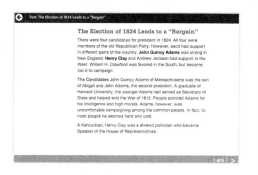

DIGITAL TEXT 3

The Presidency of John Quincy Adams

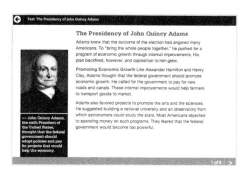

INTERACTIVE CHART

Political Parties in the Age of Jackson

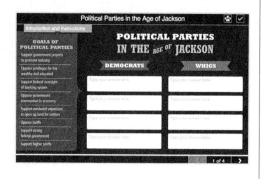

Objective 2: Identify compromises made after the 1824 election, including the roles of Henry Clay and John Quincy Adams.

Quick Instruction

In 1824, politicians had different positions, but they all belonged to the same party. There were four candidates for President, and none of them won a majority of electoral votes.

Interpret Review the image showing the constitutional process that led to the House of Representatives deciding who won 1824 presidential election. Ask students how the vote in the House was connected to the popular vote. *(In states that had a popular vote, it determined the electoral vote. The three candidates with the most electoral votes then faced a vote in the House of Representatives. However, that vote had no direct relation to the popular vote.)*

Summarize What were the roles of John Quincy Adams and Henry Clay in the congressional compromise that decided the election of 1824, and what were the effects of that compromise? *(Henry Clay urged his supporters in the House of Representatives to vote for John Quincy Adams. As a result, Adams won the election.)*

Further Instruction

Identify Cause and Effect Under what provision was the election of 1824 decided?? *(It was based on the provision of the Constitution, which states that the House is to decide presidential elections when there is no one who wins the majority of electoral votes.)*

Objective 3: Explain the origin and development of new political parties under John Quincy Adams.

Quick Instruction

Interactive Chart: Political Parties in the Age of Jackson Project the interactive chart. Ask students to consider not only which goals each party had, but also how those goals were related to one another and how they reflected the interests of each party's supporters.

Explain to students that differences between Jackson's supporters and the supporters of Adams and Clay gave rise to new American political parties during the presidency of John Quincy Adams. Explain that some of those differences were regional.

Contrast Ask student to explain the point of view of each party on the following important historic issues: the role of the federal government and tariffs? *Whigs supported a strong and active federal government; Democrats wanted a limited federal government. Whigs supported tariffs; Democrats opposed them.)*

🖳 ACTIVE CLASSROOM

Conduct a Take a Stand activity. Ask students to take a stand on the following question: During the Age of Jackson, would you have been a Whig or a Democrat?

- Ask students to divide into two groups based on their answer and move to separate areas of the classroom.

- Ask a representative from each side to present and defend the group's point of view.

Further Instruction

Identify Cause and Effect Explain the reasons for the origin and development of political parties during the presidency of John Quincy Adams. *(Jackson's supporters were angry that Adams had won the presidency even though Jackson had won more votes. Jackson's supporters differed from Adams's supporters over whether the government should have a role in the economy. Jackson's supporters opposed high tariffs and called for more political power for ordinary white men. Adams's supporters wanted the federal government to promote business and oversee banks.)*

Distinguish What role did regional interests play in the formation of political parties? *(The businesspeople who supported the Whigs and their policies of economic development were concentrated in the Northeast. Support from small farmers and workers, who backed small-government policies, gave the Democrats more influence in the South and West.)*

Jackson Wins the Presidency

DIGITAL TEXT 4

Jacksonian Democracy

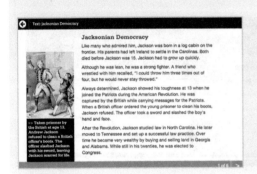

INTERACTIVE CHART

Causes and Effects of Jacksonian Democracy

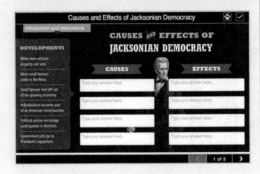

DIGITAL TEXT 5

The Spoils System

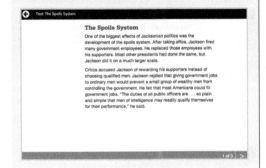

Objective 4: Describe the causes and effects of Jacksonian democracy and the impact of the election of Andrew Jackson.

Quick Instruction

Interactive Chart: Causes and Effects of Jacksonian Democracy Project the interactive chart. Ask students to think about each of the changes listed. Explicitly identify the Jackson era as a major era in U.S. history. Ask them not only to identify which changes are causes and which are effects, but also how each cause helped shape the Jackson era and how conditions during this era led to each effect.

Identify Cause and Effect After filling in the causes of the Jackson era, pick one cause and describe how that change helped shape this era. *(When white men without property gained the vote, the government became more democratic and paid more attention to ordinary people.)*

Identify Steps in a Process After filling in the effects of the Jackson era, pick one effect and describe how conditions during this era led to that effect. *(Andrew Jackson promised to help ordinary Americans. He did not think that government jobs required special qualifications, so he rewarded his supporters with government jobs.)*

📷 ACTIVE CLASSROOM

Conduct a Sequence It activity. For a key sequence of events that explain an effect of the Jackson era, give small groups of students pieces of paper and have them put the list in order.

Further Instruction

Identify Cause and Effect Explain how the impact of Andrew Jackson's election was connected to expanded suffrage? *(Jackson's Democratic Party introduced political campaigns that appealed to common people and their concerns. These campaigns motivated white men to vote and to get involved in the political process.)*

Support Ideas with Examples Describe some examples of contributions of Andrew Jackson to his country. *(He won a victory over the British and brought ordinary people into politics. However, his contributions were not all positive. For example, he took land away from Native Americans.)*

Objective 5: Explain the spoils system.

Quick Instruction

Identify Central Issues How were Jackson's political views connected with his support for the spoils system? *(Jackson believed that people with wealth, education, and connections did not deserve privilege. In his view, that meant that educated and well-connected people had no more right to government jobs than the ordinary people who supported him. Jackson believed in a powerful presidency and felt that it was his right to give his supporters jobs if he chose.)*

ELL Use the ELL activity described in the ELL chart.

Further Instruction

Draw Conclusions Explain to students that some would argue that it is wrong to give political supporters government jobs. These people would argue that only the best-qualified people should hold government jobs, regardless of their political beliefs. Others would argue that elected officials need supporters working for them in order to carry out their policies, since even the best-qualified opponent might try to undermine those policies. If time permits, ask students their opinion on this question. *(Answers will vary.)*

○ A.
○ B.
○ C.

■ SYNTHESIZE

DIGITAL ACTIVITY

Americans and Their Government

Ask students to think about each of the facts listed about citizenship and government in the Jackson era.

Discuss Ask students to think about how the relationship between Americans and their government changed under Andrew Jackson. How was that relationship connected to national identity?

■ DEMONSTRATE

DIGITAL QUIZ

Lesson Quiz and Class Discussion Board

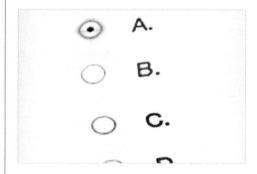

Assign the online Lesson Quiz for this lesson if you haven't already done so. Students will be offered automatic remediation or enrichment based on their score.

Pose these questions to the class on the Discussion Board:

Predict Consequences What kinds of conflicts might develop over the exclusion of some Americans from the country's democratic system? *(When an American is excluded from the democratic system, government representation and justice are lost for that person, leading to conflicts over such things as land, rights, and the benefits of being a citizen.)*

Identify Patterns What does the expansion of suffrage during this period suggest about the right to suffrage in later periods of American history? *(The expansion of suffrage suggests that even more people might be granted suffrage later in American history.)*

Topic Inquiry

Have students continue their investigations for the Topic Inquiry.

Political Conflict and Economic Crisis

Supporting English Language Learners

Use with Digital Text 2, **The Bank War.**

Reading
Prepare students for reading the text by discussing its title and headings. Encourage students to predict what background knowledge they might need in order to understand this reading. Prompt students to develop the necessary background knowledge in order to comprehend increasingly challenging language.

Beginning Develop the background knowledge students will need to comprehend the text's language by acting out the banking process. Use vocabulary from the text as you explain your actions (e.g., *bank, loan, borrow, lend*). Then have pairs of students discuss these terms and anything else they know about banking. Finally, read aloud the section titled *A Controversial Bank* as students follow along.

Intermediate Develop the background knowledge students will need to comprehend the text's language by explaining the banking process. Use vocabulary from the text to increase students' familiarity with these words. Then have pairs of students discuss what they know about banking. Finally, read aloud the text, or invite volunteers to do so.

Advanced Ask volunteers to share with their peers what they already know about banks. As they speak, record key words that will help students as they read the text. Review this vocabulary, and then have pairs of students read the text together.

Advanced High Ask volunteers to share with their peers what they already know about banks. Provide additional support by adding details about how a central bank is like and unlike a neighborhood bank. Then invite students to read the text independently.

Use with Digital Text 3, **Economic Crisis and Political Changes.**

Listening
Prompt students to understand the general meaning of spoken language ranging from situations in which contexts are familiar to unfamiliar. Provide a context for the activity by reading aloud (or revisiting) the section titled *The Panic of 1837.*

Beginning Use basic spoken language to describe the situation of the Panic of 1837. Ask students to state the general meaning of your words by completing this sentence: An economic crisis began in 1837, and Americans _____.

Intermediate Use spoken language to describe the situation of the Panic of 1837, using some details not found in the text. Ask students to state the general meaning of your words in a sentence.

Advanced Use spoken language to explain the word *depression* in the contexts of both the Panic of 1837 and the Great Depression. Ask students to state the general meaning of your words in a sentence or two.

Advanced High Use spoken language to explain the word *depression* in both familiar and unfamiliar contexts (e.g., economic and psychological). After you compare and contrast the meanings of depression in these contexts, ask students to state the general meaning of your words in a sentence or two.

◘ Differentiate Instruction

Use the Differentiated Instruction notes throughout the lesson plan to support the varied skill sets, levels of readiness, and interests in the mixed-ability classroom.

Challenge These notes include suggestions for expanding the activity for advanced students.

On-Level These notes include suggestions for modifying the activity to address different interests or learning styles.

Extra Support These notes include ideas for providing more scaffolding or reading spuport.

Special Needs These notes provide ideas for adapting instruction to support the needs of various special needs students.

■ NOTES

Objectives

Objective 1: Explain the issues of nullification and states' rights.

Objective 2: Summarize arguments regarding the banking system.

Objective 3: Identify the economic problems Martin Van Buren faced.

Objective 4: Describe the election campaigns of 1840.

LESSON 2 ORGANIZER		PACING: APPROX. 1 PERIOD, .5 BLOCKS			
				RESOURCES	
		OBJECTIVES	PACING	Online	Print
Connect					
DIGITAL START UP ACTIVITY **What Do I Need to Know?**			5 min.	●	
Investigate					
DIGITAL TEXT 1 **A Conflict Over States Rights**		Objective 1	10 min.	●	●
INTERACTIVE MAP **Tariffs and Trade**			10 min.	●	
DIGITAL TEXT 2 **The Bank War**		Objective 2	10 min.	●	●
INTERACTIVE CHART **Disagreements Over the Bank**			10 min.	●	
DIGITAL TEXT 3 **Economic Crisis and Political Changes**		Objectives 3, 4	10 min.	●	●
INTERACTIVE TIMELINE **Choosing a Presidential Candidate**			10 min.	●	
Synthesize					
DIGITAL ACTIVITY **Discuss Need-to-Know Questions**			5 min.	●	
Demonstrate					
DIGITAL QUIZ **Lesson Quiz and Class Discussion Board**			10 min.	●	

Political Conflict and Economic Crisis

■ CONNECT

DIGITAL START UP ACTIVITY
What Do I Need to Know?

Project the Start Up Activity Ask students to read the list and make a list of questions as they get settled.

Discuss To help students make their list of questions ask: What do you already know about this material? What terms do you not understand? What concepts would you like more information about?

Tell students that in this lesson they will be learning about the differences between political parties, geographic regions, and individual states during the presidency of Andrew Jackson.

Aa Vocabulary Development: Use the Interactive Reading Notepad to preview the Key Terms and Academic Vocabulary in this lesson with students.

🔁 FLIP IT!

Assign the Flipped Video for this lesson.

■ STUDENT EDITION PRINT PAGES: 313–322

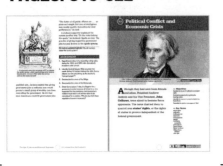

■ INVESTIGATE

DIGITAL TEXT 1
A Conflict Over States Rights

INTERACTIVE MAP
Tariffs and Trade

Objective 1: Explain the issues of nullification and states' rights.

Quick Instruction

Remind students that at this time period the United States reached as far west as Missouri. The North, South, and West (today's Midwest) were regions of importance in the United States during the nineteenth century. Each region had very different economies and political traditions. These regional differences laid the foundation for the Nullification Crisis.

Interactive Map: Tariffs and Trade Project the interactive map. Go over steps one and two of the activity with the students. Move the slider from right to left, stopping to review each step of the diagram.

Summarize How did the economies of different regions in the United States differ? *(The North's economy was based on manufacturing and trade. The South's economy was based on agriculture, while the West's featured both agriculture and livestock.)*

Apply Concepts Describe the issue of states' rights and explain the connection between that issue and John C. Calhoun's arguments for nullification. *(The issue of states' rights is a debate about how political power should be split between the federal and state governments. Calhoun believed that states had the right to nullify, or cancel, a federal law if they felt it was unconstitutional. Calhoun supported stronger states' rights.)*

💬 ACTIVE CLASSROOM

Have students complete a Jigsaw activity. Divide the class into four groups. Using the primary source on nullification, instruct two groups to read the speech by Calhoun, and two other groups to read the speech by Webster. Use the Jigsaw Strategy to help students identify different points of view of political parties and interest groups on the issue of nullification.

Further Instruction

Tariff policies impacted sections of the United States differently during the Tariff of 1828 crisis. Politicians representing different parts of the nation took part in the conflict and the resulting compromise. The argument caused southern politician John C. Calhoun to call for nullification of the federal law. Northern politician Daniel Webster argued for the tariff. In an attempt to compromise and diffuse the crisis, Henry Clay proposed a lower tariff, which Congress passed.

Contrast Have students use the Think-Pair-Share Strategy to summarize different arguments regarding protective tariffs. *(Many people in the North argued for the tariff, which assisted the economy of the North by helping northern manufacturers to sell more goods. Many people in the South argued against the tariff, which hurt the economy of the South because it caused goods to be more expensive there and reduced the amount of southern cotton that Britain bought.)*

Compare and Contrast Compare the impact of the tariff of 1828 and Henry Clay's compromise tariff. *(The tariff of 1828 raised the cost of imported goods, leading to the threat of nullification from South Carolina.)*

DIGITAL TEXT 2

The Bank War

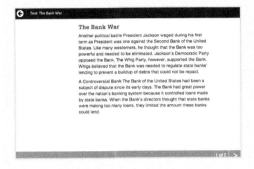

INTERACTIVE CHART

Disagreements Over the Bank

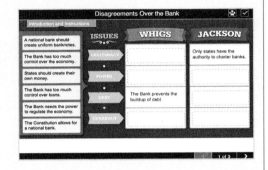

DIGITAL TEXT 3

Economic Crisis and Political Changes

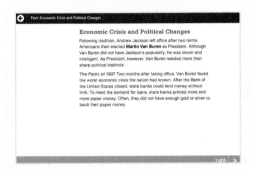

Objective 2: Summarize arguments regarding the banking system.

Quick Instruction
The first Bank of the United States closed in 1811. The second National Bank was opened in 1816 to help manage the nation's ailing economy and the debt from the War of 1812. The Bank's broad reach into the economy and occasional mismanagement made President Andrew Jackson its greatest opponent. He and other leading Democrats disagreed with the Whigs over the role of the banking system.

Interactive Chart: Disagreements Over the Bank Project the interactive chart. Have students drag a view on the Bank into its correct position based on the party that supported it.

Summarize Summarize arguments regarding the banking system. *(Supporters of the Bank believed it was needed to regulate state banks' lending and to prevent a buildup of debts that could not be repaid. Opponents thought the Bank was undemocratic, unconstitutional, and had too much power over the economy.)*

ACTIVE CLASSROOM
Have students complete a Quick Write activity to answer the question, Why did President Jackson want to change the nation's banking system?

D Differentiate: Challenge Have students split into teams of two. Conduct a series of debates on the advantages and disadvantages of the second National Bank.

ELL Use the ELL activity described in the ELL chart.

Further Instruction
Go through the Interactive Reading Notepad questions and discuss the answers with the class.

Identify Central Issues Why did the second National Bank close? *(Jackson vetoed the Bank's charter. After he was reelected, Jackson ordered the Secretary of the Treasury to stop funding the Bank.)*

Summarize What were the effects of the Bank's closing on the financial system? *(States regulated their own banking systems. Individual banks produced their own money and sometimes failed.)*

Objectives 3: List the economic problems Martin Van Buren faced; 4: Describe the campaigns of 1840.

Quick Instruction
Interactive Timeline: Choosing a Presidential Candidate Project the timeline. Have students explain how the nomination process changed over time. Then ask: Did the nominating process become more democratic with each change? Why or why not? *(The nominating of presidential candidates by party leaders or early caucuses did not make the process more democratic because it continued to be dominated by a few powerful people. The move to use conventions and then primaries did make the process more democratic because it involved many more members of the public.)*

ACTIVE CLASSROOM
Have groups of students Take a Stand on the following question: Was Martin Van Buren to blame for the economic depression during his presidency?

• Ask students to divide into two groups based on their answer and move to separate areas of the classroom.
• Ask students to talk with each other to compare their reasons for answering yes or no.
• Ask a representative from each side to present and defend the group's point of view.

Political Conflict and Economic Crisis

 **SYNTHESIZE** **DEMONSTRATE**

INTERACTIVE TIMELINE
Choosing a Presidential Candidate

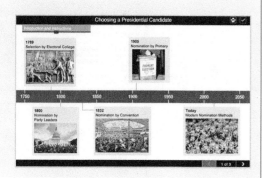

ELL Use the ELL activity described in the ELL chart.

Further Instruction
In the Panic of 1837, about 600 banks closed. This crisis turned into a full-blown depression that would have an impact on the economy of the entire United States and the reelection hopes of Martin Van Buren.

Hypothesize What strategy did the Whigs use to win the election of 1840? Would this strategy work today? *(They portrayed Harrison as a man of the people who came from humble roots. The strategy could work today because people want to relate to those they elect to office.)*

DIGITAL ACTIVITY
Discuss Need-to-Know Questions

During the Jackson era, the issues raised by the Tariff of 1828 and the arguments over the role of the second National Bank both raised questions about government's role in the economy.

Have students go over their Need-to-Know Questions with each other and then as a class. Then ask the question below.

Discuss How did President Jackson's view of the federal government's role in the economy change from the Nullification Crisis to the Bank war? *(President Jackson supported the right of federal laws over state laws in the Nullification Crisis, but during the Bank war he supported state banks over federal banks.)*

DIGITAL QUIZ
Lesson Quiz and Class Discussion Board

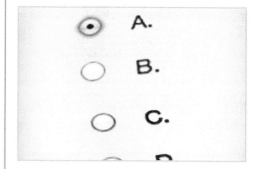

Assign the online Lesson Quiz for this lesson if you haven't already done so. Students will be offered automatic remediation or enrichment based on their score.

Pose these questions to the class on the Discussion Board:

Summarize What were the effects of the conflicts and compromises in this lesson? *(The effects of these conflicts and compromises were mixed. Tariffs and the threat of nullification divided the nation, but a compromise over the tariff resolved the issue, even though tensions remained. The Bank War, however, did not end with a compromise, which had negative effects on the nation.)*

Generate Explanations How are issues of states' rights versus federal rights still apparent today? *(Americans continue to weigh whether the federal government has the right to assert laws and enact programs that some people feel should be handled at the state level.)*

Topic Inquiry
Have students continue their investigations for the Topic Inquiry.

Native Americans on the Frontier

Supporting English Language Learners

Use with Digital Text 2, **Indian Removal.**

Listening

Familiarize students with the text's topic by reviewing or summarizing its content. Prompt students to understand the main points of spoken language ranging from situations in which topics are familiar to those in which they are unfamiliar.

Beginning Use basic spoken language to paraphrase the content of the introductory paragraph. Help students to understand your main points by having them answer these questions: What did the government want Native Americans to do? Did Native Americans sell their land?

Intermediate Use spoken language to paraphrase the content of the introductory paragraph. Have students demonstrate their understanding of what you said by stating three of your main points.

Advanced Use spoken language to give additional details about the case *Cherokee Nation* v. *Georgia* (1831), which should be a somewhat familiar topic because it is briefly mentioned in the text. Have pairs of students demonstrate their understanding of what you said by listing your main points.

Advanced High Use spoken language to tell about one of the groups affected by the Indian Removal Act (e.g., Ottawa or Potawatomi). Provide information about their way of life, both past and present. Have pairs of students demonstrate their understanding of what you said by discussing your main points.

Use with Digital Text 3, **Southern Native Americans on the Trail of Tears.**

Reading

Introduce the text by reading its title and subheadings and by predicting its content. Explain that you will be using a shared reading strategy to read part of the text together. Prompt students to demonstrate comprehension of increasingly complex English as they participate in the shared reading.

Beginning After you read aloud the introductory paragraph once, highlight words familiar to students. Then invite them to participate in a second reading of the paragraph by reading the highlighted words they encountered. Ask: Why did Native American leaders feel forced to sign new treaties?

Intermediate After you read aloud the section titled *The Chickasaw* once, invite students to participate in a second reading by saying the final clause or phrase of each sentence. Ask: Did the U.S. government pay the Chickasaw for their land? When?

Advanced After you read aloud the section titled *The Cherokee* once, invite students to participate in a second reading with you by reading every other sentence. During and after the reading, ask questions so students can demonstrate their comprehension.

Advanced High After you read aloud the section titled *The Cherokee* once, invite students to participate in a second reading by reading the entire section with you. During and after the reading, ask challenging questions so students can demonstrate their comprehension.

▷ Differentiate Instruction

Use the Differentiated Instruction notes throughout the lesson plan to support the varied skill sets, levels of readiness, and interests in the mixed-ability classroom.

Challenge These notes include suggestions for expanding the activity for advanced students.

On-Level These notes include suggestions for modifying the activity to address different interests or learning styles.

Extra Support These notes include ideas for providing more scaffolding or reading spuport.

Special Needs These notes provide ideas for adapting instruction to support the needs of various special needs students.

■ NOTES

Native Americans on the Frontier

Objectives

Objective 1: Describe the cultures of Native Americans between the Appalachians and Mississippi.

Objective 2: Explain the conflict over land occupied by Native Americans between the Appalachians and Mississippi.

Objective 3: Discuss the forced removal of Native Americans.

LESSON 3 ORGANIZER		PACING: APPROX. 1 PERIOD, .5 BLOCKS			
				RESOURCES	
		OBJECTIVES	**PACING**	**Online**	**Print**
Connect					
	DIGITAL START UP ACTIVITY **Black Hawk and the Removal of His People**		5 min.	●	
Investigate					
	DIGITAL TEXT 1 **Native Americans on the Frontier**	Objectives 1, 2	10 min.	●	●
	INTERACTIVE MAP **Selected Native American Groups, 1820**		10 min.	●	
	DIGITAL TEXT 2 **Indian Removal**	Objectives 2, 3	10 min.	●	●
	DIGITAL TEXT 3 **Southern Native Americans on the Trail of Tears**	Objective 3	10 min.	●	●
	INTERACTIVE MAP **The Trail of Tears**		10 min.	●	
Synthesize					
	DIGITAL ACTIVITY **Why Did Native Americans Move?**		5 min.	●	
Demonstrate					
	DIGITAL QUIZ **Lesson Quiz and Class Discussion Board**		10 min.	●	

■ CONNECT

DIGITAL START UP ACTIVITY
Black Hawk and the Removal of His People

Project the Start Up Activity Ask students to read the excerpt from Black Hawk's autobiography and answer the questions as they enter and get settled.

Discuss How does Black Hawk feel about his people's movement to a new home? Cite evidence from the text. *(He feels shocked—"none of our people would have believed him"—and unhappy—"miserable as the hungry, howling wolf.")* What effects might this kind of move have had on a Native American tribe and its social development, that is, on its life as a tribe? *(The tribe might have lost faith in its traditional culture and might have had to adapt to living as a minority group in a larger nation.)*

Aa Vocabulary Development: Use the Interactive Reading Notepad to preview the Key Terms and Academic Vocabulary in this lesson with students.

⚡ FLIP IT!
Assign the Flipped Video for this lesson.

■ STUDENT EDITION PRINT PAGES: 323–330

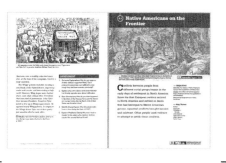

■ INVESTIGATE

DIGITAL TEXT 1
Native Americans on the Frontier

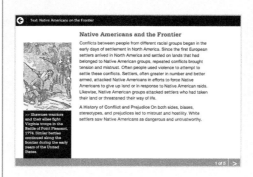

Objectives 1: **Describe the culture of Native Americans in the Southeast;** **2:** **Explain the conflict over land occupied by Native Americans in the Southeast.**

Quick Instruction
There was a long history of hostility between Native Americans on the frontier and white settlers who wanted Native Americans' land. During the Revolutionary War and the War of 1812, many Native Americans sided with the British. Later, tribes tried to win favor from the United States. None of these strategies ended the conflict with white settlers.

Interactive Map: Selected Native American Groups, 1820 Project the interactive map. Explain that the map shows Native American groups living on the frontier east of the Mississippi River in the early 1800s. Select the hot spots on the map to learn more about each of the Native American groups shown. Considering the locations of these groups.What do you think might happen as white settlers move into the areas around them? *(They would be forced, one by one, to give up their land to settlers.)*

INTERACTIVE MAP
Selected Native American Groups, 1820

👥 ACTIVE CLASSROOM

Have students complete a Graffiti Concepts activity. Ask students to reflect on the similarities and differences between the Native American groups shown on the interactive map. Have them create a visual image or set of phrases that represents those similarities and differences.

Ask students to post their "graffiti" on the board or on chart paper and them to look at all the various responses.Then, discuss similarities and differences in the responses as a group.

D Differentiate: Extra Support Ask students why relations on the frontier were tense between Native Americans and whites. Have them cite examples from the text to support their answer.

Further Instruction
Cite Evidence Did Native American groups present a national security threat—or a threat to the safety of the nation—to the leaders of the newly formed United States? Cite evidence from the reading. *(Some groups presented a national security threat because they sided with the British during the Revolutionary War and the War of 1812.)*

Identify Cause and Effect Why did some Native Americans side with the British? *(They feared that, unless they sought British help, white American settlers would take their land.)*

Native Americans on the Frontier

DIGITAL TEXT 2

Indian Removal

Indian Removal

In the eyes of government leaders, Native Americans east of the Mississippi River stood in the way of westward expansion of the United States. At first, they aimed to convince Native Americans to rely less on hunting. They wanted them to start farming cash crops such as tobacco and cotton in addition to food crops. Government leaders thought that Native Americans would then sell any land that they weren't farming to white settlers. While many Native Americans in the South did adopt cash-crop farming, they were not willing to sell their land. Meanwhile, prejudices on both sides stood in the way of white settlers and Native Americans living side by side.

1 of 6 >

DIGITAL TEXT 3

Southern Native Americans on the Trail of Tears

Southern Native Americans on the Trail of Tears

Faced with threats of military action, most Native American leaders in the South saw no choice but to sign new treaties giving up their lands. They agreed to move to what was called the **Indian Territory**. Today, most of that area is in the state of Oklahoma.

The Choctaw The Choctaw signed the first treaty in 1830. The Treaty of Dancing Rabbit Creek stated that

the United States under a grant . . . shall cause to be conveyed to the Choctaw Nation a tract of country west of the Mississippi river . .

1 of 6 >

Objectives 2: Explain the conflict over land occupied by Native Americans in the Southeast; 3: Discuss the forced removal of Native Americans.

Quick Instruction

In the years leading up to the Jackson era, more and more white settlers moved across the Appalachians into the Old Northwest (Ohio, Michigan, Indiana, Illinois, Wisconsin, Minnesota, and Iowa) and the Old Southwest (Alabama, Mississippi, Tennessee, Kentucky, Missouri, Arkansas, and Louisiana). The westward movement of these settlers increased tensions with Native Americans living in the area. Many settlers wanted the Native Americans' land. Meanwhile, the U.S. Supreme Court's *Worcester* v. *Georgia* decision made it illegal for states to take Native American land on their own. Andrew Jackson's government came up with a federal plan to move the Native Americans out of settlers' way.

Identify Cause and Effect How did the *Worcester* v. *Georgia* decision and the Indian Removal Act lead to the removal and resettlement of Native American groups such as the Cherokee from their homelands? *(The Worcester* v. *Georgia decision made it more difficult for states to clear Native American land for white settlement and made Indian removal a federal issue. However, since President Jackson ignored the ruling, the Cherokee lost any protection it provided. The Indian Removal Act provided the federal government with a legal framework for removing Native Americans from their lands and resettling them on lands west of the Mississippi River.)*

Contrast How do you see President Jackson's views on states' right differ between his response to the *Worcester* v. *Georgia* decision and his stance during the Nullification Crisis? *(President Jackson supported states' rights in the* Worcester v. Georgia *decision, but he supported the idea of a stronger federal government during the Nullification Crisis.)*

ELL Use the ELL activity described in the ELL chart.

Further Instruction

Summarize What effect did the Indian Removal Act have on the human geography of contemporary times? *(Many Native American tribes, including the Choctaw, Chickasaw, Cherokee, and Seminole, were forced to move west of the Mississippi. Therefore, in modern times few Native Americans live east of the Mississippi River.)*

Make Predictions Would the Indian Removal Act resolve conflicts between people from different racial groups in the early United States? *(Yes, offering new homelands to Native Americans so that they would leave the land desired by white settlers would resolve the conflict. No, Native Americans did not want to leave their homelands.)*

Objective 3: Discuss the forced removal of Native Americans.

Quick Instruction

The Trail of Tears was a series of forced migrations during the Age of Jackson. Faced with threats of U.S. military action, the Cherokee and other Native American groups in the present-day Southeast moved to lands west of the Mississippi. Their movement is known as the Trail of Tears because of the suffering they faced during their journeys.

Interactive Map: The Trail of Tears Project the interactive map. Explain that each map shows a different aspect of the Trail of Tears, including the original homelands of each Native American group affected, the routes they took to their new territories, and those new territories. Select the different maps to explore the Trail of Tears in detail.

INTERACTIVE MAP
The Trail of Tears

ACTIVE CLASSROOM

Use a Circle Write activity. Break students into small groups and ask them to consider this question:

At the end of the Trail of Tears, southern Native American groups were settled in a region later called Indian Territory and now part of Oklahoma. Based on what you've learned, why do you think that this region was chosen for them? *(This was an area where white settlers did not yet want to live. The land in the Indian Territory may not have been as good for farming.)*

Have students write as much as they can for 1 minute then switch with the person on their right. The next person tries to improve or elaborate the response where the other person left off. Continue to switch until the paper comes back to the first person. The group then decides which is the best response and shares that with the larger group.

ELL Use the ELL activity described in the ELL chart.

Further Instruction

Identify Cause and Effect What were the reasons for the removal and resettlement of the Cherokee in the march which became known as the Trail of Tears? *(The Cherokee resisted resettlement. In 1838, President Martin Van Buren forced the Cherokee, who had not made agreements with North Carolina, to move. The United States Army forced more than 15,000 Cherokee to march westward. In the winter of 1838–39, they went to Indian Territory, patrolled by 7,000 soldiers. The Cherokee trekked hundreds of miles over a period of several months. Thousands perished during the march that became known as the Trail of Tears.)*

Infer What does the history of the Trail of Tears indicate about the resolution of conflict between whites and Native Americans during the Jackson era? *(The conflict between whites and some Native American tribes was temporarily resolved, though not to the Native American's advantage.)*

Native Americans on the Frontier

◼ SYNTHESIZE

DIGITAL ACTIVITY
Why Did Native Americans Move?

Ask students to think about each of the questions about the reasons why Native Americans moved during the Jackson era.

Discuss Why did the Cherokee move? *(The United States military rounded them up and forced them to move.)* How have these questions changed your thinking about the Topic Essential Question: Why do people move? *(Answers should show an awareness that migration can be voluntary or involuntary. Some students may not have previously considered forced migration such as how it occurred with the Indian Removal Act.)*

◼ DEMONSTRATE

DIGITAL QUIZ
Lesson Quiz and Class Discussion Board

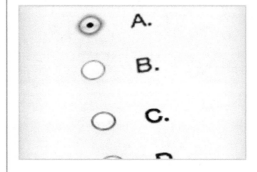

Assign the online Lesson Quiz for this lesson if you haven't already done so. Students will be offered automatic remediation or enrichment based on their score.

Pose these questions to the class on the Discussion Board:

In *Native Americans on the Frontier*, you read about the conflicts between white settlers and Native Americans, which eventually led to the forced removal of Native Americans west of the Mississippi River.

Draw Conclusions How did the relationship between Native Americans and the United States government change during the Jackson era?

Identify Patterns By the 1850s, most members of every major group of Southeastern Native Americans had been relocated to new lands in the Indian Territory west of the Mississippi. Think about the ongoing westward movement of settlers. What do you think would happen at a later date to the Native Americans in Indian Territory?

Topic Inquiry
Have students continue their investigations for the Topic Inquiry.

Westward Movement

Supporting English Language Learners

Use with Digital Text 1, **Heading Into the West.**

Listening
Read aloud the first two paragraphs of the reading *Heading Into the West* or invite a volunteer to read the passage aloud. Then prompt students to understand the main points of spoken language by completing the following tasks:

Beginning Have students work in pairs to the complete the following sentence: Settlers traveled west because they wanted _____.

Intermediate Ask students to orally name some places from which travelers often came. Then ask them to orally name some places travelers often settled. Model correct pronunciation of unfamiliar place names for students as needed.

Advanced Organize students into small groups. Have them take turns orally summarizing the passage. Direct students to restate one main point from the speaker's summary to show their understanding.

Advanced High Have students write a sentence or two that restates the main idea of the first paragraph in their own words. Then direct them to write a few sentences explaining how the details given in the second paragraph support the main idea of the first paragraph.

Use with Digital Text 4, **Canals Connect the Country.**

Reading
Have students read silently the information under the heading *An Instant Success*. After students complete the reading, use the following activities to demonstrate their comprehension of increasingly complex English by retelling or summarizing material.

Beginning Draw a Main Idea and Details graphic organizer on the board. Add the details "lowered costs of shipping," "made New York City more important," and "encouraged more canal building" to the details boxes. Then have students reread the passage and provide a main idea to summarize the details by completing the sentence starter: The Erie Canal _____.

Intermediate Have students work in small groups. Tell students to take turns rereading each sentence of the passage silently and then retelling its meaning aloud. Then direct groups to work together to write three sentences summarizing the entire passage.

Advanced Have students reread the passage and write a few sentences to summarize the effects of the opening of the Erie Canal. Have some students volunteer to retell how the canal affected both people in the West and in New York City.

Advanced High Have students reread the passage and write a short paragraph retelling the effects of the Erie Canal from the perspective of a person who shipped goods from Buffalo to New York City. The paragraph should tell how the opening of the canal changed the speed and cost of sending goods.

▣ Differentiate Instruction

Use the Differentiated Instruction notes throughout the lesson plan to support the varied skill sets, levels of readiness, and interests in the mixed-ability classroom.

Challenge These notes include suggestions for expanding the activity for advanced students.

On-Level These notes include suggestions for modifying the activity to address different interests or learning styles.

Extra Support These notes include ideas for providing more scaffolding or reading spuport.

Special Needs These notes provide ideas for adapting instruction to support the needs of various special needs students.

▉ NOTES

Westward Movement

Objectives

Objective 1: Describe how settlers traveled west.

Objective 2: List the steps Americans took to improve their roads.

Objective 3: Explain how steamboats and canals improved transportation for Americans.

LESSON 4 ORGANIZER		PACING: APPROX. 1 PERIOD, .5 BLOCKS			
				RESOURCES	
		OBJECTIVES	PACING	Online	Print
Connect					
DIGITAL START UP ACTIVITY **Heading Into the West**			5 min.	●	
Investigate					
DIGITAL TEXT 1 **Heading Into the West**		Objective 1	10 min.	●	●
DIGITAL TEXT 2 **Building Better Roads**		Objective 2	10 min.	●	●
INTERACTIVE GALLERY **New Transportation Methods**			10 min.	●	
DIGITAL TEXT 3 **The Age of Steam**			10 min.	●	●
DIGITAL TEXT 4 **Canals Connect the Country**		Objective 3	10 min.	●	●
INTERACTIVE MAP **The Erie Canal**			10 min.	●	
Synthesize					
DIGITAL ACTIVITY **What Route to Take**			5 min.	●	
Demonstrate					
DIGITAL QUIZ **Lesson Quiz and Class Discussion Board**			10 min.	●	

CONNECT

DIGITAL START UP ACTIVITY
Heading Into the West

Project the Start-Up Activity as students get settled. Have students brainstorm the types of transportation available in the 1800s and how different their lives would be without modern transportation. Then have students partner to answer one of the Connect questions. Have them share with the class or on the Class Discussion Board.

Express Problems Clearly Ask students what impact transportation in the 1800s would have on the question they selected to answer. How would it affect their day-to-day lives? *(Travel would be difficult and slow, and simple tasks would take longer.)*

Infer If the main form of transportation is a horse-drawn wagon, what would solve the problem of bad terrain? *(Developing a way to build roads through or bridges over these obstacles.)*

Aa **Vocabulary Development:** Use the Interactive Reading Notepad to preview the Key Terms and Academic Vocabulary in this lesson with students.

⇅ FLIP IT!

Assign the Flipped Video for this lesson.

STUDENT EDITION PRINT
PAGES: 331–336

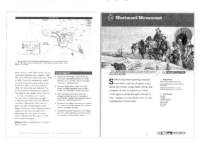

INVESTIGATE

DIGITAL TEXT 1
Heading Into the West

Objective 1: **Describe how settlers traveled west.**

Quick Instruction
While people had been exploring the land west of the original colonies for almost two centuries, the number of people looking to settle that land greatly increased in the early 1800s. The difficulties involved in large numbers of people traveling through this wild terrain created a need for new technologies and methods of transportation.

Generate Explanations Project the *New States, 1792–1819* map. Ask students to reflect on some reasons why the states formed in the order they did. Give students an appropriate amount of time to formulate a response. Ask students to pair up or turn to an assigned partner. Have them discuss their responses. *(Settlers came at different times and from different directions. They explored and settled in more easily accessible land first. Populations weren't large enough to apply for statehood.)*

D **Differentiate: On-Level** The title of this reading is *Heading Into the West*. Ask students to locate where the West was in the United States of the early 1800s. *(The West was the areas just slightly west and southwest of the original colonies.)* Are these areas what we consider the West today? *(No, they are areas that now make up the regions we call the Midwest and the South.)*

ELL Use the ELL activity described in the ELL chart.

Further Instruction
Project and discuss the Interactive Reading Notepad graphic organizer about the major routes available to settlers. Review the routes with the class and fill in the graphic organizer on the whiteboard as you go. Discuss whether these major routes were the only ways possible for people to travel at the time.

Draw Conclusions What do you think caused Americans to move westward? *(The availability of land in the West, overcrowded towns and cities in the East, desire to start anew, zest for adventure)*

Westward Movement

DIGITAL TEXT 2
Building Better Roads

Text: Building Better Roads

Building Better Roads

Settlers faced difficult journeys as they traveled to the West. Many roads were narrow dirt trails, barely wide enough for a single wagon. Trails often plunged through muddy swamps. Tree stumps stuck up in the road and often broke the wagon axles of careless travelers. The nation badly needed better roads.

Paying Tolls In the United States, as in Europe, private companies built gravel and stone roads. To pay for these roads, the companies collected tolls from travelers. At various points along the road, a pike, or pole, blocked the road. After a wagon driver had paid a toll, the pike keeper turned the pole aside to let the wagon pass. As a result, these toll roads were called **turnpikes**.

Probably the best road in the United States was the **Lancaster Turnpike**. Built in the 1790s by a private company, the road linked Philadelphia and Lancaster, Pennsylvania.

1 of 3

INTERACTIVE GALLERY
New Transportation Methods

New Transportation Methods of the Early 1800s

A flatboat was a flat-bottomed boat used for transporting passengers and cargo on rivers. Flatboats were often used for just one trip. At the end, they were broken up and the wood was reused.

1 of 2

DIGIITAL TEXT 3
The Age of Steam

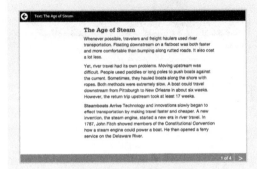

Text: The Age of Steam

The Age of Steam

Whenever possible, travelers and freight haulers used river transportation. Floating downstream on a flatboat was both faster and more comfortable than bumping along rutted roads. It also cost a lot less.

Yet, river travel had its own problems. Moving upstream was difficult. People used paddles or long poles to push boats against the current. Sometimes, they hauled boats along the shore with ropes. Both methods were extremely slow. A boat could travel downstream from Pittsburgh to New Orleans in about six weeks. However, the return trip upstream took at least 17 weeks.

Steamboats Arrive Technology and innovations slowly began to effect transportation by making travel faster and cheaper. A new invention, the steam engine, started a new era in river travel. In 1787, John Fitch showed members of the Constitutional Convention how a steam engine could power a boat. He then opened a ferry service on the Delaware River.

1 of 4

Objective 2: List the steps Americans took to improve their roads.

Quick Instruction

Interactive Gallery: New Transportation Methods Project the interactive gallery. Click through each image and ask for student volunteers to read the caption aloud. Ask students to explain the specific problems that each of these transportation methods were designed to address. *(Flatboats could be used in shallow rivers. Gravel roads were smoother and less muddy than dirt roads. Corduroy roads allowed easier travel over marshes and swampy ground. Turnpikes collected money that paid for building the roads.)*

Predict Consequences How did technological innovations, such as improved roads, affect western migration? *(Better roads meant faster and easier travel, so more people and goods could be moved.)*

> **📷 ACTIVE CLASSROOM**
>
> Use the See-Think-Wonder Strategy to have pairs of students analyze the images in the gallery and share their insights with the class.

Differentiate: Challenge
How were the construction and upkeep of state and federal roads funded? *(Through state and federal taxes)* Did building the National Road in western states, such as Illinois, have a positive consequence for a taxpayer in New England? *(Yes, because products made or grown in Illinois could be transported to New England more easily and less expensively.)*

Further Instruction

Infer One thing we take for granted today is paved roads. If drivers and their passengers get annoyed when they drive through a pothole today, think about what it must have been like to travel on unpaved roads everywhere you went. Ask students to think about the types of dangers travelers would have faced when traveling on roads in the early 1800s. *(Travelers faced mud, ruts, uneven paths, dangerous slopes, vegetation, and lack of markings.)*

Support Ideas with Evidence Did building a toll road have positive consequences for both the private owner and the traveler? Explain your reasoning. *(Yes, the owner would benefit because the cost of the road and its upkeep would eventually be surpassed by the income received in tolls. The traveler would benefit because the time saved and the ease of travel would be worth the expense of the toll.)*

Objective 3: Explain how steamboats and canals improved transportation for Americans.

Quick Instruction

The United States has a vast network of rivers and other bodies of water that connect cities and regions. They are extremely useful for getting people and goods from one place to another. Like the nineteenth century system of roads, however, travel along rivers was slow and dangerous—that is, until the advent of the steam engine.

Interactive Map: The Erie Canal Project the interactive map and click through the hotspots. Review the lock system so that students understand how it worked and how important the locks were to the success of a canal. Explicitly describe the Erie Canal as a positive consequence of human modification of the physical environment. Prompt students to analyze its impact on the growth and development of the United States. *(Expanding trade networks, access to new markets, growth of towns and cities)*

Analyze Information Ask students to explain the consequences of technological innovations, such as the steamboat. *(Steamboats made travel along rivers faster. This gave merchants and farmers a cheap way to move their goods and revolutionized travel in the West. The stump-puller helped speed the digging of the Erie Canal.)*

DIGITAL TEXT 4
Canals Connect the Country

INTERACTIVE MAP
The Erie Canal

Summarize What impact did transportation systems such as the Erie Canal have on the growth and development of the United States? *(The Erie Canal significantly decreased the cost of shipping and encouraged the continued economic growth and development of New York City.)*

⬛ ACTIVE CLASSROOM

Using the Sequence It Strategy, ask students to recreate the steps in the locks system described in the first hotspot of the interactive map. Encourage small groups to act out the sequence and to use hand or body motions to indicate the rising and lowering water at different stages in the process.

ELL Use the ELL activity described in the ELL chart.

Further Instruction
Draw Conclusions Why do you think Fulton's steamboat company succeeded when Fitch's did not? *(Because of Americans' interest in moving around the country, the timing of Fulton's steamboat may have been more advantageous.)*

Support a Point of View With Evidence Do you agree with Thomas Jefferson's belief that building the Erie Canal was "little short of madness" for the time? Why or why not? *(Considering the lack of technology and the amount of back-breaking labor building the canal would take, I agree with Jefferson that the building of the canal was something unimaginable for the time.)*

Westward Movement

SYNTHESIZE

DIGITAL ACTIVITY
What Route to Take

Tell students that by the mid-1800s Americans had a variety of routes to transport goods and people. For many, choosing a route depended on what was being transported. Project the What Route to Take activity and have students work in pairs to determine which route they think would be the best to use for the different items. Then ask the following questions:

Draw Conclusions What do you think were obstacles in transporting livestock and produce in the 1800s? *(Some possible obstacles included the cost and storage of feed for livestock, keeping livestock alive during a long trip, keeping livestock safe from injury, keeping produce fresh enough to sell at the final destination, and keeping vermin away from produce.)*

Support Ideas With Examples How have methods of transportation been improved to address those and other obstacles today? *(Today, we have faster methods of transportation to reduce feed costs, boxcar and trucks designed for livestock's comfort and safety, refrigeration methods to keep produce fresh, and sanitation methods to prevent infestation.)*

DEMONSTRATE

DIGITAL QUIZ
Lesson Quiz and Class Discussion Board

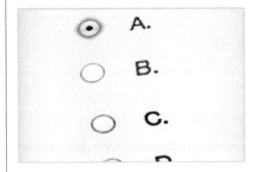

Assign the online Lesson Quiz for this lesson if you haven't already done so. Students will be offered automatic remediation or enrichment based on their score.

Pose these questions to the class on the Discussion Board:

You read about a variety of new transportation methods that developed to allow faster and more efficient movement around the United States. Although trade was one of the driving forces behind these innovations, another was the desire of many Americans to move westward.

Make Predictions What new method of transportation do you think will be developed in a later period that will be the most influential in the American quest to move even farther westward? *(The railroad)*

Draw Conclusions How will westward migration affect the growth and development of the United States? *(Americans and immigrants from around the globe will take advantage of new opportunities and will settle in areas on the frontier. The nation will grow in population and size as territories are absorbed into the United States.)*

Topic Inquiry
Have students continue their investigations for the Topic Inquiry.

Settling Oregon Country

Supporting English Language Learners

Use with Digital Text 2, **The Far West Fur Trade.**

Reading
Explain to students that they will demonstrate reading comprehension by reading from the text and referring back to it in order to respond to questions.

Beginning Have students read the first three paragraphs of the text silently. Then read aloud the passage while students follow along. After each paragraph, have students respond to one of these questions: Who traveled to Oregon to buy furs? Who caught animals for their fur? What is one interesting detail about a mountain man's appearance?

Intermediate Ask for volunteers to read aloud the first three paragraphs of the text. Then have students respond to these questions: What route might a fur trader take after leaving New England? What did a mountain man look like?

Advanced Have pairs of students read the section titled *The Fur Trade*. Then have them respond to these questions: What two main things happened at a rendezvous? What are two reasons why the fur trade died out?

Advanced High Ask students to independently read the section titled *The Fur Trade*. Have them respond to these questions on paper: What happened at a rendezvous? Why did the fur trade die out? What did some mountain men do after that? Provide time for students to discuss their answers with a partner.

Use with Digital Text 3, **The Oregon Trail**

Listening
Prompt students to understand the main points of spoken language by rereading or reviewing the text in order to gain more familiarity with it.

Beginning Use basic spoken language to describe typical daily events in a wagon train. Have students demonstrate their understanding of what you said by restating your main points. Ask: What did people do in the morning? At noon? In the evening?

Intermediate Use spoken language to describe (with some detail) the typical daily events in a wagon train. Have students demonstrate their understanding of what you said by restating your main points.

Advanced Use spoken language to describe the costs and benefits of traveling on the Oregon Trail, using details from both the text and other sources. Have students demonstrate their understanding of what you said by restating your main points.

Advanced High Use spoken language to describe the Oregon Trail in the context of its current use as a National Historic Trail. Provide details about things that visitors can do and see along the trail. Then have students demonstrate their understanding of what you said by restating your main points.

▣ Differentiate Instruction

Use the Differentiated Instruction notes throughout the lesson plan to support the varied skill sets, levels of readiness, and interests in the mixed-ability classroom.

Challenge These notes include suggestions for expanding the activity for advanced students.

On-Level These notes include suggestions for modifying the activity to address different interests or learning styles.

Extra Support These notes include ideas for providing more scaffolding or reading spuport.

Special Needs These notes provide ideas for adapting instruction to support the needs of various special needs students.

■ **NOTES**

Settling Oregon Country

Objectives

Objective 1: Explain the appeal of Oregon and the Far West.

Objective 2: Summarize how mountain men helped explore the Far West.

Objective 3: Describe the role missionaries played in Oregon.

Objective 4: Identify the hardships faced on wagon trains to the West.

LESSON 5 ORGANIZER		PACING: APPROX. 1 PERIOD, .5 BLOCKS		
			RESOURCES	
	OBJECTIVES	**PACING**	**Online**	**Print**
Connect				
DIGITAL START UP ACTIVITY **Who Is a Pioneer?**		5 min.	●	
Investigate				
DIGITAL TEXT 1 **In Search of New Territory**	Objective 1	10 min.	●	●
INTERACTIVE GALLERY **Oregon Country**		10 min.	●	
DIGITAL TEXT 2 **The Far West Fur Trade**	Objective 2	10 min.	●	●
DIGITAL TEXT 3 **The Oregon Trail**		10 min.	●	●
INTERACTIVE MAP **The Oregon Trail**	Objectives 3, 4	10 min.	●	
3-D MODEL **The Covered Wagon**		10 min.	●	
Synthesize				
DIGITAL ACTIVITY **Pioneering Success**		5 min.	●	
Demonstrate				
DIGITAL QUIZ **Lesson Quiz and Class Discussion Board**		10 min.	●	

PEARSON
realize™
www.PearsonRealize.com

Go online to access additional resources including:
Primary Sources • Biographies • Supreme Court cases •
21st Century Skill Tutorials • Maps • Graphic Organizers.

■ CONNECT

DIGITAL START UP ACTIVITY
Who Is a Pioneer?

Project the Start Up activity as students enter and get settled. Have students brainstorm what it means to be a pioneer, and how exploring new territory can be defined. Then have them share their ideas with the class by answering these questions or ask students to post their responses online on the Class Discussion Board.

Discuss If a pioneer is an explorer, what are some personality traits that make someone a good pioneer? *(Answers could include curiosity about the unknown, bravery or fearlessness, willingness to keep going in the face of danger or uncertainty.)*

Tell students that in this lesson they will be learning about Oregon and the Far West.

Aa Vocabulary Development: Use the Interactive Reading Notepad to preview the Key Terms and Academic Vocabulary in this lesson with students.

↑↓ FLIP IT!
Assign the Flipped Video for this lesson.

■ STUDENT EDITION PRINT
PAGES: 337–343

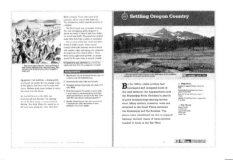

■ INVESTIGATE

DIGITAL TEXT 1
In Search of New Territory

Objective 1: **Explain the appeal of Oregon and the Far West.**

Quick Instruction
By the early 1800s, the population of the United States had moved westward as far as the Mississippi River. The plains in the middle of the continent, acquired from the Louisiana Purchase, were less hospitable for farming, which meant that explorers kept pushing westward across the Rocky Mountains and to the Pacific coast. The territory they founded, Oregon Country, was fertile and varied, but several countries wanted to lay claim to the area.

Interactive Gallery: Oregon Country Project the interactive gallery and click through the images. Discuss the features of Oregon Country that made it different from the eastern United States. *(Taller mountains, fur-bearing wildlife like beavers, open space for raising cattle, arid plains)*

INTERACTIVE GALLERY
Oregon Country

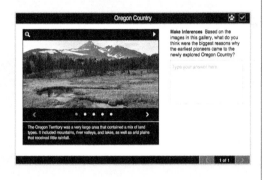

📇 ACTIVE CLASSROOM
Conduct a Think-Pair-Share activity. Project "The United States in 1830" map on the board. Ask the students to reflect on this question:

Oregon Territory is on the opposite side of the continent from the rest of the United States. Why would the United States have wanted to claim land so far away from the other states? *(Much of the land closer to the other states was considered too dry for farming. Oregon Territory also had access to resources like fur trapping and a more direct trade route to China and the Far East.)*

Ask students to pair up or turn to an assigned partner. Have them discuss their responses.

D Differentiate: On-Level The last section of the text is titled *Nations Compete*. Why would countries like Spain and Great Britain want to lay claim to Oregon Country? *(The area had resources like furs and farmland. Oregon Country was also next to territory they already possessed, Mexico and Canada.)*

Further Instruction
Make Inferences Why would trading happen at a military outpost, such as Fort Astoria? *(In largely unexplored land, military forts and bases were the safest places to buy and sell supplies and goods.)*

Settling Oregon Country

The Far West Fur Trade

The Oregon Trail

The Oregon Trail

Objective 2: Summarize how mountain men helped explore the Far West.

Quick Instruction

Some of the first people to come west to Oregon Country were fur traders, who supplied a successful trade of furs as far away as China. These trappers were known as *mountain men*, and they lived and worked individually in harsh conditions in the wild. Gathering once a year at a celebration called a rendezvous, they would compete, party, and sell their wares. When the fur trade eventually fell off, many of these mountain men found new work as explorers and guides, helping others find their way through the rough terrain of Oregon.

Infer Why would mountain men choose to endure the harsh lifestyle of a trapper? *(They were independent and self-sufficient. They sought a life that promised adventure and a good income.)*

ELL Use the ELL activity described in the ELL chart.

Further Instruction

Hypothesize After the fur trade stopped being so successful, why did people keep coming to Oregon Country? *(The wilderness lifestyle still appealed to people. There were also other opportunities for work, such as farming or raising cattle.)*

Objectives 3: Describe the role missionaries played in Oregon; **4:** Identify the hardships faced on wagon trains to the West.

Quick Instruction

The first permanent settlers in Oregon were missionaries like Marcus and Narcissa Whitman. They worked to convert the local Native Americans, set up clinics, and encouraged others to come west. Large groups of families looking to relocate in the west would join together in wagon trains. They would leave Missouri in early spring, struggling across 2,000 miles of plains and mountains to try and beat the winter snows. The way was long and difficult, but over the years thousands made it through to the other side of the continent.

Interactive Map: The Oregon Trail Project the interactive map and click through the hotspots. Review the kinds of hazards and obstacles faced by settlers traveling along the Trail, so that students can understand the determination of people trying to start a new life in the West. Ask students to explain why the Oregon Trail followed the route it did, rather than coming across farther to the north. *(The trail followed the course of several passes and rivers, such as the Snake River, through the Rocky Mountains. Getting wagons across a different part of the mountains would probably have been much more difficult.)*

3-D Model: The Covered Wagon Project the 3-D Model and click through the screens. Work with students to complete the Traveling Then and Now chart and answer the questions that follow.

Identify Cause and Effect Why did the work of missionaries increase the flow of settlers into Oregon Country? *(Missionaries sent word back to people living in the East about how good it was in the new territory. They inspired others to come and help with their mission.)*

▶ ACTIVE CLASSROOM

Conduct a Write 1 Get 3 activity. Ask: What specific problems did the pioneers face as they traveled westward? *(They had to leave their old lives behind. The journey was very long. Weather, food, and hostile locals were all potential threats. Once they arrived, they would have to build everything themselves.)*

Have students take a piece of paper and fold it into quarters, write down one response in the first box, and then go around room asking to hear other responses. If students think a response is correct, write it in one of the boxes until there are three more responses on the page. Share responses with class.

D Differentiate: Challenge Ask students to focus on a smaller portion of the Oregon Trail, such as the length from Independence Rock to Three Island Crossing. Have them research and create a more detailed map of the trail. They can present this information in a format of their choice (e.g., hand-drawn as a poster, digital art created using illustration software, a 3-D model from clay, etc.).

3-D MODEL

The Covered Wagon

ELL Use the ELL activity described in the ELL chart.

Further Instruction

Make Inferences Why would Narcissa Whitman have wanted to be one of the first pioneer women across the Rocky Mountains? *(She was a strong believer in the pioneer spirit and felt it was her duty to travel west as a missionary.)*

Infer Why did settlers travel overland along the Oregon Trail instead of by ship? *(Buying a wagon and carrying all their supplies and belongings was less expensive and faster than buying passage on a boat. Settlers also had more control over when and where they went once they reached the new territory.)*

■ SYNTHESIZE

DIGITAL ACTIVITY

Pioneering Success

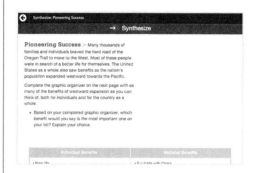

Tell the students that by the mid-1800s, a large number of Americans and others had resettled in Oregon Country. There were a number of reasons why they all chose to make the move westward. Project the Individual Benefits vs. National Benefits graphic organizer and have students work in pairs to determine what sorts of benefits came out of the settlement of Oregon Country. Then ask the following questions.

Draw Conclusions How did the westward movement of people along the Oregon Trail benefit both individuals and the United States as a whole? *(Individuals benefited the most by taking the opportunity to make a better life for themselves. The country benefited by becoming larger, with more access to resources and international trade.)*

■ DEMONSTRATE

DIGITAL QUIZ

Lesson Quiz and Class Discussion Board

Assign the online Lesson Quiz for this lesson if you haven't already done so. Students will be offered automatic remediation or enrichment based on their score.

Pose these questions to the class on the Discussion Board:

In *Oregon Country*, you read about the people who originally traveled westward to populate the new territory, what they found when they got there, and the troubles they endured while getting there. People traveled west for a variety of reasons, looking to build better and often more independent lives for themselves.

Draw Conclusions How will westward migration along the Oregon Trail affect the growth and development of the United States?

Infer What do mountain men and migrating settlers tell us about the developing personality of the American people?

Topic Inquiry

Have students continue their investigations for the Topic Inquiry.

Independence for Texas

Supporting English Language Learners

Use with Digital Text 2, **Conflict With the Mexican Government.**

Reading
Explain that students will be taking notes in order to demonstrate their comprehension of a text.

Beginning Have students read silently the section titled *Mexico Tightens Its Grip on Texas*. Then read aloud the section for students. Display the following as a bulleted list: 1830: Mexico stops _____ from settling in Texas; 1833: _____ gains power in Mexico; 1835: Santa Anna begins ruling as a _____. Have students copy and complete the notes.

Intermediate Invite volunteers to read aloud the section titled *Mexico Tightens Its Grip on Texas*. Pause the reading periodically to have students help you take notes on the section's most important points. Display the notes as a bulleted list, and have students copy them.

Advanced Have pairs of students read the section titled *Mexico Tightens Its Grip on Texas*. Explain that after every paragraph, they should stop and take notes on the most important points they have just read. Encourage them to organize their notes as a bulleted list with a heading.

Advanced High Have students independently read the text. Explain that as they read, they should pause to take notes on the most important points they encounter. Encourage them to organize their notes using the same title and subheadings as the text.

Use with Digital Text 4, **The Republic of Texas Is Born.**

Learning Strategies Listening
Review the meanings of annex and annexation in preparation for the activities.

Beginning Using the chart as a reference, explain (in basic spoken language) three reasons for the Texas annexation. To help students understand the important points of what you said, ask a literal question about each reason that students can answer with a word or phrase.

Intermediate Using the chart as a reference, explain (in spoken language) five reasons for the Texas annexation. To help students understand the important points of what you said, ask a literal question about each reason. Then ask: Which of these reasons is most important, and why?

Advanced Using the chart as a reference, explain (in spoken language) the reasons for and against the Texas annexation. Then have pairs of students discuss the important points of each side of the argument.

Advanced High Compare and contrast some basic facts about the familiar topic of the Texas annexation and the unfamiliar topic of the Hawaii annexation (e.g., reasons for it, support of inhabitants, date in history). Then have pairs of students discuss the important points you made.

▣ Differentiate Instruction

Use the Differentiated Instruction notes throughout the lesson plan to support the varied skill sets, levels of readiness, and interests in the mixed-ability classroom.

Challenge These notes include suggestions for expanding the activity for advanced students.

On-Level These notes include suggestions for modifying the activity to address different interests or learning styles.

Extra Support These notes include ideas for providing more scaffolding or reading spuport.

Special Needs These notes provide ideas for adapting instruction to support the needs of various special needs students.

■ NOTES

PEARSON
realize™
www.PearsonRealize.com

Go online to access additional resources including:
Primary Sources • Biographies • Supreme Court cases •
21st Century Skill Tutorials • Maps • Graphic Organizers.

Objectives

Objective 1: Summarize the cooperation and conflict between American settlers in Texas and the Mexican government.

Objective 2: Explain how Texas gained independence.

Objective 3: Describe how the events at the Alamo affected Texans.

Objective 4: Identify the challenges faced by the Lone Star Republic.

LESSON 6 ORGANIZER			PACING: APPROX. 1 PERIOD, .5 BLOCKS		
		OBJECTIVES	PACING	**RESOURCES**	
				Online	Print
Connect					
DIGITAL START UP ACTIVITY **I Wish to See Texas Free**			5 min.	●	
Investigate					
DIGITAL TEXT 1 **Americans Colonize Mexican Texas**		Objective 1	10 min.	●	●
INTERACTIVE MAP **The Settlement of Texas**			10 min.	●	
DIGITAL TEXT 2 **Conflict With the Mexican Government**		Objective 2	10 min.	●	●
DIGITAL TEXT 3 **Independence for Texas**		Objective 3	10 min.	●	●
INTERACTIVE GALLERY **The Defenders of the Alamo**			10 min.	●	
DIGITAL TEXT 4 **The Republic of Texas Is Born**		Objective 4	10 min.	●	●
INTERACTIVE TIMELINE **Texas: From Settlement to Statehood**			10 min.	●	
Synthesize					
DIGITAL ACTIVITY **Republic of Texas Cause-and-Effect Relationships**			5 min.	●	
Demonstrate					
DIGITAL QUIZ **Lesson Quiz and Class Discussion Board**			10 min.	●	

Topic 6 Lesson 6

Independence for Texas

CONNECT

DIGITAL START UP ACTIVITY
I Wish to See Texas Free

Project the Start Up Activity Ask students to read the quote and answer the questions as they enter and get settled. Have students share their answers with a partner, either in class or through a blog space.

Tell students that in this lesson they will be learning about how Texas became an independent republic and later a part of the United States.

Aa Vocabulary Development: Use the Interactive Reading Notepad to preview the Key Terms and Academic Vocabulary in this lesson with students.

⇅ FLIP IT!
Assign the Flipped Video for this lesson.

STUDENT EDITION PRINT
PAGES: 344–350

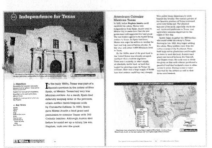

INVESTIGATE

DIGITAL TEXT 1
Americans Colonize Mexican Texas

Objective 1: Summarize the cooperation and conflict between American settlers in Texas and the Mexican government.

Quick Instruction
Interactive Map: The Settlement of Texas Project the interactive map on the whiteboard and click through the topics. Show students the region that was once part of Mexico and then became Texas. Ask students to describe the physical geography of Texas as shown on the map. Discuss how physical characteristics of the environment likely affected settlement patterns in the area.

Analyze Maps Click on the "Physical geography of Texas" layer. Ask students where they think Americans first settled in Texas, and why. *(Along rivers and near the Gulf of Mexico, where there was fertile soil for farming and waterways for transportation)*

Summarize Describe the physical characteristics of the environment that pushed people from the United States and pulled them to Mexican Texas. *(The best land in the United States was already taken, and land was expensive. Texas had large amounts of cheap, fertile land for farming.)*

INTERACTIVE MAP
The Settlement of Texas

📷 ACTIVE CLASSROOM
Have students suppose they are Stephen Austin and are trying to bring settlers to Texas. Have students use the Make Headlines activity to make a headline that captures the reasons for moving to Texas. Have students share their headlines with the class and discuss the most compelling arguments.

Further Instruction
Go through the Interactive Reading Notepad questions and discuss the answers with the class. Be sure students understand the physical and human geographic factors that shaped the early settlement of Texas.

Cite Evidence City evidence that explains why Mexico welcomed American settlers in Texas. *("Mexico was eager for settlers to develop the land and help control Indian attacks.")*

Cite Evidence Why does the physical geography of Texas remain important today? *(Increased settlement in Texas is due in part to the fertile soil that continues to ensure significant agricultural production.)*

Summarize Where was Austin's land grant? How did he divide the land to help ensure the success of the colony? *(His land grant was between the Colorado and Brazos rivers. He divided the land so colonists could access water. This decision was successful because his colony grew and more settlers came.)*

DIGITAL TEXT 2
Conflict With the Mexican Government

DIGITAL TEXT 3
Independence for Texas

Objective 2: **Explain how Texas gained independence.**

Quick Instruction

Project the image of German settlers on the whiteboard. Review the reasons settlers were drawn to Mexican Texas, including land for farming.

Identify Cause and Effect How did westward expansion cause conflict with the Mexican government? *(As more American settlers came to Texas, the Mexican government worried about losing the region to the United States. Later settlers were not loyal toward Mexico. They were Protestant, did not speak Spanish, and many supported slavery. To assert its authority, Mexico began to enforce laws that had long been ignored, including a law that banned slavery in the region. Many American settlers relied on enslaved workers to grow cotton. Settlers' anger grew when Mexico sent troops to enforce its will.)*

D **Differentiate: Extra Support** Review the definition of the key term *dictator* : a ruler with absolute power and authority. Ask students to consider what made Santa Anna a dictator. If they had settled in Texas during this time, would they have rebelled against his rule?

ELL Use the ELL activity described in the ELL chart.

Further Instruction

Go through the Interactive Reading Notepad questions and discuss the answers with the class.

Summarize Where was the first clash between Texan settlers and Mexican troops? Why did this clash occur? *(Gonzales, Texas. Texans wanted independence from Mexico; Tejanos wanted to overthrow Santa Anna.)*

Hypothesize Why do you think Texan settlers chose to go to war with Mexico instead of migrating to another region where they would be free of Santa Anna's rule? *(The settlers benefited from Texas's geography. They had fertile land and successful farms, which they did not want to leave.)*

Objective 3: **Describe how the events at the Alamo affected Texans.**

Quick Instruction

Interactive Gallery: Defenders of the Alamo Project the interactive gallery on the whiteboard and click through the images.

Analyze Images Look at the image of the Alamo compound. How did the physical geography of the region influence the events of the siege? *(The land was flat and open, making the mission the best place for the Texans to shield themselves from Santa Anna's attack. With no other natural barriers, the Mexicans could approach the mission and bombard it until they broke through. Once they broke through, there was no way for the Texans to hide or escape.)*

ACTIVE CLASSROOM

Have students use the Conversations With History Strategy and suppose they are having a conversation with William B. Travis about the siege of the Alamo. Have them write down a question they would ask, what Travis would say, and what they would say in response.

Independence for Texas

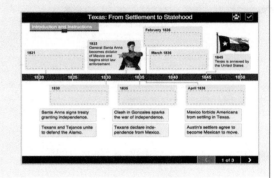

INTERACTIVE GALLERY
The Defenders of the Alamo

Built by the Spanish in 1724, this building was part of the mission of San Antonio de Valero for 70 years. It later housed Spanish troops who nicknamed it the Alamo. It went on to play a major role in Texas history.

DIGITAL TEXT 4
The Republic of Texas Is Born

The Republic of Texas Is Born

In battle, Texans had carried a flag with a single star. After winning independence, they nicknamed their new nation the Lone Star Republic. A constitution was written using the United States Constitution as a model. In September 1836, voters elected Sam Houston president of the Republic of Texas.

The new country faced several serious problems, however. First, the government of Mexico refused to accept the treaty that Santa Anna had signed. Mexicans insisted that Texas was still part of Mexico. Second, Texas was nearly bankrupt.

INTERACTIVE TIMELINE
Texas: From Settlement to Statehood

Texas: From Settlement to Statehood

Further Instruction
Go through the Interactive Reading Notepad questions and discuss the answers with the class. Be sure students understand the factors that influenced the siege of the Alamo and its significance.

Sequence Events Describe the siege of the Alamo. *(Texans waited for Santa Anna's attack from inside an old Spanish mission, the Alamo. The Texans were not equipped to hold off the attack by thousands of Mexican troops. They lasted 12 days as the Mexicans bombarded the mission. Finally, the attackers broke through the mission walls and defeated the Texans inside.)*

Objective 4: Identify the challenges faced by the Lone Star Republic.

Quick Instruction
Interactive Timeline: From Settlement to Statehood Project the interactive timeline on the whiteboard and have students read the event tiles. Ask students to state in their own words the events that led Texas to achieve independence.

Draw Conclusions How did the physical geography of Texas helped the republic grow? *(The Texan government attracted new settlers with the promise of cheap and plentiful land to farm.)*

👥 ACTIVE CLASSROOM

Have students use the Circle Write activity to write about how they think the annexation of Texas will affect the United States politically, economically, and socially. Students break into groups and write as much as they can for 1 minute, then switch with the person on their right. The next person tries to improve or elaborate on the response. Students continue to switch until the paper comes back to the first person. Have groups share the response they think is the best.

ELL Use the ELL activity described in the ELL chart.

Further Instruction
Go through the Interactive Reading Notepad questions and discuss the answers with the class.

Compare Points of View What were the arguments within the United States for and against annexing Texas? *(Because many Texans owned slaves, southerners favored annexation as a way to add another slave state to the Union. Northerners opposed annexation for this same reason. President Jackson also feared war with Mexico.)*

Make Predictions How do you think the geography of Texas might affect future relations with Mexico? *(Because they share a border, they will also share resources, such as water. They may have closer economic ties as a result; there will likely be tensions, too.)*

■ SYNTHESIZE

DIGITAL ACTIVITY

Republic of Texas Cause-and-Effect Relationships

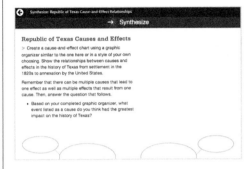

Have students review the events leading up to the annexation of Texas and fill in the chart.

Discuss Ask students to think about the important events leading up to the annexation of Texas. What geographic factors led to westward expansion into Texas? What were the effects of this expansion?

■ DEMONSTRATE

DIGITAL QUIZ

Lesson Quiz and Class Discussion Board

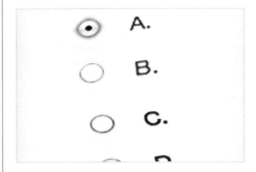

Assign the online Lesson Quiz for this lesson if you haven't already done so. Students will be offered automatic remediation or enrichment based on their score.

Pose these questions to the class on the Discussion Board:

Predict Consequences How will the annexation of Texas contribute to tensions over slavery in the United States?

Support Ideas With Examples What political, economic, social, and geographic factors led to the expansion of the United States? Give examples to support your view.

Topic Inquiry

Have students continue their investigations for the Topic Inquiry.

Manifest Destiny in California and the Southwest

Supporting English Language Learners

Use with Digital Text 2, **Manifest Destiny.**

Reading
Explain to students that using techniques to increase comprehension will help them to read silently for longer periods of time.

Beginning With students, echo read the first paragraph of the section titled *The Roots of Manifest Destiny*. Point out how some of the paragraph's information is repeated in the accompanying chart. Then ask students to silently read the same paragraph.

Intermediate Read aloud the first paragraph of the section titled *The Roots of Manifest Destiny*, modeling how to use the accompanying chart's "Social" column to support and confirm what you read. Then have students silently read the next paragraph and match the content to the chart's "Economic" column.

Advanced Display the chart titled *The Roots of Manifest Destiny* and read its content. Then ask students to silently read the section titled *The Roots of Manifest Destiny*, referring to the chart periodically to support and confirm what they are reading.

Advanced High With students, examine and discuss the three visual aids that accompany the text. Then have students silently read the text. Encourage them to refer to the visual aids as appropriate in order to increase their interest and understanding of the text.

Use with Digital Text 5, **The Effects of Migration to California.**

Listening
Introduce your speaking topic by locating California on a map and reviewing the term *gold rush*. Prompt students to understand the important details of spoken language.

Beginning Using familiar spoken language, paraphrase the first paragraph of the text. Ask: Which is a more important detail—that many different people came to California and changed its culture, or that some Australians came? That most newcomers were white Americans, or that some were Italians?

Intermediate Using mostly familiar spoken language, talk about how Native Americans fared in California. Then ask students to state the most important details you provided about Native Americans.

Advanced Using a mix of familiar and unfamiliar spoken language, talk about how Native Americans and African Americans fared in California. Then ask students to state the most important details you provided about each group.

Advanced High Using spoken language that is not linguistically accommodating and includes both familiar and unfamiliar vocabulary, talk about what Mexicans, Native Americans, Chinese, and African Americans faced in California. Challenge students to recall the most important details you provided about each group.

▶ Differentiate Instruction

Use the Differentiated Instruction notes throughout the lesson plan to support the varied skill sets, levels of readiness, and interests in the mixed-ability classroom.

Challenge These notes include suggestions for expanding the activity for advanced students.

On-Level These notes include suggestions for modifying the activity to address different interests or learning styles.

Extra Support These notes include ideas for providing more scaffolding or reading spuport.

Special Needs These notes provide ideas for adapting instruction to support the needs of various special needs students.

▪ NOTES

PEARSON
realize™
www.PearsonRealize.com

Go online to access additional resources including:
Primary Sources • Biographies • Supreme Court cases •
21st Century Skill Tutorials • Maps • Graphic Organizers.

Objectives

Objective 1: Describe life for the Spanish and Native Americans on the missions and ranches of California and New Mexico.

Objective 2: Analyze the relationship between the concept of Manifest Destiny and the westward growth of the nation.

Objective 3: List the causes and effects of the Mexican-American War.

Objective 4: Explain why the Mormons moved to Utah.

Objective 5: Describe how the gold rush affected California.

LESSON 7 ORGANIZER		PACING: APPROX. 1 PERIOD, .5 BLOCKS			
				RESOURCES	
		OBJECTIVES	**PACING**	**Online**	**Print**
Connect					
DIGITAL START UP ACTIVITY **We Are a Restless People**			5 min.	●	
Investigate					
DIGITAL TEXT 1 **New Mexico Territory and California**		Objective 1	10 min.	●	●
DIGITAL TEXT 2 **Manifest Destiny**		Objective 2	10 min.	●	●
INTERACTIVE MAP **The Growth of the West to 1860**			10 min.	●	
DIGITAL TEXT 3 **The U.S.-Mexican War**		Objective 3	10 min.	●	●
DIGITAL TEXT 4 **Settling the Mexican Cession**		Objectives 3, 4, 5	10 min.	●	●
DIGITAL TEXT 5 **The Effects of Migration to California**		Objective 5	10 min.	●	●
INTERACTIVE GALLERY **The People of California**			10 min.	●	
Synthesize					
DIGITAL ACTIVITY **Expansion of the United States**			5 min.	●	
Demonstrate					
DIGITAL QUIZ **Lesson Quiz and Class Discussion Board**			10 min.	●	

Manifest Destiny in California and the Southwest

▌ CONNECT

DIGITAL START UP ACTIVITY
We Are a Restless People

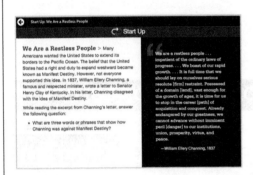

Project the Start Up activity consisting of a quotation on Manifest Destiny while the students enter and get settled. Ask students to read the quotation and answer the question. Then have them share their ideas with another student, either in-class or through an online chat or blog space.

Discuss Why was Channing against Manifest Destiny? *(He believed the rapid growth would have a negative impact on the institutions and prosperity of the Union.)*

Tell students that they will be learning about the idea of Manifest Destiny, the causes and effects of the Mexican-American War, why the Mormons moved to Utah, and events in California.

Aa Vocabulary Development: Use the Interactive Reading Notepad to preview the Key Terms and Academic Vocabulary in this lesson with students.

> **▌ FLIP IT!**
> Assign the Flipped Video for this lesson.

▌ STUDENT EDITION PRINT PAGES: 351–362

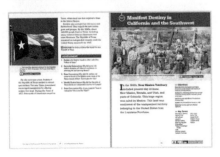

▌ INVESTIGATE

DIGITAL TEXT 1
New Mexico Territory and California

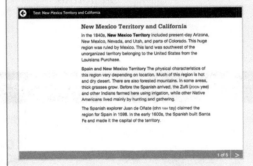

Objective 1: Describe life for the Spanish and Native Americans on the missions and ranches of California and New Mexico.

Quick Instruction

The parts of the country that we now know as California and the Southwest were part of Spain and then Mexico before they were added to the United States. Spain and Mexico established settlements along the Pacific Coast, including missions and ranches, where people of Spanish descent and Native Americans lived and worked together.

Analyze Images Project the image of Native Americans working on a Spanish mission from the reading. Ask students: How may this image reflect or differ from the reality of life on the missions? *(This image shows work that may have been done by Native Americans to help the mission function, including making rope and baskets. It does not show how hard life could be for Native Americans.)*

Summarize How did life change for Native Americans on California missions and ranches? *(Native Americans had lived in their own communities before the Spanish built their settlements. After, they lived with the Spanish on the missions and ranches. They were forced to give up their culture and did most of the work to keep the settlements functioning.)*

Further Instruction

Have students locate the different types of settlements and their locations on the regional map "Spanish Territory in North America, 1820" from the reading. Then have students answer the question below.

Compare and Contrast How did the physical geography of the New Mexico territory compare to much of the rest of the United States? *(Much of this region has a hotter, drier climate than most of the rest of the United States. Agriculture was difficult in much of this region. Before the Spanish arrived, the Zuñi (ZOON yee) and other Indians farmed here using irrigation, while other Native Americans lived mainly by hunting and gathering).* What physical characteristics of the environment attracted settlers to New Mexico and increased its population? *(Natural resources attracted settlers.)*

Draw Conclusions Ask students who was moving to California and the Southwest in the early 1800s. Have students explain the reasons these early settlers moved there. *(Spaniards moved to California and parts of the Southwest, like Santa Fe, to establish settlements and trading posts in their territory. Roman Catholic missionaries moved to convert the Native Americans. Some Americans also traveled to the Southwest.)*

DIGITAL TEXT 2

Manifest Destiny

INTERACTIVE MAP

The Growth of the West to 1860

DIGITAL TEXT 3

The U.S.-Mexican War

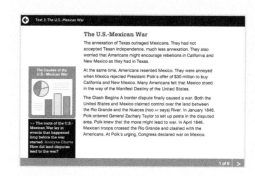

Objective 2: Analyze the relationship between the concept of Manifest Destiny and the westward growth of the nation.

Quick Instruction
Remind students that in the 1840s the United States reached as far west as the lands of the Louisiana Purchase. By this time many Americans were eager to expand the country even farther west, prompted in part by the idea of Manifest Destiny. Have students discuss the political, economic and social roots of Manifest Destiny and encourage them to identify the relationship between Manifest Destiny and westward expansion.

Interactive Map: The Growth of the West to 1860 Project the interactive map and click on the hotspots. Prompt students to connect reasons for population distribution and settlement patterns with the physical characteristics of the region.

📷 ACTIVE CLASSROOM
Conduct a Ranking Strategy activity. Ask students to rank what they think are the most important causes of westward expansion presented in the interactive map and have them explain their rationale for ranking the reasons the way they did.

D Differentiate: Extra Support Have each group of students rank the items in order of importance for one of the three categories listed in the "Roots of Manifest Destiny" table (political, economic, and social roots).

ELL Use the ELL activity described in the ELL chart.

Further Instruction
Americans who supported Manifest Destiny helped elect Polk as President in 1844. He ushered in the next era of westward expansion. Ask students to point out on a map which parts of the country were added under President Polk. *(The Oregon territory, which is now the states Oregon, Washington, and Idaho)*

Evaluate Impact Ask students how Manifest Destiny was related to the growth of the nation under President Polk. *(Polk was elected because he supported Manifest Destiny. He pushed to acquire new lands from Britain.)*

Objective 3: List the causes and results of the U.S.-Mexican War.

Quick Instruction
The U.S.-Mexican War was a turning point in growth of the United States. This war caused by a border dispute and the annexation of Texas, was fought over a vast territory from the heart of Mexico to northern California. With the lands gained from this war and the Gadsden Purchase, many Americans felt that their dream of Manifest Destiny had been fulfilled.

Identify Central Issues What were the effects of the U.S.-Mexican War? What was the impact of the U.S.-Mexican War on the growth of the United States? *(Because the United States won the U.S.-Mexican War, Mexico ceded California and the Southwest to the United States. The United States was also able to keep Texas and buy the lands of the Gadsden Purchase. These additions to the U.S. greatly expanded the western part of the country.)*

Further Instruction
The U.S.-Mexican War was the result of disputes and clashes between the United States and its neighbor Mexico. Ask the questions below before the Quick Instruction to understand the causes and details of the U.S.-Mexican War.

Manifest Destiny in California and the Southwest

DIGITAL TEXT 4

Settling the Mexican Cession

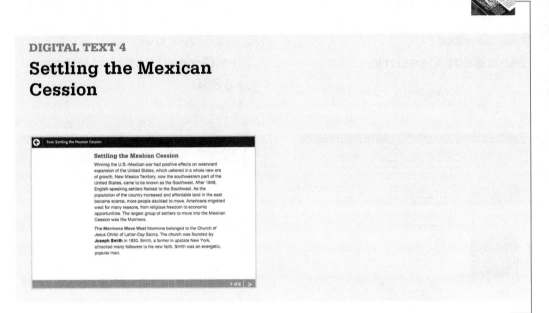

Settling the Mexican Cession

Winning the U.S.-Mexican war had positive effects on westward expansion of the United States, which ushered in a whole new era of growth. New Mexico Territory, now the southwestern part of the United States, came to be known as the Southwest. After 1848, English-speaking settlers flocked to the Southwest. As the population of the country increased and affordable land in the east became scarce, more people decided to move. Americans migrated west for many reasons, from religious freedom to economic opportunities. The largest group of settlers to move into the Mexican Cession was the Mormons.

The Mormons Move West Mormons belonged to the Church of Jesus Christ of Latter-Day Saints. The church was founded by **Joseph Smith** in 1830. Smith, a farmer in upstate New York, attracted many followers to his new faith. Smith was an energetic, popular man.

1 of 6   >

Summarize What were the causes of the U.S.-Mexican War? *(Causes included the annexation of Texas, disputes over territory, Manifest Destiny, and clashes between Mexican and American troops in disputed lands.)*

Analyze Sequence Have students record in sequential order the key events of the U.S.-Mexican War. *(The United States and Mexican armies clashed in the disputed territory in April 1846. After crossing into Mexico, American General Taylor clashed with Mexican General Santa Anna at the Battle of Buena Vista in February 1847. American General Scott sailed to Veracruz, Mexico in 1847. American General Kearny captured Santa Fe and San Diego in 1847. In 1847 General Scott reached Mexico City and was able to overtake it. In 1848 the Mexican government moved to make peace with the United States.)*

Objectives 3: List the causes and results of the U.S.-Mexican War; 4: Explain why the Mormons moved to Utah; 5: Describe how the gold rush affected California.

Quick Instruction

Once the lands of the Mexican Cession became part of the United States, Americans began to flock to the West. Early settlers came for a variety of reasons from economic opportunities provided by the gold rush to religious freedom. The physical characteristics of the environment impacted those who moved to the West and why they moved there. Immigrants came from all over the world for the economic opportunities in California. Others came to establish a new life based on farming in Utah.

Generate Explanations Ask students to compare how physical and human characteristics differed in places across the West. How were different parts of this region shaped by the people who moved there? *(Some parts of the West had good farmland while other parts had valuable resources, such as gold. People who came to the West to farm and establish lives for their families created different economies and cultures from people who came from around the world to make money mining, and then often move onwards. People who came west for religious purposes helped establish communities based on their values.)*

Further Instruction

Show and discuss the Reading Support graphic organizer about why people moved to California and Utah. Help fill in the answers by asking: Which ethnic and religious groups settled in Utah and California? Why did they move to these regions? *(Mormons moved to Utah for religious freedom. Many different ethnic groups came to California for the economic opportunities of the Gold Rush.)*

Apply Concepts What effect did human geographic factors have on the Mormon settlement of Utah? *(Mormon leader Brigham Young chose an isolated valley between the Rocky Mountains hoping the Mormons would be safe from persecution there. Young planned an irrigation system to bring water to farms. He also drew up plans for a large city, called Salt Lake City, to be built in the desert. Waves of Mormon settlers came and the settlement quickly grew.)*

DIGITAL TEXT 5

The Effects of Migration to California

INTERACTIVE GALLERY

The People of California

Objective 5: Describe how the Gold Rush affected California.

Quick Instruction

Remind students that before the Gold Rush, the population of California consisted mainly of Native Americans and people of Spanish descent. With the Gold Rush, California went through dramatic changes in its population, economy, and politics.

Interactive Gallery: The People of California Project the gallery and go over each of the images with the students.

Summarize Describe the effect of the Gold Rush and this era of western expansion on Native Americans and Mexicans living in California. *(During the 1850s and 1860s, many Mexicans and Native Americans lost their land. In 1850, about 100,000 Native Americans lived in California, but by the 1870s, the state's Native American population had dropped to 17,000.)*

📷 ACTIVE CLASSROOM

Have students use the Group Spokesperson Strategy to answer the following question: Did the opportunities provided by the Gold Rush outweigh the hardships people faced? Explain your answer with specific examples. *(For many people the opportunities provided by the Gold Rush outweighed the hardships faced. White immigrants from the United States and Europe were able to work in the mines or in other businesses, though most miners did not become rich. African Americans faced discrimination, but were able to live in a state that did not allow slavery.)*

Draw Conclusions How did the physical characteristics of the environment influence settlement patterns and population distribution in the West? *(The population of the California increased during this time, but the distribution of the population remained patchy. Locations that had gold attracted settlers. People also moved to areas with farmland.)*

■ ELL Use the ELL activity described in the ELL chart.

Further Instruction

Distinguish Identify one racial group that migrated to California. Explain their reasons for moving there, *(African Americans came to California to escape slavery in other parts of the United States, make money running businesses, and work in the mining industry.)*

Summarize How did different immigrant groups, such as the Chinese, interact with the environment in California? *(Chinese Americans shaped the environment by draining swamplands and digging irrigation systems to turn dry land into fertile farmland.)*

Manifest Destiny in California and the Southwest

SYNTHESIZE

DIGITAL ACTIVITY
Expansion of the United States

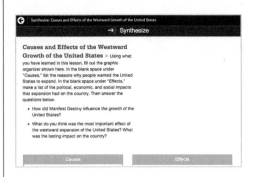

DEMONSTRATE

DIGITAL QUIZ
Lesson Quiz and Class Discussion Board

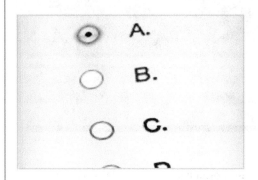

While today we picture the United States reaching from the Atlantic to the Pacific Ocean, in 1803 the nation only reached as far as the lands of the Louisiana Purchase. Many factors and major events led to the rapid growth of the country in the 1840s and 1850s. This expansion changed our nation forever.

Discuss Have partners think about the following question. What were the causes and effects of the westward growth of the United States? Ask partners to share their answers with the class.

Assign the online Lesson Quiz for this lesson if you haven't already done so. Students will be offered automatic remediation or enrichment based on their score.

Pose these questions to the class on the Discussion Board:

In *California and the Southwest*, you read about the many factors that led to the growth of the United States in a short period of time.

Apply Concepts How did Manifest Destiny influence the westward growth of the United States? *(Americans who supported Manifest Destiny were more supportive of events that led to the growth of the country, such as the Mexican-American War.)*

Topic Inquiry
Have students continue their investigations for the Topic Inquiry.

The Age of Jackson and Westward Expansion (1824–1860)

■ SYNTHESIZE

DIGITAL ESSENTIAL QUESTION ACTIVITY
Why do people move?

First, ask students to reconsider the Essential Question for the topic: Why do people move? Remind students of the reasons they considered at the beginning of the topic. For example: lack of economic, cultural, or political opportunity in their current location; expanded economic, cultural, and political opportunities in a new location; forced relocation, as in the case of many Native Americans.

Ask students, "What factors led many settlers to leave their homes and find a new home further west?"

Next, ask students to reflect on the topic as a whole and write down 1-3 questions they've thought about during the topic.

Prompt students to identify the specific push and pull factors that encouraged westward migration across the country. Ask students to work in small groups as they write a response to one of the following questions: Why did people leave their homes during this time period? What economic, cultural, or political opportunities were unavailable where they previously lived? Why did people choose to move westward to Oregon Country? Why were many Native Americans forced to move westward?

Topic Inquiry
Have students complete Step 3 of the Topic Inquiry.

■ DEMONSTRATE

DIGITAL TOPIC REVIEW AND ASSESSMENT
The Age of Jackson and Westward Expansion (1824–1860)

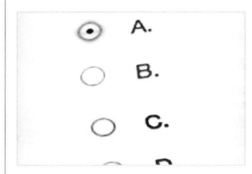

Students can prepare for the Topic Test by answering the questions in the Topic Review and Assessment online or the Assessment questions in the Print Student text. They can also prepare by reviewing their answers to the Interactive Reading Notepad questions or reviewing their notes in the Reading and Notetaking Study Guide.

DIGITAL TOPIC TEST
The Age of Jackson and Westward Expansion (1824–1860)

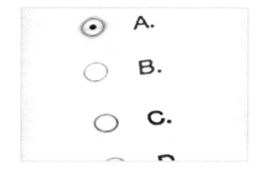

TOPIC TEST
Assign the Topic Test to assess students' understanding of topic content.

BENCHMARK TESTS
Assign these benchmark tests as you complete the relevant topics to monitor student progress toward mastering the course content and as preparation for the End-of-Course Test.

Benchmark Test 1: Topics 1–2

Benchmark Test 2: Topics 3–4

Benchmark Test 3: Topics 5–6

Benchmark Test 4: Topics 7–9

Benchmark Test 5: Topics 10–12

Benchmark Test 6: Topics 13–14

Benchmark Test 7: Topics 15–17

Society and Culture Before the Civil War (1820–1860)

TOPIC 7 ORGANIZER	PACING: APPROX. 1 PERIOD, .5 BLOCKS
	PACING
Connect	1 period
MY STORY VIDEO **Lucy Larcom, Weaving Opportunity**	10 min.
DIGITAL ESSENTIAL QUESTION ACTIVITY **Why is Culture Important?**	10 min.
DIGITAL TIMELINE ACTIVITY **Society and Culture Before the Civil War**	10 min.
TOPIC INQUIRY: DOCUMENT-BASED QUESTION **Comparing Points of View on Slavery and Abolition**	20 min.
Investigate	3–6 periods
TOPIC INQUIRY: DOCUMENT-BASED QUESTION **Comparing Points of View on Slavery and Abolition**	Ongoing
LESSON 1 The Industrial Revolution and Life in the North	30–40 min.
LESSON 2 King Cotton and Life in the South	30–40 min.
LESSON 3 Reform Movements	30–40 min.
LESSON 4 Abolitionism	30–40 min.
LESSON 5 Women's Rights	30–40 min.
LESSON 6 Arts and Literature	30–40 min.
Synthesize	1 period
DIGITAL ACTIVITY **Reflect on the Essential Question and Topic**	10 min.
TOPIC INQUIRY: DOCUMENT-BASED QUESTION **Comparing Points of View on Slavery and Abolition**	20 min.
Demonstrate	1–2 periods
DIGITAL TOPIC REVIEW AND ASSESSMENT **Society and Culture Before the Civil War**	10 min.
TOPIC INQUIRY: DOCUMENT-BASED QUESTION **Comparing Points of View on Slavery and Abolition**	20 min.

TOPIC INQUIRY: DOCUMENT-BASED QUESTION

Comparing Points of View on Slavery and Abolition

In this Topic Inquiry, students will examine primary source documents to answer the following question: What points of view did people have toward slavery and abolition? Developing a deeper understanding of these points of view, the people that held them, and the reasons for their disagreement will contribute to students' understanding of the Essential Question: Why is culture important?

STEP 1: CONNECT
Develop Questions and Plan the Investigation

Read Aloud

Divide students into pairs or small groups and have them take turns reading the speech and the poem aloud. Tell students that to answer the document-based question, they will be examining images, speeches, and lectures from pro and antislavery points of view.

Suggestion: You may want to let students read the speech and the poem to themselves beforehand. Provide a physical or online dictionary so they can look up any words they don't understand before reading aloud.

Discuss

Discuss as a class the points of view and frames of reference of the speech and the poem. Ask students to identify the point of view of each source based on the historical context surrounding the events each source discusses. Remind students that slavery and abolition were issues that divided the country in the years before the Civil War. Explain to students that this historical context shaped the frames of reference of each author and that frames of reference are the ways people think about events based on their experience and background. Discuss as a class the bias in the speech and the poem. Remind students that bias can mean prejudice. It can also mean a particular point of view. Discuss how the bias in each source reflects its author's point of view, calling on students to cite evidence for support.

Suggestion: If students are having difficulty identifying bias, have them begin rereading from the beginning of each piece. Have them stop after each line and ask themselves what the author is saying, how the author is saying it, why the author is expressing this view, and whether the piece simply states facts or whether it expresses a particular point of view, or bias.

STEP 2: INVESTIGATE
Apply Disciplinary Concepts and Tools

Analyze the Documents

Students will work individually to examine six documents and consider the different points of view they express. To guide their thinking, ask them to identify the point of view of each document based on its historical context, the frame of reference of each document's creator or author, and the bias present in each document, and then have students explain how they identified these characteristics.

Suggestion: Remind students to look up any words or phrases they do not understand. Students struggling to comprehend the documents may want to write a brief summary of each.

Check Your Understanding

Students will work individually to answer the multiple choice and short answer questions attached to each document. Answering the questions will help students identify areas in which their comprehension may be struggling. Students should review the documents as needed and correct their mistakes.

Suggestion: You may want to check students' answers for comprehension, or have students swap with a partner to check each other's work.

⏻ PROFESSIONAL DEVELOPMENT

Document-Based Question
Be sure to view the Document-Based Question Professional Development resources in the online course.

TOPIC INQUIRY: DOCUMENT-BASED QUESTION

Comparing Points of View on Slavery and Abolition *(continued)*

STEP 3: SYNTHESIZE	STEP 4: DEMONSTRATE
Evaluate Sources and Use Evidence to Formulate Conclusions	Communicate Conclusions and Take Informed Action

Write Your Essay

Students will use the documents to write essays on the following topic: What points of view did people have toward slavery and abolition? Remind students that they are being asked to think more deeply about the different points of view, frames of reference, and biases, and the ways people presented and justified their positions. Students should use their two charts to help them write their first draft.

Suggestion: Review the requirements for the essay. Students must use and mention at least four specific examples from the documents, two for each side of the argument. Essays should be clearly organized and free of errors.

Digital Topic Review and Assessment

Society and Culture Before the Civil War Students can prepare for the Topic Test by reviewing their notes for each lesson. Use the Test Bank to create your own Topic Test.

Digital Topic Test and Test Bank

TEKS Mastery Test Students can take a cumulative TEKS Mastery Test online to monitor their progress toward mastering the TEKS for this course and as preparation for the End-of-Course test.

Print Test

End-of-Course Practice Test You may want to assign the End-of-Course Practice Test found in the print Student text.

Topic Inquiry

Have students submit their essays.

INTRODUCTION

Society and Culture Before the Civil War (1820–1860)

American culture and society changed dramatically before the Civil War. New technological inventions led to industrialization and urbanization in the North. Cotton production soared in the South, bringing wealth to the region but also spreading slavery. Economic, religious, and political changes gave rise to social changes as reformers sought to improve society, end slavery, and increase women's rights. A changing society also gave rise to uniquely American forms of cultural expression.

■ CONNECT

MY STORY VIDEO
Lucy Larcom, Weaving Opportunity

Watch a video about Lucy Larcom, a worker in an early 19th century Lowell textile mill.

Check Understanding Where did many of the workers in the early textile mills come from? *(farms)*

Determine Point of View What may have accounted for the change in Lucy Larcom's view of mill work? *(Once she had grown accustomed to mill work, the novelty of it wore off. She grew to dislike the constant noise, and refused to become a slave to machines. The tedium of the labor and the need constantly to service the machines no doubt accounted for her change in view.)*

DIGITAL ESSENTIAL QUESTION ACTIVITY
Why is Culture Important?

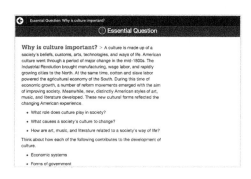

Ask students to think about the Essential Question for this topic: Why is culture important? Changes to American culture in the early 1800s impacted the nation and the American way of life.

If students have not already done so, ask them to read the list and think about how each factor contributes to the development of culture. Have students answer the questions and share their ideas with a partner.

Identify Cause and Effect What factors caused America's culture to change in the early 1800s?

Draw Conclusions How is the economy related to culture? Why would changes to the economy have a cultural impact?

DIGITAL TIMELINE ACTIVITY
Society and Culture Before the Civil War

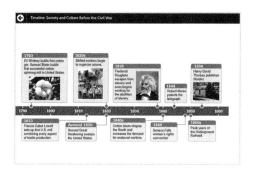

Display the timeline showing the major events before the Civil War. During this topic students will learn about all of these events and many more, but this timeline will provide a framework into which they can place the events they learn about.

Summarize Name at least two major reforms that occurred during this time. *(education; treatment for the mentally ill; women's rights; antislavery movement)*

Make Predictions How do you think the Second Great Awakening would shape American culture in the 1800s? *(It would increase religious feelings and inspire social reform.)*

Topic Inquiry
Launch the Topic Inquiry with students after introducing the topic.

The Industrial Revolution and Life in the North

Supporting English Language Learners

Use with Digital Text 2, **Factories Come to America.**

Listening
Understand the important details of spoken language like the meaning of the word credit using the familiar context of credit cards.

Beginning Use basic spoken language to paraphrase the first paragraph of the text. Then help students to understand the important details of what you said by having them complete these sentences: *During the Industrial Revolution, the banking system was _____. People could get _____ to help them start businesses.*

Intermediate Use spoken language to paraphrase the first two paragraphs of the text. Then ask students to demonstrate their understanding by identifying the most important details from what you said.

Advanced Use spoken language to explain how supply and demand influenced business and investing, using the text as a reference. Ask students to demonstrate their understanding by identifying the most important details from what you said.

Advanced High Use spoken language to discuss markets in contexts that range from familiar to unfamiliar and may or may not be included in the text (e.g., food market, labor market, free enterprise market, stock market). Ask students to demonstrate their understanding by identifying the most important detail about each kind of market.

Use with Digital Text 5, **New Technological Innovations.**

Reading
Tell students that if they read for comprehension rather than for speed, they will be able to read silently for longer periods of time.

Beginning Read aloud the first paragraph of the section titled *Farm Machines*, and explain any difficult words or phrases. Then ask students to silently read each sentence in the paragraph twice: once to decode individual words, and once to understand how the words fit together.

Intermediate Ask students to silently read the section titled *Farm Machines*. Encourage them to pause and reread any sentences they do not understand. Explain that they do not need to understand every word, but they should comprehend the general meaning of each sentence before moving on.

Advanced Ask students to silently read the section titled *A New Communications System, the Telegraph*. Encourage them to pause after each paragraph and identify its main idea, rereading it if necessary before moving on.

Advanced High Provide students with a dictionary, and ask them to silently read the text. When they encounter unfamiliar words or expressions, encourage them first to use context clues to determine their meanings. If necessary, they can also use the dictionary before resuming their reading.

D Differentiate Instruction

Use the Differentiated Instruction notes throughout the lesson plan to support the varied skill sets, levels of readiness, and interests in the mixed-ability classroom.

Challenge These notes include suggestions for expanding the activity for advanced students.

On-Level These notes include suggestions for modifying the activity to address different interests or learning styles.

Extra Support These notes include ideas for providing more scaffolding or reading spuport.

Special Needs These notes provide ideas for adapting instruction to support the needs of various special needs students.

▪ NOTES

PEARSON
realize™
www.PearsonRealize.com

Go online to access additional resources including:
Primary Sources • Biographies • Supreme Court cases •
21st Century Skill Tutorials • Maps • Graphic Organizers.

Objectives

Objective 1: Identify the Industrial Revolution and explain its effects.

Objective 2: Explain the impact of the Industrial Revolution on cities.

Objective 3: Describe how technological change affected the economy of the North.

Objective 4: Identify the impact of the Industrial Revolution on working conditions, social class, and daily life.

Objective 5: Describe the impact of immigration and attitudes toward immigrants and African Americans in the North.

LESSON 1 ORGANIZER		PACING: APPROX. 1 PERIOD, .5 BLOCKS			
				RESOURCES	
		OBJECTIVES	PACING	Online	Print
Connect					
DIGITAL START UP ACTIVITY **A Model Factory Town**			5 min.	●	
Investigate					
DIGITAL TEXT 1 **The Industrial Revolution Begins**			10 min.	●	●
DIGITAL TEXT 2 **Factories Come to America**		Objective 1	10 min.	●	●
3-D MODEL **Nineteenth-Century Textile Mill**			10 min.	●	
DIGITAL TEXT 3 **Daily Life in Factory Towns**		Objective 2	10 min.	●	●
DIGITAL TEXT 4 **Cities Expand**			10 min.	●	●
DIGITAL TEXT 5 **New Technological Innovations**			10 min.	●	●
INTERACTIVE TIMELINE **New Inventions Improve Life**		Objective 3	10 min.	●	
DIGITAL TEXT 6 **The Age of Steam Power**			10 min.	●	●
INTERACTIVE GALLERY **The Steam Locomotive**			10 min.	●	
DIGITAL TEXT 7 **Workers Respond to Challenges**		Objective 4	10 min.	●	●
DIGITAL TEXT 8 **Ethnic Minorities in the North**		Objective 5	10 min.	●	●
Synthesize					
DIGITAL ACTIVITY **A New Revolution**			5 min.	●	
Demonstrate					
DIGITAL QUIZ **Lesson Quiz and Class Discussion Board**			10 min.	●	

The Industrial Revolution and Life in the North

■ CONNECT

DIGITAL START UP ACTIVITY
A Model Factory Town

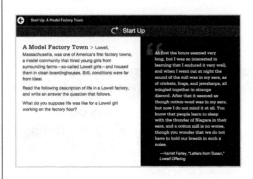

Project the Start Up Activity Ask students to read the quote and answer the questions as they enter and get settled. Have students share their answers with a partner, either in class or through a blog space.

Discuss What do you suppose life was like for a Lowell girl working on the factory floor? *(The girls worked long hours doing difficult, repetitive work, but it was exciting to learn new skills, meet other girls, and work outside the home.)*

Tell students that in this lesson they will be learning about the Industrial Revolution in the North and thetechnological innovations that changed life in the United States.

Aa Vocabulary Development: Use the Interactive Reading Notepad to preview the Key Terms and Academic Vocabulary in this lesson with students.

↕ FLIP IT!

Assign the Flipped Video for this lesson.

■ STUDENT EDITION PRINT
PAGES: 368–388

■ INVESTIGATE

DIGITAL TEXT 1
The Industrial Revolution Begins

Objective 1: Identify the Industrial Revolution and explain its effects.

Quick Instruction

The Industrial Revolution began in Britain and soon spread, along with its factories, to the United States. Americans learned to rely on the physical characteristics of the environment, such as running water, to provide fuel for factories in the early nineteenth century, or 1800s. At the beginning of industrialization, factories were built to take advantage of water power. Factors, such as increased supply, lower costs, and growing demand, brought about rapid industrialization. Inventions, such as the textile mill, the spinning jenny, and the cotton gin, allowed producers to meet the growing demand.

3-D Model: Nineteenth-Century Textile Mill Project the 3-D model of the textile mill on the whiteboard and click through the images. Have students look at the wheel. Ask what environmental feature the textile mills were dependent on. *(rivers)*

Identify Cause and Effect How did new technologies change the way goods were manufactured in the United States and elsewhere? *(Spinning jennies and power looms allowed workers to produce much more cloth than they could by hand in both the United States and Britain.)*

ELL Use the ELL activity described in the ELL chart.

DIGITAL TEXT 2
Factories Come to America

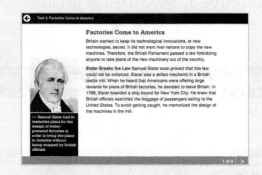

👥 ACTIVE CLASSROOM

Ask students to write brief explanations for the reasons for the increase in factories. Have students use the Write 1-Get 3 Activity and fold a piece of paper into quarters. Students write down one response in the first box and then go around asking to hear other responses. When students think a response is correct, they write it in their boxes until they have three more responses. Have students share their responses with the class.

Further Instruction

Go through the Interactive Reading Notepad questions and discuss the answers with the class. To extend the lesson, assign 21st Century Skills: Create Databases.

Generate Explanations Explain the effects of scientific and technological innovations such as the use of interchangeable parts. How did such technological innovations bring about economic growth? *(Interchangeable parts increased efficiency and saved time and money. Instead of making parts specific to each individual item, machine-made parts were identical and could be used interchangeably. This contributed to the increase in factories, which could produce the parts faster and more cheaply than small workshops. Other technological innovations, such as the steam engine, further increased efficiency and production. Because factories could sell more goods, workers and factory owners made more money and could buy more goods. This increase in supply and demand brought economic growth.)*

3-D MODEL

Nineteenth-Century Textile Mill

Early Textile Mill

Drag your cursor to explore the inner workings of an early nineteenth-century textile mill.

1 of 4

Identify Patterns What economic changes did the War of 1812 cause in the nation, and how did these changes contribute to the Industrial Revolution? *(The British blockade during the war forced Americans to build more factories to manufacture their own goods.)*

Draw Conclusions Describe the characteristics of the free enterprise system in the nineteenth century. What were the benefits of this system on the U.S. economy? *(Characteristics—few restrictions on trade or business growth; access to credit for bank loans; low taxes. Benefits—people were more easily able to finance new mills and factories; competition spurred economic growth.)*

DIGITAL TEXT 3

Daily Life in Factory Towns

Text 3: Daily Life in Factory Towns

Daily Life in Factory Towns

Slater and Whitney's innovations were just the first steps in America's Industrial Revolution. During the early 1800s, entire cities began to emerge around factories.

The Lowell Mills During the War of 1812, Francis Cabot Lowell, a Boston merchant, found a way to improve on British textile mills. In Britain, one factory spun thread and a second factory wove it into cloth. Why not, Lowell wondered, combine spinning and weaving under one roof? The new mill that he built in Waltham, Massachusetts, had all the machines needed to turn raw cotton into finished cloth.

After Lowell's death, his partners took on a more ambitious project. They built an entire factory town and named it after him. In 1821, Lowell, Massachusetts, was a village of five farm families.

>> Work in the textile mills in the early 1800s, such as the one shown here, was hard and dangerous. Workers faced long hours on their feet amid noisy machines and a risk of being caught and injured by moving parts.

1 of 6

Objective 2: **Explain the impact of the Industrial Revolution on cities.**

Quick Instruction
Project the infographic on urban industrial growth on the whiteboard. Have students consider the population growth in northern cities and explain the reasons for the increase in urbanization.

Identify Cause and Effect Identify the economic factors that brought about rapid urbanization in the nineteenth century. *(Factories increased profits, which led investors to build even more factories. These factories attracted more workers from farms who were seeking jobs and money. Cities developed and expanded around the factories as more people came to work in industries.)*

Further Instruction
Go through the Interactive Reading Notepad questions and discuss the answers with the class.

Summarize Identify the economic contributions of women to American society during the Industrial Revolution. *(Women such as the Lowell girls worked in the mills, providing labor, making products, and earning wages for their families.)*

DIGITAL TEXT 4

Cities Expand

Text 4: Cities Expand

Cities Expand

In 1800, the vast majority of Americans lived in rural areas. During the Industrial Revolution, many people left farms for cities, attracted by the job opportunities to be found in factories. As investors found that factories produced a profit, they invested those profits in building more factories, which attracted still more workers from farms. Older cities expanded rapidly, while new cities sprang up around factories. This movement of the population from rural areas to cities is called **urbanization**. Urbanization increased as industry grew.

Urbanization was a steady but gradual process. In 1800, only 6 percent of the nation's population lived in urban areas. By 1860, the number had risen to 15 percent. Not until 1920 did more Americans live in cities than in rural areas.

>> Analyze Graphs Based on the information in the graphs, what factor best explains the rapid rate of urbanization in northern cities during the mid-1800s?

1 of 4

Support Ideas with Examples Using Lowell, Massachusetts, as an example, identify how industrialization changed life in the United States. *(More people moved to cities and worked in factories, including children and girls. Mill workers put in long hours year-round, in conditions that worsened as industrialization progressed. More family members began working outside of the home to earn money. This affected women's roles, as many women took paying jobs. Women who could afford it, however, stayed home.)*

Compare and Contrast Describe the positive and negative consequences of human modification of the physical environment through urbanization. *(Positive—cities offered work opportunities and new attractions and entertainment. Negative—the streets overflowed with garbage and untreated sewage; contaminated water spread disease; coal used to power industries and homes polluted the air and caused health problems.)*

The Industrial Revolution and Life in the North

DIGITAL TEXT 5

New Technological Innovations

INTERACTIVE TIMELINE

New Inventions Improve Life

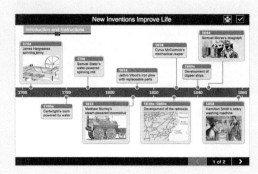

DIGITAL TEXT 6

The Age of Steam Power

Objective 3: Describe how technological change affected the economy of the North.

Quick Instruction

Interactive Timeline: New Inventions Improve Life Project the interactive timeline on the whiteboard and click through the events. Have students pick two scientific discoveries, explain their effects, and compare how they influenced daily life in the nineteenth century, or the 1800s, then have them pick two technological innovations, explain their effects, and compare how they influenced daily life in the same period.

Generate Explanations Explain the impact of communications systems such as the telegraph. How did they affect the growth, development, and urbanization of the United States? *(The telegraph contributed to the growth and development of the United States by connecting farmers and business people with different markets, increasing business opportunities and economic growth and encouraging the development of new regions.*

It contributed to urbanization, as business people located in cities with good telegraph services.) How did technological innovations such as the telegraph, the railroad, and steamships change the way goods were marketed nationally and internationally? *(Goods could now be marketed to distant customers, including customers in other countries.)*

Compare How was the locomotive an improvement over earlier railroad systems? *(The first railroads were pulled by horses or mules. The steam-powered locomotive engine pulled cars much faster. As engineering improved, locomotive railroads became safer and faster than previous forms of transportation.)*

👥 ACTIVE CLASSROOM

Have students imagine they are advertising one of the new technological innovations of the Industrial Revolution and use the Make Headlines Activity to capture the importance of the device and the impact it will have.

👥 ACTIVE CLASSROOM

Project a visual image from the steam locomotive and divide it into four numbered quadrants. Have students count off 1 to 4. Then have them look closely at the part of the image in their quadrant. Have them tell you what they see and what they learned as a result of their focus on this part of the image. Collect insights for each quadrant.

ELL Use the ELL activity described in the ELL chart.

Further Instruction

Go through the Interactive Reading Notepad questions and discuss the answers with the class. Be sure students can give examples of how technological innovations brought about economic growth. To extend the lesson, assign Personal Finance: Budgeting.

INTERACTIVE GALLERY

The Steam Locomotive

DIGITAL TEXT 7

Workers Respond to Challenges

Support Ideas with Examples Give three examples of how the free enterprise system benefited Americans during the Industrial Revolution. *(mass production lowered prices; standard of living increased; wages increased)*

Identify Cause and Effect What was the impact of transportation systems on the urbanization of the United States? *(Railroads connected cities across the United States, allowing people to migrate more easily to urban centers. Factories and businesses grew in cities with good rail connections, which further encouraged more people to move to these areas.)*

Objective 4: **Identify the impact of the Industrial Revolution on working conditions, social class, and daily life.**

Quick Instruction

Analyze Images Project the image of the factory and have students describe the working conditions visible in the image. Explain that this is an example of how industrialization changed life in the United States. Why do you think a labor reform movement developed in the United States? *(As a result of industrialization, laborers worked long hours at dangerous jobs for low wages. They organized to improve their hours, pay, and working conditions.)*

D **Differentiate: Extra Support** To understand the reasons for conflicts over labor, have students answer the following question from the point of view of a factory worker. What kinds of practices would you want the factory owner to follow? Now have them answer from the factory owner's point of view. What practices would you want to follow instead? Have students consider the different perspectives to understand how the interests of workers and owners differed.

Further Instruction

Go through the Interactive Reading Notepad questions and discuss the answers with the class.

Evaluate Arguments Evaluate the impact of the labor reform movement. Was it successful? Provide evidence to support your view. *(The movement did not completely transform working conditions, but it did meet with some*

success. Government employees won a ten-hour workday, strikes became legal, and some skilled workers won better pay.)

Summarize Based on material in this text and preceding texts, what are some examples of how industrialization changed life in the United States? *(New jobs were available in factories; people moved from farms to cities; more goods were available more cheaply; people worked long hours in factories; family life became oriented around factory work.)*

Identify Cause and Effect How did urbanization lead to conflicts between people of different social classes? *(Urban working conditions created divisions between skilled and unskilled labor and between workers, managers, and business owners. These divisions did not exist when most people were farmers. The different classes lived together in the cities, but they often had different interests and conflicting views. These differences led to conflicts such as strikes.)*

The Industrial Revolution and Life in the North

SYNTHESIZE

DEMONSTRATE

DIGITAL TEXT 8
Ethnic Minorities in the North

DIGITAL ACTIVITY
A New Revolution

DIGITAL QUIZ
Lesson Quiz and Class Discussion Board

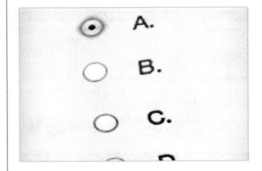

Objective 5: **Describe the impact of immigration and attitudes toward immigrants and African Americans in the North.**

Quick Instruction
Project the photo of immigrants on the whiteboard and review the reasons industrialization drew people to northern cities, including immigrants.

Identify Central Issues Identify three ethnic groups that settled in the United States during this time and explain their reasons for immigration. *(British—higher wages; Irish—freedom from hunger and British rule; Germans—fertile land, a better life, democracy)*

Further Instruction
Go through the Interactive Reading Notepad questions and discuss the answers with the class.

Identify Cause and Effect How did urbanization lead to conflicts over differences in religion? *(Most Americans during the early 1800s were Protestant, but many immigrants were Catholic or Jewish. Many immigrants came to cities, which grew increasingly diverse. Not all Americans tolerated people of different religions. This lack of tolerance led to conflict between members of the different religions.)*

Make Predictions How do you think conflicts between various ethnic groups would be resolved? *(Americans would grow more tolerant as diversity increased; immigrants would adapt to American culture.)*

Have students complete the graphic organizer and explain what they think was the most important result of the Industrial Revolution, providing evidence for support.

Discuss Ask students to review the quote from the beginning of the lesson and decide whether they think Susan's view of factory life was typical for Americans working in industry. Discuss what it was like for women, immigrants, African Americans, and skilled and unskilled laborers to work in factories as America became more urban and industrial.

Assign the online Lesson Quiz for this lesson if you haven't already done so. Students will be offered automatic remediation or enrichment based on their score.

Pose these questions to the class on the Discussion Board:

Draw Conclusions How do you think the Industrial Revolution contributed to economic differences among different regions of the United States? Explain your reasoning.

Identify Cause and Effect How did the factory system contribute to rapid industrialization? What were the effects of this innovation on the United States?

Topic Inquiry
Have students continue their investigations for the Topic Inquiry.

King Cotton and Life in the South

Supporting English Language Learners

Use with Digital Text 4, **Southern African Americans.**

Reading
Explain to students that they will be employing basic reading skills and English comprehension to locate the answers to questions provided to them beforehand.

Beginning Provide students with a list titled *Jobs of African Americans*. On the list, include some from the text's third paragraph and some not. Have students read the paragraph and demonstrate English comprehension by circling the jobs on the list that are also mentioned in the paragraph.

Intermediate Display these questions: What are two ways an African American obtained freedom? In what trades did African Americans work? Ask pairs of students to read the second and third paragraphs of the text. Then have them demonstrate English comprehension by answering the questions.

Advanced Display these questions: Why was there tension between white slave owners and free African Americans? What difficulties did free African Americans face? Ask pairs of students to read the section titled Free African Americans and demonstrate English comprehension by answering the questions.

Advanced High Provide students with a blank Venn diagram. Then ask them to read the text and demonstrate English comprehension by comparing and contrasting the work and working conditions of free and enslaved African Americans.

Use with Digital Text 5, **Slavery in the South.**

Listening
Before the activity, review the term implicit idea and provide a simple example in increasingly complex spoken language (e.g., the implicit idea in saying you are hungry is that you want to eat).

Beginning Use basic spoken language to paraphrase the first two sentences of the section titled *Hard Work*. Ask: Which idea is implicit in what I said—that enslaved workers usually worked less than 16 hours per day, worked more than 16 hours per day, or worked alongside their owners?

Intermediate Use spoken language to paraphrase the first paragraph of the section titled *Hard Work*. Ask students to identify implicit ideas about the duration and intensity of enslaved workers' workdays.

Advanced Use spoken language to paraphrase the section titled *Slave Codes*. Ask: What did slave codes forbid enslaved African Americans to do? What does this information imply about what free people could do?

Advanced High Use spoken language to paraphrase the section titled *Slave Codes*. Ask pairs of students to discuss these questions: What does this information about slave codes imply about what free people could do? What does it imply about the value given to education?

▶ Differentiate Instruction

Use the Differentiated Instruction notes throughout the lesson plan to support the varied skill sets, levels of readiness, and interests in the mixed-ability classroom.

Challenge These notes include suggestions for expanding the activity for advanced students.

On-Level These notes include suggestions for modifying the activity to address different interests or learning styles.

Extra Support These notes include ideas for providing more scaffolding or reading spuport.

Special Needs These notes provide ideas for adapting instruction to support the needs of various special needs students.

■ NOTES

King Cotton and Life in the South

Objectives

Objective 1: Identify how the development of the cotton gin affected the South.

Objective 2: Describe the agricultural economy of the South.

Objective 3: Describe southern society.

Objective 4: Compare the economic, social, and political conditions of free and enslaved African Americans.

Objective 5: Explain the impact of slavery.

LESSON 2 ORGANIZER — **PACING: APPROX. 1 PERIOD, .5 BLOCKS**

	OBJECTIVES	PACING	RESOURCES: Online	RESOURCES: Print
Connect				
DIGITAL START UP ACTIVITY **The Price of Freedom**		5 min.	●	
Investigate				
DIGITAL TEXT 1 **The Cotton Kingdom**	Objective 1	10 min.	●	●
3-D MODEL **The Cotton Gin**	Objective 1	10 min.	●	
DIGITAL TEXT 2 **Reliance on Agriculture**	Objective 2	10 min.	●	●
DIGITAL TEXT 3 **Southern Whites**	Objective 3	10 min.	●	●
DIGITAL TEXT 4 **Southern African Americans**	Objective 4	10 min.	●	●
INTERACTIVE CHART **Different Ways of Life in the South**	Objective 4	10 min.	●	
DIGITAL TEXT 5 **Slavery in the South**	Objective 5	10 min.	●	●
INTERACTIVE CHART **Lives of Free and Enslaved African Americans**	Objective 5	10 min.	●	
DIGITAL TEXT 6 **Resisting Slavery**	Objective 5	10 min.	●	●
Synthesize				
DIGITAL ACTIVITY **Cotton is King**		5 min.	●	
Demonstrate				
DIGITAL QUIZ **Lesson Quiz and Class Discussion Board**		10 min.	●	

PEARSON
realize™
www.PearsonRealize.com

Go online to access additional resources including:
Primary Sources • Biographies • Supreme Court cases •
21st Century Skill Tutorials • Maps • Graphic Organizers.

■ CONNECT

DIGITAL START UP ACTIVITY
The Price of Freedom

Project the Start Up Activity Ask students to read the quote and answer the questions as they enter and get settled. Have students share their answers with a partner, either in class or through a blog space.

Discuss What can you tell about the difficulties an enslaved person in the South faced from reading Mr. Lane's statement? Why do you think it was "politic" for him to dress poorly? *(Lane had to make sure no one would suspect that he was making money and successfully running a business. He did not want anyone to think he was preparing to buy his freedom.)*

Tell students that in this lesson they will be learning about the economic and social characteristics of life in the South.

Aa Vocabulary Development: Use the Interactive Reading Notepad to preview the Key Terms and Academic Vocabulary in this lesson with students.

⇵ FLIP IT!
Assign the Flipped Video for this lesson.

■ STUDENT EDITION PRINT
PAGES: 389–400

■ INVESTIGATE

DIGITAL TEXT 1
The Cotton Kingdom

Objective 1: Identify how the development of the cotton gin affected the South.

Quick Instruction

3-D Model: The Cotton Gin Project the 3-D model of the cotton gin on the whiteboard and click through the images. Remind students how factories changed the economy in the North. Ask how they think the cotton gin affected the economy in South.

👥 ACTIVE CLASSROOM

Have students use the Quick Write Strategy and take 30 seconds to write what they already know about the southern economy. Then have students discuss in groups or as a class how they think the rise of the cotton kingdom will impact the southern economy and way of life.

D Differentiate: Extra Support Ask students what they think is meant by the term "Cotton Kingdom." Discuss why this term describes the South in the 1800s.

Further Instruction

Go through the Interactive Reading Notepad questions and discuss the answers with the class. Be sure students explain the effects of technological developments such as the cotton gin on the economic development of the South.

3-D MODEL
The Cotton Gin

Make Generalizations Describe the economic differences between the North and South. *(The North was more industrialized and made profits from factories and manufacturing. The South was more agricultural. Wealthy southerners made so much money on cotton that they did not see a need to invest in factories.)*

Generate Explanations Explain how the cotton gin impacted economic development in both the North and South. *(South—Because the gin could clean cotton much faster than individuals could, planters began making huge profits off cotton. Agriculture spread and profits increased. North—used southern cotton to make cloth, bringing profits to the textile mills.)*

Cite Evidence that the cotton gin contributed to the rise of slavery and the plantation system. *("The huge demand for cotton, the efficiency offered by cotton gins, and southern planters' reliance on slave labor led to the growth of large plantations, each with many enslaved workers.")*

King Cotton and Life in the South

DIGITAL TEXT 2
Reliance on Agriculture

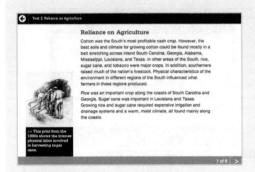

Reliance on Agriculture

Cotton was the South's most profitable cash crop. However, the best soils and climate for growing cotton could be found mostly in a belt stretching across inland South Carolina, Georgia, Alabama, Mississippi, Louisiana, and Texas. In other areas of the South, rice, sugar cane, and tobacco were major crops. In addition, southerners raised much of the nation's livestock. Physical characteristics of the environment in different regions of the South influenced what farmers in those regions produced.

Rice was an important crop along the coasts of South Carolina and Georgia. Sugar cane was important in Louisiana and Texas. Growing rice and sugar cane required expensive irrigation and drainage systems and a warm, moist climate, all found mainly along the coasts.

>> This print from the 1800s shows the intense physical labor involved in harvesting sugar cane.

Objective 2: Describe the agricultural economy of the South.

Quick Instruction

Analyze Graphs Project the infographic on cotton cultivation. Have students study the graphs and draw a conclusion about the agricultural economy of the South and the development of slavery.

Summarize Identify the key economic differences between the North and the South. *(The North relied more and more on industry and commerce. The South remained dependent on agriculture.)*

Compare and Contrast industry in the North and South. *(North—more urban, with large and diverse industries. Manufactured tools and goods made from metal and cloth. South—less industrial. The only industries served farms, by milling flour and manufacturing railroad equipment and machinery.)*

Further Instruction

Go through the Interactive Reading Notepad questions and discuss the answers with the class.

Identify Cause and Effect Identify the causes and effects of economic differences between the North and South. *(Causes— planters had invested their money in land and in enslaved African Americans to work the plantations. Because they had come to rely on those investments and made a good income from them, they saw little reason to invest in industry. Demand for factory goods was also low, as enslaved African Americans could not purchase them. By contrast, northern*

investors gained profits from investing in industry, and technological innovations and urban growth spurred growth in the North's industrial economy. Effects—poor southerners on small farms had fewer opportunities than northerners to find work outside farming; the South became dependent on northern and European industries; Southerners borrowed money from northern banks.)

Draw Conclusions How did the economic differences between the North and South lead to divisions within the nation? *(The South was largely dependent on the North for capital and for industrial goods. Many southerners were proud of the cotton economy and resented their dependence on the northern economy.)*

Summarize What physical characteristics of the environment influenced economic activities in the South? *(The South had a warm climate and rich soil for growing cotton and tobacco. Along the coast, irrigation and drainage systems and a warm, moist climate supported rice and sugar cane. Land unsuitable for crops was used for livestock.)*

DIGITAL TEXT 3
Southern Whites

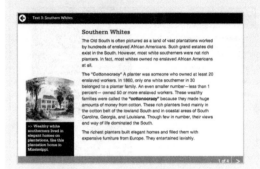

Southern Whites

The Old South is often pictured as a land of vast plantations worked by hundreds of enslaved African Americans. Such grand estates did exist in the South. However, most white southerners were not rich planters. In fact, most whites owned no enslaved African Americans at all.

The "**Cottonocracy**" A planter was someone who owned at least 20 enslaved workers. In 1860, only one white southerner in 30 belonged to a planter family. An even smaller number—less than 1 percent— owned 50 or more enslaved workers. These wealthy families were called the "**cottonocracy**" because they made huge amounts of money from cotton. These rich planters lived mainly in the cotton belt of the lowland South and in coastal areas of South Carolina, Georgia, and Louisiana. Though few in number, their views and way of life dominated the South.

The richest planters built elegant homes and filled them with expensive furniture from Europe. They entertained lavishly.

>> Wealthy white southerners lived in elegant homes on plantations, like this plantation home in Mississippi.

Objective 3: Describe southern society.

Quick Instruction

Project the images of the wealthy plantation family and the poor southern family on the whiteboard. Although the Old South is known for its grand estates, most white southerners were not wealthy planters and did not own enslaved African Americans.

Draw Conclusions How did the physical characteristics of the South influence human characteristics such as social classes in different parts of the region? *(Wealthy planters lived in the lowland and coastal areas that were best for growing cotton. Small farmers were in most parts of the South, but there were fewer in the cotton belt and coastal regions. Poor farmers lived in hilly regions north and west of the cotton belt, where the land was not suitable for cotton production and generated little wealth.)*

Further Instruction

Go through the Interactive Reading Notepad questions and discuss the answers with the class. Be sure students understand the social and economic characteristics of life for whites in the South.

Compare regions of the United States in terms of human characteristics by comparing the characteristics of northern and southern whites. *(Northerners—most whites were small farmers; the wealthiest were capitalists who made money from investing in industry; many worked in industries and lived in cities. Southerners—most were small farmers; the wealthiest were planters who made money from farming and from the labor of enslaved African Americans; few lived in cities.)*

DIGITAL TEXT 4
Southern African Americans

INTERACTIVE CHART
Different Ways of Life in the South

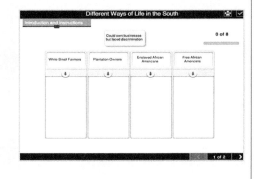

Summarize How did the upland South differ economically and socially, in terms of its human characteristics, from the lowland cotton region? *(The cotton region was wealthier and dominated the South. This was where the richest planters of the cottonocracy lived. Poor farmers lived in the upland South. Many did not own their land.)*

Objective 4: Compare the economic and social conditions of free and enslaved African Americans.

Quick Instruction

Interactive Chart: Different Ways of Life in the South Project the interactive chart on the whiteboard and have students read through the tiles. Compare the social and economic factors that influenced life for free and enslaved African Americans.

Support Ideas with Examples How did southern laws limit opportunities for free African Americans? *(They made life harder by prohibiting African Americans from voting or traveling. Many free African Americans moved to reduce the risk of being kidnapped and enslaved.)*

> 📖 **ACTIVE CLASSROOM**
>
> Have students use the Conversations with History Activity to suppose they are talking with African American inventors Norbert Rillieux or Henry Blair. Have them write down a question they would ask, what the person would say, and what they would say in response.

ELL Use the ELL activity described in the ELL chart.

Further Instruction

Both free and enslaved African Americans lived in the southern United States, but the effects of economic and social factors differed between these populations. While free African Americans faced brutal discrimination and limitations under the law, they enjoyed some rights, including the ability to own and operate businesses. On the other hand, enslaved African Americans had no rights.
As students read the text, have them compare the economic and social circumstances of enslaved and free African Americans.

Compare the family lives of free and enslaved African Americans. *(The families of enslaved African Americans could be broken up by their owners. All family members were forced to work long hours on the plantations. Free African Americans faced discrimination but were not forced to separate.)*

Determine Point of View Why did white slave owners fear the presence of free African Americans in the South? *(White owners feared they might encourage enslaved African Americans to seek freedom; they countered the slave owners' attempts to justify slavery.)*

Summarize Describe the economic contributions of free and enslaved African Americans. *(Enslaved African Americans worked on plantations, generating wealth for white owners and for the southern economy. Free African Americans owned and operated businesses, worked as farmers, developed skills and trades, and invented devices that improved southern life.)*

King Cotton and Life in the South

DIGITAL TEXT 5

Slavery in the South

INTERACTIVE CHART

Lives of Free and Enslaved African Americans

DIGITAL TEXT 6

Resisting Slavery

Objective 5: Explain the impact of slavery.

Quick Instruction

Interactive Chart: Lives of Free and Enslaved African Americans Project the interactive chart on the whiteboard and read the columns. Have students fill in the graphic organizer.

Summarize Why were enslaved African Americans kept illiterate? *(Owners thought it would be harder for enslaved African Americans to escape slavery if they couldn't read and write, because they wouldn't be able to read maps or train schedules.)*

📖 ACTIVE CLASSROOM

Ask students, "Why is Nat Turner important?" Have students use the Sticky Notes Activity and spend three minutes jotting down questions, comments, or observations about Turner and his revolt. Sort the stickies and discuss the questions as a group.

ELL Use the ELL activity described in the ELL chart.

Further Instruction

Go through the Interactive Reading Notepad questions and discuss the answers with the class.

Identify Cause and Effect What were the slave codes? What were the effects of these laws? *(The laws prohibited enslaved African Americans from gathering in large groups, leaving their owner's land without permission, owning guns, and learning to read and write. These laws made it harder for African Americans to run away or rebel.)*

Draw Conclusions Why did religion play such an important role in the lives of enslaved African Americans? *(Religion provided hope. It offered inspiring examples of other groups escaping slavery and allowed enslaved African Americans to sing about freedom in ways that were acceptable to slave owners.)*

Identify Patterns Identify the ways in which enslaved African Americans resisted slavery. *(They resisted the plantation system by breaking tools, destroying crops, and stealing food. Some tried to escape to the North. Nat Turner led a major revolt.)*

○ A.
○ B.
○ C.

■ SYNTHESIZE

DIGITAL ACTIVITY
Cotton is King

Have students examine the primary sources and answer the question.

Discuss Ask students to review the quote from the beginning of the lesson. Now that they have learned more about life in the South, have them explain the ways in which Lane's experience was and was not typical. Discuss what life in the Cotton Kingdom was like for poor and wealthy southern whites, free African Americans, and enslaved African Americans.

■ DEMONSTRATE

DIGITAL QUIZ
Lesson Quiz and Class Discussion Board

Assign the online Lesson Quiz for this lesson if you haven't already done so. Students will be offered automatic remediation or enrichment based on their score.

Pose these questions to the class on the Discussion Board:

Compare and Contrast Why did slavery develop in the South? Why do you think slavery was less extensive in the North?

Identify Cause and Effect How did slavery impact the economy and society of the South?

Analyze Information Was slavery solely a southern institution, as it is sometimes considered, or did the North contribute to its spread? Explain your reasoning.

Topic Inquiry
Have students continue their investigations for the Topic Inquiry.

Reform Movements

Supporting English Language Learners

Use with Digital Text 1, An Era of Reform.

Reading
Recall that when we summarize text, we identify the most important details and restate them in our own words.

Beginning Echo read the first two paragraphs of the section titled *The Second Great Awakening and Its Causes*. Ask students to summarize them by completing these sentences: During the colonial era, many Protestants believed their _____ was already decided. In the early 1800s, the idea of _____ became popular.

Intermediate Invite volunteers to read the first two paragraphs of the section titled *The Second Great Awakening and Its Causes*. Then ask students to summarize each paragraph in a sentence.

Advanced Invite pairs of students to read the section titled *The Second Great Awakening and Its Causes*. Then have them discuss these questions: What are the four or five most important pieces of information? How can you use them to create a summary of the section?

Advanced High Ask students to independently read the text and write a written summary of it. Encourage them to use the text's title and subheadings to help them organize their summary.

Use with Digital Text 3, The Impact of Educational Reform.

Listening
Explain to students that you will be speaking about education and educational reform in the 1800s. Discuss the meaning of *reform*.

Beginning Use basic spoken language to paraphrase the text's introductory paragraphs. Then have students demonstrate their understanding of information by answering this question: What was one characteristic of Massachusetts public schools?

Intermediate Use spoken language to explain with some detail how Massachusetts public schools changed during the 1800s, using the introduction and first section of the text as a reference. Have students demonstrate their understanding of information by answering this question: How did teacher training improve?

Advanced Use somewhat complex spoken language to paraphrase the section titled *Education Reform Gives Rise to Public Schools*. Have pairs of students demonstrate their understanding of information by answering this question: How and why did Horace Mann improve Massachusetts public schools?

Advanced High Use complex spoken language to paraphrase the section titled *Education Reform Gives Rise to Public Schools*. Have students demonstrate their understanding of information by writing a response to this question and discussing it with a partner: How were public schools alike and different in New York and Massachusetts?

D Differentiate Instruction

Use the Differentiated Instruction notes throughout the lesson plan to support the varied skill sets, levels of readiness, and interests in the mixed-ability classroom.

Challenge These notes include suggestions for expanding the activity for advanced students.

On-Level These notes include suggestions for modifying the activity to address different interests or learning styles.

Extra Support These notes include ideas for providing more scaffolding or reading spuport.

Special Needs These notes provide ideas for adapting instruction to support the needs of various special needs students.

■ NOTES

PEARSON
realize™
www.PearsonRealize.com

Go online to access additional resources including:
Primary Sources • Biographies • Supreme Court cases •
21st Century Skill Tutorials • Maps • Graphic Organizers.

Objectives

Objective 1: Explain how political and religious trends, including the Second Great Awakening, inspired reform movements.

Objective 2: Describe the impact of movements for temperance and for the reform of mental health care and prisons.

Objective 3: Explain the impact of movements for the reform of education and care for the disabled.

LESSON 3 ORGANIZER		PACING: APPROX. 1 PERIOD, .5 BLOCKS			
				RESOURCES	
		OBJECTIVES	PACING	Online	Print
Connect					
DIGITAL START UP ACTIVITY **Religious Movements and Social Reform**			5 min.	●	
Investigate					
DIGITAL TEXT 1 **An Era of Reform**		Objective 1	10 min.	●	●
DIGITAL TEXT 2 **Social Reform Movements**		Objective 2	10 min.	●	●
DIGITAL TEXT 3 **The Impact of Educational Reform**		Objective 3	10 min.	●	●
INTERACTIVE GALLERY **Changes in American Schools**			10 min.	●	
Synthesize					
DIGITAL ACTIVITY **The Impact of Social Reform**			5 min.	●	
Demonstrate					
DIGITAL QUIZ **Lesson Quiz and Class Discussion Board**			10 min.	●	

Reform Movements

■ CONNECT

DIGITAL START UP ACTIVITY
Religious Movements and Social Reform

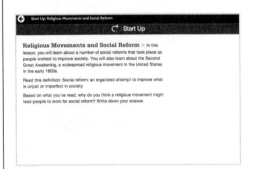

Project the Start Up Activity Ask students to read the definition and answer the question as they enter and get settled. Have students share their answers with a partner, either in class or through a blog space.

Discuss Based on what you've read, why do you think a religious movement might lead people to work for social reform? *(Religious teachings might emphasize moral action, helping others in need, or making the world a better place.)*

Tell students that in this lesson they will be learning about the causes and effects of reform movements inspired by the Second Great Awakening.

Aa Vocabulary Development: Use the Interactive Reading Notepad to preview the Key Terms and Academic Vocabulary in this Lesson with students.

↧ FLIP IT!
Assign the Flipped Video for this lesson.

■ STUDENT EDITION PRINT PAGES: 401–406

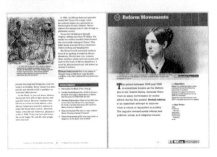

■ INVESTIGATE

DIGITAL TEXT 1
An Era of Reform

Objective 1: Explain how political and religious trends, including the Second Great Awakening, inspired reform movements.

Quick Instruction

Analyze Charts Explain to students that the period from 1815 to 1860 is sometimes known as the Reform Era. Project the chart on the whiteboard and ask how the reform movements of the nineteenth century were rooted in American cultural and political ideals.

Identify Cause and Effect Describe the causes of the Reform Era. *(Democratic ideals led to a desire to correct injustices. Industrialization and urbanization had brought hardships and challenges, and there was a need to address these. Finally, a religious movement called the Second Great Awakening aroused a desire for moral action, including helping society.)*

D Differentiate: On-Level Point out to students that a religious revival movement known as the Second Great Awakening swept the United States during the early 1800s. Ask: What were the causes of this religious revival movement? *(the spread of belief that people's fates relied on their use of their free will and their good actions rather than predestination)*

ELL Use the ELL activity described in the ELL chart.

Further Instruction
Go through the Interactive Reading Notepad questions and discuss the answers with the class.

Connect How did people of various religious groups, especially those who believed in free will, contribute to our national identity? *(By convincing people that they could be saved by their actions, preachers of free promoted practical engagement in society contributed the idea of improving society to our national identity.)*

Draw Conclusions What were the effects of the Second Great Awakening, and how did it have a religious influence on social movements? *(It encouraged the development of social reform movements because it taught that people had a religious and moral calling to improve society and reform the world.)*

DIGITAL TEXT 2

Social Reform Movements

DIGITAL TEXT 3

The Impact of Educational Reform

Objective 2: **Describe the impact of movements for temperance and for the reform of mental health care and prisons.**

Quick Instruction

Project the political cartoon on the whiteboard and have students describe what they see. Ask what values reformers hoped to instill in American society.

Analyze Cartoons How do you think religious beliefs shaped the values outlined in the cartoon? How did these values contribute to our national identity? *(Religious beliefs emphasized morality and proper living. Many Americans believed individuals should pursue goodness and knowledge and live moral lives. These values have come to shape American identity.)*

Identify Cause and Effect What were some of the effects of reform movements? *(Social reform movements led to important reforms in prisons, the care of the disabled, and also led to the temperance movement, which sought to limit alcohol consumption.)*

Further Instruction

Go through the Interactive Reading Notepad questions and discuss the answers with the class.

Summarize How did the social contributions of women affect American society? What was the impact of reform movements they led on care of the disabled? *(They worked to publicize ills and push for remedies. For example, Dorothea Dix visited jails, poorhouses, and hospitals and wrote reports about what she*

saw. *These reports convinced legislators to fund a new mental hospital. By traveling the country and raising awareness about treatment facilities, she improved care and changed the way people viewed the mentally ill.)*

Support a Point of View with Evidence Evaluate the impact of the prison reforms of the nineteenth century. What were the effects of these reforms? Do you think these reforms were successful? Support your point of view with evidence from the text. *(Prison reform was successful because it improved conditions. Some states built less crowded prisons, cruel punishments were banned, and minor crimes received shorter sentences. States also moved away from treating debtors as criminals.)*

Draw Conclusions Why do you think women were leaders in the temperance movement? Evaluate the impact of temperance reform. *(Women and children were negatively affected by men's alcohol abuse. Women therefore fought to limit or abolish drinking. As a result, nine states banned the sale of alcohol.)*

Objective 3: **Explain the impact of movements for the reform of education and care for the disabled.**

Quick Instruction

Interactive Gallery: Changes in American Schools Project the interactive gallery and click through the images. Discuss how education in the 1800s differed from education today. Have students fill in the Interactive Chart: The Reform Movement.

Identify Central Issues Why did Americans call for education reform? *(As voting rights expanded, Americans argued that citizens needed to be better educated in order to serve the nation. Few children attended school at the time, and most states did not have public education. Teachers were poorly trained, and schools were overcrowded.)*

📷 ACTIVE CLASSROOM

Use a Quick Draw strategy. Pair students for a short period (typically 30 seconds) in which to share what they know about school reform by writing with symbols or drawings.

Reform Movements

INTERACTIVE GALLERY

Changes in American Schools

👥 ACTIVE CLASSROOM

Have students pick one of the reforms they have learned about and use the Wallpaper Strategy to design a piece of wallpaper encapsulating key issues related to the reform. Have students post their wallpaper and take a gallery walk around the room, noting what others have written or illustrated. Have students jot down ideas and then discuss the reforms as a class.

Further Instruction

Go through the Interactive Reading Notepad questions and discuss the answers with the class.

Identify Cause and Effect Evaluate the impact of educational reform. *(States built new schools, extended the school year, raised teachers' pay, and provided better training for teachers. Public education spread as states established free elementary schools supported by taxes.)*

Summarize How did Horace Mann's efforts affect the public school system? *(Massachusetts already had public schools but Mann expanded the system. As head of the Massachusetts Board of Education, he convinced legislators to provide more funding for education. Massachusetts became a model for other states.)*

Cite Evidence Describe the ways in which the Second Great Awakening contributed to education reform. How did people of various religious groups contribute to American education? *(Horace Mann believed education reform would help citizens become better Christians. Samuel Gridley Howe was inspired by the movement to improve education. He founded the first American school for the blind. Prudence Crandall was a Quaker whose religious beliefs inspired her to begin a school for African American girls.)*

■ SYNTHESIZE

DIGITAL ACTIVITY
The Impact of Social Reform

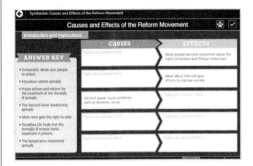

Have students fill in the chart and answer the questions. Have students discuss with a partner the reforms they think were the most important, and why.

Discuss Ask students what they think has been the lasting impact of the Reform Era. Have them review their charts and discuss the ways in which social reforms shaped the nation in the 1800s, giving examples for support. Ask how these reforms influence American society today.

■ DEMONSTRATE

DIGITAL QUIZ
Lesson Quiz and Class Discussion Board

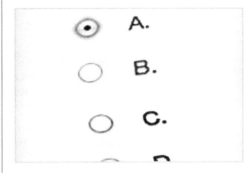

Assign the online Lesson Quiz for this lesson if you haven't already done so. Students will be offered automatic remediation or enrichment based on their score.

Pose these questions to the class on the Discussion Board:

Identify Central Issues How did the Second Great Awakening affect the American way of life?

Support Ideas with Examples How did women contribute to reform movements in the 1800s? Cite examples for support.

Topic Inquiry
Have students continue their investigations for the Topic Inquiry.

Abolitionism

Supporting English Language Learners

Use with Digital Text 2, **Abolition Gains Momentum.**

Listening
Explain that students will be following your directions in order to demonstrate their listening comprehension of spoken English.

Beginning Give the following spoken directions: Find the antislavery newspaper started by William Lloyd Garrison. After students locate *The Liberator*, discuss the strategies they used to find it.

Intermediate Describe the life of Frederick Douglass without naming him. Give the following spoken directions: Locate in the text the name of the person I described. After students have followed your directions, ask them to suggest adjectives that describe Douglass.

Advanced Give the following spoken directions: Write two sentences about Frederick Douglass, and then write two sentences about William Lloyd Garrison. After students have done so, provide time for them to share their work with a partner.

Advanced High Give the following spoken directions (in reverse order): Write two sentences contrasting Frederick Douglass and William Lloyd Garrison after you write two sentences comparing them. After students have done so, provide time for them to share their work with a partner.

Use with Digital Text 3, **Abolition Faces Opposition.**

Reading
Explain that students will demonstrate English comprehension and expand reading skills such as predicting, making connections between ideas, drawing conclusions and inferences from the text and graphic sources, and finding supporting text evidence. Review the meanings of conclusion and inference.

Beginning Echo read the last two sentences of the third paragraph. Ask students to identify the inference that could be drawn from the witness' statement: that the witness was a southerner, that he or she thought the mob was wrong, or that he or she agreed with the mob.

Intermediate Invite a volunteer to read the last two sentences of the third paragraph. Ask students to draw an inference by asking: What did the witness think about the mob's actions?

Advanced Discuss how anti-abolitionists tended to use violence against abolitionists, yet they also accused abolitionists of preaching violence. Ask: What conclusions can you draw about the fairness of those who opposed abolitionism?

Advanced High Ask pairs of students to draw conclusions by discussing this question: How much opposition to abolitionism do you think was based on racism, and how much was based on other factors, such as economy and culture? Encourage students to reference the text as needed.

▣ Differentiate Instruction

Use the Differentiated Instruction notes throughout the lesson plan to support the varied skill sets, levels of readiness, and interests in the mixed-ability classroom.

Challenge These notes include suggestions for expanding the activity for advanced students.

On-Level These notes include suggestions for modifying the activity to address different interests or learning styles.

Extra Support These notes include ideas for providing more scaffolding or reading spuport.

Special Needs These notes provide ideas for adapting instruction to support the needs of various special needs students.

■ NOTES

PEARSON
realize™
www.PearsonRealize.com

Go online to access additional resources including:
Primary Sources • Biographies • Supreme Court cases •
21st Century Skill Tutorials • Maps • Graphic Organizers.

Objectives

Objective 1: Describe the historical development of the abolitionist movement.

Objective 2: Explain the roles of Frederick Douglass and others in the abolitionist movement.

Objective 3: Identify the Underground Railroad and the role that civil disobedience played in it.

Objective 4: Describe the different points of view of interest groups on abolition.

LESSON 4 ORGANIZER		PACING: APPROX. 1 PERIOD, .5 BLOCKS			
				RESOURCES	
		OBJECTIVES	PACING	Online	Print
Connect					
DIGITAL START UP ACTIVITY **The Antislavery Movement**			5 min.	●	
Investigate					
DIGITAL TEXT 1 **Early Opposition to Slavery**		Objective 1	10 min.	●	●
DIGITAL TEXT 2 **Abolitionism Gains Momentum**		Objectives 2, 3	10 min.	●	●
INTERACTIVE MAP **The Underground Railroad**			10 min.	●	
DIGITAL TEXT 3 **Abolitionism Faces Opposition**		Objective 4	10 min.	●	●
INTERACTIVE CHART **Opposing Views on Slavery**			10 min.	●	
Synthesize					
DIGITAL ACTIVITY **The Contributions of Abolitionist Leaders**			5 min.	●	
Demonstrate					
DIGITAL QUIZ **Lesson Quiz and Class Discussion Board**			10 min.	●	

Abolitionism

CONNECT

DIGITAL START UP ACTIVITY
The Antislavery Movement

Project the Start Up Activity Ask students to read the excerpt and write down their reactions as they enter and get settled. Have students share their answers with a partner, either in class or through a blog space.

Tell students that in this lesson they will be learning about the development and impact of the abolitionist movement.

Aa Vocabulary Development: Use the Interactive Reading Notepad to preview the Key Terms and Academic Vocabulary in this lesson with students.

⇅ FLIP IT!
Assign the Flipped Video for this lesson.

STUDENT EDITION PRINT
PAGES: 407–412

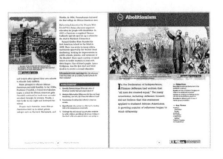

INVESTIGATE

DIGITAL TEXT 1
Early Opposition to Slavery

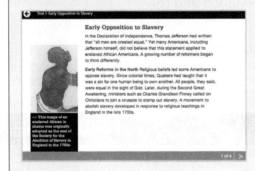

Objective 1: Describe the historical development of the abolitionist movement.

Quick Instruction
Project the antislavery medallion. The abolitionist movement began as an increasing number of northerners came to oppose slavery.

Identify Central Issues What steps did northern states take to end slavery? How effective were these efforts? Explain your reasoning. *(The northern states gradually abolished slavery. This had little impact in the South, though, where there were almost a million enslaved African Americans and little support for abolition.)*

Further Instruction
Go through the Interactive Reading Notepad questions and discuss the answers with the class.

Compare the impact of slavery on the economy and societyof the North and South. Explain the reasons for these differences. *(North—the economy was largely industrial and not dependent on slavery. South—the economy was largely based on slavery, as enslaved African Americans labored on the cotton plantations that generated the region's wealth.)*

Summarize Describe the American Colonization Society and its historical impact. *(The society established an independent colony in Liberia for freed Africans and African Americans. A few thousand African Americans moved there but most wanted to stay in their homeland in America.)*

Make a Generalization Identify how some religious groups viewed slavery, citing evidence for support. *(Some religious groups opposed slavery and wanted to abolish it—"Quakers had taught that it was a sin for one human being to own another"; "during the Second Great Awakening, ministers ... called on Christians to join a crusade to stamp out slavery.")*

DIGITAL TEXT 2

Abolitionism Gains Momentum

INTERACTIVE MAP

The Underground Railroad

DIGITAL TEXT 3

Abolitionism Faces Opposition

Objectives 2: **Explain the roles of Frederick Douglass and others in the abolitionist movement;** 3: **Identify the Underground Railroad and the role that civil disobedience played in it.**

Quick Instruction

Interactive Map: The Underground Railroad Project the interactive map on the whiteboard and click on the red circles. Have students discuss the impact of the Underground Railroad, citing evidence for support.

Generate Explanations Why did participants in the Underground Railroad choose to engage in civil disobedience, and what was the impact of that civil disobedience? *(It was illegal to help enslaved African Americans to escape. Abolitionists who helped fugitives engaged in civil disobedience against laws they felt were unjust because they saw it as the best way to free people from slavery. The impact of their civil disobedience was to free a number of African Americans from slavery.)*

D Differentiate: Extra Support Explain to students that *abolish* means to formally put an end to something. Ask what abolitionists were trying to end. Have students discuss the ways abolitionists spread their message.

📖 ACTIVE CLASSROOM

Have students work in pairs to develop a poster combining visuals with text to describe the historical development of the abolitionist movement. If time permits, students may present their posters to the rest of the class.

Further Instruction

Go through the Interactive Reading Notepad questions and discuss the answers with the class.

Summarize Describe the contributions of social leaders such as Frederick Douglass, William Lloyd Garrison, and the Grimké sisters. *(Douglass was the best-known African American abolitionist. He gave lectures in the United States and Britain about slavery and freedom and published an antislavery newspaper to promote the abolitionist cause. Garrison was an outspoken abolitionist who called for an immediate end to slavery. He published an influential antislavery newspaper and founded the New England AntiSlavery society. The Grimké sisters spoke out against slavery. Their public lectures also influenced the women's rights movement.)*

Draw Conclusions Evaluate the impact of the abolitionist movement. *(The abolitionist movement spread opposition to slavery, especially in the North. It succeeded in winning freedom for a number of African Americans, for example through the Underground Railroad. It also increased tensions between the North and the South.)*

Objective 4: **Describe the different points of view of interest groups on abolition.**

Quick Instruction

Interactive Chart: Opposing Views on Slavery Project the interactive chart on the whiteboard and have students fill in the graphic organizer.

Analyze Images Identify the different points of view on slavery presented in the political cartoon. Based on the image, evaluate the impact of the abolitionist movement on national unity. *(Northerners opposed slavery and southerners supported it; disagreements over slavery and the growing push for abolition was tearing the nation apart.)*

📖 ACTIVE CLASSROOM

Pair students to use the See-Think-Wonder Activity as they study the political cartoon. Ask: What do you see? What does that make you think about? What are you wondering about now that you've seen this? Have partners share their insights with the class.

ELL Use the ELL activity described in the ELL chart.

Abolitionism

 SYNTHESIZE

 DEMONSTRATE

INTERACTIVE CHART

Opposing Views on Slavery

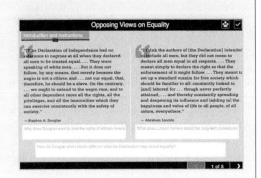

DIGITAL ACTIVITY

The Contributions of Abolitionist Leaders

DIGITAL QUIZ

Lesson Quiz and Class Discussion Board

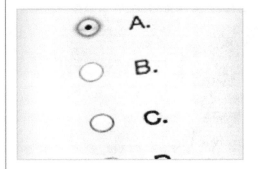

Further Instruction

Go through the Interactive Reading Notepad questions and discuss the answers with the class.

Compare and Contrast Identify the different points of views of northern interest groups on slavery. What were the reasons for these opposing viewpoints? *(Some northerners were abolitionists, but not all. Abolitionists opposed slavery because they felt that it was morally wrong. Those who depended on cotton for their livelihood, including mill owners, bankers, and merchants, supported slavery as acceptable and necessary. Some workers also feared abolition would cause African Americans north to come north and compete for their jobs.)*

Identify Central Issues The North and South increasingly had different points of view over slavery. How did social and economic factors contribute to these divisions? *(Economic—the South was more economically dependent on slavery than the North. Social— southerners feared that an attack on slavery was an attack on their way of life.)*

Have students fill in the chart and answer the questions. Have students share their charts with a partner and discuss how these abolitionist leaders contributed to the movement.

Discuss Remind students of the excerpt they read at the start of the lesson. Ask how they think passages like the one from Douglass's letter affected the abolitionist movement. Discuss how leaders like Douglass have contributed to our national identity.

Assign the online Lesson Quiz for this lesson if you haven't already done so. Students will be offered automatic remediation or enrichment based on their score.

Pose these questions to the class on the Discussion Board:

Identify Central Issues What do you think were the most important factors that led to the development of the abolitionist movement? Explain your reasoning.

Make Predictions What factors do you think would cause the abolitionist movement to gain strength leading up to the Civil War?

Support Ideas with Examples How did women contribute to the abolitionist movement? Provide examples for support.

Topic Inquiry

Have students continue their investigations for the Topic Inquiry.

Women's Rights

Supporting English Language Learners

Use with Digital Text 1, **Early Calls for Women's Rights.**

Reading
Discuss how authors' beliefs and opinions often influence the way they write about a subject, and how employing analytical skills such as evaluating written information and performing critical analyses can help a reader expand his or her reading skills.

Beginning Read this sentence from the text: Truth was a spellbinding speaker. Ask students to demonstrate English comprehension with this question: Based on this sentence, do you think the author has a positive or negative view of Sojourner Truth?

Intermediate Review the section about Sojourner Truth. Ask students to demonstrate English comprehension with this question: What opinion of Sojourner Truth do you think the author has?

Advanced Review the section about Sojourner Truth. Ask pairs of students to demonstrate English comprehension by answering these questions: What opinion of Sojourner Truth do you think the author has? Would someone who did not respect Sojourner Truth have written about her in the same way? If not, what might that person have said?

Advanced High Review the text as needed. Ask pairs of students to demonstrate English comprehension by answering these questions: Do you think the author sides with or against these women? Do you think the author gives a fair, unbiased view of the topic? Locate specific passages that support your views.

Use with Digital Text 3, **Women Gain New Opportunities.**

Listening
Prepare students for the activity by brainstorming strategies they can use to help them comprehend the key points of a spoken message (e.g., jotting down or memorizing words or phrases, retelling, or summarizing).

Beginning Pair students and have one student in each pair read aloud the first two sentences of the quotation by Elizabeth Cady Stanton. Then have the other student retell the meaning of the sentences. Have each pair work together to refine the retelling for clarity.

Intermediate Pair students and have one student in each pair read aloud the first two sentences of the quotation by Elizabeth Cady Stanton. Then have the other student summarize the sentences into one main idea. Have each pair work together to refine the summary for clarity.

Advanced Pair students and have one student in each pair read aloud the entire quotation by Elizabeth Cady Stanton. Have the other student retell the details of the quotation. Then have the pairs work together to create a summary based on the retelling.

Advanced High Read aloud the entire quotation by Elizabeth Cady Stanton. Have students create both a retelling and also a summary of the quote. Have volunteers share their summaries and retellings with the class.

D Differentiate Instruction

Use the Differentiated Instruction notes throughout the lesson plan to support the varied skill sets, levels of readiness, and interests in the mixed-ability classroom.

Challenge These notes include suggestions for expanding the activity for advanced students.

On-Level These notes include suggestions for modifying the activity to address different interests or learning styles.

Extra Support These notes include ideas for providing more scaffolding or reading spuport.

Special Needs These notes provide ideas for adapting instruction to support the needs of various special needs students.

■ NOTES

Women's Rights

Objectives

Objective 1: Describe the origins of the women's rights movement.

Objective 2: Explain the impact of the Seneca Falls Convention, including the roles of Elizabeth Cady Stanton and Susan B. Anthony.

Objective 3: Describe the impact of the women's rights movement on opportunities for women.

LESSON 5 ORGANIZER		PACING: APPROX. 1 PERIOD, .5 BLOCKS			
				RESOURCES	
		OBJECTIVES	PACING	Online	Print
Connect					
DIGITAL START UP ACTIVITY **The Struggle for Equal Rights**			5 min.	●	
Investigate					
DIGITAL TEXT 1 **Early Calls for Women's Rights**		Objective 1	10 min.	●	●
INTERACTIVE TIMELINE **The Early Women's Rights Movement**			10 min.	●	
DIGITAL TEXT 2 **A Women's Movement Organizes**		Objective 2	10 min.	●	●
DIGITAL TEXT 3 **Women Gain New Opportunities**		Objective 3	10 min.	●	●
INTERACTIVE GALLERY **New Opportunities for Women**			10 min.	●	
Synthesize					
DIGITAL ACTIVITY **Contributions of Women Leaders**			5 min.	●	
Demonstrate					
DIGITAL QUIZ **Lesson Quiz and Class Discussion Board**			10 min.	●	

■ CONNECT

DIGITAL START UP ACTIVITY
The Struggle for Equal Rights

Project the Start Up Activity Ask students to review the strategies and write down their thoughts as they enter and get settled. Have students share their responses with a partner, either in class or through a blog space.

Tell students that in this lesson they will be learning about the causes and effects of the women's rights movement.

Aa Vocabulary Development: Use the Interactive Reading Notepad to preview the Key Terms and Academic Vocabulary in this lesson with students.

⇅ FLIP IT!

Assign the Flipped Video for this lesson.

■ STUDENT EDITION PRINT PAGES: 413–418

■ INVESTIGATE

DIGITAL TEXT 1
Early Calls for Women's Rights

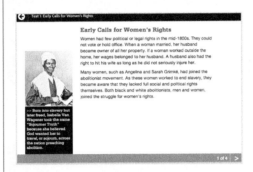

Objective 1: Describe the origins of the women's rights movement.

Quick Instruction

Interactive Timeline: The Early Women's Rights Movement Project the interactive timeline and click through the events.

Summarize Describe the contributions of Elizabeth Cady Stanton to the women's rights movement as a social leader. *(She was an active leader of the movement. When she was not allowed to actively participate in the World Antislavery Convention in London because she was a woman, she began working for women's rights.)*

📽 ACTIVE CLASSROOM

Have students use the Conversation with History Activity and suppose they are having a conversation with Elizabeth Cady Stanton after she has returned from the World Antislavery Convention in London. Have students write down a question they'd like to ask, what they think Stanton would say, and what they would say in response.

ELL Use the ELL activity described in the ELL chart.

INTERACTIVE TIMELINE
The Early Women's Rights Movement

Further Instruction

Go through the Interactive Reading Notepad questions and discuss the answers with the class. To extend the lesson, assign Primary Sources: Ain't I a Woman (Sojourner Truth).

Paraphrase Review the quote by Sojourner Truth. What was she arguing? How did her argument support the cause of women's rights? *(Truth challenged the idea that women were inferior by pointing to her experiences under slavery, where she worked as hard as men.)*

Draw Conclusions How was the women's rights movement connected to the abolitionist movement? *(While fighting for social and political rights for African Americans, women in the abolitionist movement became increasingly aware that their rights were limited as well.)*

Women's Rights

DIGITAL TEXT 2

A Women's Movement Organizes

DIGITAL TEXT 3

Women Gain New Opportunities

Objective 2: **Explain the impact of the Seneca Falls Convention, including the roles of Elizabeth Cady Stanton and Susan B. Anthony.**

Quick Instruction

Analyze Images Display the images of Elizabeth Cady Stanton and Susan B. Anthony. Describe the contributions of these two significant social leaders. *(Both women were key leaders of the women's rights movement and both were influential in promoting women's rights.)*

Summarize Describe the contributions of Elizabeth Cady Stanton and Susan B. Anthony to the women's rights movement. *(Elizabeth Cady Stanton helped organize the Seneca Falls Convention, which launched the women's rights movement. She also drafted the* Declaration of Sentiments, *which spelled out the movement's goals, for the convention. Anthony traveled the country speaking to audiences and convincing them that women deserved equal rights, especially the right to vote.)*

D Differentiate: Extra Support Explain to students that sentiments are views or feelings. Ask them what views they think the *Declaration of Sentiments* expressed and how they know.

ELL Use the ELL activity described in the ELL chart.

Further Instruction

Go through the Interactive Reading Notepad questions and discuss the answers with the class. To extend the lesson, assign the Primary Source: Seneca Falls Declaration of Sentiments and Resolutions.

Compare and Contrast Identify the political contributions of women to American society through the women's rights movement. *(Women involved in the women's rights movement contributed to American society the idea that women deserved equal rights, including the right to an education, the right to equality of opportunity in employment, and the right to vote.)*

Summarize What was the Seneca Falls Convention and why did it play such an important role in the women's rights movement? *(It was a major convention designed to draw attention to the problems women faced. It laid out demands for equality and began the organized campaign for women's rights.)*

Objective 3: **Describe the impact of the women's rights movement on opportunities for women.**

Quick Instruction

Interactive Gallery: New Opportunities for Women Project the interactive gallery on the whiteboard and click through the images. Discuss the impact of the women's rights movement on education, employment, suffrage, and property rights.

Identify Cause and Effect Evaluate the impact of the early women's rights movement. *(The early women's rights movement emphasized education to give women greater opportunities outside the home. It led women like Emma Willard and Mary Lyon to open schools and colleges for girls. This led to increased educational opportunities for women and, as a further result, to increased career opportunities.)*

📷 ACTIVE CLASSROOM

Have students imagine they are a reporter covering the Seneca Falls Convention and use the Make Headlines Activity to write a headline that captures this significant event. Have students share their headline with the class.

Further Instruction

Go through the Interactive Reading Notepad questions and discuss the answers with the class.

INTERACTIVE GALLERY
New Opportunities for Women

Compare and Contrast Identify the different points of view of interest groups on the contemporary issue of paid maternity leave. With whom do you agree, and why? *(For—groups like the National Organization for Women believe women should be paid during maternity leave to receive support during time away from their job. Against—groups like the Independent Women's Forum worry that requiring paid maternity leave might make employers not want to hire women.)*

Support Ideas with Examples Give at least three examples of how women contributed to American society through the gains during women's rights movement. *(Emma Willard— opened a high school for girls; Mary Lyon— founded Mt. Holyoke college for women; Elizabeth Blackwell—became the first women in the United States to earn a medical degree; Maria Mitchell—astronomer; Sarah Josepha Hale—magazine editor; Antoinette Blackwell— first U.S. woman ordained a minister.)*

■ SYNTHESIZE

DIGITAL ACTIVITY
Contributions of Women Leaders

Have students fill in the chart and answer the questions. Have students share their charts with a partner and discuss the major changes these leaders brought about.

Discuss Have students review what they wrote at the beginning of the lesson about effective strategies for bringing about social and political change. Ask if they would change or add to their answers now that they have read more about the women's rights movement. Have students discuss what strategies leaders of the women's rights movement used to bring about change, citing examples for support.

■ DEMONSTRATE

DIGITAL QUIZ
Lesson Quiz and Class Discussion Board

Assign the online Lesson Quiz for this lesson if you haven't already done so. Students will be offered automatic remediation or enrichment based on their score.

Pose these questions to the class on the Discussion Board:

Identify Central Issues How did the women's right movement affect American society in the 1800s? How do you think the movement's impact continues to influence American society today?

Evaluate Arguments Why do you think many of the ideas advanced by reformers such as Stanton and Anthony were considered so revolutionary at the time?

Topic Inquiry
Have students continue their investigations for the Topic Inquiry.

Arts and Literature

Supporting English Language Learners

Use with Digital Text 2, **A New Nation Finds a Voice.**

Writing
Explain that students will be learning the relationships between the sounds and letters of *ow*.

Beginning Display and read the word *Longfellow* from the text. Sound out the word with students, emphasizing the final /oe/. Ask students to complete and copy this sentence: Washington Irving wrote "The Legend of Sleepy Holl__."

Intermediate Display and read words from the text that have the letters *ow* representing /oe/ in all positions: *Longfellow, known, own*. Ask students to write sentences about 1800s American literature using these words.

Advanced Display words from the text with the final letters *ow* representing either /oe/ or /ow/: *Longfellow, hollow, how, now*. Ask pairs of students to brainstorm and sort other words ending with *ow*. Then have them write sentences about 1800s American literature with three of the words.

Advanced High Review that *ow* can represent either /oe/ or /ow/. Then say the following words while students write them: *Longfellow, however, own, brown, now, hollow*. Have students write a paragraph about 1800s American literature that uses at least three words containing *ow* (using the words above or others).

Use with Digital Text 3, **The Development of Transcendentalism.**

Listening
Review with students that some questions require a factual answer and others request an opinion. Explain that students will demonstrate listening comprehension of spoken English by responding to questions that ask for a factual answer about the text and questions that requestan opinion.

Beginning Read aloud to students the section *Henry David Thoreau and Civil Disobedience*. Ask: What did Thoreau believe each person must decide? What words would you use to describe Thoreau? Have students brainstorm words to complete this sentence: I think Thoreau was a(n) _____ person.

Intermediate Read aloud to students the sections about Emerson and Thoreau. Ask: What are the main ideas of Emerson and Thoreau? Which man's works are you more interested in reading? Why?

Advanced Read aloud to students the section *Henry David Thoreau and Civil Disobedience*. Ask: Do you agree with Thoreau that every person can and should decide for himself or herself what is right and wrong? Why or why not? How do you know what is right and wrong? Have small groups discuss their responses.

Advanced High In small groups have students read the text aloud. Then have each group consider these questions:: Do you agree that the most important truths in life cannot be understood by thinking about them? Why or why not? What do you think are the most important truths? Have students write down their responses to these questions before discussing them with the group.

▣ Differentiate Instruction

Use the Differentiated Instruction notes throughout the lesson plan to support the varied skill sets, levels of readiness, and interests in the mixed-ability classroom.

Challenge These notes include suggestions for expanding the activity for advanced students.

On-Level These notes include suggestions for modifying the activity to address different interests or learning styles.

Extra Support These notes include ideas for providing more scaffolding or reading spuport.

Special Needs These notes provide ideas for adapting instruction to support the needs of various special needs students.

■ NOTES

PEARSON
realize™
www.PearsonRealize.com

Go online to access additional resources including:
Primary Sources • Biographies • Supreme Court cases •
21st Century Skill Tutorials • Maps • Graphic Organizers.

Objectives

Objective 1: Describe American painting in the early to mid-1800s, including the Hudson River School and the work of John James Audubon.

Objective 2: Analyze American literature and music during the early to mid-1800s.

Objective 3: Describe transcendentalism.

LESSON 6 ORGANIZER		PACING: APPROX. 1 PERIOD, .5 BLOCKS			
				RESOURCES	
		OBJECTIVES	**PACING**	**Online**	**Print**
Connect					
DIGITAL START UP ACTIVITY **The Hudson Valley School**			5 min.	●	
Investigate					
DIGITAL TEXT 1 **A New American Art Style**		Objective 1	10 min.	●	●
INTERACTIVE GALLERY **Painting America**			10 min.	●	
DIGITAL TEXT 2 **A New Nation Finds a Voice**		Objective 2	10 min.	●	●
INTERACTIVE MAP **Early American Music and Literature**			10 min.	●	
DIGITAL TEXT 3 **The Development of Transcendentalism**		Objective 3	10 min.	●	●
Synthesize					
DIGITAL ACTIVITY **Themes of American Art, Music, and Literature in the 1800s**			5 min.	●	
Demonstrate					
DIGITAL QUIZ **Lesson Quiz and Class Discussion Board**			10 min.	●	

Arts and Literature

■ CONNECT

DIGITAL START UP ACTIVITY
The Hudson Valley School

Project the Start Up Activity Ask students to look at the painting and respond to the prompt as they enter and get settled. Have students share their responses with a partner, either in class or through a blog space.

Discuss How do you think this painting and others like it reflect American society in the 1800s? *(The paintings depict a romantic view of life in America. They show American landscapes, scenes from American history, important American figures, and ordinary Americans hard at work.)*

Tell students that in this lesson they will be learning about developments in art, music, and literature in the early 1800s.

Aa Vocabulary Development: Use the Interactive Reading Notepad to preview the Key Terms and Academic Vocabulary in this lesson with students.

⇅ FLIP IT!
Assign the Flipped Video for this lesson.

■ STUDENT EDITION PRINT
PAGES: 419–425

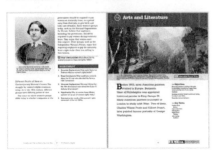

■ INVESTIGATE

DIGITAL TEXT 1
A New American Art Style

Objective 1: Describe American painting in the early to mid-1800s, including the Hudson River School and the work of John James Audubon.

Quick Instruction
Interactive Gallery: Painting America Project the interactive gallery and click through the images. Identify the Hudson River School as the first group to develop a uniquely American style of painting. Have students look through the images and describe the work of the Hudson River School artists. Discuss how the Hudson River School reflected American society in the early 1800s.

Hypothesize Why do you think art styles that were unique to American culture developed at this time? How did these art styles reflect American society during this period? *(Artists were moving away from European influences and interested in reflecting American themes. Artists were interested in the landscapes, wildlife, and people that made up the country. The approach of the Hudson River School reflected American society in the early 1800s, because like many Americans at the time, these artists were motivated by patriotism and optimism.)*

INTERACTIVE GALLERY
Painting America

■▲ ACTIVE CLASSROOM

Project the painting *Kindred Spirits* and use a whiteboard tool to divide it into four numbered sections: the mountains, the valley, the cliffs, and the figures. Have students count off 1 through 4 and use the A Closer Look Strategy to examine the part of the image in their section. Have students tell what they see and what they learned as a result of their focus on this part of the image. Have students share their insights and discuss the image as a whole.

Further Instruction
Go through the Interactive Reading Notepad questions and discuss the answers with the class.

Analyze Images Have students examine Audubon's painting of the turtle doves and describe his work. How were his paintings unique to American culture as developments in art? How did they reflect American society in the early 1800s? *(The painting is extremely detailed and lifelike. It shows the birds in their natural habitat. Audubon's work displayed the breadth and diversity of American wildlife as Americans were discovering more about different regions of the country during the early 1800s.)*

DIGITAL TEXT 2

A New Nation Finds a Voice

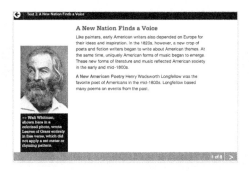

INTERACTIVE MAP

Early American Music and Literature

Compare and Contrast In what ways did fine arts in the early 1800s reflect both continuity and change in the American way of life? Why do you think these were important subjects for the artists? *(Continuity— landscape paintings showed the timelessness of the geography; paintings of Americans on farms showed traditional patterns of work and daily life. Change—paintings showing the frontier depicted the nation's expansion and the changes brought by westward movement. In capturing American society at the time, painters were showing the nation's permanence as well as its growth.)*

Objective 2: Analyze American literature and music during the early to mid-1800s.

Quick Instruction

Interactive Map: Early American Music and Literature Project the interactive map and click on the locations. Discuss how the nation's geography, diversity, and expansion influenced developments in art, music, and literature.

Draw Conclusions Describe developments in literature during the early 1800s that were unique to American culture. *(Whitman wrote about the common people of America and celebrated democracy. He wrote about the diversity of the country and its vast geography. Writers such as Longfellow, Irving, and Hawthorne wrote about themes from American history and expressed a uniquely American identity during the early 1800s.)*

📖 ACTIVE CLASSROOM

Have students use the Write 1-Get 3 activity to answer the question "Who are key American writers of the 1800s and what was their contribution to the development of American literature?"Have students fold a piece of paper into quarters, write down a response in the first box, and go around room asking to hear other responses. When students think a response is correct, have them write it in one of their boxes until they have three more responses on the page. Have students share responses with class.

ELL Use the ELL activity described in the ELL chart.

Further Instruction

Discuss answers to the Interactive Reading Notepad questions with the class. Be sure students can describe this era's developments in literature and music.

Support Ideas with Examples Give three examples of American literature of the 1800s that are unique to American culture and explain how each reflected society during this time. *(The Deerslayer and The Last of the Mohicans (Cooper) idealized frontier life. The Sketch Book (Irving) described the richness of America's past. Moby-Dick (Melville) described American whaling. The Scarlett Letter (Hawthorne) wrestled with the legacy of Puritan ideals. Clotel (Brown) described slavery and the Underground Railroad. Women writers like Sedgwick and Fern showed women who gained wealth, and the hardships of widows.)*

Identify Patterns What developments did American music undergo in the 1800s that were unique to American culture? How did these forms of music reflect society at the time? *(New American musical styles emerged as different groups came into contact with one another. They reflected American perspectives and the rise of a new middle class. African American spirituals and work songs merged European and African traditions to create uniquely American musical forms that gave rise to later forms such as blues, jazz, country, and rock.)*

Arts and Literature

DIGITAL TEXT 3

The Development of Transcendentalism

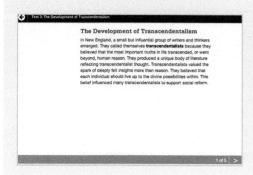

Objective 3: **Describe transcendentalism.**

Quick Instruction

Analyze Images Display the photograph of Ralph Waldo Emerson lecturing at the Summer School of Philosophy. Explain that he, and his contemporary Henry David Thoreau, were beacons of the Transcendentalist movement in literature and thought. What can you conclude about Emerson's popularity and influence based on this image and its caption? *(Emerson was a skilled lecturer and was quite popular, given the size and breadth of his audience. His thinking likely influenced most of the students and others who listened to him speak.)*

Context Clues Define *transcendentalism*. How was it unique to American culture? *(It was a movement of New England writers and thinkers who believed in nature, divinity, and the human spirit. Transcentalists produced a unique body of literature reflecting transcentdalist thought. It was unique to American culture in its emphasis on individualism.)*

Ⓓ **Differentiate: Extra Support** Remind students that *transcend* means "to go beyond." Have students reread the first paragraph of the text and explain in their own words what they think the transcendentalists were trying to "go beyond."

ELL Use the ELL activity described in the ELL chart.

Further Instruction

Go through the Interactive Reading Notepad questions and discuss the answers with the class.

Infer Why do you think transcendentalism developed in America during this time? *(Transcendentalists were reacting to industrialization and urbanization. They were also responding to the spirit of social reform that arose in the 1800s and the spread of slavery.)*

Generate Explanations Explain how Emerson and the transcendentalists reflected American society in the 1800s. *(Emerson emphasized distinctly American values such as self-reliance and individualism. Transcendentalists also prioritized social reform, a popular movement at this time.)*

Identify Cause and Effect Explain why Henry David Thoreau engaged in civil disobedience by refusing to pay taxes. Analyze what impact you think his act of civil disobedience had, citing evidence for support. *(Thoreau did not want to pay taxes to support the U.S.-Mexican War because he believed the war was wrong. This act had a strong influence. Many Americans read his essay explaining the importance of civil disobedience. Future leaders such as Mohandas Gandhi and Martin Luther King, Jr., drew on his ideas during their struggles for justice.)*

○ A.
○ B.
○ C.

■ SYNTHESIZE

DIGITAL ACTIVITY

Themes of American Art, Music, and Literature in the 1800s

Have students fill in the concept web and answer the questions. Have students share their webs with a partner and discuss their responses.

Discuss Have students review their concept webs and the examples of American art, music, and literature they read about in this lesson. Ask students what themes they think are particular to the time in which the artwork was created and what themes they think continue to influence American art, music, and literature today.

■ DEMONSTRATE

DIGITAL QUIZ

Lesson Quiz and Class Discussion Board

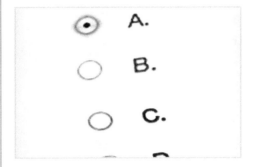

Assign the online Lesson Quiz for this lesson if you haven't already done so. Students will be offered automatic remediation or enrichment based on their score.

Pose these questions to the class on the Discussion Board:

Summarize In what ways did America develop its own unique cultural traditions in the nineteenth century? Give examples to support your views.

Draw Conclusions How do you think the development of American art, music, and literature in the 1800s helped form an American national identity at this time?

Topic Inquiry
Have students continue their investigations for the Topic Inquiry.

Society and Culture Before the Civil War (1820–1860)

■ SYNTHESIZE

DIGITAL ACTIVITY
Reflect on the Essential Question and Topic

First ask students to reconsider the Essential Question for this topic: Why is culture important? Have students make a list of three or four historical processes they learned about that changed American society, and then answer the questions.

Ask students, "How did American culture reflect these historical changes?" Have students give examples from the topic. Discuss their responses as a class or ask students to post their answers on the Class Discussion Board.

Next ask students to reflect on the topic as a whole and fill in the chart. Give students the following examples of changes in society to help them get started:

1. industrialization
2. urbanization
3. technological innovations
4. westward expansion
5. the spread of slavery

Topic Inquiry
Have students complete Step 3 of the Topic Inquiry.

■ DEMONSTRATE

DIGITAL TOPIC REVIEW AND ASSESSMENT
Society and Culture Before the Civil War (1820–1860)

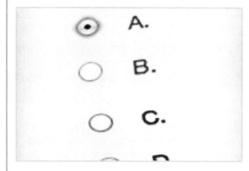

Students can prepare for the Topic Test by answering the questions in the Topic Review and Assessment online or the Assessment questions in the Print Student text. They can also prepare by reviewing their answers to the Interactive Reading Notepad questions or reviewing their notes in the Reading and Notetaking Study Guide.

DIGITAL TOPIC TEST
Society and Culture Before the Civil War (1820–1860)

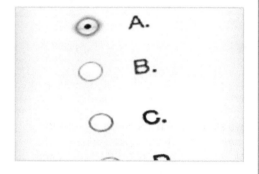

TOPIC TEST
Assign the Topic Test to assess students' understanding of topic content.

BENCHMARK TESTS
Assign these benchmark tests as you complete the relevant topics to monitor student progress toward mastering the course content and as preparation for the End-of-Course Test.

Benchmark Test 1: Topics 1–2

Benchmark Test 2: Topics 3–4

Benchmark Test 3: Topics 5–6

Benchmark Test 4: Topics 7–9

Benchmark Test 5: Topics 10–12

Benchmark Test 6: Topics 13–14

Benchmark Test 7: Topics 15–17

Sectionalism and Civil War

TOPIC 8 ORGANIZER	PACING: APPROX. 1 PERIOD, .5 BLOCKS
	PACING
Connect	1 period
MY STORY VIDEO **Robert E. Lee, The Marble Man**	10 min.
DIGITAL ESSENTIAL QUESTION ACTIVITY **When is War Justified?**	10 min.
DIGITAL OVERVIEW ACTIVITY **Sectionalism and Civil War**	10 min.
TOPIC INQUIRY: PROJECT-BASED LEARNING **Create a Website on the Impact of the Civil War**	20 min.
Investigate	3–6 periods
TOPIC INQUIRY: PROJECT-BASED LEARNING **Create a Website on the Impact of the Civil War**	Ongoing
LESSON 1 Conflicts and Compromises	30–40 min.
LESSON 2 Growing Tensions	30–40 min.
LESSON 3 Division and the Outbreak of War	30–40 min.
LESSON 4 The Course of War	30–40 min.
LESSON 5 Emancipation and Life in Wartime	30–40 min.
LESSON 6 The War's End	30–40 min.
Synthesize	1 period
DIGITAL ACTIVITY **Reflect on the Essential Question and Topic**	10 min.
TOPIC INQUIRY: PROJECT-BASED LEARNING **Create a Website on the Impact of the Civil War**	20 min.
Demonstrate	1–2 periods
DIGITAL TOPIC REVIEW AND ASSESSMENT **Sectionalism and Civil War**	10 min.
TOPIC INQUIRY: PROJECT-BASED LEARNING **Create a Website on the Impact of the Civil War**	20 min.

Topic 8

Create a Website on the Impact of the Civil War

In this Topic Inquiry students work together to build a website that promotes a fictitious museum display about the economic, social, and political impact of the Civil War. Learning how civil war impacts a country will contribute to students' understanding of the Topic Essential Question: When is war justified?

STEP 1: CONNECT
Develop Questions and Plan the Investigation

Launch the Project and Generate Questions
Review with students the *Project Launch* document, the letter from the fictitious Valley and Forest Museum. Ensure students understand that their project is to create a website to promote an exhibit, *The Impact of the Civil War in Numbers*, at the museum. In creating the website they will be transferring statistical and written information into visual representations, such as maps and charts, that will generate interest in and be representative of the museum exhibit. The website should include content related to the economic, social, and political impact of the Civil War.

Suggestion: Ensure that students can differentiate among economic, social, and political impacts. Review the examples of each. Hold a class discussion about how the three can overlap.

Prepare the Investigation
Organize the class into teams, if appropriate, and have students sign the *Project Contract.* Have students prepare by beginning the *Need-to-Know Questions* while keeping the Guiding Question in mind: In what ways did the Civil War affect the lives of Americans economically, socially, and politically?

Suggestion: Consider having students consider the points of view of various types of Americans during the Civil War. For example, How would the war most likely affect a young person in the North? A child in the South? A recent immigrant to New York? And so on.

Resources
- Student Instructions
- Project Launch
- Rubric for a Website on the Impact of the Civil War
- The Project Contract
- Need-to-Know Questions

STEP 2: INVESTIGATE
Apply Disciplinary Concepts and Tools

Research Written and Statistical Information on the Impact of the Civil War
Students will now commence their research. Begin by directing students to review the relevant *Skills Tutorials*. Remind students to keep track of their work in the *Project Tracker* as they continue to use the *Need-to-Know Questions* to guide their work. Explain that students should locate more information than they will need to complete their project. That way, they will be able to choose the statistics that are most compelling, complementary, and suitable for presenting through a variety of visual means.

Suggestion: Review applicable Internet use rules before students commence their research.

Determine How to Present Information and Statistics
Having acquired a variety of statistics about the economic, social, and political impact of the Civil War, students must now decide how to present the information. Ask students to identify the strengths and weaknesses of a variety of visual representations of quantitative information, such as different kinds of graphs, charts, tables, and maps. Assist students in effectively transferring information between different media: from written media to visual media and from statistical media to the written and visual media. Guide students in presenting factual and quantitative information visually and also in presenting quantitative information in a descriptive text.

Suggestion: Remind students that their website is being created to entice people to visit a museum exhibit, so their representations should both be accurate and visually enticing.

Resources
- Search for Information on the Internet
- Evaluate Web Sites
- Analyze Data and Models
- Identify Evidence
- Interpret Sources
- Project Tracker
- Need-to-Know Questions
- Information Organizer

⏻ PROFESSIONAL DEVELOPMENT

Project-Based Learning
Be sure to view the Project-Based Learning Professional Development resources in the online course.

STEP 3: SYNTHESIZE
Evaluate Sources and
Use Evidence to Formulate Conclusions

Select Digital Tools and Software and Create Your Visual Representations
In this step, students use a variety of digital tools to create their visual representations. A wide variety of tools are listed and suggested in the *Student Instructions.*

Suggestion: Encourage students to expand their skill sets by using digital tools that are new to them.

Create Your Website
Students create their websites using WordPress. Encourage students to include more than just their visual representations on their websites. They should include titles, captions, and information about the museum exhibit.

Revise Your Website
Review students' websites and allow them time to revise them. Encourage them to ensure that their website answers the Guiding Question: In what ways did the Civil War affect the lives of Americans economically, socially, and politically?

Suggestion: Point out to students that, like writing an essay, constructing a website requires the basic steps of planning, creating, and revising. Explain how that oftentimes revising can end up being the most time-consuming—and important—step in making anything.

Resources
• Project Tracker

STEP 4: DEMONSTRATE
Communicate Conclusions
and Take Informed Action

Present Your Website
Have students prepare their website presentations and then watch the team presentations. Limit their presentation time. To help the teams structure their time, set up a clock in the back of the room, and alert them when they have only a few minutes left.

Reflect on the Project
Conclude by reviewing the project and eliciting students' answers to these questions: What went well? What did not go so well? What are three lasting lessons you have learned from this project?

Suggestion: As an extension activity, have students learn some basics about search engine optimization (SEO), or the process of building websites that appear in Internet search engine results. How would they revise their websites to help them reach a wider audience on the Internet?

Resources
• Give an Effective Presentation

Topic (8)

INTRODUCTION

Society and Culture Before the Civil War (1820–1860)

The United States was divided by the Civil War, but the divisions had been part of American life for decades. The obvious distinction between free states and slave states was but one. The country was also divided geographically, into the North and the South. Economically, the interests of rural southerners and urban northerners regarding questions of tariffs, for example, were opposite. Social divides existed, too.Interstate and interregional travel was still rare and difficult, and truly knowing the people of a different state or region was the exception rather than the rule. All of these divisions had led to conflict and compromise. Soon, they would lead to war.

■ CONNECT

MY STORY VIDEO
Robert E. Lee, The Marble Man

Watch a video about Robert E. Lee's leadership at the Battle of Chancellorsville.

Check Understanding How was Robert E. Lee able to win victory at Chancellorsville? *(His risky decision to divide his forces resulted in a major victory for the South. However, the Confederate side suffered many casualties, among them General Stonewall Jackson.)*

Determine Point of View When the Civil War broke out, Robert E. Lee was offered command of the Union forces, but he chose to fight for the South. Why do you think he made that decision? *(A native Virginian, his desire to defend his home state from Union attack no doubt overruled his desire to see the Union be kept intact.)*

N FLIP IT!

Assign the My Story Video

DIGITAL ESSENTIAL QUESTION ACTIVITY
When is War Justified?

Ask students to think about the Essential Question for this topic: When is war justified?

Have students consider the types of factors that can divide a people: economic, political, religious, and social. Discuss which factors would justify going to war and which factors would not.

Interpret Invite a student to define a *civil war*. (A war between the citizens of the same country) Ask whether they think a civil war is ever more or less justified than a war between countries. (War against one's fellow citizens would be more difficult to justify because of the shared citizenship and cultural traits.)

Express Ideas Clearly Ask students if they think wars are generally caused by one event or factor or by several. (Wars are more likely to be caused by several factors because human relationships are complex, and more than one factor might be needed to convince people that such a deadly choice as war is justified.)

DIGITAL OVERVIEW ACTIVITY
Sectionalism and Civil War

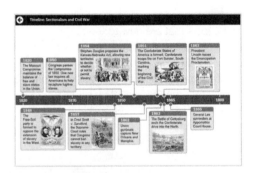

Point out that the first event in the timeline takes place more than 40 years—nearly half a century—before the beginning of the Civil War. Tell students that this reflects the fact that the Civil War did not come up "out of nowhere." It was an event long feared—and long predicted—that was the result of deep, old divisions in American society.As they learn about the Civil War, encourage students to think of it not so much as an event but as an effect, one that resulted from several causes.

Infer Ask students what all of the entries on the timeline before the Civil War have in common. (They are all concerned with slavery.) What can students infer from this? (That divisions over slavery were a major cause of the Civil War.)

Topic Inquiry
Launch the Topic Inquiry with students after introducing the Topic.

Conflicts and Compromises

Supporting English Language Learners

Use with Digital Text 4, California Reignites the Slavery Debate.

Listening
Explain to students that they will demonstrate listening comprehension of what you say through collaboration with peers.

Beginning Read the following sentences to students, then have pairs of students collaborate to explain in their own words what the sentences mean: *Calhoun insisted that slavery be allowed in the western territories. In addition, he demanded that fugitives, or African Americans who had fled slavery, be returned to their owners.*

Intermediate Orally ask students the following questions about Calhoun and Webster. In groups, have them restate the questions in their own words and then answer the questions: 1) Which man viewed slavery as evil? 2) Which man wanted to legalize slavery in the western territories? 3) Which man supported the return of fugitive slaves?

Advanced Read aloud Daniel Webster's speech excerpt from the text. Then have pairs of students demonstrate listening comprehension by collaborating to restate the excerpt into more familiar language.

Advanced High Compare and contrast the positions of Calhoun and Webster. Have pairs of students play the roles of Calhoun and Webster, state their positions in the slavery debate, and work to reach a compromise.

Use with Digital Text 6, A Book Sways the North Against Slavery.

Writing
Review the plot and popularity of *Uncle Tom's Cabin* in preparation for the activity. Prompt students to write using newly acquired basic vocabulary from the reading.

Beginning Explain the meanings of the basic vocabulary *bought, whipped,* and *refused*. Have students complete and write down this summary of *Uncle Tom's Cabin*: Simon Legree _____ a slave named Uncle Tom. Tom _____ to tell him where two runaway slaves were, so Legree _____ him.

Intermediate Discuss the meanings of the descriptive words *kindness, piety,* and *brutal*. Ask students to suggest sentences about Uncle Tom or Simon Legree using this newly acquired basic vocabulary. Record their suggestions, and have students write them down.

Advanced Discuss the meanings of the words *novel, injustice, appeal, printing,* and *translated*. Have pairs of students write an advertisement for *Uncle Tom's Cabin* that uses this newly acquired basic vocabulary.

Advanced High Discuss the meanings of the words *objected, claimed, firsthand, moral,* and *political*. Have students use this newly acquired basic vocabulary to write a paragraph explaining the importance of *Uncle Tom's Cabin*. Provide time for students to share their paragraph with a partner.

Ⓓ Differentiate Instruction

Use the Differentiated Instruction notes throughout the lesson plan to support the varied skill sets, levels of readiness, and interests in the mixed-ability classroom.

Challenge These notes include suggestions for expanding the activity for advanced students.

On-Level These notes include suggestions for modifying the activity to address different interests or learning styles.

Extra Support These notes include ideas for providing more scaffolding or reading spuport.

Special Needs These notes provide ideas for adapting instruction to support the needs of various special needs students.

■ NOTES

Topic 8 Lesson 1

Conflicts and Compromises

Objectives

Objective 1: Describe how the Missouri Compromise affected slavery.

Objective 2: Explain why conflict arose over the issue of slavery in western territories.

Objective 3: Identify why the Free-Soil party was founded.

Objective 4: Explain how the Compromise of 1850 tried to resolve the issue of slavery.

Objective 5: Summarize how Uncle Tom's Cabin affected attitudes toward slavery.

LESSON 1 ORGANIZER		PACING: APPROX. 1 PERIOD, .5 BLOCKS			
				RESOURCES	
		OBJECTIVES	PACING	Online	Print
Connect					
DIGITAL START UP ACTIVITY **The Impact of Slavery**			5 min.	●	
Investigate					
DIGITAL TEXT 1 **Henry Clay's Missouri Compromise**		Objective 1	10 min.	●	●
DIGITAL TEXT 2 **Western Expansion Heightens Tension Over Slavery**		Objective 2	10 min.	●	●
DIGITAL TEXT 3 **The Free-Soil Party Opposes Slavery in the West**		Objective 3	10 min.	●	●
DIGITAL TEXT 4 **California Reignites the Slavery Debate**			10 min.	●	●
DIGITAL TEXT 5 **Congress Reaches a Compromise**		Objective 4	10 min.	●	●
INTERACTIVE CARTOON **The Fugitive Slave Act**			10 min.	●	
DIGITAL TEXT 6 **A Book Sways the North Against Slavery**			10 min.	●	●
INTERACTIVE GALLERY *Uncle Tom's Cabin*		Objective 5	10 min.	●	
Synthesize					
DIGITAL ACTIVITY **Conflicts and Compromises Prior to the Civil War**			5 min.	●	
Demonstrate					
DIGITAL QUIZ **Lesson Quiz and Class Discussion Board**			10 min.	●	

PEARSON
realize.
www.PearsonRealize.com

Go online to access additional resources including:
Primary Sources • Biographies • Supreme Court cases •
21st Century Skill Tutorials • Maps • Graphic Organizers.

CONNECT

DIGITAL START UP ACTIVITY
The Impact of Slavery

Project the Start Up Activity Ask students
to read and respond to the excerpt as they
enter and get settled. Then have students
share their ideas in small groups.

Interpret What does George Harris say his
master does? *(Takes him away from his work,
his friends, and all that he likes; makes him
give up his wife and live with another woman)*
What does Harris suggest about the laws of
Kentucky and the nation? *(The laws should
not allow people like his master to treat other
people in this way.)* How does this excerpt and
the book *Uncle Tom's Cabin* show sectionalism
and slavery as causes of the Civil War? *(It shows
why some people opposed slavery and were
willing to fight to end slavery and win liberty.)*

Aa Vocabulary Development: Use the
Interactive Reading Notepad to preview the
Key Terms and Academic Vocabulary in this
lesson with students.

⇅ FLIP IT!
Assign the Flipped Video for this lesson.

STUDENT EDITION PRINT
PAGES: 430–438

INVESTIGATE

DIGITAL TEXT 1
Henry Clay's Missouri
Compromise

Objective 1: Describe how the
Missouri Compromise affected slavery.

Quick Instruction
Analyze Maps Project the map showing the
geographic distribution of free and slave states
prior to the Missouri Compromise. Challenge
students to consider what would happen to the
balance of free and slave states if Missouri were
admitted as a state.

Explain that in this lesson, students will explore
the provisions of the Missouri Compromise, the
role of Henry Clay, and the manner by which
the Missouri Compromise provided a peaceful,
if temporary, resolution to the challenges of
sectionalism and slavery.

Summarize What role did Henry Clay play in
achieving congressional compromise before
the Civil War? *(Henry Clay determined that the
United States could admit two states, one free
and one slave, to maintain the balance of power
between free and slave states, thereby avoiding
wider conflict. He proposed his compromise in
Congress, where it was passed and made law.)*

Further Instruction
Go through the Interactive Reading Notepad
questions and discuss the answers with the
class.

Invite students to define the term *compromise*.
Guide students to understand that a
compromise attempts to find a peaceful
resolution to a conflict by ensuring that the
parties to a conflict each give up and get
something that they want.

Recall What were the main provisions of
the Missouri Compromise? *(The Missouri
Compromise admitted Missouri as a slave*

state and Maine as a free state. It also drew an
imaginary line across the southern border of
Missouri. In the Louisiana Purchase territories,
slavery was illegal north of this line and legal
south of this line.)*

Identify Central Issues Describe how
sectionalism and slavery caused the core conflict
that the Missouri Compromise attempted to
address. How did that compromise provide a
temporary, peaceful resolution to the conflict?
*(Slavery had become a sectional issue in the
United States, whereby people in southern
states tended to support the spread of slavery
and people in northern states tended to oppose
the spread of slavery. When Missouri asked
to become a state, Congress was divided
sectionally over whether to admit Missouri as a
free or slave state, since either decision would
give more political power to one section or
another. The Missouri Compromise provided a
peaceful resolution to the immediate conflict by
admitting two states, one free and one slave, to
prevent either section from gaining more power.)*

Conflicts and Compromises

DIGITAL TEXT 2

Western Expansion Heightens Tension Over Slavery

DIGITAL TEXT 3

The Free-Soil Party Opposes Slavery in the West

Objective 2: **Explain why conflict arose over the issue of slavery in western territories.**

Quick Instruction

Prompt students to understand that the Missouri Compromise provided a guideline for slavery in the Louisiana Purchase territory, but it did not solve the question of future states or of future territories. Be sure students understand that the sectional debate over slavery originated as a conflict between northern and southern sections of the nation. However, as the nation expanded west, the sectional debate expanded, too. Each section wanted to enlarge their influence and prevent the other from gaining more influence.

Distinguish What was a primary cause of sectionalism? *(The issue of slavery and property rights continued to divide Americans across regional lines. There were many perspectives on the issue, but generally speaking, entire states felt one way or the other. These differences prompted debate over the status of western territories.)*

Infer What effect would sectionalism have on congressional conflicts over territorial gains? *(Congressional leaders from the South would likely want to allow slavery in new territories, while congressional leaders from the north would likely want to ban slavery in new territories.)*

D Differentiate: Extra Support Explain that the root of *popular* comes from the Latin for "people," and the root of *sovereignty*

comes from the Latin for "authority" or "rule." Together, *popular sovereignty* means "rule by the people." Applied to the question of slavery in territories, the phrase was used to mean that the people of the territory would decide for themselves whether to allow slavery.

Further Instruction

Analyze Cartoons Project the political cartoon on the Wilmot Proviso. Congressional leaders attemped to add the proviso to many other bills. However, the proviso failed to be adopted each time. Why is the proviso portrayed as a stumbling block in the cartoon? *(Congressional leaders kept adding the proviso to other bills, making it more difficult for Zachary Taylor to win the presidential election and for the Whigs to pass their other policy items.)*

Make Predictions What impact would slavery have on the acquisition of new territories? What challenge would it pose? *(The nation would have to decide whether to allow slavery in these territories.)*

Explain What were the provisions of the Wilmot Proviso? Why did sectionalism prevent the proviso from being adopted? *(The Wilmot Proviso would have made slavery illegal in territories gained from Mexico. This would have upset the balance between free and slave territories and states. Southern congressional leaders refused to pass the proviso in order to preserve the balance between slave and free sections of the nation.)*

Objective 3: **Identify why the Free-Soil Party was founded.**

Quick Instruction

Analyze Images Project the image of a Free-Soil Party campaign banner. Prompt students to discuss what ideas they think the Free-Soil Party represented. Explain that this lesson contrasts the point of view of the Free-Soil Party with other political parties on the historical issue of slavery.

Categorize Draw a three-column chart with the headings *Whig, Democratic,* and *Free-Soil.* List each party's 1848 presidential candidate beneath each heading. Then, list each candidate's point of view on the important historical issues of slavery. *(Whig: Zachary Taylor, did not take an official stance on slavery but was assumed to support slavery as a slave owner; Democratic: Lewis Cass, supported popular sovereignty; Free-Soil: Martin Van Buren, wanted to ban slavery in Mexican Cession)*

Further Instruction

Go through the Interactive Reading Notepad questions and discuss the answers with the class.

DIGITAL TEXT 4

California Reignites the Slavery Debate

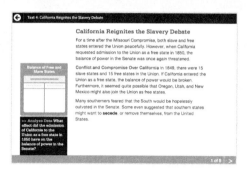

DIGITAL TEXT 5

Congress Reaches a Compromise

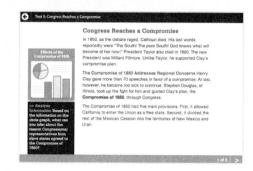

Compare Points of View Given the effects of sectionalism, why might voters have been unlikely to support Lewis Cass for president? *(Slavery was a major issue of the election, and the nation was divided largely on sectional lines. Popular sovereignty did not ensure either a balance between sections or a clear victory for either. Because popular sovereignty left the question of slavery to occupants of a territory, it was kind of risky. Neither those who supported slavery nor those who opposed it could not be sure that popular sovereignty would protect their interests. Therefore, both sides of the debate were less likely to support Cass, who promoted popular sovereignty.)*

Objective 4: **Explain how the Compromise of 1850 tried to resolve the issue of slavery.**

Quick Instruction

Prompt students to understand the roles of Henry Clay, John C. Calhoun, and Daniel Webster in compromising to achieve a peaceful resolution to the conflict between different sections of the nation. Be sure that students understand that secession, or the withdrawal of some states from the nation, was proposed prior to the Civil War. Clay, Calhoun, and Webster, in their ways, sought to prevent violent conflict and secession.

Interactive Cartoon: The Fugitive Slave Act Project the cartoon. Roll over the hotspots to reveal details about the cartoon and discuss them with students. How does this cartoon illustrate that tensions regarding the issue of slavery were rising? *(The cartoon shows the violence that surrounds the issue of slavery and the Fugitive Slave Act. People were willing to kill to recover escaped slaves, and others were willing to kill to help escaped slaves. The conflict was not just about ideas but about people's lives.)*

Compare and Contrast Summarize the roles played by John C. Calhoun, Henry Clay, and Daniel Webster in the congressional conflict over California's statehood. What did their approaches have in common, and how did they differ? *(Calhoun remained adamant that slavery must be allowed in the*

western territories and that northern states must be required to return fugitive slaves. He insisted that these demands be met to prevent secession. Webster opposed both of Calhoun's demands, but he believed it was more important to preserve the union, so he agreed to support southern demands that northerners be required to return escaped slaves. Clay proposed the Compromise of 1850 to partially meet Calhoun's demands by allowing the extension of slavery in some parts of the western territories while prohibiting it in others. The Compromise of 1850 also included a strict fugitive slave law.)

👥 ACTIVE CLASSROOM

Ask the following questions using the Circle Write Strategy: Why did people in the north, even those who did not necessarily support a ban on slavery, oppose the Fugitive Slave Act? Why did it make so many people angry? If students struggle with the questions, you may wish to model a Think Aloud: "Hmm, let me think how I would feel. If I had lived in the North, and Congress told me that I had to capture escaped slaves, whether I agreed with slavery or not, and help return them to the South, would I want to do that?"

ELL Use the ELL activity described in the ELL chart.

Conflicts and Compromises

INTERACTIVE CARTOON

The Fugitive Slave Act

DIGITAL TEXT 6

A Book Sways the North Against Slavery

INTERACTIVE GALLERY

Uncle Tom's Cabin

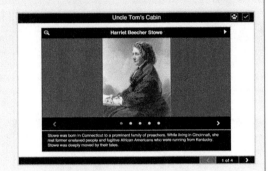

Further Instruction

Draw Conclusions Do you think the provisions of the Compromise of 1850 provided for a peaceful resolution to the conflict over slavery? Explain your reasoning. *(Like the Missouri Compromise, I think it provided a temporary peaceful resolution. States did not secede and engage in armed conflict right away, but the Fugitive Slave Act resulted in violence. Also, it did not resolve the fundamental debate over slavery in the nation, which would lead to violence eventually.)*

Objective 5: **Summarize how *Uncle Tom's Cabin* affected attitudes toward slavery.**

Quick Instruction

Interactive Gallery: *Uncle Tom's Cabin* Project the slideshow. Look at each image and source individually and discuss its meaning. Then, evaluate the collection as a whole and discuss its historical significance. Prompt students to explore how the images demonstrate the divisive nature of sectionalism and slavery in the United States leading up to the Civil War.

Summarize How did *Uncle Tom's Cabin* impact perceptions of slavery in the North? *(The publication of the novel only fueled opinions against slavery. Before the novel's publication, some northerners may have had little or no contact with people who had been enslaved. Stowe's novel made slavery and its consequences more real and personal.)*

Further Instruction

Determine Author's Purpose What did Harriet Beecher Stowe hope to convey about the effects of slavery on people in the South? *(Stowe hoped to convey the cruelty and hardship of slavery by showing how badly Tom and other enslaved persons were treated by their owners.)*

> **ACTIVE CLASSROOM**
>
> Use the Conversation With History Strategy to help students engage with the gallery. Organize students into small groups, and ask each person in the group to write and answer a question to the author of *Uncle Tom's Cabin*, Harriet Beecher Stowe.

ELL Use the ELL activity described in the ELL chart.

SYNTHESIZE

DIGITAL ACTIVITY

Conflicts and Compromises Prior to the Civil War

Ask students to review the lesson to identify key congressional conflicts that existed prior to the Civil War. Have them record these conflicts. Then, have them identify and record congressional compromises that attempted to find peaceful resolutions to these conflicts. Circulate the room to keep students on task. Ensure that students identify sectionalism and the expansion of slavery as two key conflicts and the Missouri Compromise and the Compromise of 1850 as two key compromises.

Instruct small groups to discuss how each compromise provided a peaceful resolution to a congressional conflict. Then, challenge each group to answer the question: Why do you think these proposed solutions did not solve the conflicts facing the United States at this time?

Discuss Call on each group to share ideas. Have groups record their responses to post on the class blog. Finally, tell each group to predict how sectionalism and slavery will incite the nation to war, despite attempts at compromise.

DEMONSTRATE

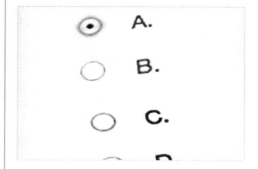

DIGITAL QUIZ

Lesson Quiz and Class Discussion Board

Assign the online Lesson Quiz for this lesson if you haven't already done so. Students will be offered automatic remediation or enrichment based on their score.

Pose these questions to the class on the Discussion Board:

In *Conflicts and Compromises*, you read about congressional conflicts driven by sectionalism and slavery that existed before the Civil War. You also learned about the roles played by legislators such as Henry Clay, John C. Calhoun, and Daniel Webster in attempting to achieve compromises. Finally, you examined two compromises that resulted in peaceful resolutions to congressional conflicts over the expansion of slavery into new states and territories. The Missouri Compromise and the Compromise of 1850 each provided temporary solutions to deep-rooted problems.

Compare Points of View Why did Clay and Webster oppose the expansion of slavery? Why did Calhoun fight so hard to promote the expansion of slavery? What incentive did all three leaders have to reach a compromise?

Make Decisions Clay and Webster decided that preserving the union was more important than restricting slavery. Do you agree that the provisions of the Compromise of 1850 were necessary? Why or why not?

Topic Inquiry

Have students continue their investigations for the Topic Inquiry.

Topic 8 Lesson 2

Growing Tensions

Supporting English Language Learners

Use with the Text 4, **The Impact of the Dred Scott Case.**

Writing
Prompt students to write about the Dred Scott case using content-based, grade-level vocabulary pertaining to the legal system.

Beginning Explain the words *case, court,* and *ruling*. Then have students use this content-based vocabulary to complete the following sentences: *Dred Scott* v. *Sanford* was a _____ in the Supreme _____. The _____ , or decision, helped the issue of slavery.

Intermediate Discuss the meanings of *Supreme Court, Justices, lawsuit, ruling,* and *decision*. Then have students write sentences using each of these terms.

Advanced Discuss the meanings of *Supreme Court, Justices, lawsuit, ruling,* and *decision*. Ask pairs of students to write a paragraph about the Dred Scott case that uses at least four of these five content-based vocabulary words.

Advanced High Discuss the meanings of *Supreme Court, Justices, lawsuit, ruling, decision, outlaw,* and *unconstitutional*. Ask students to use this content-based vocabulary to write a mock news article about the Dred Scott case that could have been printed just after the Supreme Court announced its decision.

Use with Digital Text 6, **Abraham Lincoln Leads the Republican Party.**

Listening
Review reasons for taking notes when someone is speaking, and encourage students to include only the main ideas in their notes. Prompt students to demonstrate listening comprehension of increasingly complex spoken English by taking notes commensurate with content and grade-level needs.

Beginning Display these notes as a bulleted list: born in _____ ; went to school for _____ ; studied _____ on his own; owned a _____ before going into politics. Then read aloud to students the second and third paragraphs of the text. After each sentence or two, pause so students can take notes by completing and writing down one item from the list.

Intermediate Read aloud to students the second and third paragraphs of the text. After each sentence or two, pause so students can take notes on what you have just said. Encourage students to organize their notes as a bulleted list.

Advanced Read aloud to students the fourth paragraph of the text.Have students jot down important words and phrases. Afterward, encourage them to fill in any gaps in their notes.

Advanced High Have students take notes as you read aloud the section titled "Lincoln and Douglas Debate Slavery."Afterward, encourage them to fill in any gaps or condense their notes as necessary.

D Differentiate Instruction

Use the Differentiated Instruction notes throughout the lesson plan to support the varied skill sets, levels of readiness, and interests in the mixed-ability classroom.

Challenge These notes include suggestions for expanding the activity for advanced students.

On-Level These notes include suggestions for modifying the activity to address different interests or learning styles.

Extra Support These notes include ideas for providing more scaffolding or reading spuport.

Special Needs These notes provide ideas for adapting instruction to support the needs of various special needs students.

NOTES

PEARSON
realize™
www.PearsonRealize.com

Go online to access additional resources including:
Primary Sources • Biographies • Supreme Court cases •
21st Century Skill Tutorials • Maps • Graphic Organizers.

Objectives

Objective 1: Identify the goals and outcomes of the Kansas-Nebraska Act.

Objective 2: Summarize the impact of the Dred Scott case on the nation.

Objective 3: Explain why the Republican Party was founded.

Objective 4: Explain the rapid emergence of Abraham Lincoln as a Republican Party leader.

Objective 5: Describe the reaction to John Brown's raid on Harpers Ferry.

LESSON 2 ORGANIZER		PACING: APPROX. 1 PERIOD, .5 BLOCKS			
				RESOURCES	
		OBJECTIVES	PACING	Online	Print
Connect					
DIGITAL START UP ACTIVITY **Tensions Divide the Nation**			5 min.	●	
Investigate					
DIGITAL TEXT 1 **The Question of Slavery in Kansas and Nebraska**		Objective 1	10 min.	●	●
DIGITAL TEXT 2 **Violent Clashes Over Slavery in Kansas**			10 min.	●	●
DIGITAL TEXT 3 **Violence Over Slavery Breaks Out in the Senate**			10 min.	●	●
INTERACTIVE GALLERY **The Effects of the Kansas-Nebraska Act**			10 min.	●	
DIGITAL TEXT 4 **The Impact of the Dred Scott Case**		Objective 2	10 min.	●	●
INTERACTIVE GALLERY **The Dred Scott Case**			10 min.	●	
DIGITAL TEXT 5 **The Republican Party Challenges Other Parties**		Objective 3	10 min.	●	●
DIGITAL TEXT 6 **Abraham Lincoln Leads the Republican Party**		Objective 4	10 min.	●	●
DIGITAL TEXT 7 **John Brown's Antislavery Campaign**		Objective 5	10 min.	●	●
Synthesize					
DIGITAL ACTIVITY **Tensions Divide the Nation**			5 min.	●	
Demonstrate					
DIGITAL QUIZ **Lesson Quiz and Class Discussion Board**			10 min.	●	

Growing Tensions

▉ CONNECT

DIGITAL START UP ACTIVITY
Tensions Divide the Nation

Project the Start Up Activity Ask students to answer the questions as they enter and get settled. Then, have them share their ideas in small groups.

Discuss Why might people have felt more loyalty toward their section of the country than the country as a whole? *(Many people in each section probably shared certain ways of life, economic activities, and political views. This likely made them feel closer to their friends, families, neighbors, and communities within their sections.)* How might have sectionalism increased tensions in the United States? *(Sectionalism would have encouraged people to put the interests, politics, and ideas of their own sections above the unity of the nation.)*

Aa Vocabulary Development: Use the Interactive Reading Notepad to preview the Key Terms and Academic Vocabulary in this lesson with students.

🔁 FLIP IT!
Assign the Flipped Video for this lesson.

▉ STUDENT EDITION PRINT
PAGES: 439–449

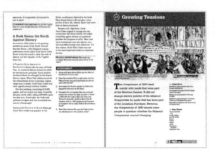

▉ INVESTIGATE

DIGITAL TEXT 1
The Question of Slavery in Kansas and Nebraska

Objective 1: Identify the goals and outcomes of the Kansas-Nebraska Act.

Quick Instruction
Interactive Gallery: The Effects of the Kansas-Nebraska Act Project the Interactive gallery and click through the items. Call on a volunteer to define *popular sovereignty*. Explain that the Kansas-Nebraska Act attempted to apply popular sovereignty to western territories. Ask students to consider how popular sovereignty might conflict with the Missouri Compromise. Prompt students to think about the effect the Kansas-Nebraska Act will have on sectionalism in the United States.

Cite Evidence that the effects of the Kansas-Nebraska Act showed the potentially violent outcomes of sectional differences over slavery. *(The Kansas-Nebraska Act's popular sovereignty provision was intended to decide the question of slavery in Kansas through a popular vote. However, pro- and antislavery forces saw it as an opportunity to tip the balance in national politics. They sent settlers to occupy Kansas and sway the vote. Settlers from both sides of the issues clashed, even on the floor of the Senate. The events demonstrated that people for and against slavery were willing to commit acts of violence to defend their positions, increasing the likelihood of war.)*

DIGITAL TEXT 2
Violent Clashes Over Slavery in Kansas

🖥 ACTIVE CLASSROOM
Have students Make Headlines for items in the Interactive gallery. Assign each student one of the pictures for which to write a headline. Then, organize students into groups so that each group has a headline for each item. Instruct students to share and revise their headlines. Discuss headlines as a class, or post them to the class blog.

Further Instruction
Begin by asking students to recall previous discussions of popular sovereignty. Draw a T-chart on the white board, and call on volunteers to list pros and cons of popular sovereignty as a solution to sectional debates about slavery. Then, display the map of the Missouri Compromise. Call on students to locate places of importance, such as the Missouri Compromise line and the unorganized territory which would eventually become the Kansas and Nebraska Territories. Point out that the Kansas-Nebraska Act changed the rules established by the Missouri Compromise by allowing citizens, not geographic boundaries, to determine the question of slavery. Explain that this circumstance posed a new precedent.

DIGITAL TEXT 3

Violence Over Slavery Breaks Out in the Senate

Be sure to point out that the Kansas-Nebraska Act was a major event in U.S. history because it exposed sectionalism and slavery as causes of strife that would lead to the Civil War. The Kansas-Nebraska Act attempted to resolve the sectional debate about slavery and avoid conflict by providing for popular sovereignty in two new territories. However, it led to more argument and violence as both sides of the issue rushed to win control of Kansas. This violence spilled over into the politics of the Senate.

INTERACTIVE GALLERY

The Effects of the Kansas-Nebraska Act

Infer What relationship do you see between the violence that occurred on the Senate floor and the fact that slavery was a cause of the Civil War? *(The fight on the Senate floor shows that Congress was unable to find a political solution to the slavery issue, leaving war as the only alternative.)*

DIGITAL TEXT 4

The Impact of the Dred Scott Case

Objective 2: Summarize the impact of the Dred Scott case on the nation.

Quick Instruction

Interactive Gallery: The Dred Scott Case Project the Interactive gallery, and click through the items. Have students write a short summary of the issues and decisions in the landmark Supreme Court case *Dred Scott* v. *Sandford*. Then, have them evaluate the impact of the case on African Americans, the slavery debate, southerners, and northerners.

Draw Conclusions What impact did *Dred Scott* v. *Sandford* have on enslaved persons and the abolitionist movement? *(This decision changed the way slavery and enslaved persons were treated in the nation. Enslaved persons could not escape from slave states and hope for protection. Moreover, abolitionists could not count on national laws to prevent the spread of slavery, because Congress could not regulate slavery within states and territories.)*

> ### 🎬 ACTIVE CLASSROOM
>
> Conduct Write 1-Get 3 about the Dred Scott aase. Ask: What are four ways that the decision in the Dred Scott Case affected the lives of people in the United States? Have students take a piece of paper and fold it into quarters, write down one response in the first box, and then go around room asking to hear other responses. If students think a response is correct, they should write it in one of the boxes until they have three more responses on the page. Have students share the responses they recorded with the class.

Growing Tensions

The Dred Scott Case

The Republican Party Challenges Other Parties

Abraham Lincoln Leads the Republican Party

D Differentiate: Extra Support Display a map of the United States at the time of the Dred Scott decision and illustrate the path of Dred Scott's travels *(from Missouri to Illinois to the Wisconsin Territory and then back to Missouri)*, pointing out where the laws of the different states and territories conflicted, leaving the Supreme Court to determine which laws applied to Dred Scott. Ask students: What does this case demonstrate about the challenges of leaving the question of slavery to individual states and territories? Have them discuss their answers in small groups.

ELL Use the ELL activity described in the ELL chart.

Further Instruction

Hypothesize If Dred Scott had left his owners or pursued his lawsuit while he was in Illinois or Wisconsin, do you think this case would have had a different outcome? Why or why not? *(I think the Supreme Court would have made the same ruling because it clearly meant to rule in favor of slavery. The court likely would have ruled that Dred Scott was property when he left Missouri and remained property wherever he went.)*

Objective 3: Explain why the Republican Party was founded.

Quick Instruction

Analyze Cartoons Display the political cartoon of Fillmore, Fremont, and Buchanan. Point out the political positions of each: Republican John Fremont, who opposed the spread of slavery; Democrat James Buchanan, who supported the spread of slavery; and American pParty candidate Millard Fillmore, who supported the Compromise of 1850. Ask students to explain how the political cartoon shows different points of view of political parties on the issue of slavery.

Further Instruction

Be sure that students understand that not all Republicans were abolitionists. Most Republicans opposed the spread of slavery to the western territories but not the existence of slavery in existing states. They were not trying to outlaw slavery throughout the nation but to contain it in the South. However, proslavery forces considered this stance a threat to their way of life.

Determine Point of View How did the points of view of the Republican and the Democratic Parties differ? How did the point of view of the American Party contrast with both? *(The Republicans opposed the expansion of slavery into western territories, while the Democrats supported the expansion of slavery into western territories. The American Party favored compromise, providing for the expansion of slavery in some territories in order to preserve the United States as a nation.)*

Objective 4: Explain the rapid emergence of Abraham Lincoln as a Republican Party leader.

Quick Instruction

Analyze Images Display the image of the Lincoln-Douglas debate and the excerpt from Lincoln's speech at Ottawa in 1858. Prompt students to interpret Lincoln's point of view in the speech. How did Lincoln feel about slavery? *(Lincoln thinks slavery is wrong because African Americans are entitled to the same natural rights as others.)* How did his point of view compare to the Republican point of view of the time? *(His views were perfectly in line with those of the Republican Party.)*

Determine Relevance What made the Lincoln-Douglas debates and their outcome such a major event in U.S. history? *(Because of its focus on the issue of slavery, the debates between Lincoln and Douglas garnered national attention. The debates not only helped elevate Lincoln's stature, preparing him to run for president, but also kept the argument over the expansion of slavery in the national spotlight. The debates themselves made slavery a central issue.)*

ELL Use the ELL activity described in the ELL chart.

DIGITAL TEXT 7

John Brown's Antislavery Campaign

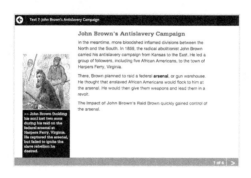

John Brown's Antislavery Campaign

In the meantime, more bloodshed inflamed divisions between the North and the South. In 1859, the radical abolitionist John Brown carried his antislavery campaign from Kansas to the East. He led a group of followers, including five African Americans, to the town of Harpers Ferry, Virginia.

There, Brown planned to raid a federal **arsenal**, or gun warehouse. He thought that enslaved African Americans would flock to him at the arsenal. He would then give them weapons and lead them in a revolt.

The Impact of John Brown's Raid Brown quickly gained control of the arsenal.

>> John Brown (holding his son) lost two sons during his raid on the federal arsenal at Harpers Ferry, Virginia. He captured the arsenal, but failed to ignite the slave rebellion he desired.

1 of 4 >

Further Instruction

Be sure that students understand Lincoln's personal views about slavery were tempered by his political motivations. Like other politicians of the time, Lincoln strove for compromise. He wanted to maintain the unity of the nation. Though he opposed slavery as a moral and social ill, he did not set out to abolish slavery where it existed throughout the nation. His primary objective as a political candidate was to prevent the spread of slavery.

Connect How did Lincoln's point of view in the debates foreshadow slavery and sectionalism as causes of the Civil War? *(Lincoln stated that he opposed slavery as a moral wrong and that enslaved persons were entitled to the same liberties as other Americans. Although he did not call for the abolition of slavery, these sentiments undermined the very existence of slavery. Such views and the reactions to those views resulted in sectional differences over slavery and highlighted the rift between North and South. Lincoln's point of view made clear that slave and free states could not continue to exist under one nation without eventually deciding the question of slavery for the entire nation.)*

Objective 5: Describe the reaction to John Brown's raid on Harpers Ferry.

Quick Instruction

Analyze Images Display the image of John Brown's raid on Harpers Ferry. Ask students to describe what they see. Recall that Brown had also been involved in the events of Bleeding Kansas. Prompt students to think about the causes and effects of the raid, including its lasting cultural legacy as developed in the song "The Battle Hymn of the Republic." Point out that the song "John Brown's Body" and the later poem "The Battle Hymn of the Republic" each celebrated antislavery themes.

Summarize Why was Brown's raid a major event in U.S. history leading up to the Civil War? *(Brown's raid at Harpers Ferry demonstrated that both sides in the sectional debates over slavery were willing to resort to violence.)*

Further Instruction

Display a map showing free and slave states in the United States around 1859. You may wish to use the map of the Missouri Compromise from the first reading in the lesson. Call on students to identify Virginia on the map and to determine whether Virginia was a free or a slave state. Then, point out the location of Harpers Ferry at the very northern tip of Virginia near the border with Maryland. Ask students why they think John Brown might have chosen this location for his raid. Discuss not only the location of the arsenal but also the area's location along the border between free and slave states.

Describe Describe the development of the "The Battle Hymn of the Republic." What makes its writing and message unique to American culture and history? *(The song began as a poem, written by Julia Ward Howe after the start of the Civil War. Howe wrote the poem after she had heard the song "John Brown's Body," which celebrated Brown as a martyr in the fight against slavery. The poem, set to the same tune as "John Brown's Body," became a popular song of the Civil War. It rallied northern troops by celebrating their cause as morally just.)*

Growing Tensions

▮ SYNTHESIZE

DIGITAL ACTIVITY
Tensions Divide the Nation

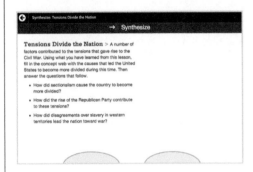

Remind students that this lesson examined the growing tensions in the nation over issues of sectionalism and slavery. Point out that violence broke out on several occasions: in Kansas, at Harpers Ferry, and even in the Senate. Have them work in pairs to complete the concept web and then review the webs as a class.

Organize students into groups to answer the following questions: How did sectionalism cause the country to become more divided? How did the rise of the Republican Party contribute to these tensions? How did disagreements over slavery in western territories lead the nation towards war? Call on each group to share one of their answers with the class.

Discuss Challenge student groups to Rank It by putting the following major events in U.S. history in order from least to most significant impact on leading the nation to war: Bleeding Kansas, Dred Scott case, Lincoln-Douglas debates, Brown's raid on Harpers Ferry. Call on groups to share and explain their rankings.

▮ DEMONSTRATE

DIGITAL QUIZ
Lesson Quiz and Class Discussion Board

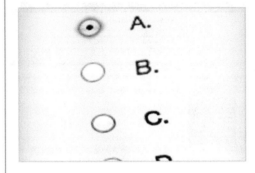

Assign the online Lesson Quiz for this lesson if you haven't already done so. Students will be offered automatic remediation or enrichment based on their score.

Pose these questions to the class on the Discussion Board:

In *Growing Tensions* , you read about the causes and effects of the following major events in U.S. history: the Kansas-Nebraska Act, the landmark Supreme Court case *Dred Scott* v. *Sandford,* the formation of the Republican Party, the Lincoln-Douglas debates, and John Brown's raid on Harpers Ferry.

Predict Consequences Which of these events most clearly elevated slavery as a national issue divisive enough to cause the Civil War? Explain your reasoning.

Synthesize Which of these events most clearly demonstrated the effects of sectionalism in the United States, and foreshadowed how sectional conflict would lead to a national civil war? Explain your reasoning.

Topic Inquiry
Have students continue their investigations for the Topic Inquiry.

PEARSON realize™
www.PearsonRealize.com
Access your Digital Lesson

Division and the Outbreak of War

Supporting English Language Learners

Use with Digital Text 1, **The Nation Moves Toward Civil War.**

Writing
Introduce the activity by showing where the following states are on a U.S. map: Alabama, Florida, Georgia, Kentucky, Louisiana, Mississippi, Missouri, South Carolina, and Texas. Prompt students to learn to spell these familiar words correctly.

Beginning Review the locations and spellings of Alabama, Florida, and Texas. Then display each word with one or more letters missing and have students complete and write the name. Repeat the activity, increasing the number of blanks in each word.

Intermediate Display two versions of the words *Florida, South Carolina, Kentucky, Georgia,* and *Louisiana*: one spelled correctly and one spelled incorrectly. Have pairs of students work to identify and write down the correct version of each word. Review the answers so students can check and correct their work.

Advanced Review the spelling of all nine states listed above. Then say the states aloud and have students write the words. Review the answers and repeat the activity so students can try to improve their accuracy.

Advanced High Provide students with a blank U.S. map with state boundaries. Say each of the nine states above, and have students try to correctly spell each name on the correct location of the map. Then display a map that students can use to check and correct their work.

Use with Digital Text 4, **Taking Sides.**

Speaking
Pronounce /shə/ and have students repeat after you. Explain that they will practice producing this sound in newly acquired vocabulary in a increasingly comprehensible manner.

Beginning Display *martial law*. Underline *-tia* in *martial*, and explain that it represents /shə/. Sound out each syllable and have students repeat after you. Repeat until students are pronouncing it correctly at regular speed.

Intermediate Display *martial, social,* and *official*. Underline *-tia* or *-cia* in each word, and explain that both letter combinations represent /shə/. Sound out each word, and have students repeat after you. Repeat until students are pronouncing the words correctly at regular speed.

Advanced Display the words *martial, official, population,* and *tension*. Underline *-tia, -cia, -tio,* and *-sio* in each word. Explain that all of these letter combinations represent /shə/. Sound out each word, and have students repeat after you. Repeat until students are pronouncing the words correctly at regular speed.

Advanced High Display the words *martial, especially, sectionalism* , and *tension*. Underline *-tia, -cia, -tio,* and *-sio* in each word. Explain that all of these letter combinations represent /shə/. Also display *decision* and demonstrate the different *-sio* sound in this word. Sound out each word and have students repeat after you.

▣ Differentiate Instruction

Use the Differentiated Instruction notes throughout the lesson plan to support the varied skill sets, levels of readiness, and interests in the mixed-ability classroom.

Challenge These notes include suggestions for expanding the activity for advanced students.

On-Level These notes include suggestions for modifying the activity to address different interests or learning styles.

Extra Support These notes include ideas for providing more scaffolding or reading spuport.

Special Needs These notes provide ideas for adapting instruction to support the needs of various special needs students.

■ NOTES

Topic **8** Lesson 3

Division and the Outbreak of War

Objectives

Objective 1: Identify how the 1860 election reflected sectional differences.

Objective 2: Explain why southern states seceded from the Union following the election of 1860.

Objective 3: Identify how the Civil War began in 1861.

Objective 4: Describe the strengths and weaknesses of the North and South as the war began.

Objective 5: Identify the leaders of each side in the war.

LESSON 3 ORGANIZER		PACING: APPROX. 1 PERIOD, .5 BLOCKS		
			RESOURCES	
	OBJECTIVES	PACING	Online	Print
Connect				
DIGITAL START UP ACTIVITY **Divisions Lead to Civil War**		5 min.	●	
Investigate				
DIGITAL TEXT 1 **Abraham Lincoln and the Election of 1860**	Objective 1	10 min.	●	●
DIGITAL TEXT 2 **The Nation Moves Toward Civil War**		10 min.	●	●
DIGITAL TEXT 3 **War Breaks Out**	Objectives 2, 3	10 min.	●	●
DIGITAL TEXT 4 **Taking Sides**		10 min.	●	●
DIGITAL TEXT 5 **Strengths and Weaknesses of the North and South**	Objective 4	10 min.	●	●
INTERACTIVE CHART **Resources in the North and the South, 1860**		10 min.	●	
DIGITAL TEXT 6 **The Leadership Roles of Lincoln and Davis**	Objective 5	10 min.	●	●
INTERACTIVE CHART **Abraham Lincoln and Jefferson Davis**		10 min.	●	
Synthesize				
DIGITAL ACTIVITY **The North and South at War**		5 min.	●	
Demonstrate				
DIGITAL QUIZ **Lesson Quiz and Class Discussion Board**		10 min.	●	

PEARSON
realize™
www.PearsonRealize.com

Go online to access additional resources including:
Primary Sources • Biographies • Supreme Court cases •
21st Century Skill Tutorials • Maps • Graphic Organizers.

■ CONNECT

DIGITAL START UP ACTIVITY
Divisions Lead to Civil War

Project the Start Up Activity Ask students to complete the activity as they enter and get settled. Then have them share their ideas with another student.

Discuss How did states' rights contribute to divisions in the nation? *(Southern states and territories considered the question of slavery and other issues to be state concerns. They did not think that the federal government had the right to restrict slavery, and they resented northern attempts to impose such laws.)*

Tell students that this lesson will take a closer look at the causes and effects of the Civil War. They will examine constitutional issues arising over states' rights and the effect of economic differences among various regions of the United States.

Aa Vocabulary Development: Use the Interactive Reading Notepad to preview the Key Terms and Academic Vocabulary in this lesson with students.

⇅ FLIP IT!
Assign the Flipped Video for this lesson.

■ STUDENT EDITION PRINT PAGES: 450–460

■ INVESTIGATE

DIGITAL TEXT 1
Abraham Lincoln and the Election of 1860

Objective 1: Identify how the 1860 election reflected sectional differences.

Quick Instruction
The outcome of the 1860 election solidified the divisions that already existed in the nation. Lincoln's election inflamed the South and gave southern secessionists a driving motivation to withdraw from the Union. However, the withdrawal itself posed a constitutional issue over states' rights: Were states entitled to leave the Union? The South said yes. Lincoln and the North said no. The disagreement over states' rights was a significant cause of the Civil War.

Connect How did the divisions in the election reflect the intensity of sectionalism as a cause of the Civil War? *(The election made clear that the nation was largely divided sectionally over the issues of slavery and states' rights, with northern support behind Lincoln and southern support against Lincoln and divided among other candidates.)*

D Differentiate: Extra Support Record the names of the presidential candidates and their political parties on the board: Abraham Lincoln (Republican), Stephen Douglas (Northern Democrat), John Breckenridge (Southern Democrat, and John Bell (Constitutional Union). List each candidate's stance on expansion of slavery. Draw a box around the three columns with Douglas, Breckenridge, and John Bell. Above the box, have them write "Split the South." Above Lincoln, have them write "Won the North." If Lincoln took

DIGITAL TEXT 2
The Nation Moves Toward Civil War

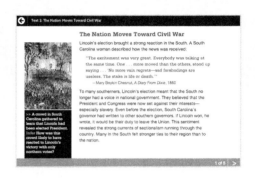

most of the northern vote, and the three other candidates had to share the southern vote, which candidate would get the most votes? *(Lincoln would get the most votes.)*

ELL Use the ELL activity described in the ELL chart.

Further Instruction
Be sure that students understand that Lincoln had solid support in the North, which had a larger population than the South. Meanwhile, citizens in the South split their votes among three candidates. This meant that Lincoln could win the election without a single electoral vote from the South, which he did.

Contrast How does Lincoln's stance on slavery contrast with southern views about states' rights? *(Lincoln's firm position against the expansion of slavery indicates that he would not support states' rights to expand and regulate slavery without federal oversight.)*

Synthesize Explain the connection between sectionalism, slavery, and states' rights as causes of the Civil War. How did the southern response to the 1860 election results demonstrate this connection? *(The nation was divided along sectional lines over the issues of slavery and states' rights. The South rallied around opposition to Lincoln's election, putting its own sectional interests and loyalties over those of the Union.)*

Division and the Outbreak of War

DIGITAL TEXT 3

War Breaks Out

DIGITAL TEXT 4

Taking Sides

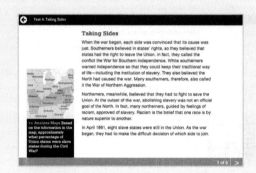

Objectives 2: **Explain why southern states seceded from the Union following the election of 1860; 3:** **Identify how the Civil War began in 1861.**

Quick Instruction

The Civil War was a major era in U.S. history. Lasting from 1861–1865, it was significant in that it was a lengthy, destructive time for the nation. The Civil War was caused by several interconnected issues that unfolded into armed conflict through a series of events. Southern states left the Union in response to Abraham Lincoln's election. War resulted from the firing on Fort Sumter after debate over the constitutional issue of states' rights to secede created conflicts over federal property.

Contrast How did Lincoln's ideas about the Union in his first inaugural address conflict with Davis's ideas about states' rights in his address? *(Lincoln asserted that the disagreeing parties in the nation must remain friends and stay united for the good of all. The Union was of paramount importance to him. In contrast, Davis asserted that the states must look firt to the preservation of their own rights and interests before considering the wider interests of the Union.)*

Contrast Lincoln's views on government with Davis's views on government from their first inaugural addresses. *(Lincoln stated that government required acquiescence, or the willingness to accept laws whether or not a person agreed with those laws. Davis emphasized that government exists only with the consent of the governed. Since southerners could no longer consent to a government they considered opposed to their interests, they had to break away and form a government to which they could consent. Davis also argued that, under the U.S. Constitution, states had the right to reclaim powers that they had given to the federal government by seceding. Lincoln took the opposite view, that states had no such right.)*

Explain What roles did Abraham Lincoln and Jefferson Davis play in the onset of war? *(Jefferson Davis was elected president of the Confederacy and helped rally people to support the newly formed nation and to find just cause in the southern states' secession. Lincoln, as President of the United States, spoke on behalf of the Union. His ideas regarding slavery as well as states' rights and secession helped bolster opposition to the Union in the South. He also made the decision to engage in war following the firing on Fort Sumter.)*

ELL Use the ELL activity described in the ELL chart.

Further Instruction

Read aloud, or call on a student to read aloud, the excerpt from Lincoln's inaugural address. Prompt students to find examples of where they see Lincoln discussing his ideas about liberty and equality in the speech. Pose questions such as: What does Lincoln mean when he says, "In YOUR hands, my dissatisfied countrymen, and not in MINE, is the momentous issue of civil war?" To whom is he speaking? Instruct students to discuss their ideas with a partner, and call on pairs to share their responses. Then ask students to explain Jefferson Davis's views on liberty and equality. *(For Davis, liberty and equality existed only between white men.)*

Hypothesize Why did the firing on Fort Sumter mark the start of the Civil War? Would the war have happened had the Confederacy not fired on Fort Sumter? Explain. *(The war started at Fort Sumter because the Confederacy fired on a federal fort and seized control of the fort from the Union. This was an overt act of aggression that Lincoln could not disregard without acknowledging secession as a legal path for southern states. I think the war still would have occurred had the firing on Fort Sumter not happened. Violence would have broken out elsewhere.)*

DIGITAL TEXT 5

Strengths and Weaknesses of the North and South

INTERACTIVE CHART

Resources in the North and the South, 1860

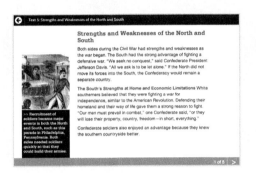

Objective 4: Describe the strengths and weaknesses of the North and South as the war began.

Quick Instruction

Interactive Chart: Strengths and Weaknesses in the North and South, 1860 Project the Interactive chart, and drag and drop resources to contrast the economic differences among different regions in the United States. At the time of the Civil War, the northern states were the industrial, financial, and manufacturing center of the United States. The southern states relied heavily on agriculture, and a large percentage of the southern population was enslaved. As the Civil War progressed, the economic differences among different regions in the United States began to have an effect.

Analyze Charts Which region, the North or the South, had the economic advantage going into the war? Why? *(I think the North had the advantage because it had industry, banking, manufacturing, shipping, and agricultural resources. The South had largely agricultural resources, much of which was not food crops, and depended on slave labor.)*

🎥 ACTIVE CLASSROOM

Have students review the Interactive chart and Take a Stand on whether the North or South was better prepared for war. Instruct students to organize into groups based on their responses and to discuss and defend their reasoning. Repeat the exercise when students have read the first section of the text. Repeat again when they have read the rest of the text. Discuss changes in the vote.

Further Instruction

Display the pie charts from the text, and compare the data with that of the interactive chart. Instruct students to draw concept webs in their notebooks, one for the Union and one for the Confederacy. As they study the charts and complete the text, have them record advantages and resources for each side of the Civil War.

Infer What was the objective of the Union in the Civil War? What was the objective of the Confederacy? Explain which of the two sides had the more difficult task, and why. *(The Union's objective was to bring the Confederacy back into the nation. The Confederacy's objective was to remain independent. I think that the Union had the more difficult challenge because it had to subdue the entire South and force it to comply with federal laws, whereas the Confederacy had to defend its lands and keep the Union out.)*

Synthesize How did the economic differences among different regions in the United States complicate the objectives of the Union and the Confederacy? Explain how economics shifted the advantage. *(The Confederacy had to remain independent, which meant it had to pay for the war and keep its economy going. This would be difficult because many southern states lacked industry, infrastructure, and other economic resources. This shifted the advantage to the Union, which had more money, industry, and infrastructure, such as transportation networks.)*

Hypothesize How would the differences in economics and objectives become manifest in the effects of the Civil War on each region of the country? *(The Union's diversified economy, larger population, and solid infrastructure would allow for the region to remain relatively intact. As an underdog, the Confederacy suffered great losses of land as a result of Union invasion as well as economic and supply difficulties. The Confederacy would be forced to diversify industry in order to survive.)*

Division and the Outbreak of War

DIGITAL TEXT 6

The Leadership Roles of Lincoln and Davis

INTERACTIVE CHART

Abraham Lincoln and Jefferson Davis

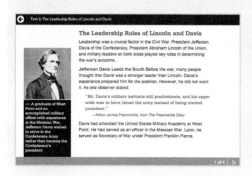

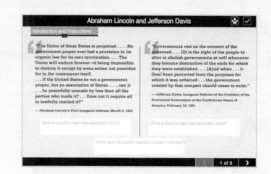

Objective 5: **Identify the leaders of each side in the war.**

Quick Instruction

Interactive Chart: Abraham Lincoln and Jefferson Davis Project the Interactive chart, and call on students to read aloud the excerpts from Lincoln's and Davis's inaugural speeches. Guide students through the Interactive graphic organizer. Point out ideas about liberty, equality, union, and government in Lincoln's Inaugural Address, and highlight key ideas in Davis's address.

Evaluate Sources How do ideas in Lincoln's Inaugural Address reflect his role as President of the United States? How do ideas in Davis's Inaugural Address reflect his role as president of the Confederacy? *(Lincoln's address places the most importance on the necessity of maintaining the Union. He make it clear that he views secession and its causes as contrary to the founding principles of liberty and equality in the United States. He also accuses secessionists of anarchy, undermining the very purpose of government. This reinforces his role as President of the United States, charged with preserving the nation and enforcing its federal laws. Davis emphasizes the importances of states' rights and interests, and makes the liberty of the southern states paramount over national interests. His concepts of liberty also apply only to southern citizens, not to all people. His words reinforce his position as president of the secessionist states, those who dissent from Lincoln's leadership.)*

📷 ACTIVE CLASSROOM

Challenge students to hold a Conversation with Lincoln and Davis. Organize the students into two groups, one for Lincoln and one for Davis. Have them script questions and answers for each. Ask one student from each group to portray Lincoln or Davis and to begin by reading aloud an excerpt from his inaugural address. Then, tell the rest of the students in each group to pose their questions, and have Lincoln and Davis respond.

Further Instruction

Prompt students to consider the qualities of good leadership as they answer the questions below.

Contrast What challenges do you think Jefferson Davis faced in his role as president of the Confederacy that Lincoln did not? What challenges do you think Lincoln faced in his role as President of the United States that Davis did not? *(Davis faced the additional challenge of building a new nation with a new government and structuring that nation's economy while defending its lands and people. Lincoln faced the challenge of rallying the North to fight a war in order to bring the southern states back into the nation.)*

Make Generalizations How did the Civil War reflect the different ideas about liberty and equality expressed in the Inaugural Addresses given by Lincoln and Davis? *(Lincoln expressed the idea that liberty and equality applied to all people and that the actions of the South undermined these principles. Davis expressed the idea that the liberties of the states were paramount and that liberty and equality applied only to recognized citizens.)*

■ SYNTHESIZE

DIGITAL ACTIVITY
The North and South at War

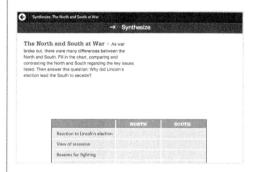

Have students work in pairs to complete the chart in which they compare the North and the South at the onset of the Civil War. Tell them to identify significant economic differences between the two regions. Then, challenge students to write a prediction about how those differences will affect the outcome of the conflict. Share students' responses in class or on a classroom blog.

Discuss Pose the question: Why did Lincoln's election lead the South to secede? Instruct students to write a response in which they use the following terms: *sectionalism, slavery,* and *states' rights.* Have them share and revise their responses in small groups. Ask each group to select the best response to share with the rest of the class. Finally, tell the student groups to answer the following question: Why did secession cause the Civil War to break out in 1861? Again, have them discuss and then share their responses.

■ DEMONSTRATE

DIGITAL QUIZ
Lesson Quiz and Class Discussion Board

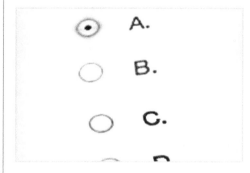

Assign the online Lesson Quiz for this lesson if you haven't already done so. Students will be offered automatic remediation or enrichment based on their score.

Pose these questions to the class on the Discussion Board:

Evaluate Arguments Why did the Confederacy fire on Fort Sumter in 1861? Why did the Union respond by going to war? Evaluate the arguments of both side of the conflict, and explain which you find to be the most just and why.

Analyze Context Lincoln and Davis made their decisions without knowing the full consequences of their actions. Summarize the motivation of both men in their roles as leaders on opposite sides of the conflict. Then, explain whether you think either would have acted differently had they known the costs of the Civil War to come. Consider whether each man could have chosen a different course of action and remained true to his principles.

Topic Inquiry
Have students continue their investigations for the Topic Inquiry.

The Course of War

Use with Digital Text 1, **North and South Adopt Different Strategies.**

Writing
Prompt students to employ English spelling rules. Explain the spelling rule that many words ending in –*y* drop that letter and add –*ies* to become plural.

Beginning Display the following pairs of words from the text: *supply, suppl _____ ; country, countr _____ ; factory, factor _____*. Have students write down each pair, completing each second word with the plural ending –*ies*.

Intermediate Display the following words from the text: *strategy, supply, country, factory*. Have students copy each word and write its plural form next to it. Then have them use three of the plural words in sentences.

Advanced Explain that some words are exceptions to the above spelling rule. Have pairs of students sort these words into a two-column chart depending on how their plurals are formed: *supply, boy, tray, country, donkey, essay, strategy, army*. Then have pairs use five of the plurals in written sentences.

Advanced High Explain that some words are exceptions to the above spelling rule. Have students sort these words into a two-column chart depending on how their plurals are formed: *supply, boy, tray, country, donkey, essay, strategy, army*. Ask: What rule can you make to explain which column a –*y* word fits into?

Use with Digital Text 4, **Union Forces Find Success in the West.**

Speaking
Display the image of General Grant to help students learn and use high-frequency English words necessary for identifying and describing people.

Beginning Display a list of high-frequency words, some describing General Grant and some not. Help students internalize the words' meanings so they can choose the words that describe Grant and use them in spoken sentences: General Grant is/looks _____.

Intermediate Ask students to brainstorm words and phrases that describe General Grant in the portrait. Expand their initial English vocabulary by adding new words and phrases to the list. Then have them use the new words and phrases in complete spoken sentences about Grant.

Advanced Introduce new high-frequency English words that might be used to describe General Grant. Have pairs of students use these words, as well as their own, to discuss and describe the portrait of Grant.

Advanced High Place students in pairs, and have them take turns drawing a portrait of General Grant based on their partner's description. Encourage speakers to use specific high-frequency words so their partners know what to draw. Then have partners compare the drawing and original portrait and identify additional details that could have been said.

▶ Differentiate Instruction

Use the Differentiated Instruction notes throughout the lesson plan to support the varied skill sets, levels of readiness, and interests in the mixed-ability classroom.

Challenge These notes include suggestions for expanding the activity for advanced students.

On-Level These notes include suggestions for modifying the activity to address different interests or learning styles.

Extra Support These notes include ideas for providing more scaffolding or reading spuport.

Special Needs These notes provide ideas for adapting instruction to support the needs of various special needs students.

▮ NOTES

Objectives

Objective 1: Describe the strategies the North and South adopted to win the war.

Objective 2: Explain how early battles dispelled hopes for a quick end to the war.

Objective 3: Identify the victories of the Confederates and the Union in the early years of the war.

LESSON 4 ORGANIZER		PACING: APPROX. 1 PERIOD, .5 BLOCKS			
				RESOURCES	
		OBJECTIVES	PACING	Online	Print
Connect					
	DIGITAL START UP ACTIVITY **A Short War?**		5 min.	●	
Investigate					
	DIGITAL TEXT 1 **The Different Strategies of the North and South**	Objective 1	10 min.	●	●
	INTERACTIVE MAP **The Union's Strategies to Win the Civil War**		10 min.	●	
	DIGITAL TEXT 2 **The Beginnings of a Long War**	Objective 2	10 min.	●	●
	DIGITAL TEXT 3 **Confederate Forces Win in the East**		10 min.	●	●
	DIGITAL TEXT 4 **Union Forces Find Success in the West**	Objective 3	10 min.	●	●
	INTERACTIVE TIMELINE **Early Battles of the Civil War**		10 min.	●	
Synthesize					
	DIGITAL ACTIVITY **Visiting Civil War Locations**		5 min.	●	
Demonstrate					
	DIGITAL QUIZ **Lesson Quiz and Class Discussion Board**		10 min.	●	

The Course of War

CONNECT

DIGITAL START UP ACTIVITY
A Short War?

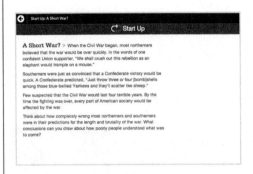

Project the Start Up Activity Tell students to consider the question as they enter and get settled. Ask: What conclusions can you make about how poorly people understood what was to come? *(Neither northerners nor southerners had any real idea of the war they were about to enter into because they had no experience with anything like it.)* Then have them share their conclusions with another student, either in class or through a chat or blog space.

Tell students in this lesson they will be learning about the course of the Civil War. They will learn about each side's strategies and how these strategies played out in dramatic battles in the East and the West.

Aa **Vocabulary Development:** Use the Interactive Reading Notepad to preview the Key Terms and Academic Vocabulary in the lesson with students.

↻ FLIP IT!

Assign the Flipped Video for this lesson.

STUDENT EDITION PRINT
PAGES: 461–467

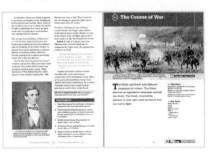

INVESTIGATE

DIGITAL TEXT 1
The Different Strategies of the North and South

Objective 1: **Describe the strategies the North and South adopted to win the war.**

Quick Instruction

Interactive Cartoon: The Union's Strategies to Win the Civil War Project the Interactive cartoon and click on the red circles to reveal the Union's strategy to win the Civil War. Ask students what the plan was called. *(The Anaconda Plan)* Why was it called this? *(It was dubbed the Anaconda Plan by the media after the snake that squeezes its victims to death.)* Explain that the plan was developed by Winfield Scott, who was soon replaced by General George McClellan.

💻 ACTIVE CLASSROOM

Have students Make Headlines for each of the strategies used by the North and the South to win the Civil War. These strategies include the North's encirclement and blockading of the South (the Anaconda Plan), its desire to capture Richmond (through the Peninsular Campaign), and the South's defensive strategy. Ask: If you were to write a headline for each of these that captured the most important aspect of it, what would that headline be? Emphasize to students that their headlines could depict a strategy as a whole or aspects of it. Allow them to use subheadings if they would like. Have students pass their headlines to a partner to review.

INTERACTIVE MAP
The Union's Strategies to Win the Civil War

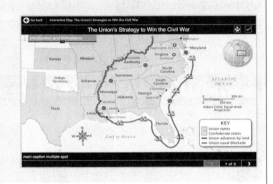

ELL Use the ELL activity described in the ELL chart.

Further Instruction

Make Generalizations Direct students to make one generalization about the Union strategy for victory in the Civil War and one generalization about the Confederate strategy. *(The Union planned to starve the Confederates into submission (Anaconda Plan) or capture the capital of Richmond and force a surrender. The Confederacy planned to hold out until popular opinion among northerners turned against the war.)*

DIGITAL TEXT 2

The Beginnings of a Long War

DIGITAL TEXT 3

Confederate Forces Win in the East

Objective 2: **Explain how early battles dispelled hopes for a quick end to the war.**

Quick Instruction

Ensure students understand that one early battle was the Battle of Bull Run, or what the Confederates called the Battle of Manassas. Invite a student to apply relative chronology by summarizing the next major event in the east, the Peninsular Campaign. *(In March 1862, McClellan led his troops up the Virginia Peninsula toward Richmond. Lee counterattacked and threatened Washington, denying McClellan additional troops and defeating his attempt to capture the Confederate capitol.)* Ask: Who won the battle between the Union ironclad *Monitor* and the Confederate ironclad *Virginia* at Hampton Roads? *(Neither; the battle was a draw.)* Conclude by asking students to explain the Battle of Antietam. What was Lee's goal? Who won the battle? *(In September 1862, General Lee took the offensive and marched his troops north into Maryland, hoping that a southern victory on northern soil would be a great blow to northern morale. General McClellan learned of the plan and attacked Lee's troops near Antietam Creek. Lee ordered his troops back into Virginia. Neither side was a clear winner. However, the North was able to claim victory, since Lee had ordered his forces to withdraw. This increased northern morale.)*

Analyze Images Display the image of Stonewall Jackson. What evidence do you see in the text and image to support the idea Jackson was a significant military leader? *(During the Battle of Manassas (Bull Run),*

Jackson rallied the Virginia troops on a hilltop. Another officer is said to have cried out "There is Jackson standing like a stone wall! Rally behind the Virginians!" Jackson became known as Stonewall Jackson after the battle concluded.)

D Differentiate: Extra Support Split students into small groups. One side in a group will represent the Union and the other the Confederacy. Walk the groups through the events described in the lesson. Structure questions to the Union group as follows: the Confederacy did this. What did you do in response? Why? Ask parallel questions of the Confederate group.

Further Instruction

Infer Based on the conclusion of the Battle of Bull Run, what could you infer about the length of the war? *(The Confederates proved they could fight against Union soldiers, which implied the war would not be as quick as many had hoped.)*

Summarize What significant contributions did General George McClellan make to the war effort? *(McClellan transformed the inexperienced recruits of the Army of the Potomac into an army of trained soldiers prepared for battle. He hoped to capture the Confederate capital of Richmond, Virginia but failed. At the Battle of Antietam, he kept Lee from victory on northern soil.)*

Infer What can students infer about the significant political and military leaders mentioned in the lesson? Ask them to list character or leadership qualities of Lincoln, McClellan, Jackson, and Lee. *(Lincoln: thoughtful; McClellan: cautious; Jackson: brave; Lee: intelligent)*

Objective 3: **Identify the victories of the Confederates and the Union in the early years of the war.**

Quick Instruction

Interactive Timeline: Early Battles of the Civil War Display the Interactive timeline. To help students interpret information from the timeline, point out that it covers battles in the early part of the war from April 1861 to May 1863. Remind students that the Union hoped to win by surrounding and splitting the Confederacy and that the Confederacy planned to fight a defensive war while outmaneuvering and defeating Union forces when they could. Discuss each battle with students in order relative to each other, as they apply absolute and relative chronology to sequence these significant events.

Draw Conclusions Review the events at the Battle of Fredericksburg and the Battle of Chancellorsville. Ask: How did the early events of the Civil War show the significance of General Lee's role in the war? *(Despite the confidence of many in the North that they could win the war quickly, Lee's skill as a military leader allowed the Confederate army to win many significant victories and inflict serious damage to the Union army.)*

Summarize Why was the Battle of Shiloh a significant victory for the Union? *(Union forces were able to gain control of the Tennessee river, cutting off one of the Confederate supply lines.)*

The Course of War

DIGITAL TEXT 4
Union Forces Find Success in the West

INTERACTIVE TIMELINE
Early Battles of the Civil War

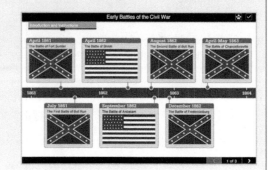

ACTIVE CLASSROOM

Have students apply absolute and relative chronology through the sequencing of significant events by making "Human Order" timelines. Give students pieces of paper and have them write the names of important early battles of the Civil War on each one, along with the date of the battle and a note of who won. Students should then get out of their seats at your signal and arrange themselves in correct chronological order. Consider having multiple groups with identical pieces of paper compete against each other.

ELL Use the ELL activity described in the ELL chart.

Further Instruction

Categorize Challenge students to identify each of the following as a Confederate victory in the East or a Union success in the West: Battle of Fredericksburg *(Confederate victory in the East);* Battle of Chancellorsville *(Confederate victory in the East);* Fort Henry and Fort Donelson *(Union success in the West);* Battle of Shiloh *(Union success in the West);* New Orleans *(Union success in the West);* Memphis *(Union success in the West).*

◼ SYNTHESIZE

DIGITAL ACTIVITY
Visiting Civil War Locations

Discuss Discuss as a class the Civil War sites students are interested in visiting. As time allows, go the federal website for each historic site and discuss what the main attractions of the site are.

Make Predictions Now that students have learned about the early course of the Civil War, how might they predict the rest of the war will proceed? *(More devastating battles will occurr for both sides before the war reaches its conclusion.)*

◼ DEMONSTRATE

DIGITAL QUIZ
Lesson Quiz and Discussion Board

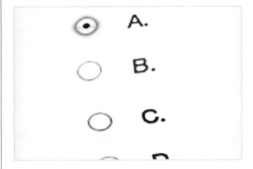

Assign the online Lesson Quiz for this lesson if you haven't already done so. Students will be offered automatic remediation or enrichment based on their score.

Pose these questions to the class on the Discussion Board:

In the *Course of War*, you learned about the early years of the Civil War. The North hoped to win the war quickly by surrounding the Confederacy or capturing Richmond, while the South planned a defensive war that they hoped would outlast the North's will to fight. The first Battle of Bull Run and the failed Peninsular Campaign disproved the notion the war would be short, however. Battles proved horrific. The Battle of Antietam made September 17, 1862 the bloodiest day in American history. Confederate victories in the East were matched by Union successes in the West. 1861 and 1862 proved to be bloody years with no end to the carnage in sight.

Compare and Contrast Do you see the North as having demonstrated any particular advantages at this point? The South?

Make Predictions How might these advantages play out as the war progresses?

Topic Inquiry
Have students continue their investigations for the Topic Inquiry.

Emancipation and Life in Wartime

Supporting English Language Learners

Use with Digital Text 2, **African Americans Fight Heroically for the Union.**

Speaking

Display the picture of 54th Regiment soldiers, and read the corresponding caption. Prompt students to expand and internalize initial English vocabulary by retelling simple stories and basic information represented or supported by pictures.

Beginning Describe what is happening in the picture to expand students' initial English vocabulary. Then have students retell basic information represented by the picture using words, phrases, or complete sentences. Encourage students to include the word *regiment* and its meaning in their retelling.

Intermediate Brainstorm words and phrases associated with the picture, such as *withdraw* and *Fort Wagner*, to help students expand and internalize their initial English vocabulary. Then have pairs of students take turns saying sentences that give basic information about the picture.

Advanced Place students in groups of three. Have each student expand and internalize initial English vocabulary by retelling the beginning, middle, or end of the story of the 54th Regiment. Explain that at least one part of the story should be represented or supported by the picture. Encourage students to use and define the words *recruit*, *withdraw*, and *Medal of Honor* in their retelling.

Advanced High Place students in pairs and have partners take turns adding sentences to an oral retelling of the story of the 54th Regiment. Explain that at least one part of the story should be represented or supported by the picture and that they should aim to expand and internalize their vocabulary by using as many specific details as possible. Encourage students to use and define the words *heroism* and *courage* in their retelling.

Use with Digital Text 6, **War Devastates the Southern Economy.**

Writing

Review subjects and verbs in a sentence in order to prepare students to edit writing for standard grammar and usage.

Beginning Display the last sentence of the text's third paragraph, and block out each instance of *was* or *were*. Have students copy and complete the sentence. Then display the past tense of *to be*. Have students edit their writing for subject-verb agreement.

Intermediate Ask students to suggest sentences using *was/were* and these subjects: war, supplies, plantations, money. Then review the past tense of *to be*. Have students edit the sentences for subject-verb agreement.

Advanced Ask pairs of students to write sentences using *was/were* and these subjects: loss, plantations, supplies, Davis. Then review the past tense of *to be*. Have students edit the sentences for subject-verb agreement. Ask: Are all nouns ending in –s plural?

Advanced High Ask students to write sentences using *was/were* and these subjects: Confederacy, plantations, money, the South, Davis. Then review the past tense of *to be*. Have students edit the sentences for subject-verb agreement. Ask: Britain is one thing representing a lot of people, land, and so on. So does it agree with *was* or *were*?

◨ Differentiate Instruction

Use the Differentiated Instruction notes throughout the lesson plan to support the varied skill sets, levels of readiness, and interests in the mixed-ability classroom.

Challenge These notes include suggestions for expanding the activity for advanced students.

On-Level These notes include suggestions for modifying the activity to address different interests or learning styles.

Extra Support These notes include ideas for providing more scaffolding or reading spuport.

Special Needs These notes provide ideas for adapting instruction to support the needs of various special needs students.

◼ NOTES

Objectives

Objective 1: Describe the purpose of the Emancipation Proclamation and its effects.

Objective 2: Explain African Americans' contributions to the war effort in the Union army and behind Confederate lines.

Objective 3: Describe conditions for Civil War soldiers.

Objective 4: Explain problems on the home front, including economic issues.

Objective 5: Identify the role women played in the war.

LESSON 5 ORGANIZER		PACING: APPROX. 1 PERIOD, .5 BLOCKS			
		OBJECTIVES	PACING	Online	Print
Connect					
DIGITAL START UP ACTIVITY **Freedom**			5 min.	●	
Investigate					
DIGITAL TEXT 1 **The Emancipation Proclamation**		Objective 1	10 min.	●	●
DIGITAL TEXT 2 **African Americans Fight Heroically for the Union**		Objective 2	10 min.	●	●
DIGITAL TEXT 3 **Soldiers Face the Horrors of War**			10 min.	●	●
INTERACTIVE GALLERY **The Hardships of Soldiers**		Objective 3	10 min.	●	
INTERACTIVE GALLERY **Photography and the Civil War**			10 min.	●	
DIGITAL TEXT 4 **Political Challenges in the North and South**			10 min.	●	●
DIGITAL TEXT 5 **War Challenges and Fuels the Northern Economy**		Objective 4	10 min.	●	●
DIGITAL TEXT 6 **War Devastates the Southern Economy**			10 min.	●	●
DIGITAL TEXT 7 **Social Contributions of Women to the War Effort**		Objective 5	10 min.	●	●
Synthesize					
DIGITAL ACTIVITY **What Do You Think of the War?**			5 min.	●	
Demonstrate					
DIGITAL QUIZ **Lesson Quiz and Discussion Board**			10 min.	●	

Emancipation and Life in Wartime

■ CONNECT

DIGITAL START UP ACTIVITY
Freedom

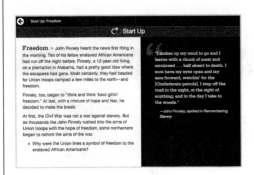

Project the Start Up Activity Tell students to read the story of John Finnely and consider the question as they enter and get settled. Ask: Why were the Union lines a symbol of freedom to the enslaved African Americans? (Slavery was illegal in most of the Union.) Extend the activity by asking students to describe the feelings that Finnely and others in his situation must have felt.

Tell students in this lesson they will be learning about the role of African Americans during the Civil War and the draft in the North and the South and how it was received. They will then turn from the political to the economic and analyze how the war affected the northern and southern economies.

Aa Vocabulary Development: Use the Interactive Reading Notepad to preview the Key Terms and Academic Vocabulary in this lesson with students.

⇅ FLIP IT!
Assign the Flipped Video for this lesson.

■ STUDENT EDITION PRINT
PAGES: 468–477

■ INVESTIGATE

DIGITAL TEXT 1
The Emancipation Proclamation

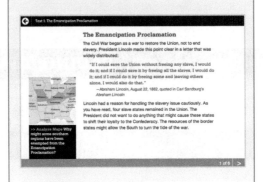

Objective 1: Describe the purpose of the Emancipation Proclamation and its effects.

Quick Instruction
Analyze Images Project the image of the Emancipation Proclamation. Explain that the announcement of the Emancipation Proclamation was one of the significant events of the Civil War. Ask: What was the Emancipation Proclamation? *(Lincoln's declaration freeing slaves in the Confederacy)* When was it issued? *(January 1, 1863)* Discuss with students the political considerations Lincoln took into account before issuing the proclamation. He prioritized saving the Union over abolition, so the proclamation only freed slaves in the Confederacy and not in Union slave states or in any Union-captured territory.

Further Instruction
Compare and Contrast How was the Emancipation Proclamation received in the North? In the South? In Europe? *(In the North it received a mixed reception. Abolitionists and free African Americans received news of it with joy. Many northerners, though, were opposed to the abolition of slavery and were unhappy about the news. In the South it was generally viewed as a fiendish destruction of property. European workers were generally in favor of it.)*

Interpret What was the significance of the announcement of the Emancipation Proclamation? *(The Emancipation Proclamation changed the dynamic of the war and broadened its purpose. It also made it less likely that Britain or any other European country would come to the aid of the South.)*

DIGITAL TEXT 2
African Americans Fight Heroically for the Union

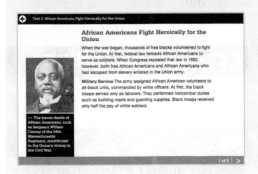

Objective 2: Explain African Americans' contributions to the war effort in the Union army and behind Confederate lines.

Quick Instruction
Generate Explanations Project the image of William Carney. Ask students to explain the role played by William Carney and the 54th Massachusetts Regiment in the Civil War. *(The courage of the 54th Massachusetts and other regiments helped to win respect for African American soldiers. Sergeant William Carney of the 54th Massachusetts was one of the first African American soldier to win the Congressional Medal of Honor in the Civil War.)* Tell them that Carney was but one of about 200,000 African Americans that had fought for the Union during the Civil War.

Sequence Events The following events are in correct chronological order. Provide them in a random order for students and challenge them to analyze the information by sequencing them correctly.

- Federal law forbids African Americans from serving as soldiers.
- Congress repeals law forbidding African Americans from serving as soldiers.
- African American troops serve only in noncombat roles.
- African American troops serve in combat and fight in major battles.
- All Union soldiers receive equal pay.

DIGITAL TEXT 3

Soldiers Face the Horrors of War

INTERACTIVE GALLERY

The Hardships of Soldiers

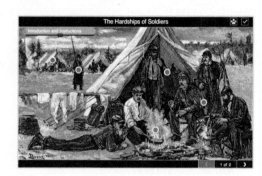

Identify Central Issues Conclude by asking students how African Americans' contributed to the Union war effort from behind Confederate line. *(They slowed down their work or refused to work at all, or escaped.)*

D Differentiate: Challenge An interested student can look up the citation for William Carney's Medal of Honor to learn what exactly he did to earn it. The student can then share what he or she learns with other students.

ELL Use the ELL activity described in the ELL chart.

Further Instruction

Summarize Ask students to describe the 54th Massachusetts Regiment. *(The 54th Massachusetts Regiment was an African American unit in the Union army. It led an attack on Fort Wagner near Charleston, South Carolina. Almost half the regiment was killed.)*

Identify Central Issues Have students complete the Biography: William Carney activity at the close of this text.

Objective 3: Describe conditions for Civil War soldiers.

Quick Instruction

Interactive Gallery: The Hardships of Soldiers Project the interactive gallery. Select the red circles to reveal details about life as a soldier. Before you select each one, ask students what they think it will reveal. Then have them compare what they expected with what they learned. Ask them how might this parallel the experience of the soldiers themselves. *(Many soldiers from the North and South had romantic ideas of what life as a soldier would be like, but the reality was much more harsh.)*

Interactive Gallery: Photography and the Civil War Project the interactive gallery. Click on each photograph to reveal the caption. Emphasize to students that Matthew Brady was a photographer, but that many photographs attributed to him were actually taken by his employees. Work your way through the photographs and invite student comment. Challenge students to identify what aspects of the Civil War the images do not reveal.

> ### 🎦 ACTIVE CLASSROOM
>
> Have students learn more about the hardships of war by letting them Act It Out. Challenge students to recreate the scene in "The Hardships of Soldiers," or a similar scene. Each student should prepare a brief speech about one aspect of life for soldiers during the Civil War.

> ### 🎦 ACTIVE CLASSROOM
>
> Have students consider the importance of photography as a way to record the experience of war by having them make Wallpaper. Direct each student to decorate a piece of printer paper with images and/ or words that capture what they feel is the most important photograph in the gallery. Post their work in the classroom. Invite individual students to give a verbal tour of the work to classroom visitors.

Further Instruction

Analyze Data Share this fact with students: One out of every seven Union soldiers and one out of every nine Confederate soldiers deserted. Direct students to express these figures as percentages. *(1/7 = 14.3 percent Union desertion rate; 1/9 = 11.1 percent Confederate desertion rate.)*

Infer What can students infer from these rates? *(Possible inferences include that life was difficult for both Union and Confederate soldiers, leading to high desertion rates, and that outside factors—such as proximity to their homes or commitment to the war effort— might be reflected in the desertion rates.)*

Emancipation and Life in Wartime

INTERACTIVE GALLERY

Photography and the Civil War

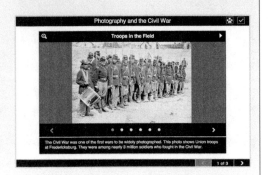

DIGITAL TEXT 4

Political Challenges in the North and South

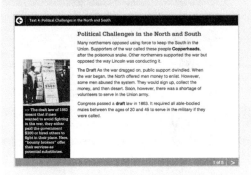

DIGITAL TEXT 5

War Challenges and Fuels the Northern Economy

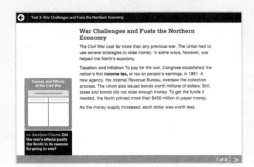

Objective 4: Explain problems on the home front, including economic issues.

Quick Instruction

Analyze Images Project the image of draft riots. Provide context for students by explaining that it is a depiction of a draft riot that took place in New York City during July 1863. Ensure they know that the draft is a law that requires people of a certain age to enlist in the military. Ask students why it led to rioting. *(Opposition to the draft in the North was rooted in opposition to the war itself, its conduct, and the fact that men of means could pay a fee and avoid the draft. Moreover, many white northerners did not want to fight against slavery, the end of which would increase competition for work and lower wages.)*

Generate Explanations Challenge students to use their knowledge of the draft riots to explain the relationship between urbanization and conflicts resulting from differences in political beliefs. *(Urbanization created areas where many people were gathered together. People of different ethnic, racial, and economic backgrounds were mixed. These different groups had different economic interests and political beliefs. For example, recent immigrants were much more likely to oppose the war, abolition, and the draft than others. These differences led to conflict, with rioters attacking free blacks and rich New Yorkers who had paid to avoid serving in the army.)*

Summarize Describe the political and economic effects of the Civil War in the South. *(The South also instituted a draft, excluding wealthy slave owners, and thereby angering some. The Civil War devastated the economy of the South, a result of taxes, inflation from overprinting money, and the dramatic reduction in income from cotton exports caused by the Union blockade.)*

ELL Use the ELL activity described in the ELL chart.

Further Instruction

Distinguish Explain that the conflict over the draft was a political effect of the Civil War in the North. What were some economic effects? *(The creation of an income tax, the printing of paper money, and the inflation that resulted from the increase in the money supply all resulted from the war. However, the wartime demand for farm equipment and clothing, shoes, guns, and other goods helped many northern industries.)*

War Devastates the Southern Economy

War Devastates the Southern Economy

For the South, war brought economic ruin. The South had to struggle with the cost of the war, the loss of the cotton trade, and severe shortages brought on by the Union blockade.

A Weak Wartime Economy To raise money, the Confederacy imposed an income tax and a tax-in-kind. The tax-in-kind required farmers to turn over one tenth of their crops to the government. The government took crops because it knew that southern farmers had little money.

Like the North, the South printed paper money. It printed so much that wild inflation set in. By 1865, one Confederate dollar was worth only two cents in gold. Prices were especially high in Richmond, where a barrel of flour was $275 in early 1864, potatoes were $25 a bushel, and butter was $15 a pound.

>> The Confederate government printed most of its currency in large denominations, such as this $500 bill. Infer Why would the government print currency in large denominations?

1 of 4 >

Interpret Ask students how the New York City draft riots might be considered an attempt to resolve conflicts between people from various racial groups. *(Northern whites wanted to avoid competing with freed blacks in the labor marketplace. The riots were an attempt to oppose the war and the freeing of enslaved African Americans.)*

Social Contributions of Women to the War Effort

Contributions of Women to the War Effort

Women of both the North and the South played vital roles during the war. As men left for the battlefields, women took jobs in industry and on farms. While men fought in the war, many women took over responsibilities of family farms and businesses. They also had to raise their families on their own.

In rare instances, some women even disguised themselves as men and enlisted in the army to fight in the war. Others served as spies and provided valuable information to military commanders. Many served in army camps, some of them choosing to accompany their husbands to war.

Women's aid societies helped supply the troops with food, bedding, clothing, and medicine. Throughout the North, women held fairs and other fundraising events to pay for supplies.

>> During the Civil War, women helped by caring for the sick and wounded. They were so successful that nursing became an accepted profession for women following the war.

1 of 3 >

Objective 5: Identify the role women played in the war.

Quick Instruction

Summarize Remind students that Matthew Brady took very few photographs of women even though they played a significant role in the Civil War. Challenge students to identify at least three important social contributions of women during the Civil War. *(Taking jobs in industry and on farms; forming aid societies that helped supply the troops with food, bedding, clothing, and medicine; working as nurses; providing comfort to fathers, brothers, sons who served as soldiers)*

Further Instruction

Generate Explanations Tell students that, before the Civil War, nursing was not an acceptable occupation for women. After the war it was. Challenge them to explain why this was so. *(Women were needed to serve as nurses during the war. They proved they were up to the task, and so it became an acceptable occupation.)*

Emancipation and Life in Wartime

▮ SYNTHESIZE

DIGITAL ACTIVITY

What Do You Think of the War?

Focus students on the individuals listed. Begin by making sure they understand who each person was. Encourage them to think from the listed people's points of view. What would each individual have to gain or lose from the Civil War?

Discuss Ask students if they think that the Civil War was the most important or memorable part of these people's lives. *(Given the monumental influence of the war on life in America, it probably was.)*

▮ DEMONSTRATE

DIGITAL QUIZ

Lesson Quiz and Discussion Board

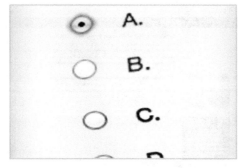

Assign the online Lesson Quiz for this lesson if you haven't already done so. Students will be offered automatic remediation or enrichment based on their score.

Pose these questions to the class on the Discussion Board:

In *Emancipation and Life in Wartime*, you learned about the Emancipation Proclamation and how it changed the course of the Civil War. You also learned about how African Americans served bravely as Union Soldiers. An outstanding example is Sergeant William Carney of the famous 54th Massachusetts Regiment, who won a Congressional Medal of Honor. African American soldiers, like all soldiers during the war, suffered terrible hardships. On the home front, the draft was resented by northerners and southerners alike. Draft riots rocked New York City. The war proved beneficial to many northern industries, even though the economy suffered from inflation. The war devastated the southern economy, which also suffered inflation and the results of the Union blockade. Women in both the North and South made valuable contributions to the war effort. An outstanding example is Union nurse Clara Barton, who later founded the American Red Cross.

Express Ideas Clearly Who is one individual from the Civil War era that you find particularly interesting, heroic, or admirable? Express your views about him or her.

Topic Inquiry

Have students continue their investigations for the Topic Inquiry.

The War's End

Supporting English Language Learners

Use with Digital Text 2, **The Battle of Gettysburg.**

Writing
Review the meaning of *pronoun* to prepare students to edit writing for standard grammar and usage of pronoun agreement commensurate with grade-level expectations.

Beginning Have students write these sentences, using pronouns in the blanks: Lee moved his army north. _____ wanted to surprise the Yankees. The Confederates fought hard, but _____ still lost. Then display the subject pronouns. Ask students to edit their writing for pronoun agreement.

Intermediate Display the following sentences: Lee moved his army north. The Confederates fought hard. Ask students to copy each sentence and write a follow-up sentence using a pronoun for the subject. Then display the subject pronouns, and have students edit their writing.

Advanced Ask pairs of students to write a paragraph about Pickett's Charge that uses at least three subject pronouns. Then display the subject pronouns, and have pairs edit their writing. Ask: Which pronoun corresponds to Pickett's Charge: he (for *Pickett*) or it (for *Charge*)?

Advanced High Ask students to write a paragraph about Pickett's Charge that uses at least three subject and three object pronouns. Then display the subject and object pronouns, and have students edit their writing. Ask: Which pronouns are the same as both a subject and an object?

Use with Digital Text 5, **Contrasting Ideas of Liberty and Union.**

Speaking
Review the concept of contrasting and discuss the vocabulary used to contrast. Prompt students to speak about Abraham Lincoln and Jefferson Davis using routine contrasting words.

Beginning Explain that the word *but* is routine language used to contrast ideas in classroom communication. Have students complete and say this sentence: Lincoln wanted slaves to be free, but Davis wanted _____.

Intermediate Explain that the words *but* and *however* are routine language used to contrast ideas in classroom communication. Have students speak using *but* and *however* to contrast the ideas of Lincoln and Davis.

Advanced Discuss how the terms *however* and *in contrast* are used to differentiate ideas in classroom communication. Have pairs of students speak using these words to contrast the ideas of Lincoln and Davis.

Advanced High Discuss how the vocabulary *by comparison* and *on the other hand* are used to contrast ideas in classroom communication. Have pairs of students use these phrases to respond to each others' statements as they discuss Lincoln and Davis.

⬛ Differentiate Instruction

Use the Differentiated Instruction notes throughout the lesson plan to support the varied skill sets, levels of readiness, and interests in the mixed-ability classroom.

Challenge These notes include suggestions for expanding the activity for advanced students.

On-Level These notes include suggestions for modifying the activity to address different interests or learning styles.

Extra Support These notes include ideas for providing more scaffolding or reading spuport.

Special Needs These notes provide ideas for adapting instruction to support the needs of various special needs students.

⬛ **NOTES**

The War's End

Objectives

Objective 1: Explain why the Union victories at Vicksburg and Gettysburg helped turn the war in the Union's favor.

Objective 2: Describe Grant's plan for ending the war and the war's outcome.

Objective 3: Identify Lincoln's hopes for the Union after his reelection.

Objective 4: Summarize why the Civil War marked a turning point in American history.

LESSON 6 ORGANIZER		PACING: APPROX. 1 PERIOD, .5 BLOCKS			
				RESOURCES	
		OBJECTIVES	**PACING**	**Online**	**Print**
Connect					
🔘	DIGITAL START UP ACTIVITY **"He Fights"**		5 min.	●	
Investigate					
🖼	DIGITAL TEXT 1 **The Siege of Vicksburg**		10 min.	●	●
🖼	INTERACTIVE MAP **The Battle of Vicksburg**		10 min.	●	
🖼	DIGITAL TEXT 2 **The Battle of Gettysburg**	Objective 1	10 min.	●	●
🖼	3-D MODEL **The Battle at Gettysburg**		10 min.	●	
🖼	DIGITAL TEXT 3 **The Gettysburg Address**		10 min.	●	●
🖼	DIGITAL TEXT 4 **Union Forces Move Southward**		10 min.	●	●
🖼	DIGITAL TEXT 6 **The Confederacy Surrenders at Appomattox**	Objective 2	10 min.	●	●
🖼	INTERACTIVE MAP **Key Battles of the Civil War**		10 min.	●	
🖼	DIGITAL TEXT 5 **Contrasting Ideas of Liberty and Union**	Objective 3	10 min.	●	●
🖼	DIGITAL TEXT 7 **The Nation Begins a New Chapter**	Objective 4	10 min.	●	●
Synthesize					
🖼	DIGITAL ACTIVITY **A Turning Point**		5 min.	●	
Demonstrate					
🔘	DIGITAL QUIZ **Lesson Quiz and Class Discussion Board**		10 min.	●	

PEARSON
realize™
www.PearsonRealize.com

Go online to access additional resources including:
Primary Sources • Biographies • Supreme Court cases •
21st Century Skill Tutorials • Maps • Graphic Organizers.

CONNECT

DIGITAL START UP ACTIVITY
"He Fights"

Project the Start Up Activity Ask students to answer the question as they enter and get settled. Then have them share their ideas with another student, either in class or through a chat or blog space.

Discuss Ask students to explain their choices of adjectives used to describe General Grant. What evidence from the text did they use to support their choices? *(Answers will vary, but students should cite specific examples from the text to explain their thinking.)*

Tell students that in this lesson they will be learning how the Battles of Vicksburg and Gettysburg turned the war's outcome in favor of the Union.

Aa Vocabulary Development: Use the Interactive Reading Notepad to preview the Key Terms and Academic Vocabulary in this lesson with students.

⮑ FLIP IT!

Assign the Flipped Video for this lesson.

STUDENT EDITION PRINT PAGES: 478–487

INVESTIGATE

DIGITAL TEXT 1
The Siege of Vicksburg

Objective 1: Explain why the Union victories at Vicksburg and Gettysburg helped turn the war in the Union's favor.

Quick Instruction
Interactive Map: The Battle of Vicksburg Project the Interactive map. Guide students to use the hints to place icons that will correctly show the outcome of the battle. Ask students how physical geographic factors affected the siege. *(The Confederate soldiers were able to defend the higher ground on the cliffs above the river, so the siege lasted longer than it otherwise would have because Grant's army had to circle around and attack by land.)*

Generate Explanations Ask students to explain the role of Ulysses S. Grant in the Union victory at the Battle of Vicksburg. *(General Grant's leadership led to the Union victory. Grant's forces had tried many times to take Vicksburg. At last, Grant devised a brilliant plan. Marching his troops inland, he launched a surprise attack on Jackson, Mississippi. Then, he turned west and attacked Vicksburg from the rear.)*

3-D Model: The Battle of Gettysburg Project the 3-D model. Explain the significant events of the Battle of Gettysburg using the student perspective near Cemetery Ridge.

INTERACTIVE MAP
The Battle of Vicksburg

Summarize Why was the Union victory at the Battle of Vicksburg a significant event of the Civil War? *(The Union army's victory at Vicksburg, combined with another victory days later, gave the North control of the Mississippi river, effectively splitting the South in two and breaking Confederate military supply lines.)*

🗪 ACTIVE CLASSROOM

Imagine that you are having a conversation with one of the soldiers who participated in the Battle of Vicksburg. Write down a question you'd like to ask, and then what that person would say to you, and what you would say in response.

🗪 ACTIVE CLASSROOM

Conduct a Circle Write activity. Break students into small groups and ask them to address this question: Why was the Battle of Gettysburg a significant event of the Civil War? Have students write as much as they can for 1 minute and then switch with the person on their right. The next person tries to improve or elaborate the response where the other person left off. Continue to switch until the paper comes back to the first person. The group then decides which is the best composition (or response) and shares that with the larger group.

The War's End

DIGITAL TEXT 2
The Battle of Gettysburg

3-D MODEL
The Battle at Gettysburg

DIGITAL TEXT 3
The Gettysburg Address

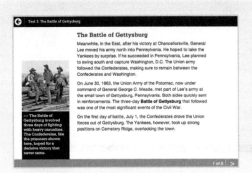

ELL Use the ELL activity described in the ELL chart.

Further Instruction

Infer In the Gettysburg Address, President Lincoln shared his ideas about liberty, equality, union, and the government. How did President Lincoln feel about these ideas based on the Gettysburg Address? Cite specific evidence from the Address in your answer. *(In the Gettysburg Address, Lincoln stated "all men are created equal" and that government should serve the people who create it, so it seems he felt strongly about equality and moving towards a country in which everyone would have a say in government. He also said that the war was a test of whether a democratic government could survive. He claimed that if the Union were to survive, then the men who died in the battle had not done so "in vain." This suggests how important he believed the Union was. In addition, he described "a new birth of freedom" in the event of a Union victory, so he believed liberty had a cost.)*

PEARSON realize™
www.PearsonRealize.com
Access your Digital Lesson

DIGITAL TEXT 4
Union Forces Move Southward

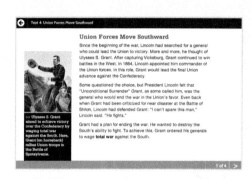

DIGITAL TEXT 6
The Confederacy Surrenders at Appomattox

INTERACTIVE MAP
Key Battles of the Civil War

Objective 2: Describe Grant's plan for ending the war and the war's outcome.

Quick Instruction

Interactive Map: Key Battles of the Civil War Project the Interactive map. Guide students through the significant events of the Civil War. Point out how the physical geographic factors of the United States affected this major historical event. The armies were fighting for territory, positioning themselves geographically, and using geographic factors, like rivers and elevated ground, to their advantage in battles. General Grant, in his role as the Union general leading the final advance against the Confederacy, planned to wage total war.

Summarize Ask students to explain Lee's surrender at Appomattox Court House. When did Lee surrender? What terms did General Grant set for the Confederate soldiers? *(Lee surrendered on April 9, 1865. Grant offered generous terms of surrender. Soldiers had to turn over their rifles, but officers could keep their pistols. Soldiers who had horses could keep them. Finally, Grant allowed the Confederate soldiers to return to their homes without fear of being pursued by U.S. authorities.)*

Support Ideas With Evidence What evidence do you see in the text to support the idea that General Grant showed honorable leadership qualities in his respectful treatment of the Confederate army after the surrender at Appomattox? *(Grant allowed former Confederate soldiers to keep their horses and ordered that they be allowed to peacefully return to their homes.)*

ACTIVE CLASSROOM

Consider performing a large-scale Act It Out with students in order to help them understand significant events of the Civil War, including the Battles of Gettysburg and Vicksburg as well as Lee's surrender at Appomattox Court House. Use sidewalk chalk to sketch out a large, rough map of the eastern United States. Have students assume the roles of the major battles of the latter part of the Civil War. Each student should give a very brief oral description—including date and outcome—of his or her battle. Have students speak in chronological order. Consider expanding the activity to have students assume the roles of armies to show large-scale, essential movements, like Sherman's March to the Sea.

Further Instruction

Identify Central Issues Focus students' attention on Grant's plan for ending the war. Ask them what "total war" means. *("Total war" is an all-out war that affects civilians at home and soldiers in combat.)*

Summarize What role did Philip Bazaar play in the Civil War? Why is he considered a hero? *(During the assault on Fort Fisher on January 15, 1865, Philip Bazaar braved terrible fire to deliver important messages between the navy and army.)*

The War's End

DIGITAL TEXT 5

Contrasting Ideas of Liberty and Union

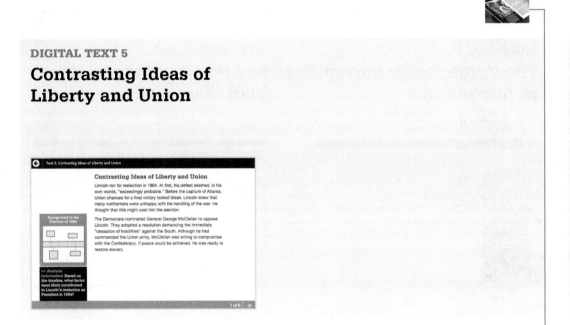

Contrasting Ideas of Liberty and Union

Lincoln ran for reelection in 1864. At first, his defeat seemed, in his own words, "exceedingly probable." Before the capture of Atlanta, Union chances for a final victory looked bleak. Lincoln knew that many northerners were unhappy with his handling of the war. He thought that this might cost him the election.

The Democrats nominated General George McClellan to oppose Lincoln. They adopted a resolution demanding the immediate "cessation of hostilities" against the South. Although he had commanded the Union army, McClellan was willing to compromise with the Confederacy. If peace could be achieved, he was ready to restore slavery.

>> Analyze Information Based on this timeline, what factor most likely contributed to Lincoln's reelection as President in 1864?

1 of 8 >

DIGITAL TEXT 7

The Nation Begins a New Chapter

The Nation Begins a New Chapter

The effect of the Civil War was immense. The Civil War years, 1861–1865, were significant on many levels. More than 360,000 Union soldiers and 250,000 Confederate soldiers lost their lives. No war has ever resulted in more American deaths. In dollars, the war's cost was about 20 billion. That was more than 11 times the entire amount spent by the federal government between 1789 and 1861.

The Civil War was a major turning point in American history. The balance of power was changed. The Democratic party lost its influence and the Republicans were in a commanding position. No longer would Americans speak of the nation as a confederation of states. Before the war, Americans referred to "these United States." After, they began speaking of "the United States." The idea that each state might secede, if it chose, was dead.

>> Analyze Data Based on the information about the human costs of the war, which side had more casualties during the war?

1 of 3 >

Objective 3: Identify Lincoln's hopes for the Union after his reelection.

Quick Instruction

Set the scene for students. 1864: an election year. The Civil War has raged for three years— much longer than anyone really expected—and northerners are unhappy with the President. Lincoln's former head of the army, cautious General George McClellan, is running against him. Lincoln fears defeat. Then, Sherman takes Atlanta, a city that symbolized the power of the South. Lincoln is reelected and expresses his hopes for the future in his Second Inaugural Address. Invite a volunteer to read excerpts from the speech aloud. Then hold a discussion in which you guide the class as they analyze Abraham Lincoln's ideas about liberty, equality, union, and government as contained in his First and Second Inaugural Addresses. Emphasize that, in both speeches, Lincoln stressed the importance of the Union of the states.

Determine Point of View Upon what document was Jefferson Davis arguing for secession from the Union in his Inaugural Address? What specific ideas did he use to support his argument? *(Davis based his arguments on the Declaration of Independence, in which the founders justified independence from Britain based on the consent of the governed. Similar about how the colonies did not want to be ruled by Britain, Davis argued for an independent Confederacy because its member states no longer wanted to be ruled by the United States government.)*

ELL Use the ELL activity described in the ELL chart.

Further Instruction

Contrast Challenge students to contrast the ideas Lincoln expressed about liberty, equality, union, and government in his First and Second Inaugural Addresses with the ideas contained in Jefferson Davis's Inaugural Address. *(While Lincoln emphasized the Union of the states based on the Constitution, Davis emphasized the fact that the Union was created by the consent of individual states and that states had the right to leave that Union and government. While Lincoln's speeches called for equality and liberty for enslaved African Americans, Davis called for the equality and liberty only of southern whites.)*

Infer What do the ideas expressed in Lincoln's and Davis's Inaugural Addresses suggest about the leadership qualities possessed by these elected U.S. leaders? *(In their Inaugural Addresses, both men show the leadership qualities of intelligence, public-speaking ability, dedication, and conviction.)*

Objective 4: Summarize why the Civil War marked a turning point in American history.

Quick Instruction

Sequence Events Share the following list with students and challenge them to identify whether each was an effect of the Civil War.

- Democrats more powerful (before the War)
- Republicans more powerful (after the War)
- country called "these United States" (before the War)
- country called "the United States" (after the War)
- state secession a valid option (before the War)
- state secession unthinkable (after the War)
- slavery allowed (before the War)
- slavery abolished (after the War)

Further Instruction

Analyze Data Display the infographic about the costs of the Civil War. Ask students to explain what this data suggests about the significance of the Civil War to American history. *(The data suggests that the Civil War was significant in its monetary and human costs. It had a major impact on the population of America and the American economy.)*

Use Context Clues Why is it significant that Americans began referring to the country as *the* United States rather than *these* United States after the Civil War? *(Americans began to think of the country as a unified whole rather than a collection of loosely joined states.)*

SYNTHESIZE

DIGITAL ACTIVITY
A Turning Point

Invite a student to explain why it is important to study the Civil War, which happened so long ago. Guide the class into understanding how the Civil War still affects us today. Everything from the status of African Americans to the power of the federal government was changed by the war.

Encourage students to spend a few minutes pre-writing before they begin their paragraphs. If students feel that all of the consequences of the Civil War were equally important, allow them to express and support that point of view.

Discuss Was the Civil War *the* most important event in American history up to that point in time? Why or why not? Encourage debate in class.

DEMONSTRATE

DIGITAL QUIZ
Lesson Quiz and Class Discussion Board

Assign the online Lesson Quiz for this lesson if you haven't already done so. Students will be offered automatic remediation or enrichment based on their score.

Pose these questions to the class on the Discussion Board:

In *The War's End*, you learned about two great battles that changed the course of the war: the Union capture of Vicksburg and the Union victory at Gettysburg. It was at Gettysburg that Lincoln gave his famous address expressing American ideals. Soon after, Union forces moved deep into the South, eventually forcing the Confederacy to surrender at Appomattox Court House. The Civil War was over. It had cost many lives and great amounts of money, and it changed the country in ways that are still apparent today.

Make Generalizations What do you think are the "lessons" of the Civil War for Americans today?

Express Ideas Clearly What aspect of the Civil War do you find most interesting? The military? The politics? Something else? Explain why.

Topic Inquiry
Have students continue their investigations for the Topic Inquiry.

Sectionalism and Civil War

▮ SYNTHESIZE

DIGITAL ACTIVITY
Reflect on the Essential Question and Topic

First ask students to reconsider the Essential Question for the Topic: When is war justified? Remind students of the factors that might justify going to war that they considered at the start of the Topic:

- economic factors
- religious factors
- political factors
- social factors

Ask students to reconsider their answers in light of what they've learned about the Civil War. Do they think the South was justified in going to war against the North? Do they think the North was justified in going to war against the South? What factors were involved?

Next ask students to reflect on the Topic as a whole and jot down one to three questions they've developed while learning about the Civil War. Share these examples if students need help getting started:

- Which factor or combination of factors— economic, religious, political, social—led to the Civil War?
- Do you think people of the time thought the war was caused by the same things that historians today would say caused the war?
- How can disagreements rooted in sectionalism be resolved without going to war?

You may ask students to share their questions and answers on the Class Discussion Board.

Topic Inquiry
Have students complete Step 3 of the Topic Inquiry.

▮ DEMONSTRATE

DIGITAL TOPIC REVIEW AND ASSESSMENT
Sectionalism and Civil War

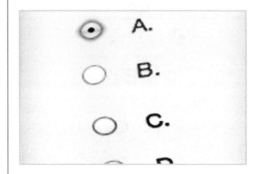

Students can prepare for the Topic Test by answering the questions in the Topic Review and Assessment online or the Assessment questions in the Print Student text. They can also prepare by reviewing their answers to the Interactive Reading Notepad questions or reviewing their notes in the Reading and Notetaking Study Guide.

DIGITAL TOPIC TEST
Sectionalism and Civil War

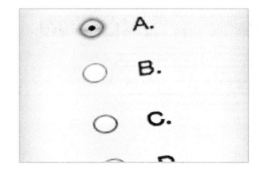

TOPIC TEST
Assign the Topic Test to assess students' understanding of topic content.

BENCHMARK TESTS
Assign these benchmark tests as you complete the relevant topics to monitor student progress toward mastering the course content and as preparation for the End-of-Course Test.

Benchmark Test 1: Topics 1-2

Benchmark Test 2: Topics 3-4

Benchmark Test 3: Topics 5-6

Benchmark Test 4: Topics 7-9

Benchmark Test 5: Topics 10-12

Benchmark Test 6: Topics 13-14

Benchmark Test 7: Topics 15-17

The Reconstruction Era

TOPIC 9 ORGANIZER	PACING: APPROX. 1 PERIOD, .5 BLOCKS
	PACING
Connect	**1 period**
MY STORY VIDEO — NBC LEARN **Born into Slavery**	10 min.
DIGITAL ESSENTIAL QUESTION ACTIVITY **How Should We Handle Conflict?**	10 min.
DIGITAL TIMELINE ACTIVITY **The Reconstruction Era**	10 min.
TOPIC INQUIRY: CIVIC DISCUSSION **Ending Reconstruction**	20 min.
Investigate	**3–7 periods**
TOPIC INQUIRY: CIVIC DISCUSSION **Ending Reconstruction**	Ongoing
LESSON 1 Early Reconstruction	30–40 min.
LESSON 2 Radical Reconstruction	30–40 min.
LESSON 3 Reconstruction and Southern Society	30–40 min.
LESSON 4 The Aftermath of Reconstruction	30–40 min.
Synthesize	**1 period**
DIGITAL ACTIVITY **Reflect on the Essential Question and Topic**	10 min.
TOPIC INQUIRY: CIVIC DISCUSSION **Ending Reconstruction**	20 min.
Demonstrate	**1–2 periods**
DIGITAL TOPIC REVIEW AND ASSESSMENT **The Reconstruction Era**	10 min.
TOPIC INQUIRY: CIVIC DISCUSSION **Ending Reconstruction**	20 min.

TOPIC INQUIRY: CIVIC DISCUSSION

Ending Reconstruction

In this Topic Inquiry, students work in teams to examine different perspectives on this issue by analyzing several sources, arguing both sides of a Yes/No question, then developing and discussing their own point of view on the question: **Should the United States have ended Reconstruction in 1877?**

STEP 1: CONNECT
Develop Questions and Plan the Investigation

Launch the Civic Discussion

Divide the class into groups of four students. Students can access the materials they'll need in the online course or you can distribute copies to each student. Read the main question and introduction with the students.

Have students complete Step 1 by reading the Discussion Launch and filling in Step 1 of the Information Organizer. The Discussion Launch provides YES and NO arguments on the main question. Students should extract and paraphrase the arguments from the reading in Step 1 of their Information Organizers.

Next, students share within their groups the arguments and evidence they found to support the YES and NO positions. The group needs to agree on the major YES and NO points and each student should note those points in their Information Organizer.

Resources
- Student Instructions
- Information Organizer
- Discussion Launch

⏻ PROFESSIONAL DEVELOPMENT

Civic Discussion
Be sure to view the Civic Discussion Professional Development resources in the online course.

STEP 2: INVESTIGATE
Apply Disciplinary Concepts and Tools

Examine Sources and Perspectives

Students will examine sources with the goal of extracting information and perspectives on the main question. They analyze each source and describe the author's perspective on the main question and key evidence the author provides to support that viewpoint in Information Organizer Step 2.

Ask students to keep in mind:

- **Author/Creator:** Who created the source? An individual? Group? Government agency?
- **Audience:** For whom was the source created?
- **Date/Place:** Is there any information that reveals where and when the source was created?
- **Purpose:** Why was the source created? Discuss with students the importance of this question in identifying bias.
- **Relevance:** How does the source support one argument or another?

Suggestion: Reading the source documents and filling in Step 2 of the Information Organizer could be assigned as homework.

Resources
- Student Instructions
- Information Organizer
- Source documents

STEP 3: SYNTHESIZE
Use Evidence to Formulate Conclusions

Formulate Compelling Arguments with Evidence

Now students will apply perspectives and evidence they extracted from the sources to think more deeply about the main question by first arguing one side of the issue, then the other. In this way students become more prepared to formulate an evidence-based conclusion on their own.

Within each student group, assign half of the students to take the position of YES on the main question and the others to take the position of NO. Students will work with their partners to identify the strongest arguments and evidence to support their assigned YES or NO position.

Present Yes/No Positions

Within each group, those assigned the YES position share arguments and evidence first. As the YES students speak, those assigned NO should listen carefully, take notes to fill in the rest of the Compelling Arguments Chart (Step 3 in Information Organizer) and ask clarifying questions.

When the YES side is finished, students assigned the NO position present while those assigned YES should listen, take notes, and ask clarifying questions. Examples of clarifyin questions are:

- I think you just said [x]. Am I understanding you correctly?
- Can you tell me more about [x]?
- Can you repeat [x]? I am not sure I understand, yet.

Suggestion: You may want to set a 5 minute time limit for each side to present. Provide a two-minute warning so that students make their most compelling arguments within the time frame.

Switch Sides

The students will switch sides to argue the opposite point of view. To prepare to present the other position, partners who first argued YES will use the notes they took during the NO side's presentation, plus add any additional arguments and evidence from the reading and sources. The same for students who first argued the NO position.

STEP 4: DEMONSTRATE
Communicate Conclusions and Take Informed Action

Individual Points of View

Now the students will have the opportunity to discuss the main question from their own points of view. To help students prepare for this discussion, have them reflect on the YES/NO discussions they have participated in thus far and fill in Step 4 of their Information Organizers.

After all of the students have shared their points of view, each group should list points of agreement, filling the last portion of Step 4 on their Information Organizers.

Reflect on the Discussion

Ask students to reflect on the civic discussion thinking about:

- The value of having to argue both the YES and NO positions.
- If their individual views changed over the course of the discussion and why.
- What they learned from participating in the discussion.

Resources

- Student Instructions
- Information Organizer

INTRODUCTION

The Reconstruction Era

Following the Civil War, Congress instituted sweeping political, economic, and social changes in the former Confederate states. During this period of Reconstruction, African Americans gained many rights. They were still, however, denied full equality, especially in the South.

■ CONNECT

MY STORY VIDEO
Born into Slavery

Watch a video about what it was like to be born into slavery and the changes that came with emancipation.

Check Understanding What was the basis for the descriptions of slavery in this video? *(interviews in the 1930s with formerly enslaved African Americans)*

Assess Credibility How credible a view does the video present of slavery and its aftermath? *(Because the video is based on the recollections of people who endured slavery, their first-hand accounts must be taken as credible, even though the passage of time may have affected their memories.)*

DIGITAL ESSENTIAL QUESTION ACTIVITY
How Should We Handle Conflict?

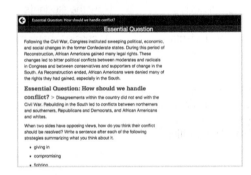

Ask students to think about the Essential Question for this topic: How should we handle conflict? Point out that disagreements continued after the Civil War over how to rebuild the South.

If students have not already done so, ask them to read the list and write a sentence about each strategy. Have students share their ideas with a partner.

Support Ideas with Examples Why do you think Americans continued to face conflicts following the Civil War? Name three areas in which you think conflict occurred and why.

Make Predictions What strategies do you think Americans will use to address conflicts following the Civil War? Explain your reasoning.

DIGITAL TIMELINE ACTIVITY
The Reconstruction Era

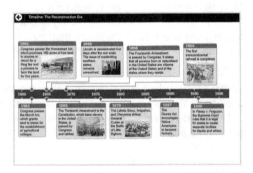

Display the timeline showing the major events of the Reconstruction era. During this topic, students will learn about all of these events and many more, but this timeline will provide a framework into which they can place the events they learn about.

Summarize What three amendments were passed following the Civil War and how did they impact the nation? *(Thirteenth—abolished slavery; Fourteenth—granted African Americans citizenship; Fifteenth—forbade states from denying citizens the right to vote because of race)*

Identify Cause and Effects Based on this timeline, how do you think Lincoln's assassination affected Reconstruction? *(His mild plan was not implemented and Reconstruction became harsher.)*

Topic Inquiry
Launch the Topic Inquiry with students after introducing the topic.

PEARSON realize™
www.PearsonRealize.com
Access your Digital Lesson

Early Reconstruction

Supporting English Language Learners

Use with Digital Text 2, **The Causes and Effects of Reconstruction.**

Speaking
Prompt students to speak using a variety of grammatical structures such as appositives. Explain that an appositive is a grammatical structure that renames, explains, or identifies a noun next to it.

Beginning Display this sentence: Reconstruction, a time of rebuilding, followed the war. Point out the appositive *a time of rebuilding,* and brainstorm alternatives. Have students say the sentence aloud using one of the alternatives.

Intermediate Read aloud the sentences from the text that include the boldface terms *Wade-Davis Bill* and *Freedmen's Bureau*. Help students to identify the appositive in each. Then have students say additional sentences about the boldface terms that include appositives for them.

Advanced Read aloud the sentences from the text that include the boldface terms *Wade-Davis Bill* and *Freedmen's Bureau*. Ask students to identify the appositive in each. Then have pairs of students say sentences that include appositives for these words: *Lincoln, Reconstruction.*

Advanced High Read aloud the sentences from the text that include the boldface terms *Wade-Davis Bill* and *Freedmen's Bureau*. Ask students to identify the appositive in each. Then have pairs of students discuss Reconstruction using at least two appositives.

Use with Digital Text 4, **President Johnson's Reconstruction Plan.**

Writing
Discuss how editing writing for standard grammar and usage of appropriate verb tenses improves communication and avoids misunderstanding.

Beginning Display these sentences: The Thirteenth Amendment (bans/banned) slavery. Slavery (is/was) still illegal today. Have students choose between each pair of verbs and write down the sentences. Then discuss the present and past tenses, and have students edit their writing for appropriate verb tenses.

Intermediate Display these sentences: The Thirteenth Amendment _____ slavery. Slavery _____ still illegal today. Have students write down and complete the sentences. Then discuss the present and past tenses, and have students edit their writing for appropriate verb tenses.

Advanced Ask pairs of students to write a paragraph about the Thirteenth Amendment that uses the present, past, and future tenses. Then review each tense and answer students' questions. Have pairs edit their writing for appropriate verb tenses.

Advanced High Ask students to write a paragraph about the Thirteenth Amendment that uses the present, past, and future tenses and includes these verbs: approve, forbid, be, overturn. Then review each tense and answer students' questions. Have students edit their writing for appropriate verb tenses.

◨ Differentiate Instruction

Use the Differentiated Instruction notes throughout the lesson plan to support the varied skill sets, levels of readiness, and interests in the mixed-ability classroom.

Challenge These notes include suggestions for expanding the activity for advanced students.

On-Level These notes include suggestions for modifying the activity to address different interests or learning styles.

Extra Support These notes include ideas for providing more scaffolding or reading spuport.

Special Needs These notes provide ideas for adapting instruction to support the needs of various special needs students.

■ NOTES

Early Reconstruction

Objectives

Objective 1: Describe the nation's economic, political, and social problems after the Civil War.

Objective 2: Identify the early steps that were taken during Reconstruction.

Objective 3: Explain how the assassination of Lincoln and the inauguration of a new President led to conflict.

LESSON 1 ORGANIZER		PACING: APPROX. 1 PERIOD, .5 BLOCKS			
				RESOURCES	
		OBJECTIVES	PACING	Online	Print
Connect					
	DIGITAL ACTIVITY **Predicting Postwar Problems**		5 min.	●	
Investigate					
	DIGITAL TEXT 1 **Effects of the Civil War**	Objective 1	10 min.	●	●
	BEFORE AND AFTER **The Downfall of the Southern Economy**		10 min.	●	
	DIGITAL TEXT 2 **The Causes and Effects of Reconstruction**	Objective 2	10 min.	●	●
	DIGITAL TEXT 3 **The Assassination of Abraham Lincoln**		10 min.	●	●
	DIGITAL TEXT 4 **President Johnson's Reconstruction Plan**	Objective 3	10 min.	●	●
	INTERACTIVE GALLERY **Lincoln and Reconstruction**		10 min.	●	
Synthesize					
	DIGITAL ACTIVITY **Events that Affected Reconstruction**		5 min.	●	
Demonstrate					
	DIGITAL QUIZ **Lesson Quiz and Class Discussion Board**		10 min.	●	

PEARSON
realize™
www.PearsonRealize.com

Go online to access additional resources including:
Primary Sources • Biographies • Supreme Court cases •
21st Century Skill Tutorials • Maps • Graphic Organizers.

CONNECT

DIGITAL ACTIVITY
Predicting Postwar Problems

Project the Start Up Activity Ask students to read the questions and make a prediction as they enter.

Discuss How will both sides work together to run the federal government? *(There will be major disagreements; the North will be politically dominant.)* How should the federal government treat the states that seceded from the Union? *(Ensure that the states that seceded are loyal to the Union and will follow its laws outlawing slavery.)* What economic issues might there be in the South? *(losses from the war; lack of industrialization; downturns in agricultural production; the expense of rebuilding)* What needs to be resolved regarding slavery? *(the political and social status of African Americans)*

Aa Vocabulary Development: Use the Interactive Reading Notepad to preview the Key Terms and Academic Vocabulary in this lesson with students.

⇅ FLIP IT!
Assign the Flipped Video for this lesson.

▉ STUDENT EDITION PRINT
PAGES: 492–498

INVESTIGATE

DIGITAL TEXT 1
Effects of the Civil War

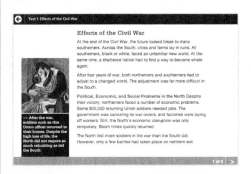

Objective 1: Describe the nation's economic, political, and social problems after the Civil War.

Quick Instruction
Before and After: The Downfall of the Southern Economy Project the Before and After activity and use the slider to show how prices and dollar values changed in the South during the war.

Analyze Graphs Describe the effects of the Civil War on the Confederate dollar. *(the dollar weakened until it was almost worthless)*

📷 ACTIVE CLASSROOM
Have students use the Quick Write Strategy and take 30 seconds to write what they know about the political, social, and economic issues facing the nation as a result of the Civil War.

Further Instruction
Go through the Interactive Reading Notepad questions and discuss the answers with the class.

Compare and Contrast the economic problems faced by the North and South following the Civil War. What caused the economic differences between these two regions? *(North—returning soldiers needed jobs and factories were laying off workers. South—cities and farms lay in ruins, Confederate money was worthless, loans were never repaid, and banks closed. Causes— fighting mostly took place in the South; the North had industries to return to, whereas the South could not rebuild its plantation system)*

BEFORE AND AFTER
The Downfall of the Southern Economy

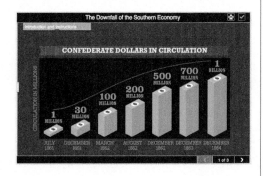

Generate Explanations Explain the social and political problems faced by the South after the war. *(Social—The South had millions of new freedmen but no legal systems to protect them. Political—There was no clear structure for running the state governments. Many Confederates were barred from office and feared African Americans gaining political power.)*

Make Predictions How do you think the economic differences between the North and South will affect Reconstruction? *(They will make it difficult for the South to rebuild; many southerners will resent wealthier and more economically stable northerners dictating Reconstruction polities.)*

Early Reconstruction

DIGITAL TEXT 2

The Causes and Effects of Reconstruction

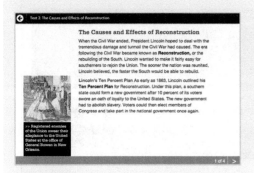

DIGITAL TEXT 3

The Assassination of Abraham Lincoln

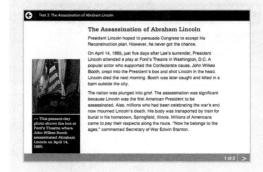

Objective 2: Identify the early steps that were taken during Reconstruction.

Quick Instruction

Project the image of the African American school. Define Reconstruction as the era of rebuilding the South following the Civil War. Explain that the Civil War resulted in extensive damage economically, politically, and socially, which caused there to be a Reconstruction period to repair and heal. Explain that Reconstruction also had many effects, such as building schools like this one for freedmen.

Summarize How did the Freedman's Bureau impact African Americans? *(It provided food and clothing to formerly enslaved people, helped freedmen find jobs, and set up schools for African Americans.)*

D Differentiate: Extra Support Explain that to reconstruct means to rebuild, or to build something again after it has been destroyed. Ask students what was destroyed that needed to be rebuilt after the Civil War. Discuss why they think the term Reconstruction is used to describe this era.

ELL Use the ELL activity described in the ELL chart.

Further Instruction

Go through the Interactive Reading Notepad questions and discuss the answers with the class.

Compare and Contrast the Wade-Davis Bill and Lincoln's Ten Percent Plan and explain how each proposed to address political, economic, and social problems during Reconstruction. What do the differences between these bills reveal about the nation's political problems following the Civil War? *(Ten Percent—proposed that southern states would form new governments and rejoin the Union after 10 percent of voters swore a loyalty oath; required the abolition of slavery; offered amnesty to former Confederates who had not been leaders. Wade Davis—proposed a majority of white men to swear a loyalty oath; prohibited Confederates from voting or holding office. The Wade-Davis Bill was harsher than Lincoln's plan, suggesting many Republicans disagreed with his policies and felt he was being too easy on the South.)*

Cite Evidence Describe Lincoln's leadership qualities following the Civil War, citing evidence for support. *(generous toward the South and concerned about the nation's future after the war—"Lincoln wanted to make it fairly easy for southerners to rejoin the Union. The sooner the nation was reunited, Lincoln believed, the faster the South would be able to rebuild." Willing to stand up to Republicans with whom he disagreed—"Lincoln refused to sign the Wade-Davis Bill because he felt it was too harsh.")*

Objective 3: Explain how the assassination of Lincoln and the inauguration of a new President led to conflict.

Quick Instruction

Interactive Gallery: Lincoln and Reconstruction Project the interactive gallery and discuss the images with students.

Generate Explanations Explain the significance of Lincoln's assassination on the course of Reconstruction. *(Lincoln was not able to implement his more moderate Ten Percent Plan. Johnson became President and also took a moderate approach, but Republicans who wanted harsher measures were able to take control.)*

> **💬 ACTIVE CLASSROOM**
>
> Ask students to Take a Stand on the following question: "Were Republicans right to demand harsher measures against the South during Reconstruction?" Ask students to divide into two groups based on their answer and move to separate areas of the room. Ask students to talk with each other to compare their reasons for answering yes or no. Have representatives from each side present and defend the group's point of view.

ELL Use the ELL activity described in the ELL chart.

Further Instruction

Go through the Interactive Reading Notepad questions and discuss the answers with the class.

DIGITAL TEXT 4

President Johnson's Reconstruction Plan

INTERACTIVE GALLERY

Lincoln and Reconstruction

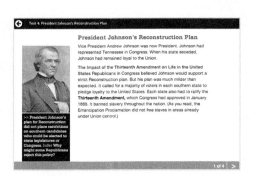

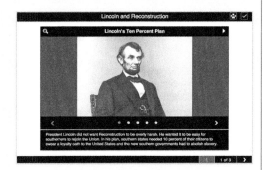

Identify Cause and Effect Describe the impact of the Thirteenth Amendment on life in the United States. *(It banned slavery throughout the nation, overturning previous rulings. This created a new social and economic system in the South. African Americans were hired as workers and many migrated North.)*

Make Predictions Analyze the leadership qualities of Andrew Johnson. How do you think he will fare in the showdown against Republicans? Explain your reasoning. *(Johnson was not as strong a leader as Lincoln. He had not been elected President and was not the leader who won the war. Given that the Republicans are organizing against him, he will probably not be able to prevent Congress from implementing a harsher reconstruction plan.)*

Early Reconstruction

▮ SYNTHESIZE

DIGITAL ACTIVITY
Events that Affected Reconstruction

Have students make a timeline and choose one of the events to write about. Have students share their timelines with a partner and discuss their responses.

Discuss Have students review the predictions they made at the beginning of the lesson. Ask how they would revise their answers now that they have learned more about the causes and effects of early Reconstruction.

▮ DEMONSTRATE

DIGITAL QUIZ
Lesson Quiz and Class Discussion Board

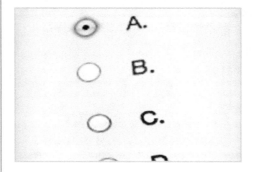

Assign the online Lesson Quiz for this lesson if you haven't already done so. Students will be offered automatic remediation or enrichment based on their score.

Pose these questions to the class on the Discussion Board:

Summarize Describe the causes and effects of Reconstruction.

Compare and Contrast How did Reconstruction impact different groups in the South, including African Americans, poor whites, and former Confederates? Give examples for support.

Topic Inquiry
Have students continue their investigations for the Topic Inquiry.

Radical Reconstruction

Supporting English Language Learners

Use with Digital Text 1, **Reconstruction Difficulties Persist.**

Writing
Display the first sentence of the text. Prompt students to employ increasingly complex grammatical structures such as using the possessive case. Point out the apostrophe -s in *Johnson's*, and explain the relationship between Johnson and the Reconstruction plan.

Beginning Display this sentence: The South black codes did not allow freedmen to _____. Have students write down the sentence, add an apostrophe -s to employ the possessive case correctly, and fill in the blank with an appropriate word or phrase.

Intermediate Ask students to suggest sentences that use the possessive case (apostrophe –s) correctly using the following words: The South's, Freedmen's. Record students' suggestions, and have students write down the sentences.

Advanced Ask pairs of students to write a paragraph about the challenges of Reconstruction by using the possessive case (apostrophe –s) correctly with these words: Reconstruction's, Tennessee's, Johnson's, protest's. Have pairs read their paragraphs to one another.

Advanced High Ask students to write a paragraph about the challenges of Reconstruction using the possessive case (apostrophe –s) correctly at least three times. Have partners read each other's paragraphs and explain each instance of the possessive case that they encounter.

Use with Digital Text 4, **Political Problems and a New President.**

Speaking
Have students speak using a variety of sentence lengths with increasing accuracy and ease as they acquire more English.Explain that varying sentence length, or using a mix of shorter and longer sentences, can make spoken language more interesting and understandable.

Beginning Display this sentence: The House impeached Johnson. Brainstorm a list of prepositional phrases that could be added to the sentence in order to lengthen it. Ask students to add one of the phrases and say the new sentence aloud.

Intermediate Display this sentence: The House impeached Johnson. Ask students to think of ways that prepositional phrases could be added to the beginning and to the end of this sentence in order to lengthen it. Have students share these sentences aloud.

Advanced Display this sentence: The House impeached Johnson. Have pairs of students practice speaking with a variety of sentence lengths by adding prepositional phrases and independent clauses to the original sentence.

Advanced High Display this sentence: The House impeached Johnson. Ask pairs of students to practice speaking with a variety of sentence lengths by adding a dependent clause to the original sentence, as well as changing the original to a dependent clause and then adding a new independent clause to it.

◩ Differentiate Instruction

Use the Differentiated Instruction notes throughout the lesson plan to support the varied skill sets, levels of readiness, and interests in the mixed-ability classroom.

Challenge These notes include suggestions for expanding the activity for advanced students.

On-Level These notes include suggestions for modifying the activity to address different interests or learning styles.

Extra Support These notes include ideas for providing more scaffolding or reading spuport.

Special Needs These notes provide ideas for adapting instruction to support the needs of various special needs students.

◼ NOTES

Radical Reconstruction

Objectives

Objective 1: Describe how Congress reacted to the passage of black codes in the South.

Objective 2: Explain how Radical Republicans gained power in Congress.

Objective 3: Identify why President Johnson was impeached.

LESSON 2 ORGANIZER		PACING: APPROX. 1 PERIOD, .5 BLOCKS			
				RESOURCES	
		OBJECTIVES	PACING	Online	Print
Connect					
	DIGITAL START UP ACTIVITY **Causes of Radical Reconstruction**		5 min.	●	
Investigate					
	DIGITAL TEXT 1 **Reconstruction Difficulties Persist**	Objective 1	10 min.	●	●
	DIGITAL TEXT 2 **Reforms of the Radical Reconstruction Congress**	Objective 2	10 min.	●	●
	DIGITAL TEXT 3 **Political and Social Problems During Reconstruction**		10 min.	●	●
	INTERACTIVE GALLERY **The Massacre of New Orleans**	Objective 3	10 min.	●	
	DIGITAL TEXT 4 **Political Problems and a New President**		10 min.	●	●
Synthesize					
	DIGITAL ACTIVITY **The Effects of Radical Republicans in Congress**		5 min.	●	
Demonstrate					
	DIGITAL QUIZ **Lesson Quiz and Class Discussion Board**		10 min.	●	

■ CONNECT

DIGITAL START UP ACTIVITY

Causes of Radical Reconstruction

Project the Start Up Activity. Ask students to read the definition and answer the question as they enter and get settled. Have students share their responses with a partner, either in class or through a blog space.

Discuss Why do you think the black codes led Republicans in Congress to take charge of Reconstruction in the South? *(The Republicans felt the South was trying to preserve their power over African Americans and not make changes to its politics or society.)*

Tell students that in this lesson they will be learning about the Radical Reconstruction and the new legislative reforms of the Radical Reconstruction Congress.

Aa Vocabulary Development: Use the Interactive Reading Notepad to preview the Key Terms and Academic Vocabulary in this lesson with students.

⤺ FLIP IT!

Assign the Flipped Video for this lesson.

■ STUDENT EDITION PRINT
PAGES: 499–505

■ INVESTIGATE

DIGITAL TEXT 1

Reconstruction Difficulties Persist

Objective 1: Describe how Congress reacted to the passage of black codes in the South.

Quick Instruction

Project the image of African American sharecroppers on the whiteboard. Define the black codes as laws that severely limited the rights of freedmen. Discuss how the black codes impacted African Americans by making it harder to escape the plantation system.

Summarize How did Radical Republicans react to the black codes passed in the South? *(Radical Republicans thought Reconstruction had been too lenient. They believed Reconstruction policies didn't force the South to change its politics, allowing the states to pass unjust laws. Radical Republicans vowed to take control of Reconstruction.)*

ELL Use the ELL activity described in the ELL chart.

Further Instruction

Go through the Interactive Reading Notepad questions and discuss the answers with the class. Be sure students understand the effects of Lincoln's and Johnson's Reconstruction plans and the causes of Radical Reconstruction.

Support Ideas with Examples How did the black codes impact African Americans socially, economically, and politically? Provide examples for support. *(The codes limited freedmen's political power by preventing them from voting or holding public office. In many states the codes limited their economic power by allowing them to work only as servants or farm laborers. They had to sign contracts or be forced to work on a plantation. Socially, the codes kept freedmen from achieving equality.)*

Identify Cause and Effect Describe the social and political problems during Reconstruction that caused Radical Republicans to seek control of Congress. *(Black codes limited the rights of freedmen; violence broke out against African Americans in Memphis and New Orleans; Johnson ignored a report by the Joint Committee on Reconstruction about conditions in the South.)*

Radical Reconstruction

Reforms of the Radical Reconstruction Congress

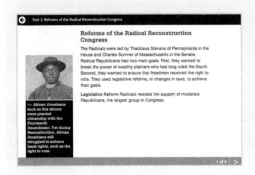

>> African Americans such as this laborer were granted citizenship with the Fourteenth Amendment. Yet during Reconstruction, African Americans still struggled to achieve basic rights, such as the right to vote.

Political and Social Problems During Reconstruction

>> This cartoon shows the terror of the New Orleans riots of 1866. Analyze Political Cartoons What meaning can you infer from the way President Johnson is portrayed in this cartoon?

Objective 2: Explain how Radical Republicans gained power in Congress.

Quick Instruction

Project the image of the African American laborer. Explain that the Radical Reconstruction Congress passed a number of legislative reforms, including Constitutional amendments, that impacted African Americans during Reconstruction.

Make Generalizations What were the effects of the Radical Reconstruction Congress on Reconstruction? *(Reconstruction became harsher toward the South. The South had to follow more reforms. Legislation passed to ensure greater equality for African Americans.)*

D Differentiate: Extra Support The Radical Reconstruction Congress wanted a tougher approach toward the South. Explain that radical can mean *thorough, different,* or *extreme*. It can also refer to a complete social or political change. Have students give one example of a reform that the Radical Reconstruction Congress passed and explain why it was considered radical.

Further Instruction

Go through the Interactive Reading Notepad questions and discuss the answers with the class.

Draw Conclusions Describe the impact of the Fourteenth Amendment on life in the United States. *(The amendment protected the citizenship of African Americans. It overturned the Dred Scott ruling and made it illegal to deny voting rights to African Americans on the basis of race. However, the amendment did not fully protect the rights of African Americans or change the discrimination African Americans faced until many years later.)*

Evaluate Arguments Evaluate the legislative reform programs of the Radical Reconstruction Congress. Were the Civil Rights Act of 1866 and the Fourteenth Amendment effective? Why or why not? *(the reforms were not effective in combating discrimination and ensuring equality at the time. However, they set an important foundation for African Americans to achieve greater rights as citizens in the future.)*

Objective 3: Identify why President Johnson was impeached.

Quick Instruction

Interactive Chart: Legislation and Reform During Reconstruction Project the interactive chart and read through the tiles. Have students fill in the chart and discuss their answers.

Interactive Gallery: The Massacre of New Orleans Project the interactive gallery about the Massacre of New Orleans. What political problems does the cartoon depict? *(the failed policies of Reconstruction; disagreements between Johnson and the Radical Republicans; ongoing violence against African Americans in the South)*

> **📷 ACTIVE CLASSROOM**
>
> Ask students to complete a Make Headlines Activity. Have students write a headline that captures a main idea associated with the Massacre of New Orleans. Ask: If you were to write a headline right now that captured the most important aspect of the Massacre of New Orleans, what would that headline be? Pass your headline to a partner for them to review—they can keep yours or ask for theirs back.

INTERACTIVE GALLERY

The Massacre of New Orleans

DIGITAL TEXT 4

Political Problems and a New President

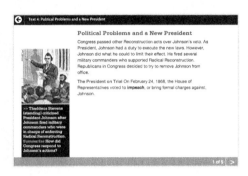

ACTIVE CLASSROOM

Have students use the Sticky Notes Strategy and spend three minutes jotting down their response to this question on sticky notes: "Why did the Radical Reconstruction Congress impose additional legislative reforms on the South?" Ask students to post their sticky notes on the board or on chart paper and look at the various responses. Discuss similarities and differences in the responses as a group.

ELL Use the ELL activity described in the ELL chart.

Further Instruction

Go through the Interactive Reading Notepad questions and discuss the answers with the class.

Compare the impacts of the Fourteenth and Fifteenth Amendments. How were these amendments intended to address social and political problems during Reconstruction? Why were their impacts limited? *(Fourteenth— African Americans were citizens. Fifteenth— citizens could not be denied the right to vote based on race. The amendments were meant to grant social and political equality to African Americans but states found ways around them initially.)*

Summarize What were the Military Reconstruction Acts of 1867 and how did they impact southern whites, northern Republicans, and African Americans? *(The Acts divided southern states into military districts. Southern whites had less power to rule themselves, especially since former Confederates could not vote. African Americans had their right to vote protected by the army. Northern Republicans won state elections because African Americans voted Republican while many southern whites were not allowed to vote or refused in protest.)*

Identify Cause and Effect Describe the causes and effects of political tensions between President Johnson and Congress. *(Causes— Johnson opposed Radical Reconstruction and vetoed the Reconstruction Act. Congress passed other acts over his veto, but Johnson tried to limit their effects. Effects—Johnson fired military commanders who supported Radical Reconstruction, so Republicans tried to impeach him. Republican Ulysses S. Grant easily won the 1868 presidential election.)*

Radical Reconstruction

■ SYNTHESIZE

DIGITAL ACTIVITY
The Effects of Radical Republicans in Congress

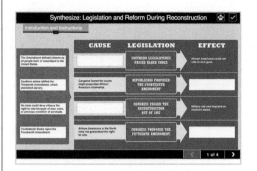

Have students complete the concept web and choose one of the changes to write about. Have students share their webs with a partner and discuss their responses.

Discuss Have students review the answers they wrote at the beginning of the lesson about why the black codes led Republicans to take charge of Reconstruction in the South. Ask how they would revise or add to their answers now that they have learned more about the rise of Radical Reconstruction. Discuss the additional factors that caused the Radical Reconstruction Congress to come to the power and the effects this had on the nation.

■ DEMONSTRATE

DIGITAL QUIZ
Lesson Quiz and Class Discussion Board

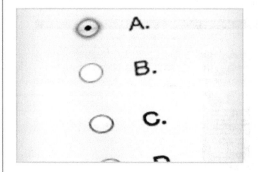

Assign the online Lesson Quiz for this lesson if you haven't already done so. Students will be offered automatic remediation or enrichment based on their score.

Pose these questions to the class on the Discussion Board:

Identify Cause and Effect How did the Fourteenth and Fifteenth Amendments impact the rise of the Republicans in state and federal government?

Evaluate Arguments Do you think Republicans were right to impose harsher Reconstruction policies than President Johnson against the South following the Civil War? Explain your reasoning, providing examples for support.

Topic Inquiry
Have students continue their investigations for the Topic Inquiry.

Reconstruction and Southern Society

Supporting English Language Learners

Use with Digital Text 1, **New Political Groups in the South.**

Speaking
Explain that using a variety of sentence types adds clarity and interest to spoken language. Review the four main sentence types (exclamatory, interrogative, imperative, declarative), and prompt students to practice speaking using terms from the text, with the goal of increasing their speaking accuracy and ease.

Beginning Briefly summarize information presented in the text about scalawags. Ask students to say a declarative sentence that borrows information from your summary.

Intermediate Say a declarative sentence about the scalawags, and ask students to say an interrogative sentence that borrows information from it (or has the declarative sentence as its answer). Encourage students to use a rising inflection at the end of their questions.

Advanced Ask: Why might carpetbaggers have moved to the South? Have pairs of students practice using the exclamatory sentence type as they answer this question.

Advanced High Ask pairs of students to discuss what motivated carpetbaggers to move to the South. Encourage each partner to use a variety of sentence types during the discussion by including each type at least once.

Use with Digital Text 3, **Political Problems and Legislative Reform.**

Writing
Display the text's second paragraph, and highlight each sentence in a different color. Point out the variety of sentence lengths. Have students write using a variety of grade-appropriate sentence lengths in increasingly accurate ways.

Beginning Display these sentences: After the war, the South built _____. Taxes also _____. Have students use words or phrases to create sentences of varying lengths and write the sentences down.

Intermediate Ask pairs of students to write about Reconstruction in the South using a variety of grade-appropriate sentence lengths. Have them include a sentence under five words, one between five and nine words, and one of at least ten words (which could consist of two independent clauses).

Advanced Ask pairs of students to write a cohesive paragraph about Reconstruction in the South using a variety of grade-appropriate sentence lengths. Encourage them to include one sentence under five words and one of at least ten words.

Advanced High Ask students to write a cohesive paragraph about Reconstruction in the South using a variety of grade-appropriate sentence lengths. Then have partners read each other's work and discuss not only the variety of sentence lengths, but also how they are distributed within the paragraph.

Ⓓ Differentiate Instruction

Use the Differentiated Instruction notes throughout the lesson plan to support the varied skill sets, levels of readiness, and interests in the mixed-ability classroom.

Challenge These notes include suggestions for expanding the activity for advanced students.

On-Level These notes include suggestions for modifying the activity to address different interests or learning styles.

Extra Support These notes include ideas for providing more scaffolding or reading spuport.

Special Needs These notes provide ideas for adapting instruction to support the needs of various special needs students.

■ NOTES

Topic ⑨ Lesson 3

Reconstruction and Southern Society

Objectives

Objective 1: Identify new forces in southern politics.

Objective 2: Describe how southern conservatives resisted Reconstruction.

Objective 3: Analyze the economic, political, and social challenges facing Reconstruction governments.

Objective 4: Explain why sharecropping led to a cycle of poverty.

LESSON 3 ORGANIZER		PACING: APPROX. 1 PERIOD, .5 BLOCKS			
		OBJECTIVES	**PACING**	**RESOURCES**	
				Online	Print
Connect					
DIGITAL START UP ACTIVITY **Social, Political, and Economic Challenges in the South**			5 min.	●	
Investigate					
DIGITAL TEXT 1 **New Political Groups in the South**		Objective 1	10 min.	●	●
DIGITAL TEXT 2 **Conservatives Resist Reform**		Objective 2	10 min.	●	●
INTERACTIVE GALLERY **Reconstruction-Era Political Groups**			10 min.	●	
DIGITAL TEXT 3 **Political Problems and Legislative Reform**		Objective 3	10 min.	●	●
DIGITAL TEXT 4 **Economic Problems During Reconstruction**		Objective 4	10 min.	●	●
INTERACTIVE CHART **The Cycle of Poverty**			10 min.	●	
Synthesize					
DIGITAL ACTIVITY **Differing Views of Reconstruction**			5 min.	●	
Demonstrate					
DIGITAL QUIZ **Lesson Quiz and Class Discussion Board**			10 min.	●	

PEARSON
realize™
www.PearsonRealize.com

Go online to access additional resources including:
Primary Sources • Biographies • Supreme Court cases •
21st Century Skill Tutorials • Maps • Graphic Organizers.

■ CONNECT

DIGITAL START UP ACTIVITY
Social, Political, and Economic Challenges in the South

Project the Start Up Activity Ask students to read the activity and write down their responses as they enter and get settled. Have students share their responses with a partner, either in class or through a blog space.

Discuss Write down one social problem, one political problem, and one economic problem that you think the South will continue to face as Reconstruction progresses. *(racial inequality; conflicts with Republicans in power in state and federal governments; the cost of rebuilding.)* Then make a prediction about how you think one of these problems will affect life in the reconstructed states. *(African Americans will face discrimination and violence; southern whites will seek to regain power; the South will diversify its industries in an effort to make the economy grow)*

Aa Vocabulary Development: Use the Interactive Reading Notepad to preview the Key Terms and Academic Vocabulary in this lesson with students.

↱ FLIP IT!
Assign the Flipped Video for this lesson.

■ STUDENT EDITION PRINT
PAGES: 506–512

■ INVESTIGATE

DIGITAL TEXT 1
New Political Groups in the South

Objective 1: **Identify new forces in southern politics.**

Quick Instruction
Project the image of Hiram Rhodes Revels, the nation's first African American senator. Discuss the ways in which Revels's election impacted the nation.

Summarize Identify the three new groups that took over southern politics during Reconstruction. *(Scalawags—white southern Republicans, largely businesspeople rebuilding the South. Carpetbaggers—northerners who came to the South for profit, to help freedmen, and because they loved the land. African Americans—voted in large numbers for the first time and were elected to public offices.)*

ELL Use the ELL activity described in the ELL chart.

Further Instruction
Go through the Interactive Reading Notepad questions and discuss the answers with the class. To extend the lesson assign the Biography: Hiram Rhodes Revels.

Compare Points of View Contrast the views of white southern Democrats and white southern Republicans on Reconstruction, citing evidence for support. *(White southern Democrats did not support Reconstruction, as evidenced by their use of the derogatory term scalawags to describe white southern Republicans who did. White southern Democrats thought the scalawags were traitors. White southern Republicans supported Reconstruction because many of them had opposed secession and wanted to forget the war and rebuild.)*

Analyze Information Reread the last paragraph of the text. Evaluate the impact of Hiram Rhodes Revels's election in light of what you learned. *(Revels's election was a significant victory that reflected the social and political changes taking place in the South, but it did not change the fact that African Americans still faced discrimination and had a limited voice in government.)*

Reconstruction and Southern Society

DIGITAL TEXT 2

Conservatives Resist Reform

INTERACTIVE GALLERY

Reconstruction-Era Political Groups

DIGITAL TEXT 3

Political Problems and Legislative Reform

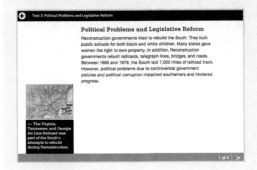

Objective 2: **Describe how southern Conservatives resisted Reconstruction.**

Quick Instruction

Interactive Gallery: Reconstruction-Era Political Groups Project the interactive gallery on the whiteboard and click through the images. Identify the different points of view of Republicans and Democrats on Reconstruction.

Cite Evidence that southern Conservatives opposed Reconstruction, and why. ("These Conservatives resented the changes imposed by Congress and enforced by the military. They wanted the South to change as little as possible.")

> ### ACTIVE CLASSROOM
>
> Have students use Cartoon It Strategy and create a quick copy of one compelling image from the text or the interactive gallery. Have students turn their image into a political cartoon that illustrates a key concept or main idea about the Reconstruction-era political groups.

D Differentiate: Extra Support Explain to students that the terms Republican and Democratic did not have the same meaning in the 1800s as they do today. Have students review the text and identify the points of view of Republicans and Democrats during Reconstruction.

Further Instruction

Go through the Interactive Reading Notepad questions and discuss the answers with the class.

Draw Conclusions What social, political, and economic factors do you think caused the rise of conservative feelings in the South? (Social— the strong measures taken by Republicans to change southern society led to resentment. Many southerners saw the Republicans as outsiders. Political—Conservatives wanted to return to a time when they held power. Economic—planters wanted African Americans to work on plantations and small farmers and laborers did not want to compete with African Americans for jobs.)

Summarize the social and political impact of the Ku Klux Klan on African Americans in the South. (Klan members terrorized African Americans, making many people afraid to vote.)

Analyze Information Reread the quotes from the U.S. Senator and African American voters in the text. Based on this evidence, explain the social and political problems that emerged during this portion of Reconstruction and evaluate the impact on southern whites and African Americans. (Southern whites felt the country belonged to them and did not want to share political power with African Americans. Secret societies like the KKK used violence and fear to keep African Americans and white allies from voting and holding office.)

Objective 3: **Analyze the economic, political, and social challenges facing Reconstruction governments.**

Quick Instruction

Project the image on the whiteboard and discuss the steps Reconstruction governments took to rebuild the South.

Summarize Give three examples of how Reconstruction governments brought improvements to southern states. (They built public schools, gave women the right to own property in many states, and rebuilt infrastructure including railroads, telegraph lines, bridges, and railroads.)

Draw Conclusions What political problems hindered progress of rebuilding in the South? (There was political corruption within governments and some former Confederates were taxed without representation. Voting rights also remained an issue, particularly for African Americans.)

Support Ideas with Evidence How did economic differences between the North and South affect attitudes toward Reconstruction? Cite evidence for support. (Reconstruction raised taxes, creating resentment among southerners. The financial burden caused some landowners to lose their land. Southerners also opposed corruption by Reconstruction governments.)

ELL Use the ELL activity described in the ELL chart.

PEARSON

realize™

www.PearsonRealize.com
Access your Digital Lesson

DIGITAL TEXT 4

Economic Problems During Reconstruction

INTERACTIVE CHART

The Cycle of Poverty

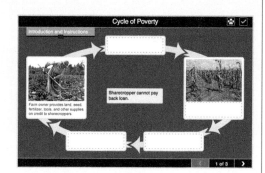

Further Instruction

Go through the Interactive Reading Notepad questions and discuss the answers with the class.

Draw Conclusions Identify the legislative reform programs of the reconstructed state governments and evaluate whether they were effective in rebuilding southern states. *(New state constitutions put in place adult male suffrage, took away restrictions for holding office, reinstated elections for public officials, and increased power of the executive branches. These measures allowed the southern states to form new governments but did not lead to changes in the power structure, as states imposed new voting restrictions against African Americans, allowed former Confederates to vote and hold office, and forced African Americans from office.)*

Objective 4: Explain why sharecropping led to a cycle of poverty.

Quick Instruction

Interactive Chart: The Cycle of Poverty
Project the interactive chart and have students read through the tiles. Discuss the ways in which sharecropping created a cycle of poverty for African Americans and poor whites.

Generate Explanations Explain the economic problems African Americans and poor white southerners faced that led them to become sharecroppers. *(African Americans left plantations after the Civil War but did not have other economic opportunities. Most African Americans and poor whites did not have money to become landowners and so had to rent land as sharecroppers instead.)*

👥 ACTIVE CLASSROOM

Have students use the Write 1-Get 3 Strategy to answer the question: What are 4 key characteristics of sharecropping? Have students take a piece of paper and fold it into quarters, write down 1 response in the first box, and then go around room asking to hear other responses. If they think a response is correct, have them write it in one of their boxes until they have three more responses on their page. Call on students to share their responses with class.

Further Instruction

Go through the Interactive Reading Notepad questions and discuss the answers with the class.

Analyze Information Describe the effects of Reconstruction on economic opportunities for African Americans. Why did one freedman say those who had been enslaved received "nothing but freedom"? *(Reconstruction did not create many new economic opportunities for African Americans. They had little chance to become landowners and work their way out of poverty. The freedman meant that African Americans had received freedom but no additional opportunities or support to help them become self-sufficient.)*

Identify Cause and Effect Describe the positive and negative effects of sharecropping on African Americans. *(They had greater independence and could hope to become landowners, but many instead fell into debt.)*

Reconstruction and Southern Society

■ SYNTHESIZE

DIGITAL ACTIVITY
Differing Views of Reconstruction

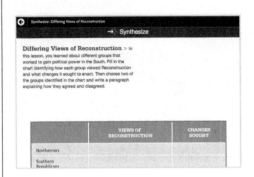

Have students fill in the chart and choose two of the groups to write about. Have students share their charts with a partner and discuss their responses.

Discuss Have students review the predictions they made at the beginning of the lesson about the social, political, and economic problems the South faced as Reconstruction progressed. Ask students how accurate their predictions were and whether they would revise their list of problems now that they have learned more. Have students discuss how the problems they listed were addressed during Reconstruction.

■ DEMONSTRATE

DIGITAL QUIZ
Lesson Quiz and Class Discussion Board

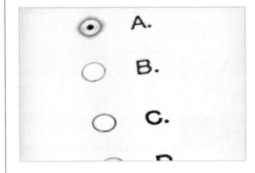

Assign the online Lesson Quiz for this lesson if you haven't already done so. Students will be offered automatic remediation or enrichment based on their score.

Pose these questions to the class on the Discussion Board:

Identify Cause and Effect How did Reconstruction cause the political landscape of the South to change?

Summarize What social, political, and economic problems did African Americans continue to face during Reconstruction?

Topic Inquiry
Have students continue their investigations for the Topic Inquiry.

The Aftermath of Reconstruction

Supporting English Language Learners

Use with Digital Text 1, **Reconstruction Ends.**

Speaking
Explain that using a variety of connecting words can make spoken language easier to follow.

Beginning Display and read aloud the last sentence of the text's second paragraph. Explain how the word *but* shows that the two independent clauses contradict each other. Then have students complete and say this sentence: Tilden won the popular vote, but _____.

Intermediate Display and read aloud the last sentence of the text's second paragraph. Explain that *but* connects contradictory ideas, while *and* suggests agreement. Have students complete and say this sentence two ways: Congress passed the Amnesty Act, but/and _____.

Advanced Explain the use of *however*, both at the beginning and in the middle of sentences. Then have pairs of students discuss the 1876 election using *however* in both the beginning and middle of sentences.

Advanced High Point out the phrase *at the same time* used in the text's third and last paragraphs. Then have students use the phrases, *as well as*, *but*, and *however* in a discussion about the end of Reconstruction. Ask: Can you use *but*, *however*, and *as well as* interchangeably? Why or why not?

Use with Digital Text 3, **The "New South" Moves Toward Industry.**

Writing
Explain that knowing a variety of sentence patterns can help students write original, grammatically correct sentences on any topic.

Beginning Display these sentences: Cotton is important. Cotton is a crop. Explain that *important* and *crop* describe *cotton*. Then have students complete these sentences with descriptive words or phrases and write them down: Henry Grady was _____. James Duke was _____.

Intermediate Display this sentence: Cotton production recovered _____. Ask: What words or phrases could be added to describe how, when, or where cotton production recovered? Have students complete and write down the sentence three different ways.

Advanced Display this sentence: James Duke used new machinery in North Carolina. Point out the subject, verb, object, and adverbial phrase. Then have pairs of students write additional sentences about the "New South" using this sentence pattern.

Advanced High Display this sentence: In the South, textiles gave the economy a boost. Discuss how the phrase in the South could be relocated to the end of the sentence, as well as how the direct and indirect objects might be reversed. Then have students create additional sentences about the "New South" using this sentence pattern and its variations.

▣ Differentiate Instruction

Use the Differentiated Instruction notes throughout the lesson plan to support the varied skill sets, levels of readiness, and interests in the mixed-ability classroom.

Challenge These notes include suggestions for expanding the activity for advanced students.

On-Level These notes include suggestions for modifying the activity to address different interests or learning styles.

Extra Support These notes include ideas for providing more scaffolding or reading spuport.

Special Needs These notes provide ideas for adapting instruction to support the needs of various special needs students.

■ NOTES

The Aftermath of Reconstruction

Objectives

Objective 1: Summarize the events that led to the end of Reconstruction.

Objective 2: Explain how the rights of African Americans were restricted in the South after Reconstruction.

Objective 3: Identify industries that flourished in the "New South."

LESSON 4 ORGANIZER		PACING: APPROX. 1 PERIOD, .5 BLOCKS		
			RESOURCES	
	OBJECTIVES	PACING	Online	Print
Connect				
DIGITAL START UP ACTIVITY **The Rise of Segregation**		5 min.	●	
Investigate				
DIGITAL TEXT 1 **Reconstruction Ends**	Objective 1	10 min.	●	●
DIGITAL TEXT 2 **New Legislation Restricts African American Rights**	Objective 2	10 min.	●	●
INTERACTIVE TIMELINE **Oppression of African Americans**		10 min.	●	
DIGITAL TEXT 3 **The "New South" Moves Toward Industry**	Objective 3	10 min.	●	●
BEFORE AND AFTER **Change in Southern Industry**		10 min.	●	
Synthesize				
DIGITAL ACTIVITY **The Effects of Reconstruction**		5 min.	●	
Demonstrate				
DIGITAL QUIZ **Lesson Quiz and Class Discussion Board**		10 min.	●	

PEARSON
realize™
www.PearsonRealize.com

Go online to access additional resources including:
Primary Sources • Biographies • Supreme Court cases • 21st Century Skill Tutorials • Maps • Graphic Organizers.

CONNECT

The Rise of Segregation

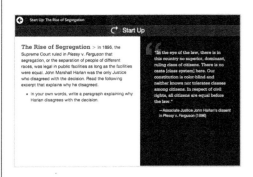

Project the Start Up Activity Ask students to read the quote and write down their response as they enter and get settled. Have students share their responses with a partner, either in class or through a blog space.

Discuss In your own words, write a paragraph explaining why Harlan disagreed with the decision. *(Harlan believed the Constitution applies equally to all citizens. He did not think segregating people based on race was legal because it treated citizens differently under the law.)*

Tell students that in this lesson they will be learning about the political, social, and economic impact of Reconstruction following the end of the Reconstruction Era.

Aa Vocabulary Development: Use the Interactive Reading Notepad to preview the Key Terms and Academic Vocabulary in this lesson with students.

⇅ FLIP IT!

Assign the Flipped Video for this lesson.

■ STUDENT EDITION PRINT PAGES: 513–518

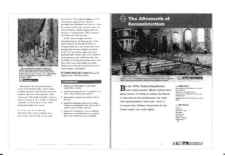

INVESTIGATE

Reconstruction Ends

Objective 1: Summarize the events that led to the end of Reconstruction.

Quick Instruction

Project the image of the political cartoon on the whiteboard and have students describe what they see. Ask students to use the cartoon to make a prediction about how attitudes toward Reconstruction will lead to the end of this era.

Summarize What factors caused Reconstruction to end? *(Radical Republicans were losing power; many northerners did not want to keep trying to reform the South; corruption hurt the Republican party; Hayes won the presidential election and agreed to end Reconstruction if the South did not contest his victory.)*

ELL Use the ELL activity described in the ELL chart.

Further Instruction

Go through the Interactive Reading Notepad questions and discuss the answers with the class.

Infer Evaluate the legislative reform programs of the reconstructed state governments and their impact based on the following sentence: "It was time to let southerners run their own governments, they said—even if it meant that African Americans in the South might lose their rights." *(The sentence suggests the legislative reform programs did not have a lasting impact if rights for African Americans were eroded as soon as Reconstruction came to an end.)*

Identify Cause and Effect Explain the causes and effects of the Democratic rise to power in the South. *(Causes—Congress passed the Amnesty Act giving nearly all white southerners the right to vote, and they voted solidly Democratic. Threats of violence kept many African Americans who would have voted Republican from the polls. Effects—Democrats became a powerful bloc and won the popular vote in the presidential election. They agreed to give the disputed election to Hayes in exchange for an end to Reconstruction. The Democratic party became a stronghold in the South and African Americans lost most political rights.)*

The Aftermath of Reconstruction

DIGITAL TEXT 2	INTERACTIVE TIMELINE	DIGITAL TEXT 3
New Legislation Restricts African American Rights	**Oppression of African Americans**	**The "New South" Moves Toward Industry**

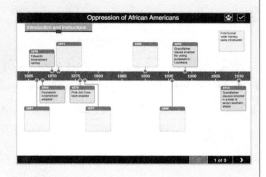

Objective 2: **Explain how the rights of African Americans were restricted in the South after Reconstruction.**

Quick Instruction

Interactive Timeline: Oppression of African Americans Project the interactive timeline and read through the events. Discuss the political problems that led to the erosion of African American rights.

Support Ideas with Examples Give three examples of new laws passed in the South and explain their impact on African Americans. *(poll taxes—required voters to pay to vote; kept poor people, including many African Americans, from voting. Literacy tests—required voters to read and explain a section of the Constitution; many African Americans had little education and could not pass the tests. Grandfather clauses—if voters had a father or grandfather eligible to vote in 1867, they were exempt from the literacy test; allowed illiterate white voters to vote but not African Americans; Jim Crow laws—instituted segregation.)*

📖 ACTIVE CLASSROOM

Have students take 30 seconds and use the Quick Write Strategy to write down their responses to the quote by George Washington Cable about segregation.

D **Differentiate: Extra Support** Explain to students that to segregate means to separate or isolate. Have them explain the system of segregation in their own words.

Further Instruction

Go through the Interactive Reading Notepad questions and discuss the answers with the class. To extend the lesson assign the Landmark Supreme Court Case: *Plessy v. Ferguson.*

Summarize How did the Plessy case address conflicts between African Americans and southern whites? *(The case legalized segregation, creating separate facilities for African Americans and whites and ensuring discrimination would continue.)*

Draw Conclusions What were the effects of Reconstruction on African Americans' social and political rights? *(African Americans wound up losing many of the rights they had gained in the early years of Reconstruction. Laws kept them from voting and segregation was used to prevent social equality.)*

Objective 3: **Identify industries that flourished in the "New South."**

Quick Instruction

Before and After: Change in Southern Industry Project the interactive activity on the whiteboard and move the slider to show the changes. Have students locate the new southern industries on the map.

Identify Cause and Effect How did the Civil War and Reconstruction cause the South to develop new industries? *(The war destroyed many farms and plantations and ended the plantation system; even when cotton production recovered, southerners wanted to build up southern industry instead of depending on the North.)*

📖 ACTIVE CLASSROOM

Pair students and have them use the See-Think-Wonder Strategy to study the interactive map. Have students use the slider to view both maps. Then ask: What do you see? What does that make you think? What are you wondering about now that you've seen this? Have students share their insights with the class.

ELL Use the ELL activity described in the ELL chart.

Further Instruction

Go through the Interactive Reading Notepad questions and discuss the answers with the class.

BEFORE AND AFTER
Change in Southern Industry

Draw Conclusions How did the physical characteristics of the environment influence economic activities in the South during the nineteenth century? *(The South developed industries based on its natural resources. It grew cotton and tobacco, mined for minerals, and developed industries in oil and steel. The South also built factories to take advantage of its lumber supply.)*

Summarize Describe the positive consequences of human modification of the physical environment on the South. *(Clearing land, using natural resources, and building farms and factories provided jobs and opportunities that helped the economy recover after the war.)*

 SYNTHESIZE

DIGITAL ACTIVITY
The Effects of Reconstruction

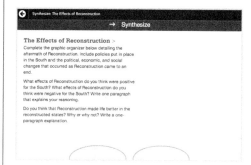

Have students fill in the graphic organizer and answer the questions. Have students share their graphic organizers with a partner and discuss their answers.

Discuss Have students share their views about the overall effectiveness of Reconstruction and the ways it changed life in the South. Ask students to consider the effects of Reconstruction on white southerners and African Americans, and how it impacted relations between the North and South. Remind students to use examples to support their views.

DEMONSTRATE

DIGITAL QUIZ
Lesson Quiz and Class Discussion Board

Assign the online Lesson Quiz for this lesson if you haven't already done so. Students will be offered automatic remediation or enrichment based on their score.

Pose these questions to the class on the Discussion Board:

Identify Central Issues Why did Reconstruction come to a close? What were the effects of its ending?

Make Generalizations How did Reconstruction change life for African Americans socially and politically?

Identify Patterns In what ways did a "New South" develop following the Civil War?

Topic Inquiry
Have students continue their investigations for the Topic Inquiry.

The Reconstruction Era

■ SYNTHESIZE

DIGITAL ACTIVITY
Reflect on the Essential Question and Topic

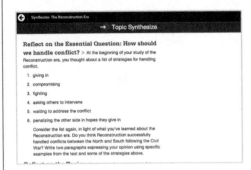

First ask students to reconsider the Essential Question for this topic: How should we handle conflict? Have students consider the list of strategies for handling conflict in light of what they have learned. Then ask students to answer the question using specific examples and at least two of the strategies.

Ask students, "What were the conflicts that arose during Reconstruction? How were they resolved?" Have students give examples from the topic. Discuss their responses as a class or ask students to post their answers on the Class Discussion Board.

Next ask students to reflect on the topic as a whole and write down three important changes that Reconstruction and westward expansion brought, and how each of these changes shaped the nation. Give students the following examples of changes to help them get started:

1. changes in political leadership
2. economic developments
3. new legislation
4. social shifts
5. advancements and setbacks to civil rights
6. population, migration, and settlement patterns

Topic Inquiry
Have students complete Step 3 of the Topic Inquiry.

■ DEMONSTRATE

DIGITAL TOPIC REVIEW AND ASSESSMENT
The Reconstruction Era

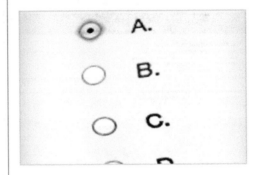

Students can prepare for the Topic Test by answering the questions in the Topic Review and Assessment online or the Assessment questions in the Print Student text. They can also prepare by reviewing their answers to the Interactive Reading Notepad questions or reviewing their notes in the Reading and Notetaking Study Guide.

DIGITAL TOPIC TEST
The Reconstruction Era

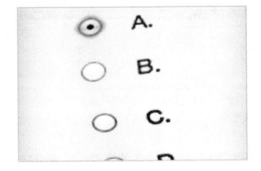

TOPIC TEST
Assign the Topic Test to assess students' understanding of topic content.

BENCHMARK TESTS
Assign these benchmark tests as you complete the relevant topics to monitor student progress toward mastering the course content and as preparation for the End-of-Course Test.

Benchmark Test 1: Topics 1–2

Benchmark Test 2: Topics 3–4

Benchmark Test 3: Topics 5–6

Benchmark Test 4: Topics 7–9

Benchmark Test 5: Topics 10–12

Benchmark Test 6: Topics 13–14

Benchmark Test 7: Topics 15–17

END-OF-COURSE TESTS
Assign End-Of-Course Test 1 or 2 to measure students' progress in mastering the course content.